Buying or selling CSA bonds?

Nobody has more experience than R.M. Smythe & Dr. Douglas Ball

R.M. Smythe & Co. is the leading resource for Confederate States of America bonds. In 1997 alone, R.M. Smythe in auctions or by private treaty sold more CSA bonds than any other firm in the world. This included the record price for a single CSA bond—$22,275 paid at the Memphis 1997 auction for the Essai Bond of April 12, 1862, from the John Ford Collection.

R.M. Smythe is the only firm to have sold rare cotton warrants (B-151, B-152, B-155) or to have handled every one of the 14 known examples. And we are also the only firm that has had the privilege of selling a B-141 or B-142 loan bond, an issued $100 B-269 bond, or all of the issued $500 B-273 bonds.

In addition, R.M. Smythe maintains a large and diverse inventory of Confederate bonds. And of course, no other firm can offer you the knowledge, integrity, and experience of Dr. Douglas B. Ball, the leading authority on Confederate financial history.

Dr. Douglas B. Ball is the author of *Financial Failure and Confederate Defeat; Confederate Interim Depository Receipts and Funding Certificates in the Commonwealth of Virginia, 1861–1865;* and numerous articles on Confederate bonds in *Numismatist* and *Bank Note Reporter.* He holds a B.A., Wooster; M.A., Yale; M.B.A., Columbia; and Ph.D., University of London. Dr. Douglas Ball is Vice President and Director of Research at R.M. Smythe.

Buying or selling Confederate bonds? Contact Dr. Douglas Ball.

R.M. SMYTHE

212-943-1880
www.rm-smythe.com

26 Broadway, Suite 271
New York, NY 10004-1701

800-622-1880
dball@rm-smythe.com

Comprehensive Catalog and History of Confederate Bonds

Douglas B. Ball, Ph. D.

with foreword by

John J. Ford

BNR Press

in association with

R. M. Smythe & Co., Inc.

Other Civil War titles from the same publisher:

Comprehensive Catalog of Confederate Paper Money (Grover Criswell, 1996)
Civil War Encased Stamps (Fred Reed, 1995)

Other current works from the same publisher:

Comprehensive Catalog of U. S. Paper Money Errors (Frederick J. Bart, 1994)
U. S. Essay, Proof, and Specimen Notes (Gene Hessler, 1977)
Comprehensive Catalog of U.S. Paper Money (Gene Hessler, 1997)
Comprehensive Catalog of U.S. Large Size Star Notes (Doug Murray, 1996)
An Illustrated History of U. S. Loans 1776-1892 (Gene Hessler, 1988)
The Engraver's Line (Gene Hessler, 1993)
College Currency: Money for Business Training (Herb and Martha Schingoethe, Neil Shafer, editor, 1993)
Stocks and Bonds of North American Railroads (Terry Cox, 1995)
Prisoner of War and Concentration Camp Money, second edition (Lance Campbell, 1993)
World War II Remembered: history in your hands, a numismatic study (C. Frederick Schwan and Joseph E. Boling, 1995)
Comprehensive Catalog of Military Payment Certificates (Fred Schwan, 1996)
American Automotive Stock Certificates (Lawrence Falater, 1997)

9 8 7 6 5 4 3 2 1

ISBN 0-931960-58-4

BNR Press
132 East Second Street
Port Clinton, Ohio 43452-1115

phone	(419) 732-NOTE (6683)
	(800) 793-0683
	(419) 734-6683 (message service only)
fax	(419) 732-6683
	(800) 793-0683
e-mail	BNR Press@aol.com

since 1977

CONTENTS

Foreword

Sometime in the early spring of 1962, Charles Wormser, my colleague in the operation of New Netherlands Coin Company, called me at home, where I was cataloging our June sale. He suggested that I find time to come into the office as he had a young man, a serious "Professor type" potential client who wanted to look over our firm's large stock of CSA currency. C.M.W. was not cognizant of the numerous varieties of Confederate treasury notes, and thought that I could best handle our possible customer. The man with whom Charles had made an appointment to meet me, (the company's resident expert) at New Netherlands, was a graduate student at Yale, Charles' alma mater. His name was Douglas B. Ball.

New Netherlands had a large stock of CSA paper money as I had had an interest in that series for most of my life. Moreover, I thought it good business to have a stock on hand for the Civil War Centennial. In 1953-4, we purchased the McCoy Collection formed in Washington D.C. and the F.C.C. Boyd collection. By 1962 we were also helping the Historical Society of Pennsylvania liquidate the legendary John C. Browne collection, the basis for the original Bradbeer book in 1915. When Doug Ball discovered us, we had more than a half dozen Montgomery sets and a number of other left over $50 and $100 Montgomery bills, that together with thousands of other notes, constituted our stock. The conglomeration was all neatly arranged by Bradbeer-Criswell numbers together with penciled notations on each envelope by our own super expert, the brilliant and ill-fated Walter Breen. The McCoy collection was kept in three yard long file boxes behind our protective screen; the Pennsylvania Historical Society holdings were stored in black boxes kept in the deep drawers of the desk in my office.

At the age of nine, I, in common with many of my peers, collected stamps. After a few years, I fell behind hinging and mounting stamps in my albums. So in 1936, I was only too eager to discover coins and paper money. Late in that year, accompanied by my mother, I purchased my first Confederate currency item, a $10 type 68 note, for 15 cents. At the same time, I also bought the $50 and $100 card proofs of the Powell Bank of Newburgh, New York, for 25 cents each. In all events, in the following year, 1937, I was buying CSA notes from Kenneth W. Lee of Los Angeles and Tom Elder, probably from their ads in the numismatic section of Lightner's *Hobbies* magazine.

I remember that Ken Lee and his dad offered groups of ten different Confederate notes at $2.50 per offering in their ads. I ordered as many of these lots as my meager weekly income of $3-4 (paper route money) would permit. I was surprised at the number of 1861 notes in these 10 piece groups and the multitude of what appeared to be different varieties. Early in 1938, while becoming a pest at the firm of Stack's at their newly established offices on 46th Street in New York City, the brothers Stack made a serious mistake. They introduced an eager 14 year old to William W. Bradbeer's magnum opus of 1915 on *Confederate and Southern States Currency.* Quickly realizing that the book was the "bible" and having ascertained that it was relatively rare, I borrowed from Stack's their reference library copy and arranged with a school friend (and fellow collector) whose aunt was proficient with a typewriter, to have the entire book typed. Armed with this innocuous-appearing manuscript, I promptly proceeded to comb through the Stack inventory, pulling out for purchase all the Whatman, Hodgkinson & Company, Wookey Hole Mill, N(ew)Y(ork) watermarked notes and other rare varieties (then not much esteemed), usually at a small discount from Wayte Raymond's current price list. My interest slowly waned however, as I eventually cleaned Joe and Morton Stack out of sleepers and became more and more interested in United States pattern coins. However, it is true what they say; if you learn well when you are young a good part of your knowledge will stick with you. Thus I thought that I was more or less prepared for Mr. Ball.

I was at least an hour late for my carefully arranged meeting with Douglas. I had missed one train and the next one was late or a problem arose with my house renovation then in progress. My partner, C.M.W., was irate at my tardy appearance; but Douglas Ball seemed quite placid, having read a good portion of the *New York Times,* by the time I had arrived. Eventually, having mollified Charles, I carried the Browne collection boxes from my office out to our sales counter. After Charles had made the requisite introductions and had retired behind our security screen, I got down to business.

I soon found out that I was not dealing with a run of the mill neophyte seeking the usual selection of type notes. Instead, I was confronted by a specialist intent upon acquiring every possible variety of note of the 1861-1864 Confederate issues. It was not long before I learned that thanks to his father, George W. Ball and his influence with the Library of Congress (the senior Ball was second man in the State Department from December 1961 until September 1966), that Douglas had procured a Photostat copy of Raphael P. Thian's *Register of the Confederate Debt.* I had an original of this extremely rare publication (one of five known) in my library, but had never found time to peruse thoroughly its contents. On the other hand, Doug Ball had apparently put his copy of the Thian book to better purpose.

On top of having the use of the Thian, Douglas had also been in touch with Philip H. Chase, an authority on CSA paper, who had published a definitive work on *Confederate Treasury Notes* in 1947. Chase's book did not catch on, even though his knowledge was considerable. His approach was too much that of the cerebral engineer, and was not adjusted for the benefit of the average collector. However, much his knowledge had registered with Doug Ball. I found this out early on when D.B.B corrected me about the quantity emitted of a note whose issue figures were published in Thian.

It would not be difficult to draw a parallel between this writer, armed with a copy of Bradbeer, doing business with Stack's in 1938-1940 and Douglas Ball, having digested much of the data in Thian, doing business at New Netherlands Coin Co., with an older and hopefully wiser John Ford, twenty-two or more years later. However, that was not to be the case. Doug Ball negotiated and bought with completely uncharacteristic candor and honesty, seldom encountered in the numismatic trade. When I attempted to exaggerate either rarity or importance of a note, he politely corrected me; on the other hand, when I priced a note too low, he told me that I was in error and offered a more realistic figure. D.B.B.'s modus operandi paid off. Within two years after we commenced doing business, I purchased an unpublished hoard of CSA proofs and essai notes that I sold directly to specialist Ball at a modest mark-up, while he was undergoing advanced individual training in the U. S. Army Reserve at Fort Benning. In addition, Douglas eventually bought the bulk of the McCoy and Browne rarities from us, putting together probably the finest and most comprehensive CSA treasury note collection ever assembled. His Confederate fiscal paper and bond holdings ended up on the same scale, the bonds being helped by the purchase of the entire Criswell collection in October of 1980.

I purchased my first Confederate bond in the late 1940's. It was a framed February 17, 1864 $1000 coupon bond that long found a home on my Rockville Centre office wall. While attending the American Numismatic Association convention in Omaha, Nebraska, in 1955, I got in touch with D.O. Barrett, who operated a sort of paper money museum at Boystown. Always carrying U.S. obsolete bank notes with me to major conventions, I offered a number to Mr. Barrett who found some of our small selection to be important. I ended up trading notes with him for a small (25 or so) group of Confederate bonds. That was the beginning of my collection.

A couple of years later, wrapping up my late office lunch hour, I stopped in to visit with Vernon Brown at the Chase Bank Money Museum located on Sixth Avenue, just around the corner from the New Netherlands office. Vernon welcomed my occasional visits as he invariably had an inquiry or two, which he liked to run by me. One day, probably in 1958, he showed me a sample group of CSA bonds sent to the Chase by a British institution which wanted to know if they had any value, however small. The bank in London was cleaning house, and wondered if they should trash what they believed to be worthless paper. Naturally, we corresponded directly with the bank and ended up purchasing close to two hundred bonds at around $3 apiece. Most of these were interesting August 19, 1861 Act issue variants (hence the "generous" price for the time and place).

My interest stimulated, I went back to my friend, Vernon Brown, and asked him to obtain from the proper department within his bank a list of long established banking institutions in London and Paris. Soon, armed with a list of a couple of dozen banks, we wrote to each, soliciting bonds. Douglas Ball tells the story of how I got four pairs of Cotton Warrents, how I traded the outside pair to Grover Criswell, who used them in his 1961 book, and the tragic destruction of the other 1492 bonds in 1964. At any rate, New Netherlands, based on our inquiries, was able to import thousands of Confederate bonds and related material.

Charles M. Wormser had little interest in my bond machinations and gave me carte blanche to build up my personal collection. However, his interest perked up when, as I recall, I sold 500 $1000 Stonewall Jackson bonds of February 20, 1863, all pink paper originals, to a Virginia mail organization named the Stonewall Jackson Memorial Association. That organization was trying to raise money to refurbish the general's home in Winchester, and the bonds were sold at a sharp price increase to raise funds for this project. From that time on, New Netherlands Coin Company stocked Confederate bonds.

During this time, between 1962 and 1964, I was offered a pair of sample specimen cotton warrants to which a letter of Jefferson Davis' addressed to the Confederate Senate was attached. I had already sold Ball a complete set of the then rare Erlanger Bonds for $600 and he was beginning to form a bond collection of his own. He was a willing buyer of the sample pair.

His interest in Confederate bonds and certificates soared to an elevated level when he lived in London to attend the University of London's School of Economics and Political Science, where he got a PhD in Economics in 1974. During his stay in London, Doug discovered the existence of the Confederate Bondholders Committees. In the years after the Civil War, the idea behind these organizations being that if enough people got together to pressure the American government, they might get something for their bonds. But the major organized committee had apparently disappeared without a trace.

In the meantime, in January 1974, Doug completed his thesis required for a PhD: *Confederate War Finance, 1861-1865: Economic Policy-Making in the South during the American Civil War.* Clearly, student and researcher Ball, not only built up a large collection of bonds and fiscal paper of the Confederacy, but unlike most collectors, he knew the background of these items intimately and analyzed the reasons why various issues were authorized, what happened to them and why. The thesis was a relatively modest effort, consisting of 426 pages of carefully typed paper, reduced to a length conforming with the University requirements. Over the years, D.B.B. kept adding to his critical knowledge of Confederate finance, revising and rewriting his thesis as occasion offered.

In 1991, the University of Illinois Press published a revision of Dr. Ball's thesis, carefully edited and more readable that the original text of nearly twenty years earlier. The Illinois title was *Financial Failure and Confederate Defeat.* This book received a mix of kudos and criticisms, some holding that his attacks on the Confederate leadership were unfair. One reviewer even took him to task for being an advocate of slavery and rebellion because he had suggested that the Confederacy's finances might have been better managed. Yet I believe that every collector and student interested in CSA bonds and other tangible relics of the South's valiant but futile efforts to support financially their four year war effort, will find Doug's facts and theories of extreme interest and importance, particularly today when America's finances are so poorly managed.

While Doug was in London, he built up a relationship with several London firms, especially Stanley Gibbons, to whom he sold duplicate Confederate notes. It was Chris Stocker at Stanley Gibbons, after that firm suffered disastrous losses and had to be liquidated, that put Doug into contact with Coutt's Bank and its hoard of Confederate bonds in 1981. It was NASCA's purchase of over 20,000 of these bonds that allowed Doug to use the representative group involved for some large scale research, which proved quite illuminating. I well remember him calling me up excitedly to tell me of the discovery of some new bond or that a certain bond, based on his holdings, was no longer rare.

As long ago as 1963, Doug had confided in me his hope of researching and publishing a comprehensive catalog on all aspects of Confederate money, bonds and fiscal paper. I thought at the time that this goal was commendable, but I warned Doug that he had taken on a very ambitious task. I observed that there were a lot more areas than he had heretofore taken into account and that such a work would involve many years of hard research and much time. Moreover, I knew that he would need to finish his education and get a job, which would necessarily delay his hope of getting such a work in print.

His lack of success in getting and keeping a foothold in an academic career and his able cataloging of the Charles J. Affleck Collection of Continental and Colonial paper money in 1975 suggested to me the need for him to turn a part time hobby into a full time career. At my suggestion and with help from myself and my friends, Douglas opened his own company, NASCA (Numismatic and Antiquarian Service Corporation of America) at the end of May 1976. Since NASCA was located in my home town of Rockville Centre, New York, and as I had withdrawn from New Netherlands in 1971, I was able to take an active advisory role in NASCA's affairs.

Unfortunately, the executive manager's personality change and disastrous business decisions following a well nigh fatal heart attack in 1981, and his resignation at the end of that year, coupled with serious losses and the need to put the firm into liquidation from 1982-1984, left Doug with no time for literary projects. Then followed Doug's need to help his father, former Deputy Secretary of State, George W. Ball, finish his last book, on the Middle East (1985-1993). Finally, there were the sudden deaths first of Doug's mother later in 1993 and then his father in May 1994, which further diverted Doug's energies. It was not until late 1995, when the liquidation of his father's estate was essentially complete that he was able to return to his long delayed project.

The sale and breaking up of the Coutts Bank Confederate bond hoard (the substantial residue of the major CSA bondholder's committee), in 1987-1989, coupled with the intrinsic attraction of the Confederate bond area and the discovery of so many new varieties of bonds, rendered the original Kerksis work, which I had helped bring to fruition in 1960, out of date and comparatively obsolete. Thus it was obvious that this should be the first subject area that might be quickly tackled. Happily, it is now completed, although Doug, always the good student, modestly declares that it is still work in progress.

As I stated earlier, I have known Douglas B. Ball for over 35 years and am pleased that I have been asked to write an introduction to this, the first of what I trust will be a whole series of well prepared and dependable catalogs of Confederate paper numismatic artifacts.

John J. Ford, Jr.

Introduction

In bringing this, the first of his books, to the public's attention, the author would like to encourage collectors and dealers to be in touch with him regarding any new varieties seen, any discrepancies in reported number ranges, signers, papers, and dates, or to provide any other constructive comments. Although the data contained may appear to be comprehensive, new information is continually surfacing, and I would like to include such in a future edition. I may be reached through R. M. Smythe & Company at Suite 271, 26 Broadway, New York, NY 10004-1701 or by telephone at 1-800-622-1880 or (212) 908-4642.

Preface

Like the Confederate currency, Confederate bonds have been collected since the end of the Confederate War. Price lists were put out and partial catalogs prepared by the pioneers in the field, among them Haseltine, Massamore, Thian, and others. It was not until 1966 that Ben Douglas, a Washington, DC dealer, together with one of his friends and customers, Charles J. Affleck of Winchester, Virginia, published a modest pamphlet that attempted for the first time a comprehensive listing of Confederate bonds.

Simultaneously, Sidney C. Kerksis (whose manuscript of the Confederate and Southern States currency, a revision of Bradbeer, had been published by the Criswell brothers) prepared a Southern States bond list partially based on Raphael P. Thian's *Register of the Confederate Debt, Funded and Unfunded....* The back pages of Thian's work furnished information on the quantities of Confederate bonds reportedly issued. Later, this manuscript was also conveyed to Grover Criswell and published by him in 1961 as Volume II of his currency series, just in time for the Civil War centennial. Criswell revised this book in 1980 and brought out an abridged soft cover version with only the Confederate bonds in 1992/1993.

While certainly an improvement over earlier efforts, the author has never been particularly happy with the Kerksis-Criswell approach to the cataloging of the Confederate bond issues. Being something of a purist at heart, I prefer to have bonds listed in the order in which they appeared rather than in the order in which their existence was discovered. In addition, many bonds are not listed, the extensive issue of the Trans-Mississippi bonds is ignored, and there are errors in the numbers of bonds reported issued, due to incomplete work done by Thian. Finally, there are listings of bonds that do not exist, omissions of bonds that do exist, and *ad hoc* use of serial letters after catalog numbers indicating afterthoughts in listings. I have attempted to leave room in the present simple numbering system for the appearance of possible new varieties whose existence seems possible.

The Coutts Bank hoard

Undoubtedly the watershed event in the collecting of Confederate bonds was the discovery and sale by Coutts Bank of the bonds held over from the Confederate Bond Holders Committee. The story of how these bonds came into the bank's possession and their disposal is fascinating.

After the Union victory in 1865, many British subjects remained convinced that the United States government was in some manner legally obligated to redeem the Confederate debt. This view was first advanced by the holders of the Erlanger bonds (whose story will be told hereafter), who claimed that the Confederate cotton had been pledged to them and they must be paid off from the proceeds of the sale of that cotton. Since many Southerners cancelled the sales and sequestered the cotton for themselves, the Federal government managed to retrieve very little of this cotton, as Ambrose Bierce's memoirs conclusively demonstrate. Later, those Britishers who held other issues claimed that the United States was the successor to the Confederacy and its assets and was therefore obligated to discharge its debts.

Not surprisingly, this view found no acceptance in Washington, where the Confederacy was declared to be a totally illegal experiment in rebellion and its debts null and void *ab initio*. The United States, both in America and in Europe, took the position that the creditors of the Confederacy were not entitled to a cent and that all the assets of the Confederacy were the lawful property of the government in Washington. While this view prevailed in the American courts, the French and British courts entertained a different opinion. Thus, in Britain, efforts to force the firm of Fraser, Trenholm, the Confederates' depositary in Europe, to hand over the Confederate assets that trickled in after the war were repelled and the United States was assessed legal costs. The courts held that the firm had used those assets as an offset to claims that it had against the Confederacy. The United States, it was said, could not have a better claim to the Confederate assets than the Confederacy itself had.

Jefferson Davis, president of the Confederate States of America.

Faced with these claims and the possibility that the Democrats might again gain control of the Congress and repudiate the Federal debt incurred in suppressing the Confederate rebellion, or, worse, that they might assume the Confederate debt, the Radicals added section five to the Fourteenth Amendment. This specifically required the payment of the Federal debt and prohibited payment of the Confederate debts (national, state, or local) by the Federal, state, or local governments. This, the Radicals thought, ought to dispose of this contentious issue permanently.

However, from 1879 to 1884, the question arose again in Great Britain. Despite warnings from men like former Secretary of State Judah P. Benjamin, who was living in Britain and practiced law there, that such debts would not be paid, the notion gained ground that the bonds would be redeemed by the Federal government. Speculators began to buy such bonds at $20 in gold for every $1000 face value in bonds. A bond holders committee was organized, forms for receiving deposits of bonds pending collection were prepared and issued to depositors, and funds equal to 0.75% of the face value of the deposited bonds were collected from the depositors to defray the expense of making representations in London and Washington.

Bonds poured into London from those Southerners anxious to salvage something from the debacle. Indeed, some persons acquired remainder bonds that they proceeded to complete with fictitious or forged signatures and send off to Britain, where they were eagerly bought up. Such was the demand that when the supply coming in from the South proved inadequate, various enterprising persons in the Netherlands began to make counterfeits that were eagerly bought by gullible Britons.

The most extensively copied bond was the February 20, 1863 7% bond with the portrait of Stonewall Jackson. Not having any pink paper available, the counterfeiters, to allay possible inquiries, put "Second" or "Third" series on their wood pulp paper products, going to some trouble to replicate the red as well as the embossed treasury seal. Somewhere between $10 million and $15 million face value of fake bonds were made and sold, to judge from the contents of the London hoard. Most of the counterfeits were made in the $1000 denomination, for obvious reasons. As there was no longer a Confederate treasury nor any of its officers on hand to denounce these bonds as impostors, the counterfeiters appear to have escaped unscathed. Such bonds were not contemporaneous with the Confederacy nor did they have anything whatsoever to do with it.

The Atlantic and Western Railroad depot in Atlanta.

After 1885, this madness waned. About a third of the bonds lodged with the committee were returned to their depositors after it was realized that nothing useful was going to happen. Those bonds that remained passed by corporate succession to Coutts Bank, where they gathered coal dust and rotted from high paper acidity as the years passed.

In 1979, Coutts resolved to empty its vaults of this unwelcome and unremunerative burden. That part of the bonds whose current owners could be traced (obviously all the original depositors were dead), amounting to about 21,000 pieces, were sold to NASCA, now part of R. M. Smythe & Company. These arrived from London in early 1982 and had to be cleaned and pressed. Many hours were spent soaking these bonds in my bathtub and draining the water off them on the tiled bathroom walls. They were then placed on unpatterned blotting paper to dry, being pressed by the weight of the other bonds on top of them. Very few bonds were lost. My late mother even took a hand in these proceedings, doing over 4,000 of them in her home in Princeton. Asked how she was getting on with this project, she replied with a pardonable pun that she was still in bondage.

This group proved to be quite exciting. Besides the fact that it contained massive quantities of bonds heretofore thought to be extremely rare, it also had many low numbered bonds and an astonishing quantity of discovery pieces. I spent many hours enjoying my research with this group. My only regret was that the condition of my firm necessitated the speedy sale of as many bonds as possible in order to meet our corporate obligations as they came due.

The residue, amounting to 87,000 pieces, whose owners could not be located, then had to be disposed of. I spent some weeks in the vault of Coutts Bank doing a census of the bonds with a view to forming an opinion as to the quantities in the holdings, what their conditions were, and how much should be offered for them. So much sulfuric acid was in the paper (a prime cause of paper decomposition) that the bank officer who was assisting me in the examination had his hands covered with blisters by the end of the first day and had to wear gloves thereafter. I washed my hands frequently, but I had to take brief fresh air breaks because of the odor.

Eventually, to meet its fiduciary responsibilities, Coutts arranged to auction the 87,000 remaining pieces in one lot in London in November 1987. It was bought by a two-firm consortium for a sum in excess of £350,000. Most of the better pieces were sold through R. M. Smythe during 1988 and 1989. The residue were marketed by the partners directly to the public.

Confederate cannon at Pensacola.

Unfortunately, many of the more delicate pieces, particularly the Stonewall Jackson counterfeits, were destroyed because those to whom the Texas partner gave them to be ironed did not realize that the brittle paper could not tolerate such treatment; the bonds simply disintegrated. Probably 6,000 pieces were lost in this manner.

General Robert E. Lee.

Approach to cataloging

In the 1960s, with the encouragement of Ben Douglas, Charles Affleck, and Neil Shafer, I started the research that I thought would lead to a complete catalog of Confederate currency, fiscal paper, and bonds. But a project that I thought would only take a few years went on and on. Time went by, there was one diversion after another, and some thirty years have passed since the dinner in Washington where I broached my plans to the three men. Publication has been constantly delayed because of the discovery of new items and facts. A great deal of exciting information came from extensive research in the National Archives. There was also a pile of new material that came to light as a result of the Coutts hoard. Further information came to light from the sale of the American Bank Note Company archives in the early 1990s.

There will no doubt be many who will find the detailed information in this catalog exhausting and of marginal interest. But this information, if used, will forever pull aside the veil of ignorance and misinformation that has covered this area. It will also render intelligent collecting less difficult. What I have tried to do is to level the playing field by making everyone aware of what exists and what it is worth.

The reader will quickly note that there has been a massive overhaul both in terms of completeness of listings and the order in which the bonds are arranged. The August 19, 1861 bonds are listed by their due date, arrayed by denominations from low to high. This allows the collector to note the similarity in designs of many of the due date series bonds. Registered bonds are listed for the first time broken out into their various designs in the order in which they were issued. Not only are the quantities of each design given, but also the numbers issued of each denomination within that bond design.

Dates of issue are provided, where available, but these are not always provided for the coupon bonds. The bonds of the Act of August 19, 1861 are particularly annoying in this regard. Their dates are frequently the date of the purchase, not the date emitted; thus it has been necessary to leave this information out.

There is also a wholly new listing of the registered bonds of August 19, 1861, which have various due dates, together with the quantities that are thought to have been emitted. For some reason, almost certainly on the orders of Secretary Memminger, such bonds primarily mature in January; those falling due in July are quite rare.

Coupon alignment and the signer for the register are also listed, together, where known, with the number ranges in which those signatures exist. Again, some signatures do not exist for several bonds and others are quite rare. The detail may seem overwhelming, but will become less so with experience and regular use.

This revised mode of listing leads to new recognition of many rarities.

Readers will also note that while it has been the practice to put rarities on each bond, there has not been, until recently, a published scale as to what those numbers mean for Confederate items. I have adopted a rarity 1 to 8 system in keeping with the generally accepted practice in obsolete bank note catalogs. However, the amounts of Confederate notes and bonds available so far exceed the usual availability of obsolete bank notes that I have had to create my own number ranges. To further differentiate more precisely the various gradations of rarity of the bonds available, I have also introduced pluses and minuses, each with its own number range, to allow collectors to calculate with greater precision the availability of any bond. Many bonds are reasonably available; others are practically nonexistent. The numbers reportedly issued, even when revised from the previously reported Thian-Kerksis figures, do not provide an infallible guide as to availability.

Descriptive details

Bond sizes

The bonds illustrated herein are various fractions of actual size. Bond sizes range from 164 x 95mm up to 428 x 730mm. Because of the limitations of page size, it has not proved practicable to photograph all the bonds with all the attached coupons. Some full length pieces have been included for informational purposes.

Printers

There were quite a number of firms that produced registered and coupon bonds, call certificates, certificates of indebtedness, and the like for the Confederate Treasury. Following are brief histories of these firms, listed in alphabetical order.

1) **American Bank Note Company**. This firm's name first came into use in 1855 as a name for Draper, Welsh and Company. By the merger agreement of 1858, this firm absorbed most of the other prominent firms of the time and gained a near monopoly of the security printing business. Bonds were prepared for the Confederacy by this firm in New York, prior to the outbreak of war. The plates for these bonds were then seized by a U.S. marshal. Subsequently, more bonds were printed at the New Orleans branch office headed by Samuel Schmidt.

2) **Archer & Daly** (Archer & Halpin). This firm was set up in Richmond, Virginia in 1863. John Archer was an engraver from the North who had worked for Harper Brothers, the book printers, as a plate engraver. Joseph Daly is thought to have been (at least according to August Dietz I, who interviewed some of the old printers) a Richmond plasterer of means who put up the money for the Archer firm in its various forms. However, Paterson visited Richmond in August 1862 and reported to Secretary Memminger that Archer was absent at a Virginia spa and that Daly was in charge of the shop in his absence. Daly, it seems, was doing some of the Confederate stamps by the stereograph process, probably the De La Rue 5¢ blue stamps with Davis on them. It would therefore seem that Dietz to the contrary, Daly was in fact a printer and engraver, and not merely a financial backer.

In 1863 Frederick Halpin had been ignominiously booted out of the Keatinge and Ball premises in Columbia, South Carolina for alleged complicity in Blanton Duncan's false accusations against Edward Keatinge. Halpin then moved to Richmond, where he joined the Archer firm. He appears to have been a man in his early 60s who had also been a Northern engraver for Harper Brothers.

This firm, in its various guises, produced stamps, notes, and bonds for the Confederacy until September 1864, when its equipment was seized for alleged inefficiency. Subsequently, its men and materials were shipped to Columbia, South Carolina where most of the workmen took service with Keatinge and Ball. Evans and Cogswell seem to have been assigned most of the bond plates and printed all the bonds originally engraved by Archer.

3) **John Douglas** was an engraver and printer in New Orleans, Louisiana. He produced three bonds, some government warrants, and other fiscal paper, not to mention state notes and private scrip. His one-man shop had a limited productive capacity, and after the capture of New Orleans on April 24, 1862, he was cut off from further business with the Confederacy.

4) **Blanton Duncan** was the son of Kentucky Congressman Garrett Duncan, who moved to Europe in 1861 in order to avoid having to take sides in the impending conflict. His son was made of sterner stuff. At 35, he formed the first Confederate Kentucky regiment as its executive officer (with no previous military experience). He went with his unit eastward and joined General Joseph Johnston's forces near Winchester, Virginia. He was present at First Manassas (Bull Run) where he was men-

The famous bridge at Antietam/Sharpsburg.

tioned by General Beauregard in his dispatches. He next went back to Kentucky to help organize the secession convention (of which he was a member). While he was thus engaged, he also helped Secretary Memminger in his search for men and security printing materials, particularly paper.

In January 1862 he appeared once more in Richmond, Virginia, where he joined the bar and opened a printing shop. Mary Boykin Chesnut reported meeting him at a dinner party at this time and found him quite fascinating. Even at this early time he had trouble with his workmen, who took off "blue Mondays" for getting drunk and to seek opportunities for amorous indulgence. After he appealed for help from the provost marshal, General Winder, these men were arrested and forced to return to their presses. By way of thanks to the general, Duncan put his portrait on a $1000 bond.

In May 1862 he moved his printing operation to Columbia, South Carolina where he ruled his workers with a rod of iron and compelled them to be more efficient. However, his blatant efforts to eliminate the competition by seizing their supplies and manpower under pretended military authority got him into major trouble with state governments (who had contracts with those firms) and with Secretary Memminger, who had to deal with their vehement complaints. Among the firms victimized was F. W. Bournemann's shop in Charleston, which worked for that city and also for the state of North Carolina. Even the firm of Evans and Cogswell, with whom Secretary Memminger was well acquainted, and who had been induced by him to undertake contracts with the government, suffered from Duncan's depredations.

Duncan's campaign to monopolize the security printing business even extended to an effort to corner the ice supply (needed to cool off printing plates) as well as to the interception of the ink and paper arriving in Charleston consigned to Keatinge & Ball. This devious activity was discovered purely by accident, when Joseph Daniel Pope, a prominent South Carolina lawyer from Beaufort, who had been the former statewide commissioner for the war tax and who was in charge of the printers from April 1862 to April 1863, visited Duncan's premises during his absence. Conducted on a tour of inspection of the building, Pope literally stumbled upon the missing materials in Duncan's attic.

Federal railroad bridge in Virginia.

Interior View of **FORT SUMTER** *on the 14th April 1861, after its evacuation by* Maj. Robert Anderson, *1st Art. U.S.A. Com'd. Showing the north end of West Barracks, with the two tiers of Casements and Barbette of adjacent north channel face.*

Curiously, while Pope was making this discovery, Duncan was on a flag of truce ship near Richmond. He was trying to induce a Major Schenk of the United States Army to become his partner and help him procure badly needed printing supplies by running them through the blockade. Schenk reported this proposition to his superiors under the mistaken impression that something of the sort must have been going on prior to Duncan's surprise approach. This led to such a bitter wrangle between the War and Treasury Departments that Lincoln had to step in and settle the controversy personally.

These and other annoying habits resulted in the loss of Duncan's government contracts in early 1863. In May 1862 Duncan had set up a steam press for printing books and documents, and many items bear his imprint. He also continued for a few weeks in 1863 as a note contractor for various state and local governments, most notably those in Louisiana. When his state contracts were completed, Memminger seized the equipment and supplies that the government had given to Duncan, and Duncan later sold out the residue of his business. He rejoined the Army in Wilmington, North Carolina for the duration of the war. He was still alive in 1896, when he was reportedly visiting California during the winters.

5) **George Dunn and Company** was formed in 1863. Dunn had come over to Wilmington aboard the *Giraffe* in early 1862 as part of the group of Scottish lithographers hired by Major Benjamin F. Evans in London during late 1861. His talents and skills at working without the usual equipment brought him to Secretary Memminger's attention. He was accordingly encouraged to set up his own shop, separate from that of the government in Richmond.

He designed some of the "December 2, 1862" $5 note, and later won contracts to engrave quite a few bonds and call certificates. He also did some of the late warrants. His limited printing capacity often compelled him to sublet the printing end of his business. For example, while he designed and engraved the March 23, 1863 4% coupon bonds, the bonds were actually printed by Hoyer & Ludwig, and most of his other work was printed by Evans & Cogswell.

Dunn was, next to Edward Keatinge, without doubt the best engraver within the Confederacy. He remained in Richmond and did some private engraving and printing work when his government contracts permitted. He probably returned to Britain in early 1865 along with the other printers who had three-year contracts. The postwar Richmond directories make no mention of him.

Ruins of Richmond.

6) **Evans & Cogswell**. This Charleston, South Carolina firm was formed in 1836 originally under the style of Walker and Cogswell. In 1860, James Walker took a back seat as a silent partner and was replaced by Major Benjamin Evans. The firm was renamed Evans & Cogswell. Evans went to Europe in late 1861 and at great risk procured badly needed manpower and supplies. While doing so, he used the offices of the famous firm of Thomas De La Rue and Company as his headquarters. He is described in that firm's history as a large, charming but businesslike man. On his way back, he had the curious distinction of having no less than three ships founder beneath him, making him the Jonah of the Confederacy. His revolver, which he took with him on this trip, turned up in the 1970s and was sold to a collector.

His junior partner, Harvey Cogswell I, continued in his role as the firm's general manager. Walker tried to help out (and avoid the draft) by going to Britain in 1863. Operating under instructions furnished by Secretary Memminger, he contracted with S. Straker and Sons for the production of the Chemicograph backs, which were intended to be used as the new backs for the 1864 note issue. Unfortunately, the plates were captured while running the blockade, although Walker himself managed to return safely by another ship.

The firm printed a few bonds starting in late 1861, only to have their materials and personnel seized by Blanton Duncan in May 1862. Duncan then bought them out, Harvey Cogswell being under the misapprehension that Duncan was running a *bona fide* government establishment and that he was selling his plant to the government. When Major Evans' men arrived from Britain with supplies, the firm was started up again, and was active doing large scale work for the Confederacy from 1862 on. It printed notes and bonds for state, city and private corporations, particularly early during the war; it also used its steam printing press for book and other commercial printing.

When the Union blockade tightened around Charleston and shells from Morris Island began to land in the city (one hit the State Bank building on the corner of Bay and Broad Streets, right next door to the Evans & Cogswell offices), the firm moved to Columbia. There it took over Kintsler's Hall, a large, airy, multistory building, where it continued its operations until the fall of Columbia to General Sherman in February 1865.

The firm returned to Charleston, where under the resumed name of Walker, Evans and Cogswell (WECO) it continued in business after the war despite the loss of much of its equipment in the reported burning of its Columbia premises in 1865. It was still doing security printing work early into the 20th century. A history of WECO was published in 1936. More recently, this firm survived as an office supply store. In the late 1980s Harvey Cogswell V sold his plant and then conveyed the trade name to a young couple, who failed within a year or so in North Charleston.

7) **Fred Geese** (originally styled Friederich Giesse), was a lithographer from Bavaria. He came to America and went to work in 1859 for Ludwig Hoyer. He moved from Richmond in 1864 and ended by working for Evans & Cogswell. He engraved one set of Confederate bonds, which bear his name, for Evans & Cogswell in 1864. After the war, unable for reasons unknown to make a living as a lithographer, he and his wife ran a grocery store in Richmond. He is buried in Richmond's Hollywood Cemetery, just to the right across the street from the Ludwig family plot.

8) **Hoyer & Ludwig**. This firm consisted of two persons, Ludwig Hoyer and Charles Ludwig. Hoyer was born in 1820 in Bavaria and moved to Richmond where, by 1860, he was a successful jeweler and real estate investor. He hired Geese and then Ludwig to work for the business card printing operation associated with his jewelry store. His firm also printed labels for cigar boxes and other tobacco products.

Charles Ludwig, 1829-1874, also came originally from Bavaria, via Sweden. He had been orphaned at an early age, but he claimed to have been brought up by an aunt who was a lady-in-waiting to Eugene de Beauharais's daughter, who became the queen of Oscar I of Sweden. He learned the lithographic engraving business, was well educated and came over to the United States. He married a Culpepper, Virginia woman, Henrietta Koeckler, had four sons and moved to Richmond, where he worked for a while for Ritchie & Dunnavant, the Commonwealth's official printers. He did some bonds and ballots for them in the 1856-1859 period. In early 1860, he went to work for Hoyer.

In July 1861, at the time of the Confederate government's removal from Montgomery, Alabama to Richmond, the treasury, for lack of anything better in the way of security printers, contracted with Hoyer & Ludwig to print the notes and bonds authorized by the Act of May 16, 1861. Subsequently, the firm also printed notes and bonds authorized by the Act of August 19, 1861. When not engaged in that business, the firm printed notes for states such as Virginia and Florida and a number of local governments in Virginia. They also did Virginia scrip notes and the occasional bank note.

With the Union attack on Richmond in the spring of 1862, Secretary Memminger decided that the security printers should be moved to some less vulnerable site. If the capital should be captured, it would be impossible to move the printers out with their heavy equipment on short notice. If these plants were captured, the Confederacy would be deprived of the means to pay the army or any other government expenses, particularly with treasury notes. Accordingly, Memminger decreed that all the printers must move to Columbia, South Carolina.

Hoyer & Ludwig declined to make this move. Both men were closely associated with Richmond and they may have thought that, despite Memminger's firm insistence on the point, they could still get government contracts. Moreover, they were filling orders for others and they may have thought that that business, which was not trammeled by Memminger's low margin contracts, would pay them better. In any case, they did not move and were compelled to sell their government-supplied equipment and materials to James T. Paterson of Augusta, Georgia, who moved that portion of the plant to South Carolina.

The departure of the printers to Columbia did not, as Secretary Memminger had intended, mean an end to the relationship between Hoyer & Ludwig and the treasury. The firm was still busy finishing up contracts for coupon and registered bonds, call certificates and other debt instruments, and Ludwig continued to do postal warrants for Postmaster General Reagan, who was not bound by Memminger's rules.

Moreover, in August 1862 Ludwig got a secret contract for one Confederate note of his design (the Type 46, $10). Later he received printing contracts for the $1 and $2 bills, from late 1862 to 1865. Ludwig also did some of the bond printing that George Dunn could not handle. Then, ironically, in early 1865, when the Union captured Columbia and broke up the other printing firms, Hoyer & Ludwig enjoyed a brief monopoly of the printing contracts. Hoyer also rented some of his buildings to the Confederacy to use as offices.

After the war, Hoyer retired from business. His wife had died in 1865 and he decided to devote himself to his investments and the rearing of his sole surviving child. In the 1870 census, he was reportedly living with his 16 year-old daughter and owned over $100,000 worth of real estate at depressed postwar values, exclusive of other investments. He was, by the standards of the day, a wealthy man, and his daughter, whatever her personal attractions or accomplishments, was an eligible heiress.

With Hoyer's retirement, the firm was broken up and Ludwig established a new firm. Under this arrangement, he worked for over a year with Edward Keatinge, the erstwhile Confederate currency engraver, as his junior partner. The two men produced a few bonds and some checks under the Ludwig & Keatinge imprint. When things quieted down and it was once more safe to go north, Keatinge moved back to New York. Ludwig carried on for a few more years as a sole proprietor. His efforts to incorporate a Southern security printing firm fell through, and he died of renal failure in 1874.

9) **Dr. James T. Paterson** was a Scottish dentist who moved with his brother George to Augusta, Georgia in the 1850s. There he set up his dental office in a smart part of town just opposite, as it turned out, Augusta's foremost house of assignation.

In the course of his professional activities with his brother, he came to know a number of prominent Georgians including Vice President Alexander H. Stephens. Confronted by the Conscription Act in early 1862 and anxious to avoid the draft as a foreigner, Paterson entered the security engraving business, taking over the contracts and much of the manpower and equipment of the Richmond firm of Hoyer & Ludwig. He set up two shops, one in Columbia to meet his Confederate contracts and another in his home town of Augusta to handle an extensive business in state notes and bonds, local scrip, and book printing.

Paterson's chief function was to take over where Ludwig had left off. In addition to the note printing, he did a few Confederate registered bonds and call certificates, as well as warrants. Duncan and Evans & Cogswell took over all the Confederate coupon bond printing business.

Paterson's position was a very uncomfortable one. Hoyer & Ludwig had off-loaded on him their oldest equipment and least efficient workmen. He got trapped in the general intrigues among the printers, which involved bribing workmen to switch employers. The fact that Paterson was absent, more often than not, in Augusta, left his Columbia plant in the hands of his foreman. On at least one occasion, after high words, Edward Keatinge pulled Paterson's foreman off his horse and gave him a sound thrashing, protected from the Paterson workmen by a shotgun-wielding Thomas A. Ball, Keatinge's manager.

Paterson lost his Confederate contracts in April 1864 and was replaced as a printer by Evans & Cogswell. He continued in Augusta with his general printing business and his state currency and bond work, chiefly for Mississippi, until 1865. After the war, he invested his capital in a lumber company near Savannah. When that firm failed, he committed suicide in 1870.

10) **Ritchie & Dunnavant**. This firm and that of Tyler and Allegre were the public printers for the Commonwealth of Virginia in the years prior to the Confederate War. They had, in addition to their public printing, done a few bonds, ballots and the like. Charles Ludwig, as noted, had worked for them.

During the war the firm printed some registered bonds for Virginia. In 1864, they appear to have printed the pink paper funding forms. Later, they prepared the call certificates under the Act of February 17, 1864. This was the only group of bonds done by them.

11) **Wagner & Company**. Very little is known about this firm, which was a father and son printing concern in Nashville, Tennessee. These men came to Blanton Duncan's attention in the fall of 1861, when Duncan was passing through on his way to the December 1861 Kentucky secession convention. Duncan bought out the Wagners, brought them to Richmond with their equipment, and from the design and workmanship of Duncan's bonds they appear to have had a major influence on that part of his work. Only one bond bears their imprint, probably an error which the egotistical Duncan would have been unlikely to tolerate.

12) **George Wojciechowski**. Wojciechowski was a Polish lithographer who worked and subcontracted for Evans & Cogswell. Otherwise, we know very little about him. He apparently did the engraving work as opposed to the actual printing, the quality of his work being considerably lower than that of the Scottish lithographers imported in 1862. His name appears on a number of 1863 bonds.

Bond engravers

Collectors will note that there are comments in the catalog text on names that appear on the bonds, which apparently identify the engravers. Some of these names will be familiar to those who collect Confederate or Louisiana state currency, where such names appear on the faces and backs of the notes in the margins. Unfortunately, we know very little about these men, as they are seldom mentioned in the Confederate correspondence; efforts to learn more about them would be very time consuming and likely unproductive.

Paper

The paper used for the Confederate bonds varied considerably in quality. At the beginning, the traditional hard-wearing red silk fiber paper was used, but the supply of this was soon exhausted and a thick bond paper was used that proved very unsuitable because of its tendency to split. Then other miscellaneous white papers were employed, some of mottled or oil stained texture.

Much of this early paper came from a mill near Nashville, with which Duncan had contracted in late 1861. This source was lost in early 1862 as a result of General Grant's successful offensive. The quality of the paper it put out was not good, and John Douglas was of the opinion that much of it was unsuitable even for wrapping new shoes.

In 1863, there was an improvement in paper quality as paper from Europe and particularly from Britain came in. Thin, bluish-white banknote paper was used, and house stationery from the firm of "C. Ansell" came into use on the $1000 8% bonds of February 20, 1863. Because of an error, at least one sheet of paper watermarked "CSA" in block letters and some sheets of "J. Green & Sons, 1862" watermarked paper, originally intended for currency printing, were diverted to the printing of some $100 bonds.

Pink paper was also ordered from the Belvidere Mill in Richmond and was used for the 7% February 20, 1863 bonds and the 1864 call certificates as well as Treasury notes. The Confederate printers used the wet printing process, for which the paper was soaked in vats before going to press. The early sheets had the distressing habit of disintegrating in the vats or in the printing presses before Belvidere got the hang of making this paper. As a result, much precious time was wasted in removing the fibers from the printing plates.

Later, thick and thin paper from the Belvidere works was used on the 1864 bonds. Much of this paper was heavily sized; in consequence, many bonds are brittle and tend to split easily.

Richmond in ruins.

In early 1864, with the printing and issue of massive quantities of new bonds anticipated under the February 17, 1864 act, security considerations came to the fore. The new bonds would not be redeemable for thirty years and the danger of their being counterfeited rose accordingly. Therefore, the Belvidere paper works in Richmond, with or without instructions, prepared a deckle with a wavy line and a copy of the Confederate seal (the equestrian statue of George Washington, lying to the west of the Virginia capitol building) located at the center. Some sheets of paper were made from the deckle and sent to the treasury for approval. However, this was done too late and it was decided not to use this watermarked paper after all. A few of these fascinating paper samples still exist.

Bond signers

Under United States law, which was carried over by the Confederacy, the Register of the Treasury was responsible for signing all transfer drafts, treasury warrants, bonds, bond coupons, treasury notes and other debt instruments. His office, which had quite a number of clerks in it, was also responsible for keeping accurate records of the public debt. In mid-1861, when the register was freed from the necessity of personally signing treasury notes, a substantial force, under his supervision, remained responsible for signing on his behalf all the treasury notes and for keeping a record of the notes issued and cancelled. The Register's Office was thus an important part of the Treasury Department. The chief personnel of that office, insofar as they pertained to the issue of bonds, were as follows:

1) **Alexander Clitherall** served as first Register of the Treasury from February 1861 until July 24, 1861. At that time, with the government moving to Richmond, Clitherall, an Alabamian, decided not to go and resigned his post. He held a number of minor state offices after the war. His signature appears only on the February 28, 1861 act bonds.

2) **Charles T. Jones**, Acting Register. Jones had been the Chief Clerk of the register's office in Washington under Secretary Howell Cobb. He came to Montgomery with a pile of forms (thereby providing an invaluable continuity in bureaucratic tradition and operation *vis-a-vis* the Washington regime) and assumed the same office under the Confederacy from February 1861 until April 1865. He could only sign bonds as "Acting Register" when the register was absent. This first came about when Clitherall resigned. Later, when Robert Tyler was absent from the office for whatever reason, Jones was pressed into service.

The CSS *Virginia* in Hampton Roads engaging the Union fleet.

When, as noted, two assistant registers were appointed in 1863, the need for Jones to sign bonds diminished greatly. Jones' signature occurs on the February 28, 1861, May 16, 1861 and August 19, 1861 bonds as well as on scattered bonds in 1862 and early 1863. His initials may also be found at the left on bonds as proof that they had been registered on the treasury records.

3) **Robert Tyler** (1816-1877), the second register, was a son of U.S. President John Tyler by his first wife. Tyler was head of the Democratic party in Pennsylvania and a personal friend of President James Buchanan before he had to flee to the Confederacy. Through his father's influence, he procured the post of Register of the Treasury, which he held from August 13, 1861 to the end of the war.

Sinking of the ironclad CSS *Atlanta.*

The massive proliferation of warrants, transfer drafts, bonds, call certificates, and the like created a tidal wave of work, which Tyler could not handle. After Tyler had an altercation with Secretary Memminger, who claimed that Tyler was wasting valuable time wandering around the hallways of the executive office building (the former U.S. customs house), President Davis intervened. He agreed with Tyler that he had other things to do besides signing coupon bonds and the upshot of the matter was that Congress was asked to approve the appointment of two assistant registers. These men did most of the bond signing work in 1863 and a larger part of it still in 1864. It was also helpful when the Congress allowed the coupons of each bond to bear Tyler's printed signature instead of requiring, as had heretofore been the case, that one of his clerks sign each and every coupon.

At the end of the war Tyler moved with his family to Alabama, where he became a newspaper editor. He also became the head of the Democratic party in Alabama, thus becoming one of the select few to have had a political career in more than one state.

4) **Charles A. Rose**, Assistant Register. Little is known of him but that he was 53 in 1863 when he was appointed and he was a Richmond notary public. He had earlier worked for the department and his initials, CAR, appear on a number of bonds. He remained as assistant register until the end of the War.

5) **E. Apperson** was the other assistant register. Nothing is known at present of this man, who signed most of the 1864 bonds.

6) **Henry Dickson Capers**. Capers was the reporter for a Charleston newspaper at Montgomery when C. G. Memminger hired him as his chief clerk. Capers held this job for the one year's duration of the Provisional Congress, before he left to join the artillery. His full name and later his initials, HDC, frequently appear at the left on the early bonds. The initials of other minor members of the register's office appear at the left when and as required on all the bonds. After Memminger's death in 1888, Capers wrote his biography.

Bond coupons

The Confederate coupon bonds come three ways: those that are complete, those that are "as issued" (described below), and those having coupons from July 1, 1865 on. A few bonds have extra coupons dated between September 1, 1861 and April 1, 1865. Such bonds command a small premium over those with the usual number of coupons. Bonds with less than the proper number of coupons sell for somewhat less than the usual prices. Bonds with all their coupons or "as issued" go for premiums, particularly those bonds issued in the first two years. The premium is smaller for the 1863-4 bonds, of which quite a few have turned up in pristine condition.

Because the Confederacy did not wish to pay interest on bonds prior to the date on which they were sold, the last coupon frequently does not have any fixed denomination. Instead, there is a handwritten denomination. Where the bond has been issued after the due date of the first coupon, that coupon is either clipped off or is pen cancelled and the second coupon is hand altered to reflect the sale date. This is what is called "as issued." This practice became established after the fiasco with the February 28, 1861 act bonds, where the printers printed fixed denomination first coupons, assuming that interest would be paid from May 1, 1861. This produced bonds with first coupons for $1.33, $2.66, $13.33 and $26.66, sums that could not be paid as there was not, nor has there ever been, a coin for a third or two thirds of a cent.

There are also instances where the bonds were prepared too late to be sold in a timely way (this chiefly happened with the February 20, 1863 and February 17, 1864 bonds). The government therefore had bonds prepared with the first coupon maturing six months later. Thus the February 20, 1863 bonds, when complete, have first coupons for July 1863 and January 1864, while the February 17, 1864 bonds have first coupons for July 1864 and January 1865.

All bond coupons were signed by clerks of the treasury department staff (in particular those in the register's office) until 1864, when the printed signature of Robert Tyler appears. This arose because Congress permitted the Secretary of the Treasury to issue bonds "with such authentication as the Secretary of the Treasury may prescribe." Among the anomalies are the *Indian Princess* bonds issued after July 1, 1863, which have three hand-drawn coupons signed by Robert Tyler in person, although the bonds are all signed by Charles T. Jones. These bonds were evidently prepared after the funding act of October 1862 required that bonds be prepared to draw in the July 25, 1861 dated notes. Since the bonds called for a ten-year maturity date and it was already 1863, the three coupons were added to meet that requirement.

Bond numbering systems

As might be expected, bonds were numbered by hand and start with number 1 until the issue was complete. However, there are exceptions to this rule. Some bonds, although authorized by a particular act, continue with the numbers used for another bond act. On other occasions, there is a big skip in numbers where there was a changeover in acts. In the early 1861 bonds, the numbering system starts at one for each denomination and goes on until the end. With the August 19, 1861 registered bonds, bond number one starts with the date due; hence the listing by due dates.

Those who are interested in low numbered bonds, particularly number one items, will find that quite a few of these have survived. Those who moved quickly during the dispersal of the London hoard had a chance to acquire quite a number of these. When these groups are broken up in the fullness of time, others will have similar opportunities.

Trans-Mississippi overprints

Bonds shipped to the far west were overprinted in red with restrictive texts that made them invalid until they were endorsed by a duly authorized depositary. This was to prevent their use by the Union in the event of their diversion or capture. Two principal styles of overprint were used. The two-line text reads: "This Bond NOT TO BE VALID, until endorsed/by the Depositary who issues it." The three-line text reads: "This Bond not to be valid until/endorsed by the Depositary to/whom it is to be issued." Additional endorsements were often applied at the issuing office, usually stating the geographic location of the office.

Lieutenant General "Stonewall" Jackson.

Lieutenant General "JEB" Stuart.

Catalog numbering system

Since most collectors have collected bonds using the Kerksis-Criswell numbering system, a cross-referenced number list has been furnished that allows the collector to translate the old Criswell numbers into the Ball numbers appearing in this book. Since quite a few Ball listings are not included in Criswell, there will be many items not appearing with an independent Criswell number.

Values

In keeping with the general hobby practice, I have included values for bonds in fine and very fine condition to the right of the listings. Values have been put on great rarities simply by way of an extrapolation of earlier reported prices. They do not, in such cases, represent current market prices based on current sales, as is the case with the values for more common pieces. The values quoted are intended as guides for collectors in buying and selling Confederate bonds. They are the author's best estimate of the current market conditions. Various prices prevail in different markets. They also go up and down.

I would have preferred to have put the values in a separate booklet, as was done with the first Criswell bond book. Such an approach might prevent this book's becoming dated soon after publication because of changes in the market for collectors' bonds. The publisher objected to this pointing out among other things that most collectors prefer to have all of the information available in one concise package. Since my firm publishes price lists of Confederate bonds at least twice a year, in the spring and late fall, those wishing to keep abreast of price developments can easily do so by writing or calling R. M. Smythe & Co. Inc. at 26 Broadway, Suite 271, New York, NY 10004-1701, phone 800-622-1880.

Table of rarities

Each bond is assigned a rarity value in the catalog. These values are a quick way to indicate the scarcity of a particular bond. Although there is a correlation, keep in mind that rarity and value are not the same thing. The quantities listed for the respective rarities are the number estimated to still exist.

rarity		**extant**
8	=	1-3
7+	=	4-10
7	=	11-20
7-	=	21-35
6+	=	36-50
6	=	51-75
6-	=	76-100
5+	=	101-200
5	=	201-350
5-	=	351-500
4+	=	501-750
4	=	751-1000
4-	=	1001-1500
3+	=	1501-2500
3	=	2501-5000
3-	=	5001-7500
2+	=	7501-10,000
2	=	10,001-20,000
2-	=	20,001-35,000
1+	=	35,001-50,000
1	=	50,001-100,000
1-	=	100,000+

Acknowledgments

There were many people and institutions which had a hand in the production of this book. I would like first to thank in alphabetical order those persons or institutions which furnished information, made useful suggestions or otherwise provided general assistance. Among these were Charles J. Affleck†, my parents George W.† and Ruth M. Ball†, Coutts Bank, Arnold Cowan†, Grover C. Criswell, Ben Douglas†, John J. Ford, Jr., Paul Gibson, Stephen L. Goldsmith, Diana and John Herzog, Kevin Jackson, Donald King, Hardie Maloney, Eddie Nash, Ronald Payne, Fred Schwan, Ritchie Self, Michael Sherman, Hugh Shull, Guy Swanson, Duke University, The National Archives, The Smithsonian Institution, Museum of the Confederacy, and Karen Vasudeva, not to mention the many others who helped in various ways.

I would like to thank Karen Vasudeva, my father's former assistant, who typed the various editions of my manuscript and who also deciphered my handwriting.

Thanks are also due to Joseph E. Boling for his painstaking reading of my manuscript. He made many suggestions for improvements and found discrepancies in data presented at that stage. I am also indebted to Fred Schwan who made many useful suggestions regarding the format of my book.

I would like to pay particular homage to Diana and John Herzog, Stephen L. Goldsmith, and R. M. Smythe & Company. They all encouraged the publication of this volume and gave me time off to complete my research, finish my manuscript and otherwise complete this long-delayed task.

All this said, I assume sole responsibility for anything appearing in this book. If there is anything good here, those who contributed to it are welcome to take such credit as their services warrant; if there are any errors, they are mine alone.

† deceased

Bull Run.

CATALOG OF CONFEDERATE STOCKS AND BONDS

Manassas (Bull Run) Battlefield.

I. ACT OF FEBRUARY 28, 1861

The first Confederate bond issue, for $15 million, was authorized by the Confederate Congress on February 28, 1861. It was a small issue and one clearly not seriously intended for the defense of the Confederate States; it was simply intended as bridge financing to meet the temporary needs of the government.

Since relations with the United States were uncertain at best and with Lincoln due to be inaugurated on March 4th, Secretary Memminger was anxious not to place this order in the North, where the bonds might be intercepted. Instead, he sent an agent to New Orleans, who contracted with Samuel Schmidt, the resident manager of American Bank Note Company, to have the whole of this issue of $50, $100, $500 and $1000 coupon bonds and registered bonds (known as "stock" at the time) done in the South.

Time passed and war broke out at Fort Sumter on April 12, 1861. Shortly after that event, Memminger received a telegram from New York announcing the completion of his order for registered bonds and informing him that they were on their way to Montgomery by express. Since the whole purpose of contracting for this work in New Orleans had been to avoid having it done in New York, Memminger immediately contacted New Orleans to find out what was going on.

Schmidt, it seems, with only himself, his son and another workman in his shop, did not have the plates or manpower to fill Memminger's order. Since the treasury agent had failed to make it clear that all this work was to be done on the premises, Schmidt had followed the usual procedure of passing the order along to New York for execution. For its part, the New York office, also apparently in keeping with long established practice, had filled the order for the registered bonds using an imprint that said that those bonds had been engraved and printed in New Orleans, whereas they had actually been done in New York. Thus while the whole procedure looks suspiciously as if the New York office was anticipating probable Federal objections to its having filled this order, there was nothing, from a purely internal company policy view, that was in any way objectionable or out of the ordinary.

The books of registered bonds, four books of 250 bonds each for each of the four denominations, were dispatched as stated, but they all did not arrive. The last book of the $50s never turned up; nor did two books of the $500s, and a book of the $100s, according to the letters of transmittal between Secretary Memminger and the register's office. The plates were seized in New York shortly after this shipment by the U.S. marshal.

It should also be noted that with war having broken out, work on the coupon bonds ceased in New York. Only the $500 bond was in proof form (less the coupons, which had not yet been engraved); the $1000 was still an all-written mockup with pasted-in vignettes, and there is no evidence that work had even started on the $50 and $100 denominations. In any case, Memminger had to make immediate arrangements to have the coupon bonds printed in the South.

Cut off from the New York office, Schmidt had no choice but to start belatedly preparing the $1000 and $500 coupon bonds. The lettering was handsome, as were the green protectors. But very significantly, Schmidt nowhere put his name nor that of American Bank Note on any of these bonds, nor did he use the name "Southern Bank Note Company," which he used on the notes that he made. Whether this was done to conceal his role in the production, as many suspect, is unknown.

In the meantime, the lower denomination bonds were farmed out to John Douglas, a New Orleans engraver with a small shop. His $100 and $50 bonds look well enough, but he had to get his red silk fiber paper from Schmidt's shop. When the supply was exhausted, about half way through the contract, Douglas had to use a thick bond paper that he did not consider suitable. This explains the use of two kinds of paper for these bonds.

James Denegre, President of the New Orleans Canal and Banking Company, suggested to Secretary Memminger that the bond holders should be given the added assurance of payment through the creation of a sinking fund from the one-tenth of a cent per pound of cotton export duty that was authorized along with the bonds, but the revenue from that act was inadequate for the purpose indicated. Moreover, this idea was advanced so late that only a portion of the $500 coupon bonds of this act had the sinking fund text printed on their backs.

Note that all of the coupon bonds, regardless of the printer, have a line at the left calling for the register to list the city where the interest would be payable. The idea behind this was that the treasury could estimate how much coin it would need to send to each assistant treasurer or pay depositary. However, the idea behind a coupon bond is that it is transferable by delivery, and tying the bond to a particular place where it must be paid would defeat the whole purpose of such bonds. Thus the blanks were not filled in, nor were they used again.

It should be noted that while complete bonds of other issues turn up with some regularity, the author knows at present of only seven such bonds of this act, one $1000 and a few $50s and $100s. The oddity of their coupon denominations, as noted above, makes them doubly attractive, hence the large premium paid for them.

In addition to the printed coupon and registered bonds, there was also an issue of manuscript bonds, as a stopgap measure while bonds were being prepared. This was particularly true of registered bonds in denominations in excess of $1000. The issue of manuscript bonds was imperative because there was no time to prepare regular bonds and the Treasury urgently needed cash with which to meet its needs. Most of the manuscript bonds are made payable to banks, savings banks, or insurance companies. Most seem to have been taken up when the Ball 18 (Cr. 9) bonds were issued, starting sometime in August 1861, although some remained outstanding for the entire war.

A. 8% coupon bonds due September 1, 1871
Amount authorized: $15 million
Total amount issued (all types): $10,636,850

TYPE 1 **$50**

Total number issued (all varieties): 7,835[1]
Rarity (3+)
Dates of issue: April 17 - October 31, 1861
Imprint: "Douglas, Engr. N. Orleans"

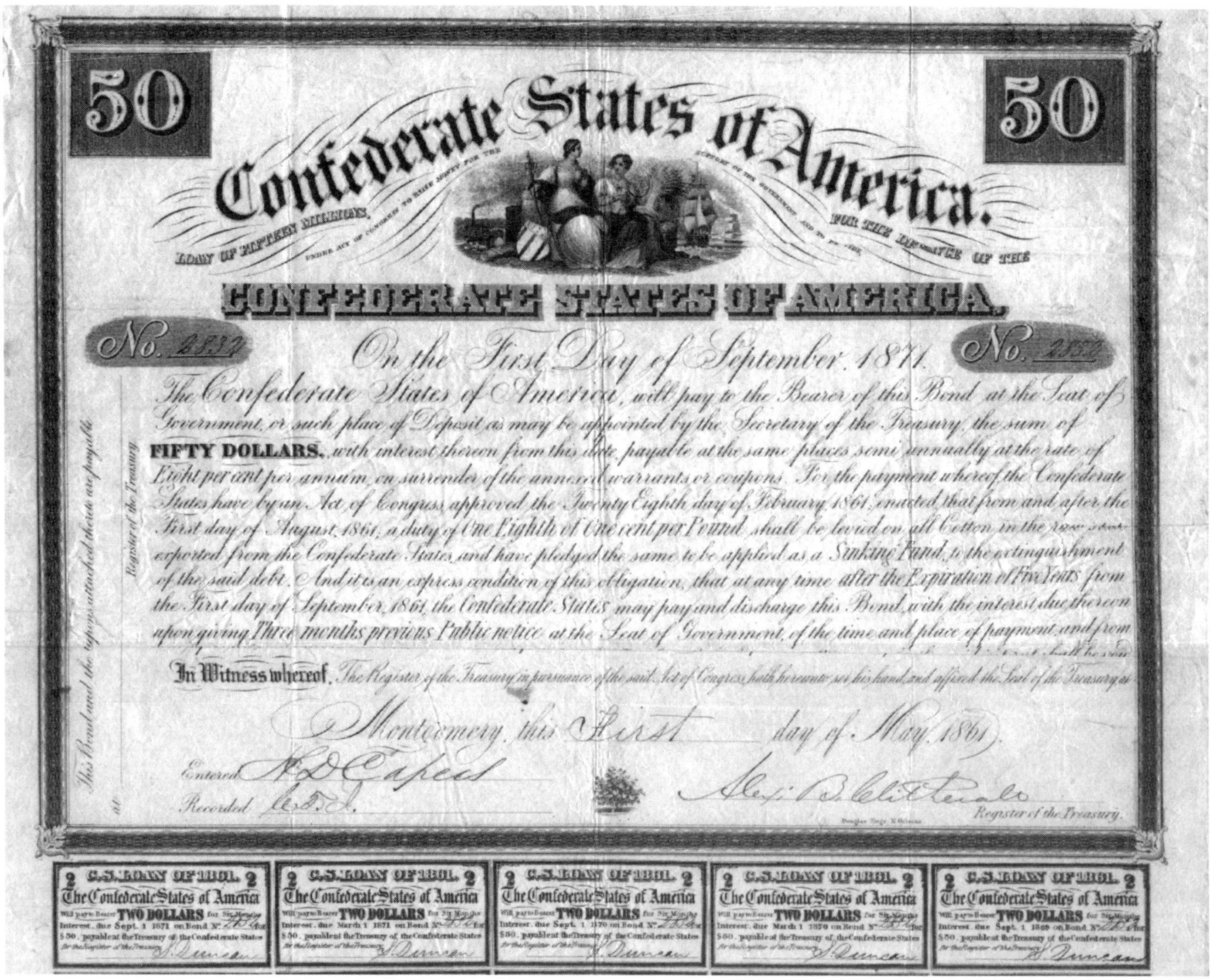

(Two women, Columbia/Commerce, left; Ceres/agriculture, right.)

				fine	very fine
1.	$50	Printed on thin red silk fiber paper. Number issued: c. 4,700 (#1-4700) Dates of issue: c. April 17 - May 1, 1861 Signed by Clitherall, Jones.	Rarity (4-)	$60	$75
2.	$50	Same, but printed on thick bond paper. Number issued: c. 3,135 (#4701-7835) Dates of issue: May 1 - October 31, 1861 Signed by Jones, Tyler.	Rarity (4)	$65	$80

Atlanta rail yard in ruins.

TYPE 2 **$100**

Total number issued (all varieties): 7,950[2] Rarity (3+)
Dates of issue: April 17 - September 30, 1861
Imprint: "Douglas, Engr. N. Orleans"

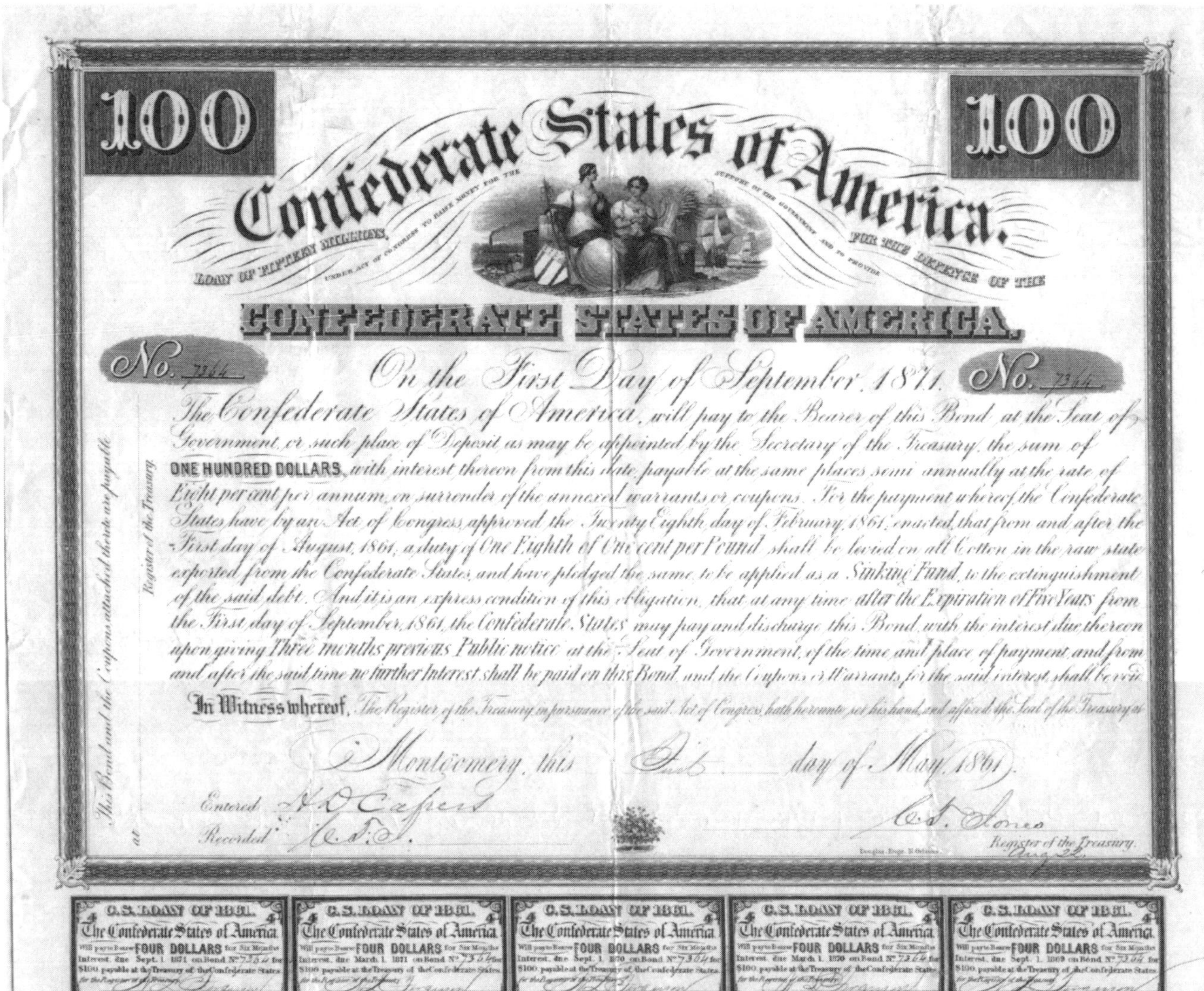

100 Confederate States of America. 100

Loan of Fifteen Millions, under act of Congress to raise money for the support of the Government and to provide for the defence of the

CONFEDERATE STATES OF AMERICA.

No. 7364 On the First Day of September 1871. No. 7364

The Confederate States of America, will pay to the Bearer of this Bond at the Seat of Government or such place of Deposit as may be appointed by the Secretary of the Treasury, the sum of ONE HUNDRED DOLLARS, with interest thereon from this date payable at the same places semi annually at the rate of Eight per cent per annum, on surrender of the annexed warrants or coupons. For the payment whereof the Confederate States have by an Act of Congress approved the Twenty Eighth day of February, 1861, enacted that from and after the First day of August, 1861, a duty of One Eighth of One cent per Pound shall be levied on all Cotton in the raw state exported from the Confederate States, and have pledged the same to be applied as a Sinking Fund, to the extinguishment of the said debt. And it is an express condition of this obligation, that at any time after the Expiration of Five Years from the First day of September, 1861, the Confederate States may pay and discharge this Bond, with the interest due thereon upon giving Three months previous Public notice at the Seat of Government, of the time and place of payment, and from and after the said time no further Interest shall be paid on this Bond and the Coupons or Warrants for the said interest shall be void.

In Witness whereof, The Register of the Treasury in pursuance of the said Act of Congress hath hereunto set his hand and affixed the Seal of the Treasury at Montgomery, this [illegible] day of May 1861.

Entered [illegible]
Recorded [illegible]

Register of the Treasury.

Douglas Engr. N. Orleans

This Bond and the Coupons attached thereto are payable at Register of the Treasury.

C.S. LOAN OF 1861. The Confederate States of America Will pay to Bearer FOUR DOLLARS for Six Months Interest, due Sept. 1. 1871 on Bond No 7364 for $100 payable at the Treasury of the Confederate States. for the Register of the Treasury.

C.S. LOAN OF 1861. The Confederate States of America Will pay to Bearer FOUR DOLLARS for Six Months Interest, due March 1. 1871 on Bond No 7364 for $100 payable at the Treasury of the Confederate States. for the Register of the Treasury.

C.S. LOAN OF 1861. The Confederate States of America Will pay to Bearer FOUR DOLLARS for Six Months Interest, due Sept. 1. 1870 on Bond No 7364 for $100 payable at the Treasury of the Confederate States. for the Register of the Treasury.

C.S. LOAN OF 1861. The Confederate States of America Will pay to Bearer FOUR DOLLARS for Six Months Interest, due March 1. 1870 on Bond No 7364 for $100 payable at the Treasury of the Confederate States. for the Register of the Treasury.

C.S. LOAN OF 1861. The Confederate States of America Will pay to Bearer FOUR DOLLARS for Six Months Interest, due Sept. 1. 1869 on Bond No 7364 for $100 payable at the Treasury of the Confederate States. for the Register of the Treasury.

(Two women, Columbia/Commerce, left; Ceres/agriculture, right.)

				fine	very fine
3.	$100	Printed on thin red silk fiber paper. Number issued: c. 4,700 (#1-4700) Dates of issue: c. April 17 - May 1, 1861 Signed by Clitherall, Jones.	Rarity (4-)	$50	$75
4.	$100	Same, but printed on thick bond paper. Number issued: c. 3,250 (#4701-7950) Dates of issue: c. May 1 - September 30, 1861 Signed by Clitherall, Jones, and Tyler.	Rarity (4)	$60	$85

TYPE 3 **$500**

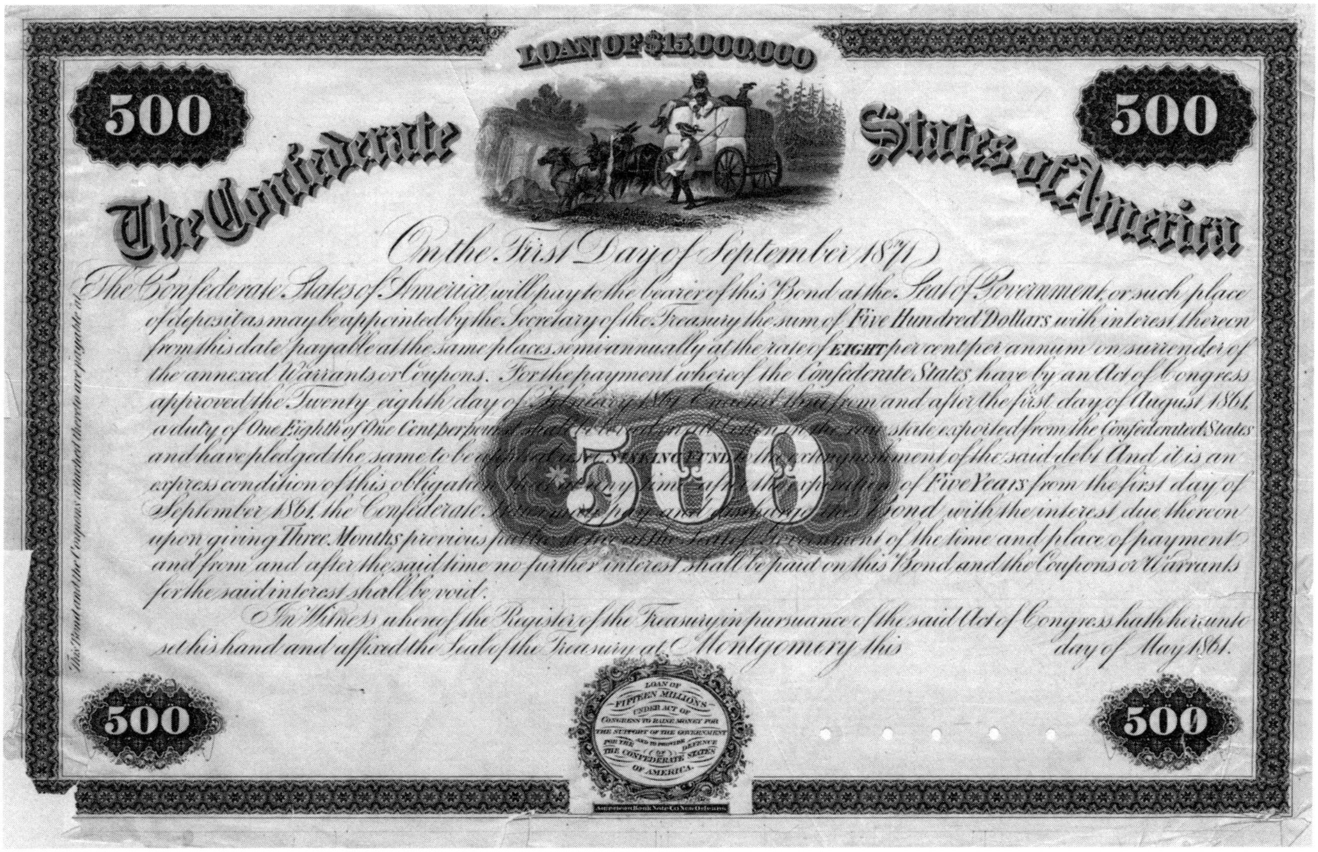

Imprint: none (prepared by American Bank Note Company, New York)

(Slaves on mule-pulled cotton wagon, top center)

"500" medallions in each corner: "500" green protector, center.

As noted in the introduction, the coupon bond order was erroneously placed in New York by Samuel Schmidt at the American Bank Note Company, New Orleans office. The company engraved the bond, printed one impression on India paper before war broke out and work ceased on the order. This piece was filed in the archives from which it emerged in 1992.

5.	$500	Printed on India paper. Number prepared: 1 (unique) Prepared prior to April 21, 1861.[3]	([4])

TYPE 4 **$500**

Total number issued (all varieties): 5,250 Rarity (3+)

Dates of issue: May 1 - November 1, 1861

Imprint: none; however, known to have been printed by Samuel Schmidt (resident manager of the American Bank Note Company branch at New Orleans). The imprint was possibly omitted to prevent the tracing of these bonds to Schmidt's shop.

$15,000,000.

500. CONFEDERATE STATES OF AMERICA. 500.

Loan of FIFTEEN MILLIONS, under Act of Congress to raise money for the Support of the Government, and to provide for the Defence of the CONFEDERATE STATES OF AMERICA.

No. 1249 On the First Day of September, 1871, No. 1249.

The CONFEDERATE STATES OF AMERICA, will pay to the Bearer of this Bond at the Seat of Government, or such place of Deposit as may be appointed by the Secretary of the Treasury, the sum of FIVE HUNDRED DOLLARS, with interest thereon from this date, payable at the same places semi-annually, at the rate of EIGHT PER CENT. per annum, on surrender of the annexed warrants or coupons. For the payment whereof the Confederate States have by an Act of Co[illegible] of February, 1861, enacted, that from and after the First day of [illegible] ONE EIGHTH OF ONE CENT PER POUND shall be levied on all Cotton in the raw state exported from th[illegible] same to be applied as a SINKING FUND, to the extinguishment of the sa[illegible]tion of this obligation, that at any time after the Expiration of Five Years, from the [illegible] the CONFEDERATE STATES may pay and discharge this Bond, with the interest due thereon, upon giving THREE MONTHS' PREVIOUS PUBLIC NOTICE at the Seat of Government, of the time and place of payment, and from and after the said time NO FURTHER INTEREST SHALL BE PAID ON THIS BOND, and the Coupons or Warrants for the said interest shall be void.

In Witness Whereof, The Register of the Treasury, in pursuance of the said Act of Congress, hath hereunto set his hand, and affixed the Seal of the Treasury, at Montgomery, this First day of May, 1861.

Entered A. D. Capers

Recorded C. T. S.

Register of the Treasury.

Register of the Treasury.

This Bond and the Coupons attached thereto, are payable at

C. S. LOAN OF 1861. The Confederate States of America Will pay to Bearer Twenty Dollars for SIX Months Interest, due [illegible] No. 1249 for $500, payable [illegible] Confederate States. For the Register of the Treasury. $20

(Green tint on engraved text)

				fine	very fine
6.	$500	Printed on thin red silk fiber paper. Number issued: c. 3,500 (1-3000; 3401-3700; 4001-4200) Dates of issue: April 17 - September 10, 1861 Signed by Clitherall, Jones, Tyler.	Rarity (4-)	$65	$85

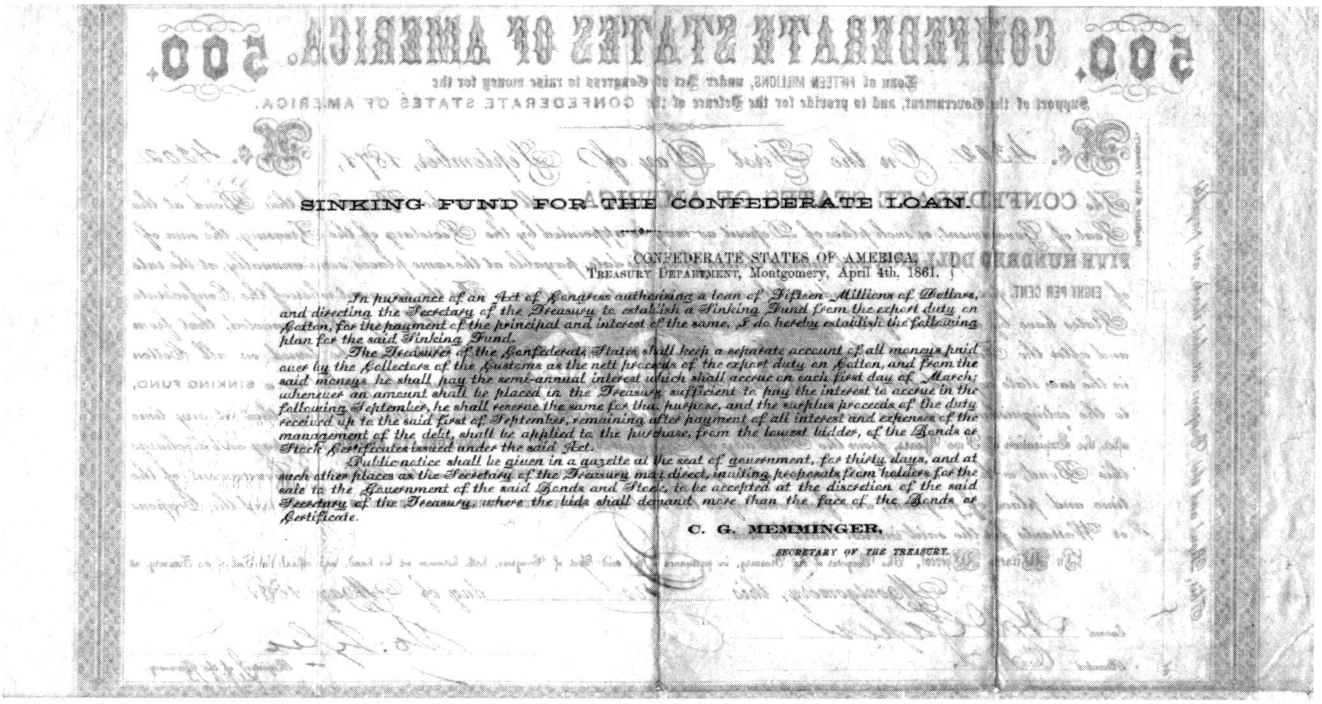

7.	$500	Same, but "Sinking fund for the Confederate Loan..." etc. printed in blue on the back.[5] Number issued: c. 1,750 (3001-3400; 3701-4000; 4201-5250) Dates of issue: September 11 - November 1, 1861 Signed by Jones, Tyler.	Rarity (4+)	$90	$125

TYPE 5 **$1,000**

Essay, handwritten mock-up with engraved vignettes, slaves and mule-pulled cotton wagon top center, *Justice* bottom; both engraved vignettes glued to text.

American Bank Note began work on this bond with an all handwritten text and some proof vignettes pasted on at appropriate points. The outbreak of hostilities ended all further work on this project and the bond was placed in the American Bank Note Company archives from which it emerged in 1992.

LOAN OF $15000000.

Loan of Fifteen Millions, under Act of Congress to raise Money for the support of the Government and to provide for the Defence of the Confederate States of America

CONFEDERATE STATES OF AMERICA

1000 No. No. 1000

On the First Day of September 1871

The Confederate States of America will pay to the Bearer of this Bond at the seat of Government, or such place of Deposit as may be appointed by the Secretary of the Treasury, the sum of ONE THOUSAND DOLLARS with interest thereon from this date, payable at the same places semiannually, at the rate of Eight per cent per annum, on surrender of the annexed warrants or Coupons. For the payment whereof the Confederate States have by an Act of Congress approved the Twenty eighth day of February 1861, Enacted, that from and after the First day of August 1861, a duty of one eighth of one cent per pound shall be levied on all Cotton in the raw state exported from the Confederate States, and have pledged the same to be applied as a Sinking Fund to the Extinguishment of the said debt, And it is an express Condition of this Obligation, that at any time, after the expiration of five years, from the first day of September 1861, the Confederate States may pay and discharge this Bond, with the interest due thereon, upon giving Three Months previous public notice at the Seat of Government, of the time and place of payment, and from and after the said time no further interest shall be paid on this Bond and the Coupons or Warrants for the said interest shall be void.

In Witness whereof the Register of the Treasury in pursuance of the said Act of Congress hath hereunto set his hand, and affixed the Seal of the Treasury at Montgomery this day of May 1861.

1000 Entered Recorded Register of the Treasury 1000

American Bank Note Co. New Orleans

8. $1,000 Written on regular paper. (6)
Number prepared: 1 (unique)
Prepared prior to April 21, 1861.

TYPE 6 **$1,000**

Total number issued (all varieties): 7,071 (7,161 printed)   Rarity (3+)
Dates of issue: May 1 - October 31, 1861

Imprint: none; however, known to have been printed by Samuel Schmidt (resident manager of the American Bank Note Company branch at New Orleans). The imprint probably was omitted to prevent the tracing of these bonds to Schmidt's shop.

			fine	very fine
9.	$1,000	Printed on thin red silk fiber paper.		
		Number prepared: 7,071 (#1-4614, 7654-7077, 7151-7161)[7] Rarity (3+)	$65	$85
		Dates of issue: May 1 - October 31, 1861		
		Signed by Clitherall, Jones, and Tyler.		

B. Stock certificates due September 1, 1871
Total amount issued (all types): $6,674,200

TYPE 7 **$50**

Total number issued: 391 (1,000 printed)[8] Rarity (6)
Dates of issue: April 17, 1861 - March 1, 1865
Imprint: "American Bank Note Company, New Orleans." The real printer was the company's New York office, which shipped the stock certificates South after the outbreak of hostilities. The use of an imprint other than that of the actual producer may or may not have been intended to keep the New York office out of trouble. What Samuel Schmidt thought of this when he was printing bonds anonymously and printing bank notes and Confederate treasury notes under a resurrected *nom de guerre* (Southern Bank Note Co.) is not recorded.

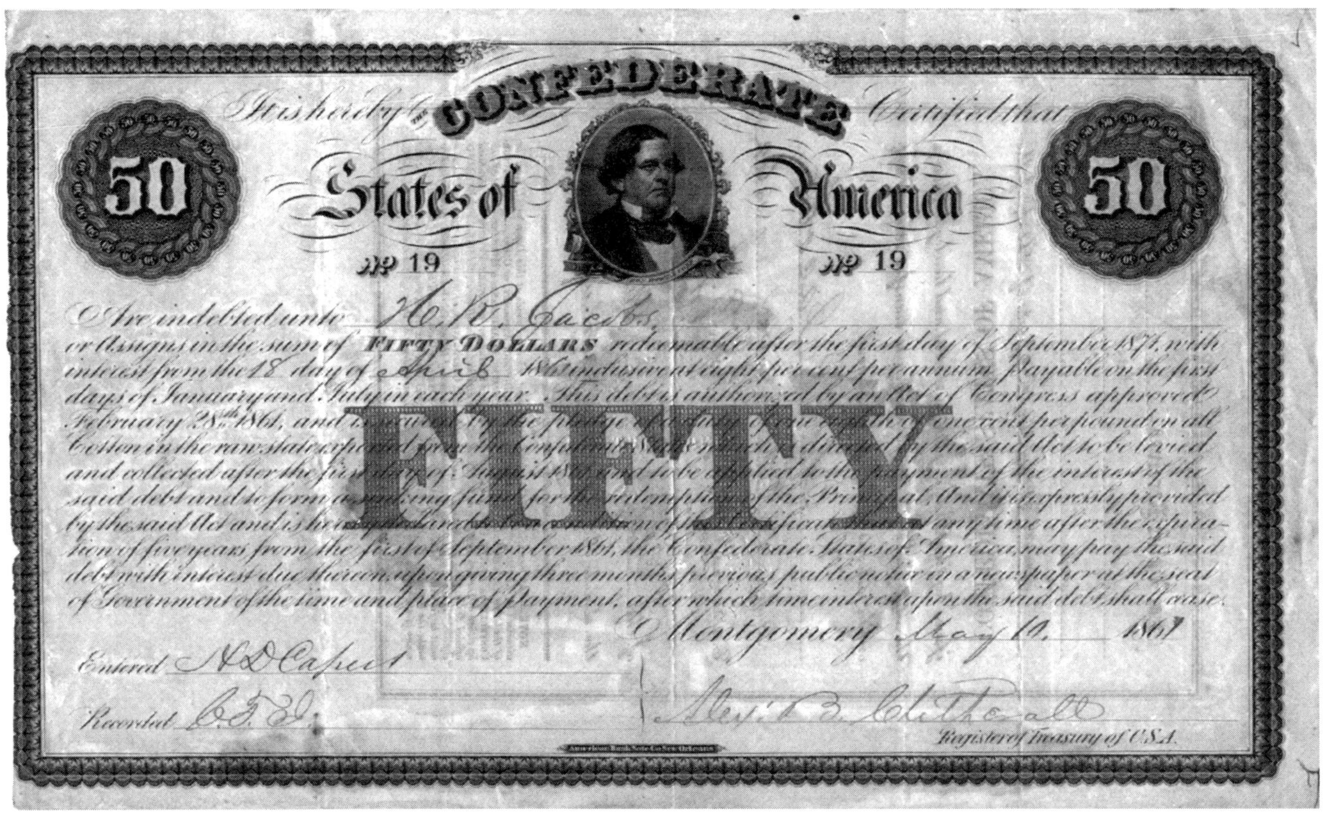

Signed by Clitherall, Tyler.

(Howell Cobb, president of the Confederate Provisional Congress)

				fine	very fine
10.	$50	Printed on plain white paper. Number issued: c. 250 (#1-250) Dates of issue: c. April 11 - May 16, 1861 Signed by Clitherall.	Rarity (6+)	$1,500	$2,200
11.	$50	Same, but "Montgomery" crossed out and "Richmond" written in its place. Number issued: c. 141 (#251-391) Dates of issue: c. May 17, 1961 - March 1, 1865	Rarity (8)[9]	$3,500	$4,500

TYPE 8 **$100**

Total number issued (all varieties): 750 (1,000 printed)[10] Rarity (6)
Dates of issue: April 17, 1861 - March 5, 1865
Imprint: "American Bank Note Company, New Orleans."

(Andrew Jackson, center)

No.	Denomination	Description	Rarity	fine	very fine
12.	$100	Printed on plain white paper. Number issued: c. 250 (#1-250) Dates of issue: c. April 17 - May 20, 1861 Signed by Clitherall.	Rarity (7-)	$2,500	$3,000
13.	$100	Same, but "Montgomery" crossed out and "Richmond" written in. Number issued: c. 500 (#251-750) Dates of issue: c. May 21, 1861 - July 5, 1862 Signed by Clitherall.	Rarity (6+)	$4,500	$5,750

TYPE 9 **$500**

Total number issued (all varieties): 491 (1,000 printed)[11] Rarity (6+)
Dates of issue: April 17, 1861 - March 1, 1865
Imprint: "American Bank Note Company, New Orleans."

(John C. Calhoun, center)

				fine	very fine
14.	$500	Printed on plain white paper. Number issued: c. 177 (#1-177) Dates of issue: April 17 - May 28, 1861 Signed by Clitherall.	Rarity (7-)	$1,800	$2,500
15.	$500	Same, but "Montgomery" crossed out and "Richmond" written in.[12] Number issued: c. 314 (#178-491) Dates of issue: May 29, 1861 - February 8, 1865. Signed by Tyler.	Rarity (7)	$1,500	$2,000

TYPE 10 **$1,000**

Total number issued (all varieties): 1,000 — Rarity (5+)
Dates of issue: April 17 - August 6, 1861
Imprint: "American Bank Note Company, New Orleans."

(Jefferson Davis as a U.S. senator, center)

				fine	very fine
16.	$1,000	Printed on plain white paper.			
		Number issued: c. 810 (#1-810)	Rarity (6-)	$650	1,000
		Dates of issue: April 17 - June 30, 1861			
		Signed by Clitherall.			
17.	$1,000	Same, but "Montgomery" crossed out and "Richmond" written in.[13]			
		Number issued: c. 190 (#811-1000)	Rarity (7)	$750	$1,250
		Dates of issue: July 1 - August 6, 1861			
		Signed by Clitherall, Jones, and Tyler.			

TYPE 11 various (written) denominations

Total number issued (all varieties): c. 515 Rarity (6)
Dates of issue: April 17, 1861 - January 1, 1863
Imprint: "Hoyer & Ludwig, Richmond, Va."

It is hereby Certified that THE CONFEDERATE States of America

No. 1050. No. 1050.

Are indebted unto Mechanics Savings Society, Petersburg Va. or assigns in the Sum of One Thousand Dollars redeemable after the first day of September 1871 with interest from the 22 day of August 1861 inclusive at eight per cent per annum payable on the first days of January and July in each year. This debt is authorized by an Act of Congress approved February 28th 1861 and is secured by the pledge of a duty of one eighth of one cent per pound on all Cotton in the raw state exported from the Confederate States which is directed by the said Act to be levied and collected after the first day of August 1861 and to be applied to the payment of the interest of the said debt and to form a sinking fund for the redemption of the Principal, and it is expressly provided by the said Act and is hereby declared to be a condition of this Certificate that at any time after the expiration of five years from the first of September 1861 the Confederate States of America may pay the said debt with interest due thereon upon giving three months previous public notice in a Newspaper at the Seat of Government of the time and place of payment, after which time Interest upon the said debt shall cease.

Richmond Va. August 22, 1861.

Entered H. D. Capers
Recorded C. T. J.

C. T. Jones
Register of Treasury of C.S.A.

HOYER & LUDWIG RICHMOND, VA.

(*Confederacy*, left; Benjamin Franklin, center)

18. Printed on plain white paper.

Number issued: 515 (see chart) Rarity (6)

fine	very fine
$2,500	$3,500

Signed by Tyler with a few scattered Jones signatures.

Denomination		Approximate number issued	Serial #(s)	Rarity
A	$250	51	1-51	7
B	$800	21	1-21	8
C	$1,000	212	1001-1212	7
D	$2,000	54	1-54	7
E	$2,400	3	1-3	8
F	$3,000	26	1-26	8
G	$4,000	12	1-12	8
H	$5,000	49	21-61[14]	8
I	$6,000	4	1-4	—
J	$10,000	38	1-38	—
K	$15,000	8	1-8	—
L	$20,000	13	1-13	8
M	$24,000	2	1-2	—
N	$26,000	1	1	—
O	$30,000	7	1-7	—
P	$35,000	1	1	—
Q	$40,000	1	1	—
R	$50,000	4	1-4	—
S	$100,000	5	1-5	—
T	$200,000[15]	1	1	—
U	$230,000	1	1	—
V	$300,000	1	1	—
		515		

Items without rarity numbers are not known to exist and may therefore not be collectable.

A Union patriotic cover.

TYPE 12 various (written) denominations

Total number issued (all varieties): c. 445 Rarity (7-)
Dates of issue: January 10, 1863 - March 9, 1865
Imprint: "J.T. Paterson & Co., Columbia, S.C."

(*Confederacy*, left; farm man and woman, center)

			fine	very fine
19.	Printed on plain white paper. Number issued: c. 445 Signed by Tyler.	Rarity (7-)	$3,000	$4,500

Denomination		Approximate number issued	Serial #(s)	Rarity
A	$100	87	751-837	8
B	$250	2	52-53	—
C	$800	14	22-35	8
D	$1,000	161	1213-1373	7
E	$2,000	17	55-71	8
F	$3,000	39	27-65	8
G	$4,000	19	13-31	8
H	$5,000	43	62-104	8
I	$10,000	29	39-67	8
J	$15,000	6	9-14	—
K	$20,000	23	14-36	8
L	$100,000	5	6-10	—
		445		

Items without rarity numbers are not known to exist and may therefore not be collectable.

Table of rarities

8	=	1-3
7+	=	4-10
7	=	11-20
7-	=	21-35
6+	=	36-50
6	=	51-75
6-	=	76-100
5+	=	101-200
5	=	201-350
5-	=	351-500
4+	=	501-750
4	=	751-1000
4-	=	1001-1500
3+	=	1501-2500
3	=	2501-5000
3-	=	5001-7500
2+	=	7501-10,000
2	=	10,001-20,000
2-	=	20,001-35,000
1+	=	35,001-50,000
1	=	50,001-100,000
1-	=	100,000+

TYPE 13

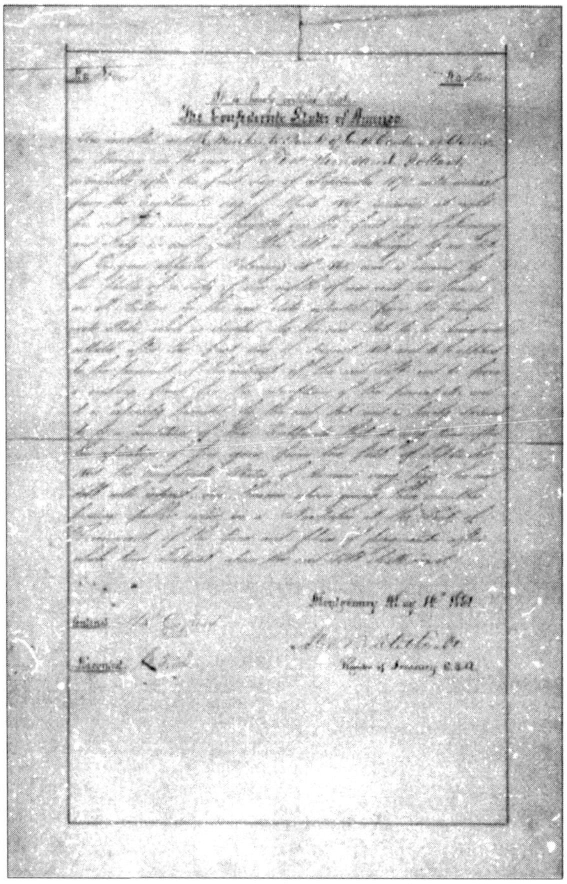

20. Handwritten bonds (usually on lined or hand-ruled thick paper).
Number issued: c. 28 (various #s) Rarity (7+) $4,000
Dates of issue: May 18 - August 6, 1861
Signed by Clitherall, Tyler.

N.B. Some of these bonds may have been exchanged for regularly printed bonds, though some were unexchanged or paid by 1865.

Denomination	Approximate number issued	Serial #(s)	Rarity
A $5,000	20	1-20	7+
B $10,000	2	1-2	—
C $100,000	5	1-5	—
D $200,000	1	1	—
	28		

Items without rarity numbers are not known to exist and may therefore not be collectable.

II. ACT OF MAY 16, 1861

In the meantime, the Confederate Congress had passed an act on May 16, 1861 authorizing two sets of bonds; one loan, for $30 million, was to be used for produce loan subscriptions, and the other was to fund the $20 million of notes authorized by the same act. (Produce loans were subscribed by planters who pledged the proceeds of future sales of crops, principally cotton, as payment for the bonds.) The produce bond contracts were apparently awarded to Douglas, who started on the $100 denomination. In the fall of 1861, he reported his progress on this project (some complete bonds had been done, but most had been partially prepared either as coupons or the bond itself). It was only then that he learned that the Act of August 19, 1861 had superseded that part of the May 16, 1861 act pertaining to the produce loan and that the text of the bonds was no longer valid.

The bonds were junked and their existence only came to light in the 1960s when two were discovered back to back, double framed, in a Charleston, South Carolina dealer's shop. One ended in the John J. Ford collection and the other ultimately passed to Grover Criswell, who illustrated it in his book. It was sold with his collection in October 1980. A few more have subsequently surfaced and been sold at auction.

Meanwhile, the seat of government had been moved to Richmond, and Hoyer & Ludwig, as noted earlier, entered the bond printing business. From July 1861 until May 1862 this firm was busy preparing notes, and from November 1861 on, bonds of section two of the May 16, 1861 act as well.

Under the terms of section two of this act, $20 million of treasury notes were authorized. These were fundable into ten year 8% bonds, which were more nearly call certificates, since they could be redeemed in $100 increments up to the time that the notes matured on July 25, 1863. Thereafter, they had to be held until they became payable in July 1871.

At this time, the treasury did not provide close supervision of the printers except insofar as security and deliveries were concerned. No effort was made to direct what vignettes were to be used. Indeed, at this time, plates were received from the Bank of Charleston and other banks for the use of the Confederate government. Just as some of these plates were modified and used for the production of notes, so Hoyer & Ludwig used the Bank of Charleston $5 and $10 Draper, Toppan and Longacre plates for some of their bonds. For example, Ludwig used the *Indian prince* and *Indian princess* vignettes from the $5 bill on the $500 bond, while the *Indian prince* turned up on the $1000 bond. The *Athena* vignette at the right of the $1000 appeared on some of the Bank of Charleston $20 notes.

In addition to the selection of vignettes, there was the matter of error coupons. The last coupon on both denominations was supposed to be dated July 1871, but because Ludwig only got started on these bonds in November, he assumed that the bonds would not fall due until January 1872. That is why the coupons with that date on the $1000 bond were pen cancelled. One can only assume that the $500 bond's last coupon was not cancelled because of an oversight.

The maturity date of the July 25, 1861 notes having come and gone two years later and the government not having the coin with which to redeem them, the Congress ordered that all such notes should be funded. Interest was therefore allowed on the $1000 bonds to January 1872 and the coupons ceased to be cancelled.

The $500 bonds had apparently been sold up to number 319 when the fresh effort at funding was ordered. Taking advantage of the wide margin between the bond proper and the coupons, some clerk drew in three more coupons ending July 1873, the coupons which matured in 1862 and early 1863 being cut off. Each coupon was signed in person by Robert Tyler.

These bonds were long unknown and the $500 bond, based on the incomplete Thian figures (the second group was found registered elsewhere than where one would have expected to find it), was one of the great rarities of the Confederate bond series. Then the first part of the London hoard came to light when NASCA purchased part of it in December 1981. Apparently, all of the second variety of the $500 bonds, and many of the other varieties of May 16, 1861 act bonds, had been sent to London so that no one had had any occasion to see them. This was one of several discoveries made as a result of the sale of that holding.

When Hoyer & Ludwig refused to move to Columbia, James T. Paterson took up their contracts and filled the orders for registered bonds of this act. However, Paterson in turn left in early 1864 and the work was passed on to Evans & Cogswell, who produced a different certificate of their own (Ball 28, Cr. 16). The reason for this last certificate was not only that the July 25, 1861 notes were still being belatedly funded under the funding acts, but that those who owned registered bonds had occasion to sell or transfer them to other parties. Every time this happened or someone died, a new certificate had to be prepared for the new owner or heir. However, by this time most newly emitted bonds were being issued under the authority of the Act of June 13, 1864, so relatively few of the older series bonds printed by Evans and Cogswell were issued; they are scarce.

Manuscript bonds were also issued under the May 1861 act, clearly as an interim measure to take in funds while the printed bonds were still in course of preparation. Once the bonds were prepared, no more manuscript bonds were issued under this act, and those that had been put out were, for the most part, taken up and exchanged for regular bonds.

A. 8% coupon bonds due November 1, 1881
Amount Authorized: $50 million
Total Amount issued: none

TYPE 14 **$100**

Total number issued (all varieties): none. Approximately 3,000 were printed, some only partially, by the fall of 1861. Eight are known to exist at present.

Imprint: "Douglas, New Orleans."

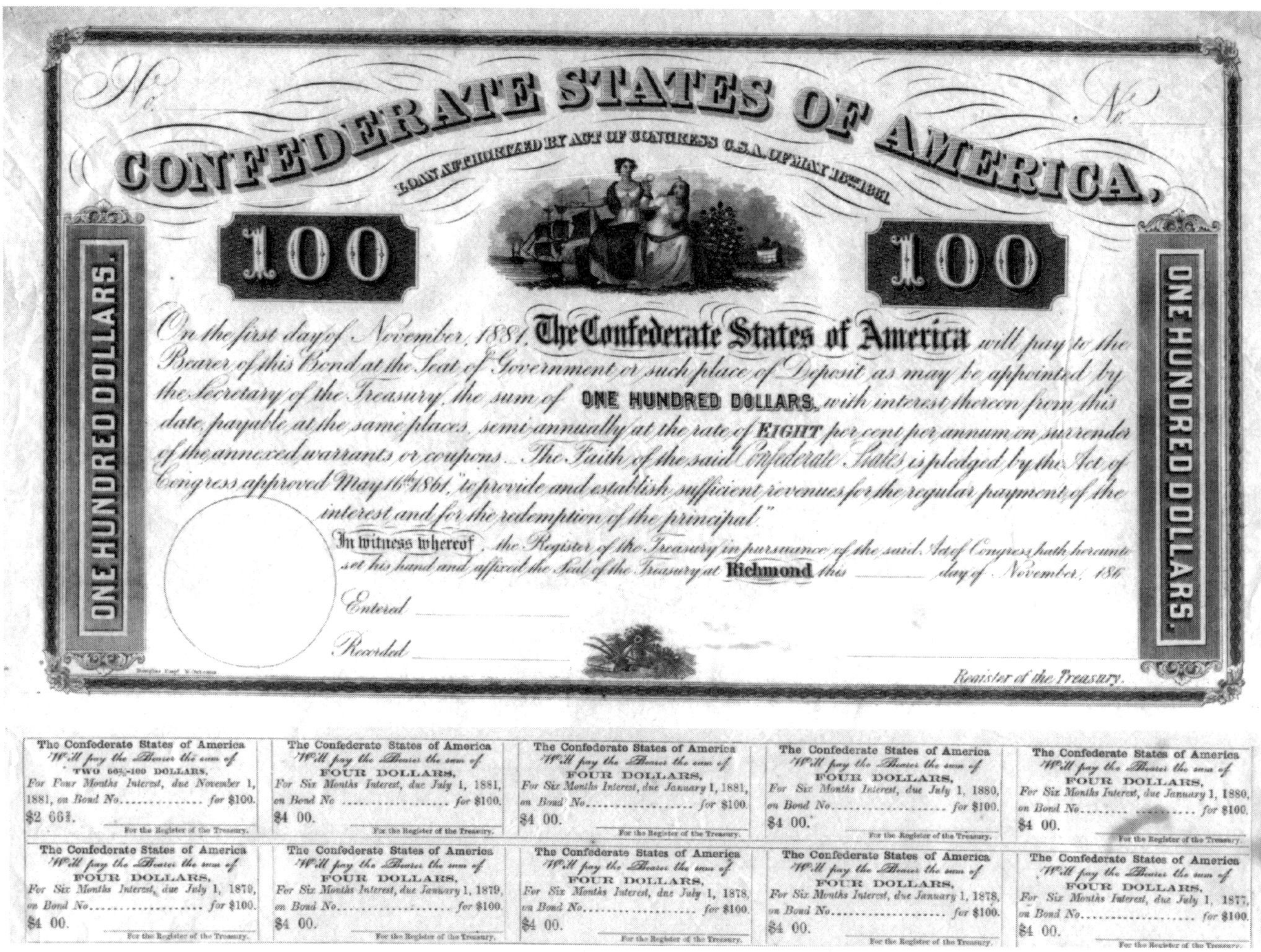
No. No.
CONFEDERATE STATES OF AMERICA.
LOAN AUTHORIZED BY ACT OF CONGRESS C.S.A. OF MAY 16th 1861
100 100
ONE HUNDRED DOLLARS. ONE HUNDRED DOLLARS.
On the first day of November, 1881, The Confederate States of America will pay to the Bearer of this Bond at the Seat of Government or such place of Deposit as may be appointed by the Secretary of the Treasury, the sum of ONE HUNDRED DOLLARS, with interest thereon from this date, payable at the same places, semi-annually at the rate of EIGHT per cent per annum on surrender of the annexed warrants or coupons. The Faith of the said Confederate States is pledged by the Act of Congress approved May 16th 1861, "to provide and establish sufficient revenues for the regular payment of the interest and for the redemption of the principal."
In witness whereof, the Register of the Treasury in pursuance of the said Act of Congress hath hereunto set his hand and affixed the Seal of the Treasury at Richmond this ______ day of November, 186
Entered
Recorded
Register of the Treasury.

The Confederate States of America Will pay the Bearer the sum of TWO 66⅔-100 DOLLARS, For Four Months Interest, due November 1, 1881, on Bond No............ for $100. $2 66⅔. For the Register of the Treasury.
The Confederate States of America Will pay the Bearer the sum of FOUR DOLLARS, For Six Months Interest, due July 1, 1881, on Bond No............ for $100. $4 00. For the Register of the Treasury.
The Confederate States of America Will pay the Bearer the sum of FOUR DOLLARS, For Six Months Interest, due January 1, 1881, on Bond No............ for $100. $4 00. For the Register of the Treasury.
The Confederate States of America Will pay the Bearer the sum of FOUR DOLLARS, For Six Months Interest, due July 1, 1880, on Bond No............ for $100. $4 00. For the Register of the Treasury.
The Confederate States of America Will pay the Bearer the sum of FOUR DOLLARS, For Six Months Interest, due January 1, 1880, on Bond No............ for $100. $4 00. For the Register of the Treasury.
The Confederate States of America Will pay the Bearer the sum of FOUR DOLLARS, For Six Months Interest, due July 1, 1879, on Bond No............ for $100. $4 00. For the Register of the Treasury.
The Confederate States of America Will pay the Bearer the sum of FOUR DOLLARS, For Six Months Interest, due January 1, 1879, on Bond No............ for $100. $4 00. For the Register of the Treasury.
The Confederate States of America Will pay the Bearer the sum of FOUR DOLLARS, For Six Months Interest, due July 1, 1878, on Bond No............ for $100. $4 00. For the Register of the Treasury.
The Confederate States of America Will pay the Bearer the sum of FOUR DOLLARS, For Six Months Interest, due January 1, 1878, on Bond No............ for $100. $4 00. For the Register of the Treasury.
The Confederate States of America Will pay the Bearer the sum of FOUR DOLLARS, For Six Months Interest, due July 1, 1877, on Bond No............ for $100. $4 00. For the Register of the Treasury.

(*Commerce & Ceres* with ship in background)

				fine	very fine
21.	$100	Printed on thick bond paper. Number issued: none Dates of issue: unissued and unsigned	Rarity (7+)	$4,500	$6,500

B. 8% coupon bonds due July 1, 1872
Amount Authorized: $20 million
Total Amount issued: $1,185,000

TYPE 15 **$500**

Total number issued: c. 772 (#1-772)
Dates of issue: October 17, 1861 - July 1, 1863
Imprint: “Hoyer & Ludwig, Richmond, Va.”; lithographed.

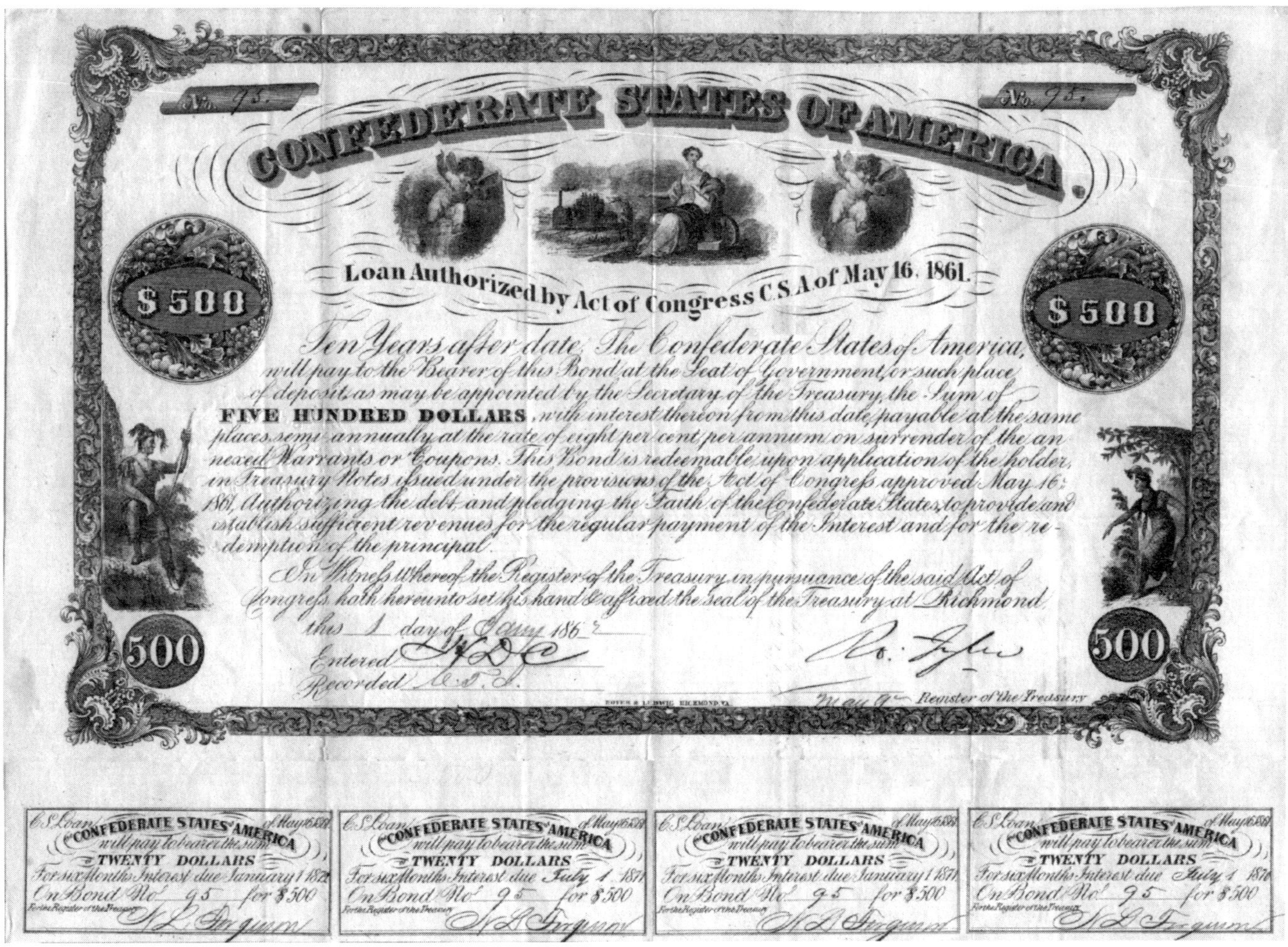
No. 95
CONFEDERATE STATES OF AMERICA.
$500
Loan Authorized by Act of Congress C.S.A. of May 16, 1861.
Ten Years after date The Confederate States of America, will pay to the Bearer of this Bond at the Seat of Government, or such place of deposit as may be appointed by the Secretary of the Treasury, the Sum of FIVE HUNDRED DOLLARS, with interest thereon from this date, payable at the same places semi annually at the rate of eight per cent per annum on surrender of the annexed Warrants or Coupons. This Bond is redeemable upon application of the holder, in Treasury Notes issued under the provisions of the Act of Congress approved May 16, 1861, authorizing the debt and pledging the Faith of the Confederate States, to provide and establish sufficient revenues for the regular payment of the Interest and for the redemption of the principal.
In Witness Whereof the Register of the Treasury in pursuance of the said Act of Congress hath hereunto set his hand & affixed the seal of the Treasury at Richmond this 1 day of Jany 1862
Entered
Recorded
Register of the Treasury
HOYER & LUDWIG RICHMOND VA.
500

C.S. Loan of May 16 1861 CONFEDERATE STATES AMERICA will pay to bearer the sum TWENTY DOLLARS For six Months Interest due January 1 1872 On Bond No. 95 for $500 For the Register of the Treasury

C.S. Loan of May 16 1861 CONFEDERATE STATES AMERICA will pay to bearer the sum TWENTY DOLLARS For six Months Interest due July 1 1871 On Bond No. 95 for $500 For the Register of the Treasury

C.S. Loan of May 16 1861 CONFEDERATE STATES AMERICA will pay to bearer the sum TWENTY DOLLARS For six Months Interest due January 1 1871 On Bond No. 95 for $500 For the Register of the Treasury

C.S. Loan of May 16 1861 CONFEDERATE STATES AMERICA will pay to bearer the sum TWENTY DOLLARS For six Months Interest due July 1 1870 On Bond No. 95 for $500 For the Register of the Treasury

(*Indian Prince*, left; *Commerce*, flanked by cupids, center; *Indian Princess*, right)[16]

No.	Denom.	Description	Rarity	fine	very fine
22.	$500	Printed on thick bond paper. Number issued: 319 (#1-319) Dates of issue: October 17, 1861 - June 30, 1863 Signed by Jones (c. #1-50) and Tyler (c. #51-319).	Rarity (5+)	$75	$125
23.	$500	As last; three handwritten coupons under bond signed by Robert Tyler. Number issued: c. 453 (#320-772) Date of issue: July 1, 1863 Signed by Jones.	Rarity (5)	$110	$150

TYPE 16 **$1,000**

Total number issued: 799 (#1-799) Rarity (5)
Dates of issue: September 17, 1861 - June 30, 1862
Imprint: “Hoyer & Ludwig, Richmond, Va.”; lithographed.

(*Indian Prince,* left; men loading wagon, flanked by sailing ships, center; *Minerva,* right)[17]

				fine	very fine
24.	$1,000	Printed on thick bond paper, last coupon pen cancelled in red ink. Number issued: c. 584 (#36-619) Dates of issue: September 17, 1861 - November 30, 1861 Signed by Tyler.	Rarity (5+)	$175	$300
25.	$1,000	As last, but coupon not cancelled. Number issued: c. 215 (#1-35; 620-799) Dates of issue: December 1, 1861 - June 30, 1862 Signed by Tyler.	Rarity (6)	$250	$400

C. 8% registered bonds due July 1, 1872
Amount Authorized: $20 million
Total Amount issued (all types): $8,365,200

TYPE 17 various denominations
Imprint: "Hoyer & Ludwig, Richmond, Va."

No. 537 No. 537

It is hereby Certified that The Confederate States of America are indebted unto William D. Hall or assigns in the sum of Five Hundred Dollars redeemable after ten years from this date, with interest from the 22d day of July 1862 inclusive, at Eight per cent per annum payable on the first days of January and July in each year. This debt is authorized by an Act of Congress approved May 16 1861 and upon application of the holder of this certificate redeemable in Treasury Notes issued under the provisions of said Act. The faith of the Confederate States is pledged to provide and establish sufficient revenues for the regular payment of the interest, and for the redemption of the principal.

Richmond July 1. 1862

Entered

Recorded

Ro. Tyler
Register of the Treasury

July 22, 1862

Eight per cent

Act of May 16 1861

Hoyer & Ludwig Richmond Va.

(*Agriculture and Commerce* with urn, center)

26.	Printed on regular white paper.		fine	very fine
	Number issued: c. 1,136 (#1-1136)[18]	Rarity (5+)	$200	$300
	Dates of issue: c. September 17, 1861 - January 7, 1863.			
	Signed by Tyler, Jones.			

Denomination	Number issued	Rarity	Denomination	Number issued	Rarity
$100	8	—	$10,500	1	—
$200	8	—	$11,000	7	—
$300	8	—	$11,500	1	—
$400	8	—	$12,000	7	—
$500	233	6+	$13,000	4	—
$600	6	—	$15,000	8	—
$700	2	8	$16,000	3	—
$800	8	—	$17,000	3	—
$900	2	—	$17,500	1	—
$1,000	243	6+	$18,000	3	—
$1,200	4	—	$19,000	1	—
$1,400	2	—	$19,500	1	—
$1,500	42	8	$20,000	18	—
$1,700	3	8	$23,000	1	—
$2,000	135	7-	$24,000	1	—
$2,400	1	—	$25,000	7	—
$2,500	19	—	$25,500	1	—
$2,600	3	—	$26,000	2	—
$2,800	1	—	$30,000	4	—
$3,000	58	8	$30,500	1	—
$3,500	2	—	$32,000	2	—
$4,000	35	8	$34,000	1	—
$4,500	4	—	$40,000	5	—
$5,000	62	8	$50,000	18	—
$5,500	10	—	$58,000	1	—
$5,900	6	—	$60,000	3	—
$6,000	14	—	$80,000	1	—
$6,500	2	—	$100,000	9	—
$7,000	12	—	$166,000	1	—
$8,000	15	—	$200,000	1	—
$8,500	3	—	$317,000	1	—
$9,000	9	—	$417,000	1	—
$10,000	49	8			

Items without rarity numbers are not known to exist and may therefore not be collectable.

TYPE 18 various denominations
Imprint: "J.T. Paterson & Co., Columbia, S.C."; lithographed.

$300 $300

It is hereby Certified that THE CONFEDERATE States of America

No. 1278 No. 1278

Are indebted unto Wm D. Nutt or assigns in the sum of Three Hundred Dollars redeemable after ten years from this date, with interest from the 27 day of February 1863 inclusive, at Eight per cent per annum payable on the first days of January and July in each year. This debt is authorized by an Act of Congress approved May 16 1861 and upon application of the holder of this certificate redeemable in Treasury Notes issued under the provisions of said Act. The faith of the Confederate States is pledged to provide and establish sufficient revenues for the regular payment of the interest, and for the redemption of the principal.

Eight per cent

Act of May 16 1861

Richmond January 1. 1863

Entered
Recorded

Register of the Treasury Mar 3/63

(*Ceres & Commerce* with urn, center)

27.	Printed on regular white paper.		fine	very fine
	Number issued: c. 1,914 (#1137-3050)	Rarity (5+)	$175	$250
	Dates of issue: January 8, 1863 - November 16, 1863			
	Signed by Tyler.			

Denomination	Number issued	Rarity	Denomination	Number issued	Rarity
$100	330	7-	$2,700	1	—
$200	161	7	$2,800	2	—
$300	952	7	$3,000	47	8
$400	64	7	$3,200	3	—
$500	333	7-	$3,300	1	—
$600	34	8	$3,400	2	—
$700	29	8	$3,500	9	—
$800	18	8	$3,600	3	—
$900	6	—	$3,700	1	—
$1,000	269	7-	$3,800	3	8
$1,100	11	—	$4,000	24	—
$1,200	9	8	$4,100	1	—
$1,300	12	—	$4,200	1	—
$1,400	6	—	$4,300	1	—
$1,500	17	8	$4,500	4	—
$1,600	6	—	$4,600	3	—
$1,700	5	—	$4,700	1	—
$1,800	3	—	$4,800	1	—
$1,900	2	—	$5,000	55	8
$2,000	121	7	$5,100	1	—
$2,100	6	—	$5,500	2	—
$2,200	3	—	$5,800	1	—
$2,300	1	—	$5,900	2	—
$2,500	30	8	$6,000	10	—
$2,600	4	—	$6,300	2	—

Items without rarity numbers are not known to exist and may therefore not be collectable.

Denomination	Number issued	Rarity	Denomination	Number issued	Rarity
$7,000	17	—	$19,000	5	—
$7,500	1	—	$20,000	4	—
$8,000	9	8	$21,000	4	8
$8,200	1	—	$23,000	1	—
$8,500	2	—	$24,000	1	—
$8,800	1	—	$25,000	3	—
$9,000	4	—	$26,000	1	—
$9,300	1	—	$30,000	2	8
$9,400	1	—	$32,000	1	—
$9,600	2	—	$34.000	1	—
$10,000	17	—	$35,000	1	—
$10,200	1	—	$40,000	1	—
$10,500	3	—	$45,000	1	—
$10,800	1	—	$45,500	1	—
$11,000	2	—	$48,000	1	—
$12,000	4	8	$50,000	1	—
$13,000	2	—	$60,000	1	—
$15,000	8	—	$62,400	1	—
$15,300	1	—	$75,000	1	—
$15,500	1	—	$80,000	1	—
$16,000	1	—	$162,000	1	—
$18,000	4	—			

Items without rarity numbers are not known to exist and may therefore not be collectable.
Note: 35 additional pieces are not included in the table.

TYPE 19 various denominations
Imprint: "Evans & Cogswell, Columbia, S.C."; lithographed.

IT IS HEREBY CERTIFIED THAT THE CONFEDERATE STATES OF AMERICA

$500 No 3431 $500 No 3431

Are indebted unto Mrs Ann G Williams or assigns in the sum of Five Hundred Dollars redeemable after ten years from this date, with interest from the 1 day of January 1864 inclusive, at Eight per cent per annum payable on the first days of January and July in each year. This debt is authorized by an Act of Congress approved May 16 1861 and upon application of the holder of this certificate redeemable in Treasury Notes issued under the provisions of said Act. The faith of the Confederate States is pledged to provide and establish sufficient revenues for the regular payment of the interest and for the redemption of the principal.

Richmond July 1 1862

Entered
Recorded
Ro. Tyler
Register of the Treasury April 14/64

EVANS & COGSWELL, COLUMBIA, S.C.

(*Science,* center)

			fine	very fine
28.	Printed on white, waxy paper.			
	Number issued: c. 503 (#3051-3553)	Rarity (7-)	$3,500	$4,500
	Dates of issue: November 17, 1863 - March 20, 1865[19]			
	Signed by Tyler.			

Denomination	Number issued	Rarity	Denomination	Number issued	Rarity
$100	51	8	$2,300	1	—
$200	31	8	$2,500	7	—
$300	20	8	$2,600	1	—
$400	19	8	$2,700	1	—
$500	64	7+	$3,000	28	8
$600	9	—	$3,200	1	—
$700	14	—	$3,400	2	—
$800	5	—	$3,500	3	—
$900	6	8	$3,800	1	—
$1,000	68	7+	$4,000	13	—
$1,100	4	—	$4,200	1	—
$1,200	6	—	$4,500	4	—
$1,300	4	—	$4,600	1	—
$1,400	1	—	$4,700	1	—
$1,500	15	8	$5,000	16	8
$1,600	1	—	$5,500	3	—
$1,700	5	—	$5,800	2	—
$1,800	1	—	$5,900	1	—
$1,900	4	—	$6,000	7	—
$2,000	25	8	$6,700	1	—
$2,100	2	—	$6,900	1	—
$2,200	1	—	$7,000	6	8

Items without rarity numbers are not known to exist and may therefore not be collectable.

Denomination	Number issued	Rarity	Denomination	Number issued	Rarity
$7,500	2	—	$18,000	1	—
$7,800	2	—	$19,000	2	—
$8,000	3	—	$19,900	1	—
$9,000	3	—	$20,500	1	—
$10,000	6	—	$22,500	1	—
$10,200	1	—	$23,000	1	—
$10,800	1	—	$25,000	4	—
$11,000	2	—	$28,000	1	—
$12,000	1	—	$36,600	1	—
$13,000	3	—	$38,300	1	—
$14,000	2	8	$50,000	1	—
$15,000	2	—	$50,700	1	—
$16,000	1	—	$217,000[20]	1	—

Items without rarity numbers are not known to exist and may therefore not be collectable.

Note: the table contains one more piece than was recorded issued.

TYPE 20 various denominations

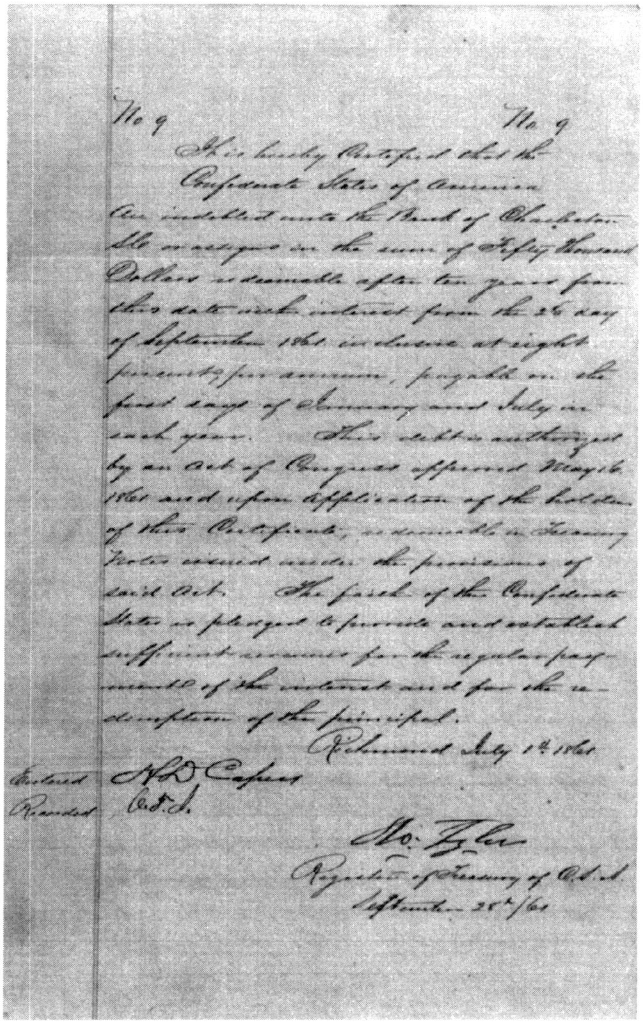

No 9 No 9

It is hereby Certified that the Confederate States of America are indebted unto the Bank of Charleston S.C. or assigns in the sum of Fifty Thousand Dollars redeemable after ten years from this date with interest from the 26 day of September 1861 inclusive at eight per cent per annum, payable on the first days of January and July in each year. This debt is authorized by an Act of Congress approved May 16 1861 and upon application of the holder of this Certificate, redeemable in Treasury Notes issued under the provisions of said Act. The faith of the Confederate States is pledged to provide and establish sufficient revenues for the regular payment of the interest and for the redemption of the principal.

Richmond July 1st 1861

Entered N.D. Capers
Recorded C.T.S.

Ro: Tyler
Register of Treasury of C.S.A.
September 26th/61

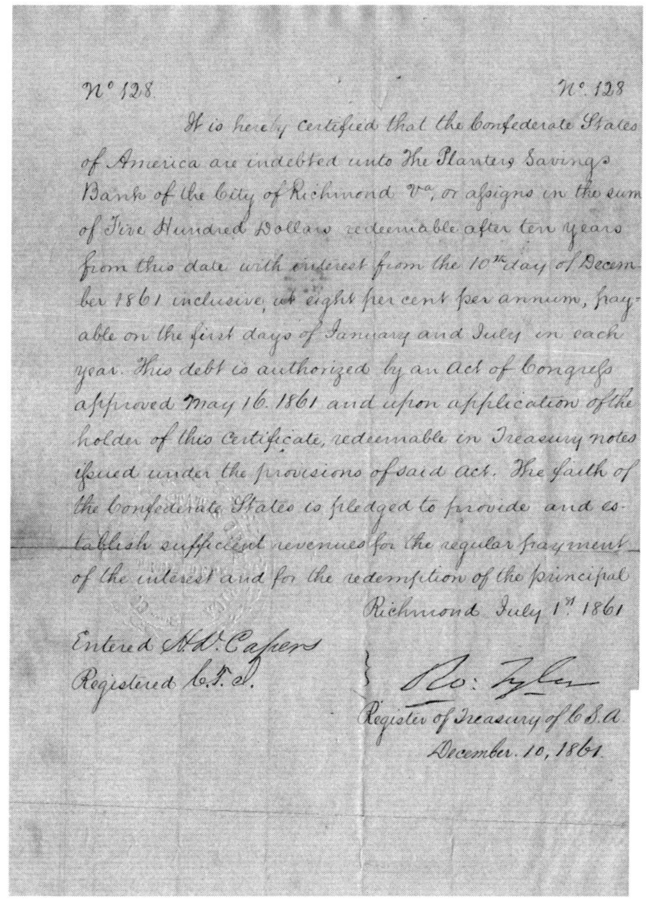

No. 128 No. 128

It is hereby certified that the Confederate States of America are indebted unto The Planters Savings Bank of the City of Richmond Va, or assigns in the sum of Five Hundred Dollars redeemable after ten years from this date with interest from the 10th day of December 1861 inclusive, at eight per cent per annum, payable on the first days of January and July in each year. This debt is authorized by an Act of Congress approved May 16. 1861 and upon application of the holder of this Certificate, redeemable in Treasury notes issued under the provisions of said Act. The faith of the Confederate States is pledged to provide and establish sufficient revenues for the regular payment of the interest and for the redemption of the principal.

Richmond July 1st 1861

Entered N.D. Capers
Registered C.T.S.

Ro: Tyler
Register of Treasury of C.S.A.
December. 10, 1861.

29.	All handwritten certificates on white or blue wove bond paper.		fine	very fine
	Number issued: c. 150 (#1-150)	Rarity (7+)	$5,000	$6,500
	Dates of issue: c. May 16, 1861 - December 31, 1861			
	Signed by Tyler.			

III. ACT OF AUGUST 19, 1861

The Act of August 19, 1861 was the first of a series of war acts, intended to place at the Confederacy's disposal the means needed to wage a war to maintain its independence. It called for the issue of $100 million of treasury notes, fundable into 8% bonds, redeemable in not more than twenty years.

The Confederate congressmen, many of whom had served in Washington, had at least learned something from the United States' experience with the Mexican War debt. Millions of dollars of bonds had been floated and were outstanding, but the government was unable to avail itself of its surpluses to redeem the bonds without paying a large premium. James G. Holmes, a stockbroker who had handled a Charleston City loan, suggested to Secretary Memminger the idea of having serial maturities, a novelty then, but quite common now. Thus instead of having a balloon note where all the principal fell due at one time with inconvenient effects on the government's finances, some of the loan would mature every year, allowing the government to retire its debt year by year and reducing the bond premium in the open market.

Secretary Memminger thought that this was a good idea and let the Provisional Congress, of which he was a member, know about his plans. An examination of the Thian *Register of the Confederate Debt...*, pages 182-184, discloses the exact form in which the treasury carried out Holmes' idea. Due dates ranged from January 1, 1864 to July 1, 1881. No coupon bonds matured in January 1864, 1866, 1869, 1870, 1872, 1874, 1876 and 1881. Registered bonds or "stock" matured in January 1864-1881, with July maturities (all very small in amount and therefore rare) in July 1864, 1865, 1870, 1873 and 1881. It should be noted that the amounts maturing grew with each year, the assumption being that there would be a substantial floating debt to clear off, particularly treasury notes, so that large scale redemptions could best be afforded later.

Purchasers of these bonds preferred buying readily transferable coupon bonds to registered bonds by 3-1, or roughly $75 million to $25 million. It should also be noted that no provision was made in the original act for the emission of registered bonds. As a result, a supplementary act was passed August 24, 1861 for that purpose.

Having secured authority for the issue of bonds and having arranged for their time of redemption, there remained the pressing question of what to do about their denominations and who was to prepare them. The bankers, headed by James D. Denegre of New Orleans, felt that any bond under $500 was a waste of time. The Congress, in the original produce loan act of May 16, 1861, had hoped to get small lenders into the picture and had provided for a $100 denomination. Under the August 19, 1861 act, produce subscriptions could be for sums as small as $50, and $50 bonds were provided for that purpose. However, the number of such bonds and their value (8,707 pieces worth $435,350) clearly indicates that not much help was expected from the small subscriber, and this denomination was not repeated in later acts when inflation had made it all but useless.

Instead, fixed denominations of $1000, $500, and some $100 bonds were decided upon. No higher denomination in coupon bonds was authorized. However, registered bonds existed from denominations as low as $50 up to six figures, as an examination of the catalog lists will show. The average was over $2500 per certificate.

The next problem was to sell such bonds or to get people to fund their notes into bonds, coupled with a need to get the bonds prepared. Sales of the bonds totalled $16 million by the end of the Provisional Government. Sales began around October 22, 1861 and continued to February 22, 1862. A few manuscript bonds were prepared and issued, and some registered bonds were produced by Hoyer & Ludwig and distributed to the purchasers. The coupon bonds were another matter.

Hoyer & Ludwig was primarily responsible for currency production. Leggett, Keatinge & Ball had only gotten into production in a small way in October 1861. Blanton Duncan did not open his shop until January 1862, and Evans & Cogswell had only begun their discussions with Secretary Memminger about doing some bonds for him the fall of 1861. The chief burden of producing the Confederate bonds therefore fell to Hoyer & Ludwig.

Apparently, the assignments to do the printing of the August 19, 1861 bonds were as follows: Evans & Cogswell was to do those maturing from July 1, 1864 to July 1, 1865, $100 to $1000. Hoyer & Ludwig was assigned the bonds that matured from January 1, 1867 to July 1, 1868. With the exception of a stray bond done by Ludwig and two scattered bonds done by Evans & Cogswell, all the other bonds of this series were printed by Blanton Duncan.

It is also indicative that all the Duncan bonds have first coupons either dated July 1, 1862 or January 1, 1863. We may therefore safely date their production after Duncan reached Columbia, South Carolina, and we may equally safely speculate that the Hoyer & Ludwig bonds were done before the move to Columbia.

It should also be noted that Evans & Cogswell, in keeping with their professed difficulty in doing engraving work as opposed to printing, used the same design, *Liberty* with shield and a ship behind, for all of their bonds. As for Hoyer & Ludwig, that firm used all different designs, but these were available from the bank note plates lent to the government or were drawn, for the most part, from the standard printing stocks of the time. The only $50 bond's central vignette was drawn from the T-17 Confederate note; so too was the portrait of Washington on the $100; the pictures of *Ceres* and *Commerce* on the $500 bond; and the train on the $1000 bond. All but the *Ceres* vignette came from Confederate notes, and *Ceres* was used on the Florida notes.

The $1000 bond with the picture of *Commerce* with cornucopia came from a Bank of Charleston note plate lent to the government.

Some effort at originality was made on a few bonds, particularly on the $100 vignette of *City Hall* (which took quite some time to identify) and the portrait of Postmaster General Reagan. Indeed, as the war progressed, there was increasingly a tendency to use Confederate officials' portraits, not only to be more distinctively Confederate but also to throw off would-be counterfeiters, by compelling them to copy such work from the ground up. They could not simply obtain a plate previously used for an obsolete bank note and transfer the engraving to a bond plate.

The work of Blanton Duncan on the August 19, 1861 act bonds is shrouded in silence and confusion, the effort at analysis made more difficult by the current mode of listing these bonds by denomination and due date, rather than by due date then denomination. When the latter system is used, one is immediately struck by the fact that the bonds of each due date are essentially the same. That is, with the exception of the portrait used, the border elements and text are identical for each bond. Every bond has one of three groups of elements around the portrait: three women, two women with a squared off scene, or a wreath of flowers and curved borders. Even the bond number medallions were the same for each denomination.

Such uniformity may have been intended as a security device, but is more likely to be related to the fee paid for each bond plate. If the bond plates could be reduced to three masters, where only the portrait and denomination elements were different, the difficulty, labor and expense of producing a bond plate would be greatly reduced. Further, if the portraits were reused in varying permutations and combinations, there would be a further economy in that regard. By these means the profit, at a fixed rate per new bond plate, would be greatly increased.

The persons whom Duncan chose to honor reflected those who were in a position of power in Richmond and whom Duncan might well wish to influence in his own favor. Thus out of sixty-two bonds designed by Duncan, ten were in honor of Judah P. Benjamin, whose influence over President Davis was widely talked about; eight honored Secretary Memminger, Duncan's employer; seven R.M.T. Hunter, the President Pro-tem of the Senate and chairman of the Senate finance committee. President Davis was honored only three times, which was matched by the number of times his secretary, Burton Harrison (misidentified as General Beauregard) appeared on these bonds. The Attorneys General, Thomas Bragg and Thomas Watts, appeared on six and two bonds respectively. Secretary of the Navy Mallory appears five times. Secretary of War Randolph appears three times and former Secretary of State Toombs, twice. Those honored but once include the treasurer, Edward Elmore; Samuel Preston Moore, the surgeon general; Vice President Stephens (evidently considered to be out of the loop in decision making); Lucy Pickins, wife of the South Carolina governor; and General Winder, the provost marshal, who, we earlier pointed, out had helped Duncan put down a revolt by his printers. Four portraits were of an unknown man.

Identifying these personages has not always been easy. Hugh Shull found the portrait of General Winder that allowed his name to be attached to Ball 101 (Cr. 94). I came across, by pure happenstance, the portrait of Surgeon General Moore. Guy Swanson, former librarian of the Museum of the Confederacy, made the connection with Burton Harrison, whose portrait in oil hangs in the museum.

This selection of persons suggests a number of things besides politics. It also shows the influence of the location of Duncan's firm. During his stay in Richmond, Duncan obviously had the chance to meet many prominent people; hence the portraits of the cabinet officers and some of the lesser personnel in the capital. On the other hand, Mrs. Pickins would clearly belong to Duncan's Columbia period, since he would have seen her there and she was a woman of some prominence. In any case, he alone made the choice of who would or would not appear on his bonds. I have never found any correspondence instructing the chief clerk, Joseph Daniel Pope, to order the printers to use a particular portrait, except in the case of the $100 Type 49 bills, where Secretary of War Randolph's angry resignation in November 1862 made honoring him at that time singularly awkward for Secretary Memminger. However, as no alternate portrait of an appropriate character was ready, the note had to proceed as originally planned.

Another anomaly arises from the fact that some of the Duncan bonds do not bear any imprint, and when the imprint does occur, it varies between those professedly printed in Richmond and Columbia. Why did this happen?

One possibility is that the engravers had no idea that an imprint on the bonds was a Treasury Department requirement. From the distribution of these, it appears that five bonds had no imprint at all, mostly concentrated among those bonds with late 1870s due dates, with scattered bonds elsewhere. Then there are no less than five bonds that appear with and without imprints. All of these, when they do have an imprint, have their origin professedly at Columbia. By that time, the engravers should have known what they were doing.

Then there is the matter of the bonds that bear the Richmond imprint. These are mostly located in the 1869-1872 period. However, there are also bonds from the 1880-1881 period. This out-of-order production reflects a demand for the most distant due dates rather than the early maturities, and indicates that their production had to be expedited.

In seeking an explanation for all this, one must keep in mind that the printers considered their removal to Columbia to be a temporary expedient and fully expected to be recalled to Richmond when the danger from the Union armies blew over. This is reflected in the $20 T-20 notes Duncan produced at about this time.

I should guess that Duncan's firm began by producing the early maturity dated bonds and the last bonds, moved to Columbia, left the name off through oversight, and then followed up with the Columbia imprinted bonds. How this happened or why is not explained in any of the official correspondence.

Production of these bonds proceeded slowly throughout 1862, not being finished until the end of the year. An issue of new bonds was clearly going to be needed by the end of 1862, because the amount of notes outstanding under the authority of the Act of August 19, 1861, as amended, greatly exceeded the quantity of bonds authorized under the same act. Moreover, the Congress was trying to draw all these notes in and more bonds were clearly needed to carry out this forced funding program.

Amount authorized: $100 million of 8% Bonds
Various due dates, January 1, 1864 to July 1, 1881
Total amount issued (all types): $74,880,050

A. 8% coupon bonds due July 1, 1864
Engraved by "Evans and Cogswell"
Printed by Evans and Cogswell (low numbers) and B. Duncan (higher numbers)
Vignette of *Liberty,* Confederate flag on shield, ships.

TYPE 21 **$100**

				fine	very fine
30.	$100	Printed on white paper.			
		Number issued: 598 (#1-598)[21]	Rarity (6-)	$150	$225
		Signed by Tyler (c. #1-200) and Jones (#201-598).			

TYPE 22 **$500**

				fine	very fine
31.	$500	Same, but for denomination. Number issued: 700 (#1-700) Signed by Tyler and Jones (scattered).	Rarity (5+)	$250	$350

TYPE 23 **$1,000**

32.	$1,000	Same, but for denomination. Number issued: 927 (#1-927)[22] Signed by Tyler (#1-300) and Jones (#301-927).	Rarity (5+)	$200	$300

B. 8% coupon bonds due January 1, 1865
Engraved by "Evans & Cogswell"
Printed by Evans & Cogswell (low numbers) and B. Duncan (higher numbers)
Vignette of *Liberty,* Confederate flag on shield, ships.

TYPE 24 **$100**

				fine	very fine
33.	$100	Similar to the above, printed on white paper.			
		Number issued: 449 (#1-449)[23]	Rarity (6-)	$225	$350
		Signed by Tyler and Jones (c. #140-280)			

500 500 500 500
No 108 No 108
Confederate States LOAN of America.
$500 $500
Authorized by the Act of Congress C.S.A. of August 19 1861.
EIGHT PER CENT
JANUARY 1st 1865
On the first day of January 1865 The Confederate States of America will pay to the Bearer of this Bond at the Seat of Government, or such place of Deposit as may be appointed by the Secretary of the Treasury the sum of FIVE HUNDRED DOLLARS, with interest thereon from this date payable at the same places semi-annually at the rate of Eight per cent per annum, on surrender of the annexed Warrants or Coupons. This debt is authorized by an act of Congress approved August 19, 1861, entitled, "An Act to authorize the issue of Treasury Notes, and to provide a War Tax for their redemption."
In Witness Whereof the Register of the Treasury in pursuance of the said Act of Congress hath hereunto set his hand and affixed the seal of the Treasury at RICHMOND, this 22 day of Mar. 1862
REGISTER OF THE TREASURY.

C.S. Loan of Aug 19. 1861
THE CONFEDERATE STATES OF AMERICA
WILL PAY TO BEARER
TWENTY DOLLARS
For Six Months Interest due January 1, 1865
On Bond No 108 for $500
For the Register of the Treasury

C.S. Loan of Aug 19. 1861
THE CONFEDERATE STATES OF AMERICA
WILL PAY TO BEARER
TWENTY DOLLARS
For Six Months Interest due July 1, 1864
On Bond No 108 for $500
For the Register of the Treasury

C.S. Loan of Aug 19. 1861
THE CONFEDERATE STATES OF AMERICA
WILL PAY TO BEARER
TWENTY DOLLARS
For Six Months Interest due January 1, 1864
On Bond No 108 for $500
For the Register of the Treasury

C.S. Loan of Aug 19. 1861
THE CONFEDERATE STATES OF AMERICA
WILL PAY TO BEARER
TWENTY DOLLARS
For Six Months Interest due July 1, 1863
On Bond No 108 for $500
For the Register of the Treasury

C.S. Loan of Aug 19. 1861
THE CONFEDERATE STATES OF AMERICA
WILL PAY TO BEARER
TWENTY DOLLARS
For Six Months Interest due January 1, 1863
On Bond No 108 for $500
For the Register of the Treasury

C.S. Loan of Aug 19. 1861
THE CONFEDERATE STATES OF AMERICA
WILL PAY TO BEARER
TWENTY DOLLARS
For Six Months Interest due July 1, 1862
On Bond No 108 for $500
For the Register of the Treasury

TYPE 25 **$500**

				fine	very fine
34.	$500	Illustrated Number issued: 381 (#1-381)[24] Signed by Tyler.	Rarity (6)	$150	$250

TYPE 26 **$1,000**

35.	$1,000	Similar to the above. Number issued: 671 (#1-671)[25] Signed by Tyler and Jones.	Rarity (5+)	$115	$200

C. 8% coupon bonds due July 1, 1865[26]
Engraved by "Evans & Cogswell"
Printed by Evans & Cogswell (lower numbers) and B. Duncan (higher numbers).
Vignette of *Liberty,* Confederate Flag on shield, ships.

TYPE 27 **$100**

				fine	very fine
36.	$100	Similar to the above, printed on white paper.			
		Number issued: 614 (#1-614)[27]	Rarity (6-)	$100	$150
		Signed by Tyler (c. #41-614) and Jones (c. #1-40).			

TYPE 28 **$500**

37. $500 Similar to the above.
Number issued: 742 (#1-742)[28] Rarity (5+) $75 $160
Signed by Tyler (c. #31-742) and Jones (c. #1-30).

TYPE 29 **$1,000**

38. $1,000 Illustrated.
Number issued: 993 (#1-993)[29] Rarity (5) $110 $135
Signed by Tyler (c. #1-300) and Jones (c. #301-993).

D. 8% coupon bonds due July 1, 1866[30]
Imprint: "B. Duncan, Columbia S.C."

(Judah P. Benjamin, center, | (Thomas Bragg) | (Samuel Preston Moore, Surgeon General, CSA)

TYPE 30 **$100**

100 ONE HUNDRED 100

JULY 1, 1866. EIGHT PER CENT.

CONFEDERATE STATES OF AMERICA
LOAN.

No 144 No 144

AUTHORIZED BY THE ACT OF CONGRESS, C.S.A. OF AUGUST 19, 1861.

On the first day of July 1866 The Confederate States of America will pay to the Bearer of this Bond, at the Seat of Government, or such place of Deposit as may be appointed by the Secretary of the Treasury, the sum of ONE HUNDRED DOLLARS with Interest thereon from this date, payable at the same place semi-annually at the rate of Eight per Cent per annum, on surrender of the annexed Warrants or Coupons. This debt is authorized by an Act of Congress approved August 19, 1861, entitled "An Act to authorize the issue of Treasury Notes, and to provide a War Tax for their redemption."

In Witness whereof the Register of the Treasury, in pursuance of the said Act of Congress, hath hereunto set his hand and affixed the seal of the Treasury at RICHMOND.
this 2[illegible] day of Dec 1862

Entered [illegible]
Recorded [illegible]

Register of the Treasury.

100 ONE HUNDRED 100

C.S. LOAN OF AUG. 19, 1861. THE CONFEDERATE STATES OF AMERICA, Will pay to Bearer FOUR DOLLARS FOR SIX MONTHS INTEREST, DUE JULY 1, 1866. On Bond No 144 for $100 For the Register of the Treasury

C.S. LOAN OF AUG. 19, 1861. THE CONFEDERATE STATES OF AMERICA, Will pay to Bearer FOUR DOLLARS FOR SIX MONTHS INTEREST, DUE JANUARY 1, 1866. On Bond No 144 for $100 For the Register of the Treasury

C.S. LOAN OF AUG. 19, 1861. THE CONFEDERATE STATES OF AMERICA, Will pay to Bearer FOUR DOLLARS FOR SIX MONTHS INTEREST, DUE JULY 1, 1865. On Bond No 144 for $100 For the Register of the Treasury

				fine	very fine
39.	$100	Illustrated, printed on white paper. Number issued: 594 (#1-594) Signed by Tyler.	Rarity (6-)	$150	$250

TYPE 31 **$500**

40.	$500	Similar to the above, but for Thomas Bragg portrait. Number issued: 831 (#1-831) Signed by Tyler.	Rarity (5+)	$60	$125

ONE THOUSAND
JULY 1, 1866.
EIGHT PER CENT.
CONFEDERATE STATES OF AMERICA
LOAN.
No 205
No 205
AUTHORIZED BY THE ACT OF CONGRESS, C.S.A. OF AUGUST 19, 1861.
On the first day of July 1866 The Confederate States of America will pay to the Bearer of this Bond, at the Seat of Government or such place of Deposit as may be appointed by the Secretary of the Treasury, the sum of ONE THOUSAND DOLLARS with Interest thereon from this date, payable at the same place semi annually, at the rate of Eight per Cent per annum, on surrender of the annexed Warrants or Coupons. This debt is authorized by an Act of Congress, approved August 19, 1861, entitled "An Act to authorize the issue of Treasury Notes and to provide a War Tax for their redemption."
In Witness whereof the Register of the Treasury in pursuance of the said Act of Congress hath hereunto set his hand and affixed the seal of the Treasury at RICHMOND this 27 day of Nov 1862
Entered
Recorded
Ro: Tyler
Register of the Treasury.
ONE THOUSAND

TYPE 32 **$1,000**

41.	$1,000	Similar, but for Samuel Preston Moore portrait.[31] Number issued: 1,093 (#1-1093) Signed by Tyler.	Rarity (5)	$60	$75

E. 8% coupon bonds due January 1, 1867[32]
Imprint: "Hoyer & Ludwig, Richmond, Va."

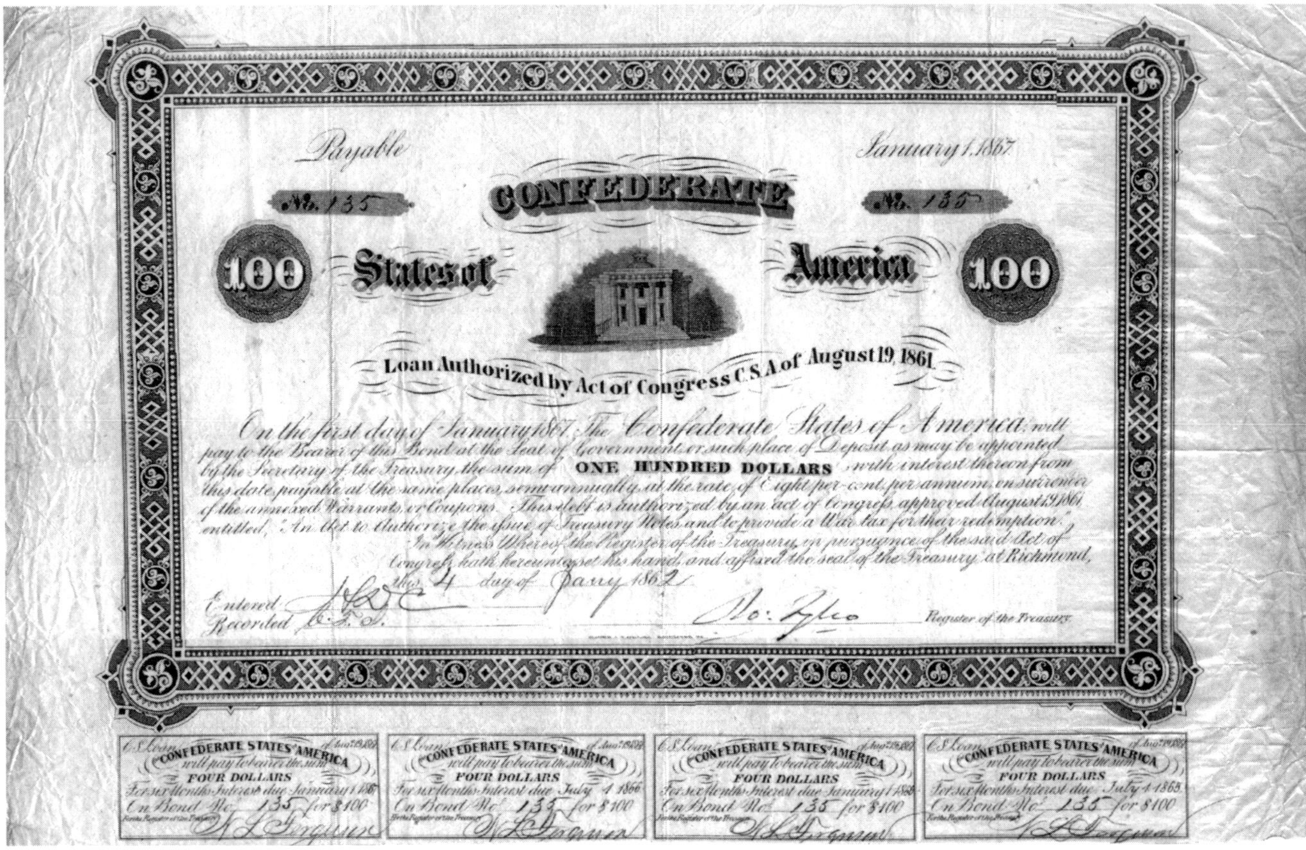

(Richmond City Hall, 1861)

TYPE 33 **$100**

				fine	very fine
42.	$100	Illustrated, printed on white paper.			
		Number issued: 358 (#1-358)	Rarity (6-)	$350	$550
		Signed by Tyler.			

FIVE HUNDRED FIVE HUNDRED

Payable January 1, 1867

CONFEDERATE STATES OF AMERICA

$500 $500

Loan Authorized by Act of Congress C.S.A of August 19, 1861

On the first day of January 1867 The Confederate States of America will pay to the Bearer of this Bond at the Seat of Government or such place of Deposit as may be appointed by the Secretary of the Treasury the sum of FIVE HUNDRED DOLLARS with interest thereon from this date payable at the same places semi-annually at the rate of Eight per cent per annum on surrender of the annexed Warrants or Coupons. This debt is authorized by an act of Congress approved August 19, 1861 entitled, "An Act to Authorize the issue of Treasury Notes and to provide a War tax for their redemption."

In Witness Whereof the Register of the Treasury in pursuance of the said Act of Congress hath hereunto set his hand and affixed the seal of the Treasury at Richmond, this 9 day of Jany 1862.

Entered

Recorded

Register of the Treasury

BOYER & LUDWIG RICHMOND

FIVE HUNDRED FIVE HUNDRED

(Woman and children looking at safe labeled "Confederate States Treasury")

TYPE 34 **$500**

				fine	very fine
43.	$500	Illustrated, printed on white paper. Number issued: 866 (#1-866) Signed by Tyler and Jones.	Rarity (5+)	$120	$200

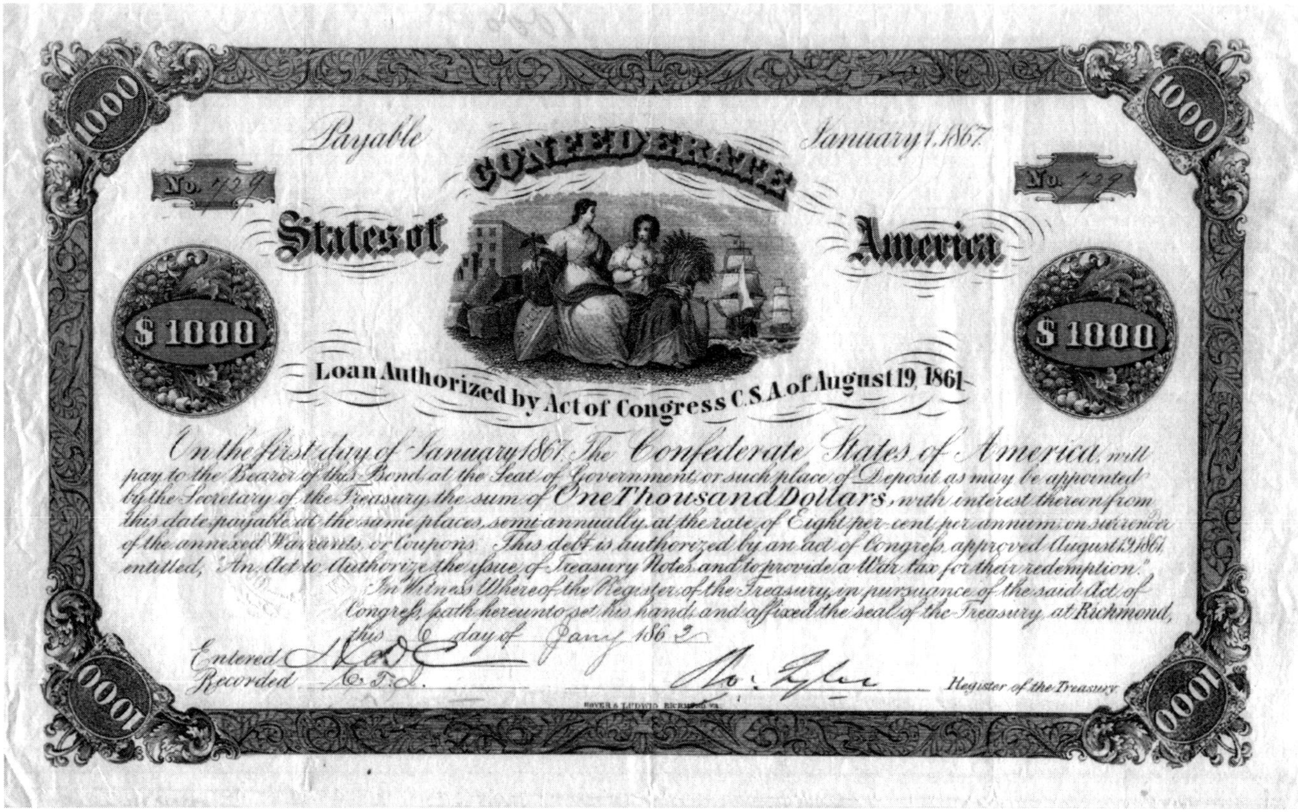

1000

Payable January 1, 1867

No. 729

Confederate States of America

$1000

Loan Authorized by Act of Congress C.S.A. of August 19, 1861

On the first day of January 1867 The Confederate States of America will pay to the Bearer of this Bond at the Seat of Government or such place of Deposit as may be appointed by the Secretary of the Treasury, the sum of One Thousand Dollars, with interest thereon from this date payable at the same places semi-annually at the rate of Eight per cent per annum on surrender of the annexed Warrants or Coupons. This debt is authorized by an act of Congress approved August 19, 1861, entitled, "An Act to Authorize the issue of Treasury Notes and to provide a War tax for their redemption."

In Witness Whereof the Register of the Treasury, in pursuance of the said Act of Congress, hath hereunto set his hand and affixed the seal of the Treasury at Richmond, this 6 day of Jany 1862

Entered

Recorded

Ro. Tyler — Register of the Treasury

(*Commerce and Ceres* center, with British shield)

TYPE 35 **$1,000**

				fine	very fine
44.	$1,000	Illustrated, printed on thick bond paper.			
		Number issued: 1,000 (#1-1000)	Rarity (5-)	$90	$125
		Signed by Tyler.			

F. 8% coupon bonds due July 1, 1867[33]
Imprint: "Hoyer & Ludwig, Richmond, Va."

(*Commerce, Ceres & Navigation,* center)

TYPE 36 **$50**

				fine	very fine
45.	$50	Illustrated, printed on white paper.			
		Number issued: 926 (#1-926)	Rarity (5)	$100	$160
		Signed by Tyler (c. #1-140; 511-926) and Jones (c. #141-510).			

Confederate States LOAN of America

$500 $500

Authorized by the Act of Congress C.S.A. of August 19 1861

EIGHT PER CENT

JULY 1 1867

No. 413 No. 413

On the first day of July 1867 The Confederate States of America will pay to the Bearer of this Bond at the Seat of Government or such place of Deposit as may be appointed by the Secretary of the Treasury the sum of FIVE HUNDRED DOLLARS, with interest thereon from this date payable at the same places semi annually at the rate of Eight per cent per annum on surrender of the annexed Warrants or Coupons. This debt is authorized by an Act of Congress approved August 19 1861, entitled, "An Act to authorize the issue of Treasury Notes and to provide a War tax for their redemption."

In Witness Whereof the Register of the Treasury in pursuance of the said Act of Congress hath hereunto set his hand, and affixed the seal of the Treasury at Richmond, this 25 day of Jany 1862

Entered

Recorded

C. T. Jones, Actg Register of the Treasury

HOYER & LUDWIG RICHMOND VA.

(*Ceres,* center)[34]

TYPE 37 **$500**

				fine	very fine
46.	$500	Illustrated, printed on white paper.			
		Number issued: 901 (#1-901)	Rarity (5)	$125	$175
		Signed by Tyler (c. #1-155; 600-901) and Jones (c. #156-600)			

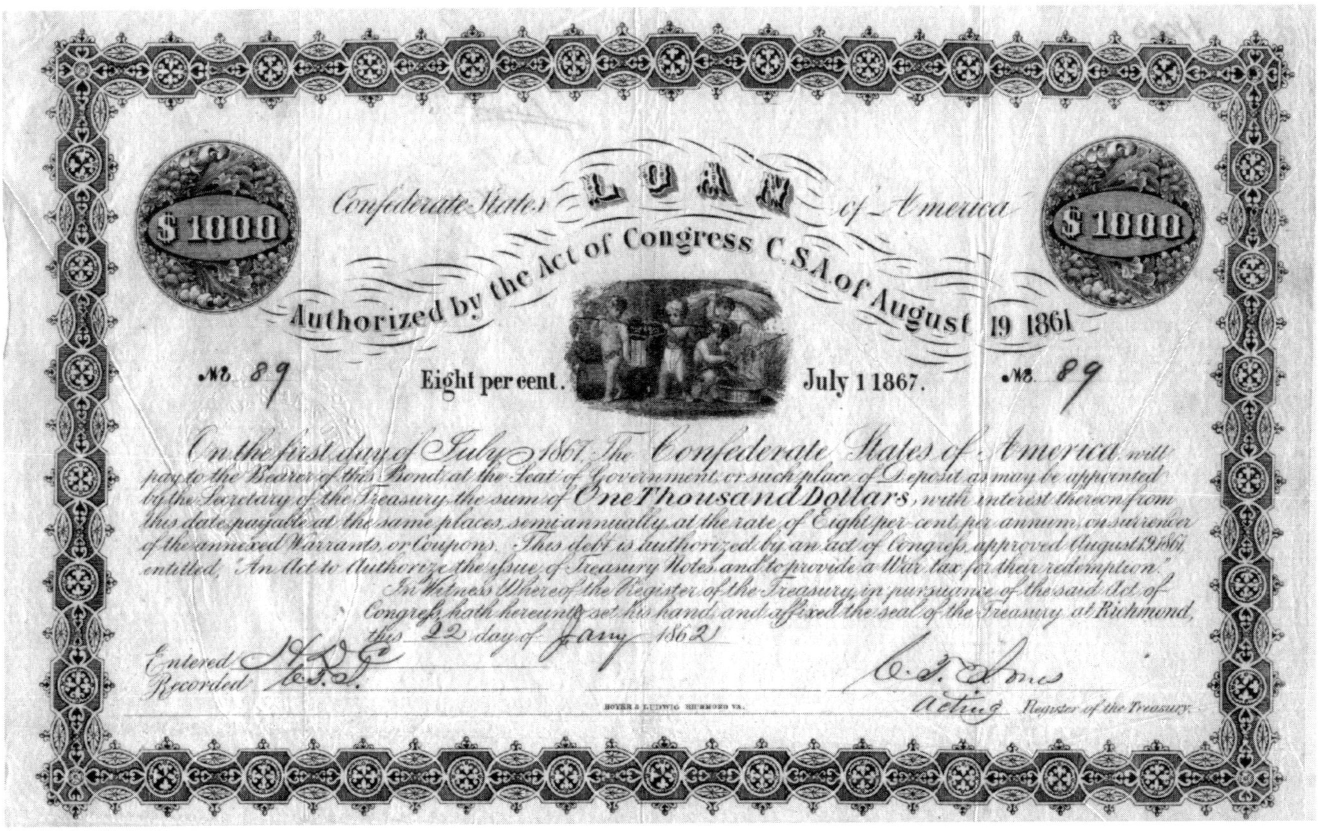

(Four boys as Bacchus, Mercury, etc.)

TYPE 38 **$1,000**

				fine	very fine
47.	$1,000	Illustrated, printed on white paper.			
		Number issued: 1,199 (#1-1199)	Rarity (5-)	$85	$125
		Signed by Jones (c. #1-900) and Tyler (c. #901-1199).			

G. 8% coupon bonds due January 1, 1868[35]
Imprint: "Hoyer & Ludwig, Richmond, Va."; lithographed.

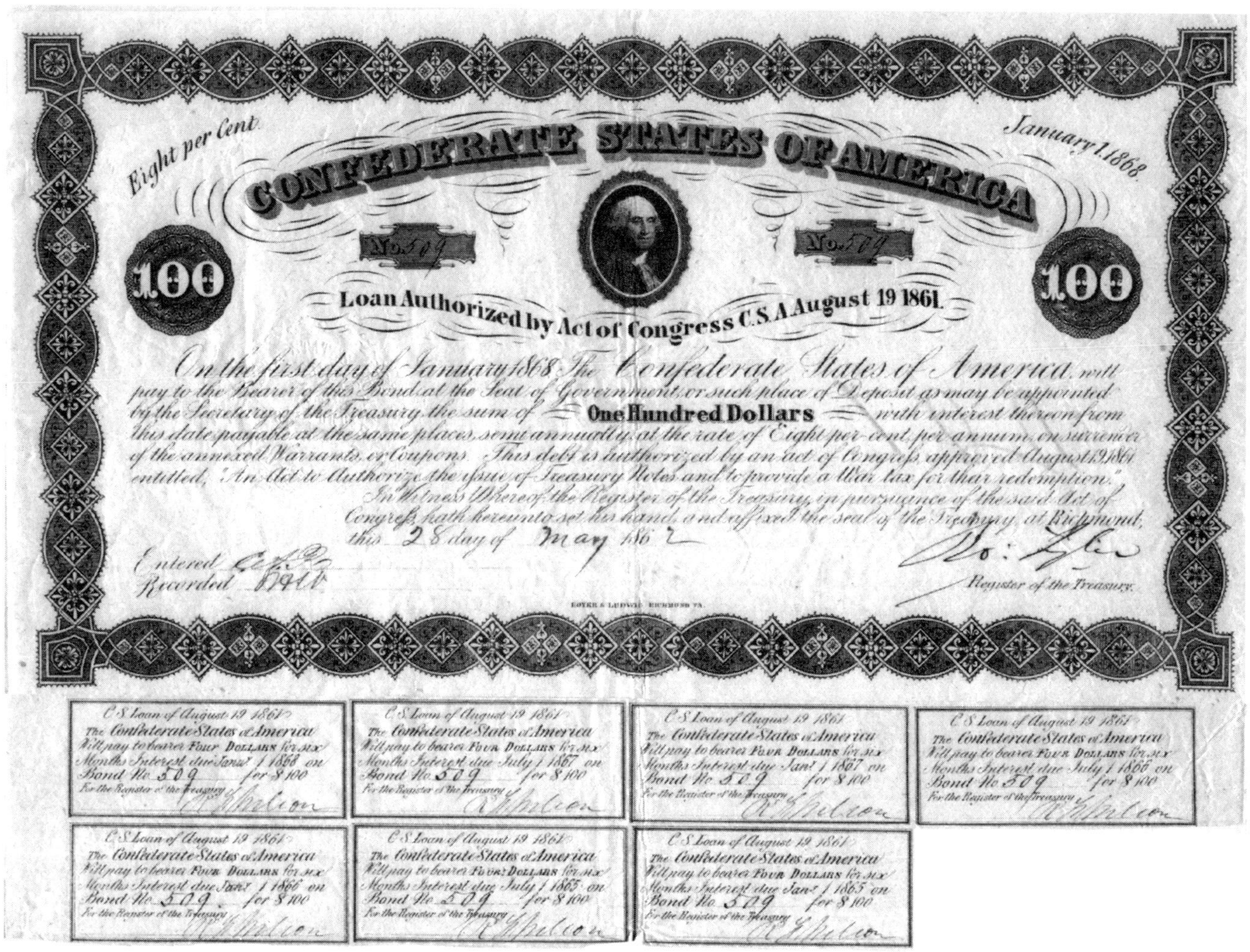

(Washington, center)

TYPE 39 **$100**

				fine	very fine
48.	$100	Illustrated, printed on white paper.			
		Number issued: 628 (#1-628)	Rarity (5)	$175	$250
		Signed by Tyler.			

Eight per Cent

January 1 1868

CONFEDERATE STATES OF AMERICA

No 1108 No 1108

$500 $500

Loan Authorized by Act of Congress C.S.A August 19 1861.

On the first day of January 1868 The Confederate States of America will pay to the Bearer of this Bond at the Seat of Government or such place of Deposit as may be appointed by the Secretary of the Treasury the sum of Five hundred Dollars with interest thereon from this date payable at the same places semi annually at the rate of Eight per cent per annum on surrender of the annexed Warrants or Coupons. This debt is authorized by an act of Congress approved August 19 1861, entitled "An Act to Authorize the issue of Treasury Notes and to provide a War tax for their redemption."

In Witness Whereof the Register of the Treasury, in pursuance of the said Act of Congress hath hereunto set his hand and affixed the seal of the Treasury at Richmond, this 29 day of May 1862

Entered

Recorded

Register of the Treasury

(*Commerce* on a bale, center)

TYPE 40 **$500**

				fine	very fine
49.	$500	Illustrated, printed on white paper.			
		Number issued: 1,132 (#1-1132)[36]	Rarity (4+)	$100	$125
		Signed by Tyler (c. #1-800; 901-1132) and Jones (c.#801-900).			

(Equestrian statue of Washington on the capitol grounds in Richmond)

TYPE 41 **$1,000**

				fine	very fine
50.	$1,000	Illustrated, printed on white paper. Number issued: 1,094 (#1-1094) Signed by Tyler.	Rarity (5-)	$80	$115

H. 8% coupon bonds due July 1, 1868[37]
Imprint: "Hoyer & Ludwig, Richmond, Va."

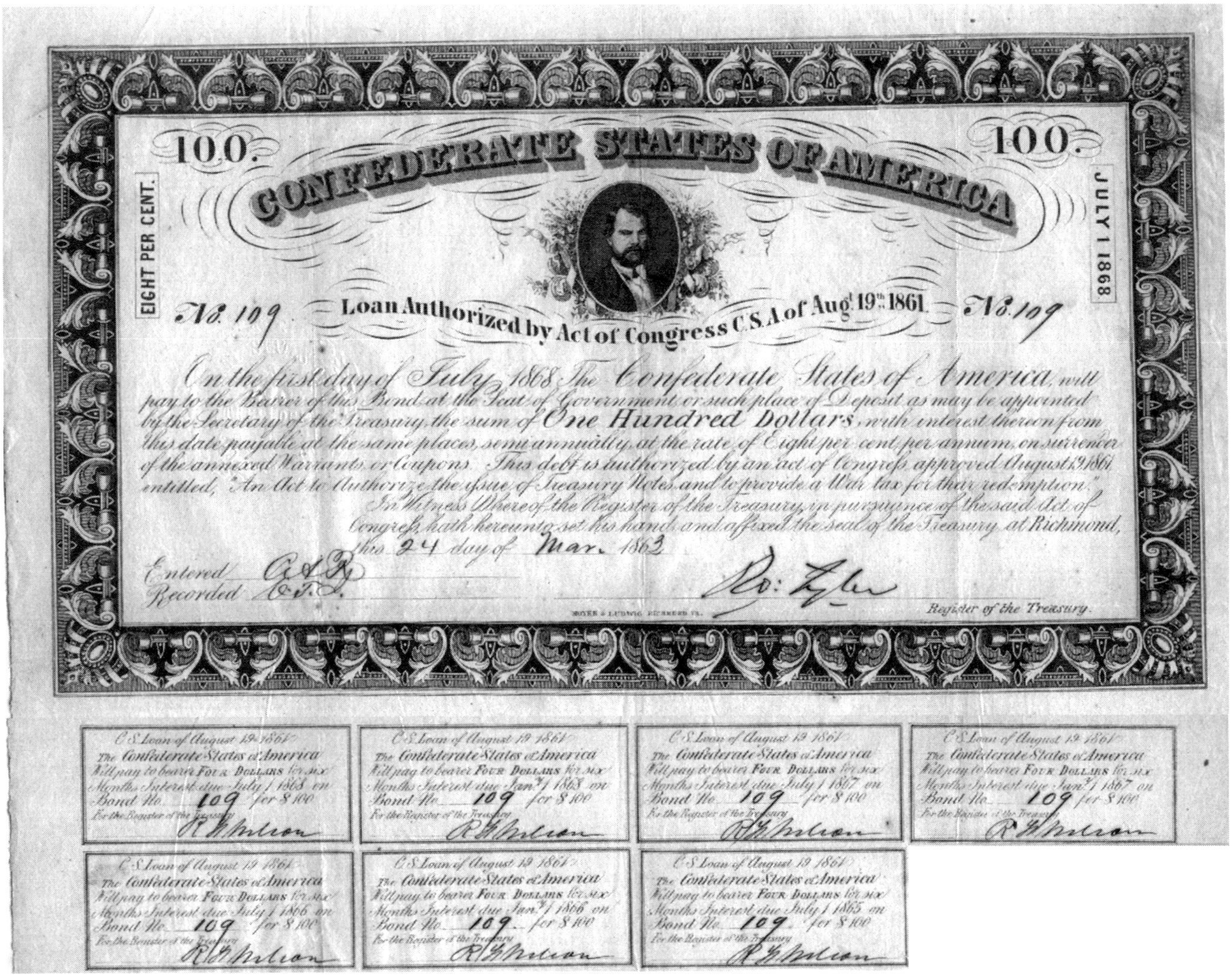

100. CONFEDERATE STATES OF AMERICA 100.

EIGHT PER CENT. JULY 1 1868

No. 109 Loan Authorized by Act of Congress C.S.A. of Aug. 19th 1861. No. 109

On the first day of July 1868 The Confederate States of America will pay to the Bearer of this Bond at the Seat of Government or such place of Deposit as may be appointed by the Secretary of the Treasury, the sum of One Hundred Dollars, with interest thereon from this date payable at the same places, semi annually, at the rate of Eight per cent per annum, on surrender of the annexed Warrants or Coupons. This debt is authorized by an act of Congress approved August 19 1861, entitled, "An Act to Authorize the issue of Treasury Notes and to provide a War tax for their redemption."

In Witness Whereof the Register of the Treasury, in pursuance of the said Act of Congress, hath hereunto set his hand and affixed the seal of the Treasury at Richmond, this 24 day of Mar. 1862

Entered

Recorded

Ro: Tyler

Hoyer & Ludwig Richmond Va.

Register of the Treasury.

C.S. Loan of August 19 1861 The Confederate States of America will pay to bearer Four Dollars for six Months Interest due July 1 1868 on Bond No. 109 for $100 For the Register of the Treasury

C.S. Loan of August 19 1861 The Confederate States of America will pay to bearer Four Dollars for six Months Interest due Jan. 1 1868 on Bond No. 109 for $100 For the Register of the Treasury

C.S. Loan of August 19 1861 The Confederate States of America will pay to bearer Four Dollars for six Months Interest due July 1 1867 on Bond No. 109 for $100 For the Register of the Treasury

C.S. Loan of August 19 1861 The Confederate States of America will pay to bearer Four Dollars for six Months Interest due Jan. 1 1867 on Bond No. 109 for $100 For the Register of the Treasury

C.S. Loan of August 19 1861 The Confederate States of America will pay to bearer Four Dollars for six Months Interest due July 1 1866 on Bond No. 109 for $100 For the Register of the Treasury

C.S. Loan of August 19 1861 The Confederate States of America will pay to bearer Four Dollars for six Months Interest due Jan. 1 1866 on Bond No. 109 for $100 For the Register of the Treasury

C.S. Loan of August 19 1861 The Confederate States of America will pay to bearer Four Dollars for six Months Interest due July 1 1865 on Bond No. 109 for $100 For the Register of the Treasury

(Postmaster General Reagan, center)

TYPE 42 **$100**

				fine	very fine
51.	$100	Illustrated, printed on white paper.			
		Number issued: 727 (#1-727)	Rarity (5)	$100	$150
		Signed by Tyler.			

(Virginia state arms, Athena trampling a tyrant center)

TYPE 43 **$500**

				fine	very fine
52.	$500	Illustrated, printed on white paper.			
		Number issued: 957 (#1-957)	Rarity (5-)	$100	$175
		Signed by Tyler (c. #1-900; 926-957) and Jones (c. #901-925).			

(Locomotive with straight steam)

TYPE 44 **$1,000**

				fine	very fine
53.	$1,000	Illustrated, printed on white paper.			
		Number issued: 1,283 (#1-1283)	Rarity (4+)	$90	$150
		Signed by Tyler and Jones (c. #241-300; #1221-1250).			

I. 8% coupon bonds due July 1, 1869
Imprint: "B. Duncan, Columbia, S.C."

(R.M.T. Hunter)

(J.P. Benjamin)

(C.G. Memminger)

ONE HUNDRED

100

CONFEDERATE STATES OF AMERICA

LOAN.

No 2447

AUTHORIZED BY THE ACT OF CONGRESS, C.S.A. OF AUGUST 19, 1861.

EIGHT PER CENT.

JULY 1, 1869.

On the first day of July 1869. The Confederate States of America will pay to the Bearer of this Bond, at the Seat of Government, or such place of Deposit as may be appointed by the Secretary of the Treasury, the sum of ONE HUNDRED DOLLARS with Interest thereon from this date, payable at the same place, semi-annually, at the rate of Eight per Cent. per annum, on surrender of the annexed Warrants or Coupons. This debt is authorized by an Act of Congress, approved August 19, 1861, entitled "An Act to authorize the issue of Treasury Notes, and to provide a War Tax for their redemption."

In Witness whereof the Register of the Treasury, in pursuance of the said Act of Congress, hath hereunto set his hand and affixed the seal of the Treasury at RICHMOND, this 26 day of apr 1862

Entered [illegible]
Recorded [illegible]

Register of the Treasury.

B. DUNCAN, RICHMOND.

ONE HUNDRED

TYPE 45 **$100**

				fine	very fine
54.	$100	Illustrated, printed on white paper.			
		Number issued: 8,884 (#1-8884)[38]	Rarity (3+)	$35	$45
		Signed by Tyler (c. #1-8000 and Jones (c. #8001-8884).			

TYPE 46 **$500**

55.	$500	Illustrated, printed on white paper.			
		Number issued: 1,005 (#1-1005)	Rarity (5-)	$60	$75
		Signed by Tyler (c. #1-900) and Jones (c. #901-1005).			

TYPE 47 **$1,000**

56.	$1,000	As preceding, but for number medallions and Memminger portrait.			
		Number issued: 593 (#1-593)	Rarity (5)	$80	$100
		Signed by Tyler (c. #1-584) and Jones (c. #585-593).			

J. 8% coupon bonds due July 1, 1870
Imprint: "B. Duncan, Columbia, S.C."[39]

(Thomas Watts flanked by *Law, Justice,* woman with flag)

(Thomas Bragg)

(Jefferson Davis)

TYPE 48 **$100**

				fine	very fine
57.	$100	Illustrated, printed on white paper. Number issued: 877 (#1-877) Signed by Tyler.	Rarity (5)	$180	$250

TYPE 49 **$500**

				fine	very fine
58.	$500	As above, but for medallions and Bragg portrait. Number issued: 1,126 (#1-1126) Signed by Tyler.	Rarity (5-)	$45	$65

59.	$500	As preceding, hand reissued on the back in red ink by James Sorley, CSA depositary in Houston, Texas. Number issued: unknown (#900 range) Dates of issue: December 1863 Signed by Tyler.	Rarity (6)	$110	$150
60.	$500	Same, hand reissued on the back by Wood & Power.[40] Number issued: unknown (#900 range) Date of issue: January 28, 1863 Signed by Tyler.	Rarity (7+)	$300	$450
61.	$500	As preceding, hand reissued by A.W. McRae, "Asst. CSA agent." Number issued: unknown (#720 range) Signed by Tyler.	Rarity (7+)	$175	$250

TYPE 50 **$1,000**

62.	$1,000	As above, but for Davis portrait. Number issued: 1,491 (#1-1491) Signed by Tyler.	Rarity (4+)	$100	$125

K. 8% coupon bonds due January 1, 1871[41]
Imprint: "B. Duncan, Columbia, S.C."

(C.G. Memminger)

(J.P. Benjamin, center)

(Jefferson Davis)

TYPE 51 **$100**

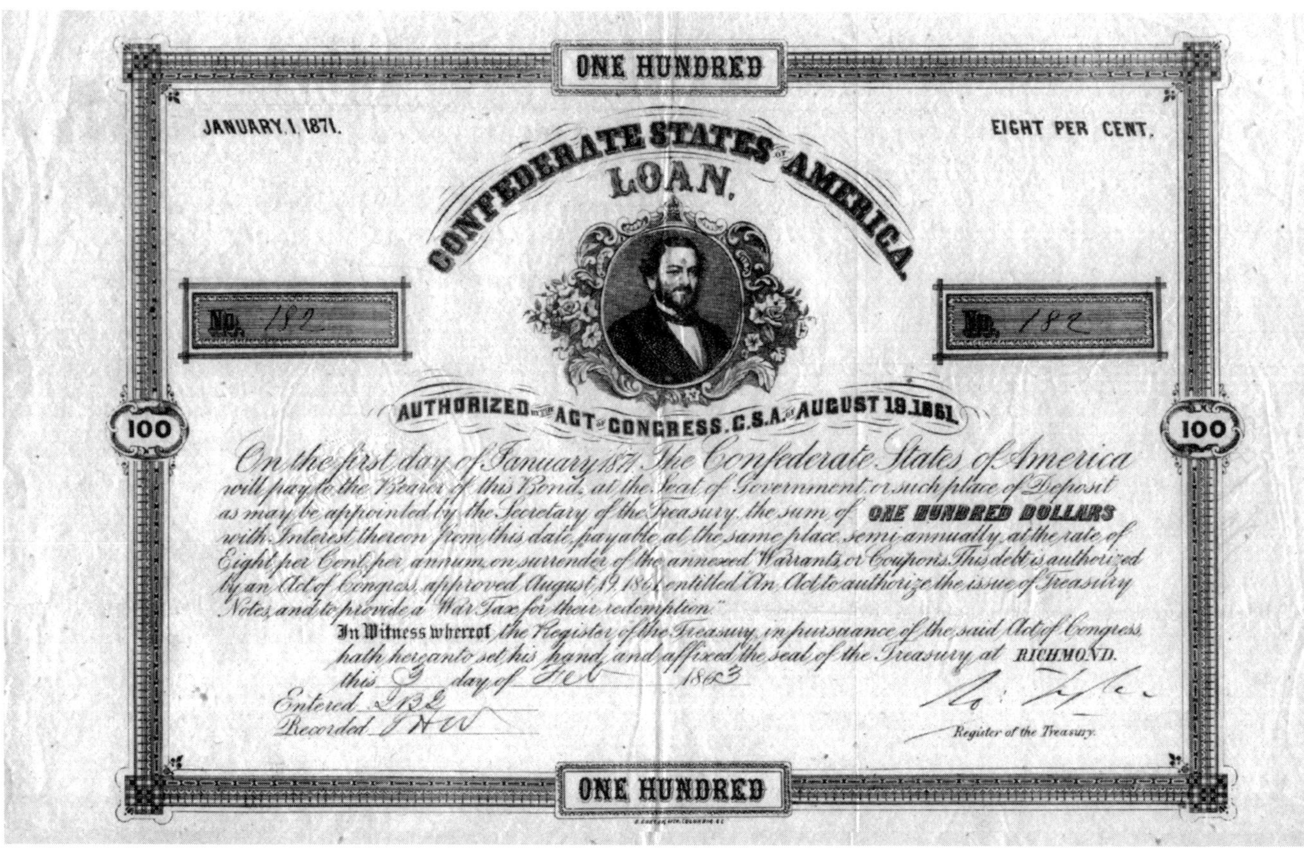

ONE HUNDRED

JANUARY 1, 1871. EIGHT PER CENT.

CONFEDERATE STATES OF AMERICA LOAN.

No. 182 No. 182

100 100

AUTHORIZED BY THE ACT OF CONGRESS. C.S.A. OF AUGUST 19, 1861.

On the first day of January 1871 The Confederate States of America will pay to the Bearer of this Bond, at the Seat of Government or such place of Deposit as may be appointed by the Secretary of the Treasury, the sum of ONE HUNDRED DOLLARS with Interest thereon from this date, payable at the same place semi-annually, at the rate of Eight per Cent. per annum, on surrender of the annexed Warrants or Coupons. This debt is authorized by an Act of Congress approved August 19, 1861, entitled "An Act to authorize the issue of Treasury Notes, and to provide a War Tax for their redemption."

In Witness whereof the Register of the Treasury, in pursuance of the said Act of Congress, hath hereunto set his hand and affixed the seal of the Treasury at RICHMOND. this 3 day of Feb 1863

Entered

Recorded

Register of the Treasury.

ONE HUNDRED

				fine	very fine
63.	$100	Illustrated, printed on white paper.			
		Number issued: 896 (#1-779; 800-916)	Rarity (5)	$100	$135
		Date of issue: February 3, 1863			
		Signed by Tyler.			

				fine	very fine
64.	$100	Same, no imprint. Number issued: 22 (#780-799 plus others, scattered) Date of issue: February 3, 1863 Signed by Tyler.	Rarity (7-)	$250	$350

TYPE 52 **$500**

65.	$500	As above, but Memminger portrait. Number issued: 1,080 (#1-1080) Signed by Tyler.	Rarity (5-)	$50	$65

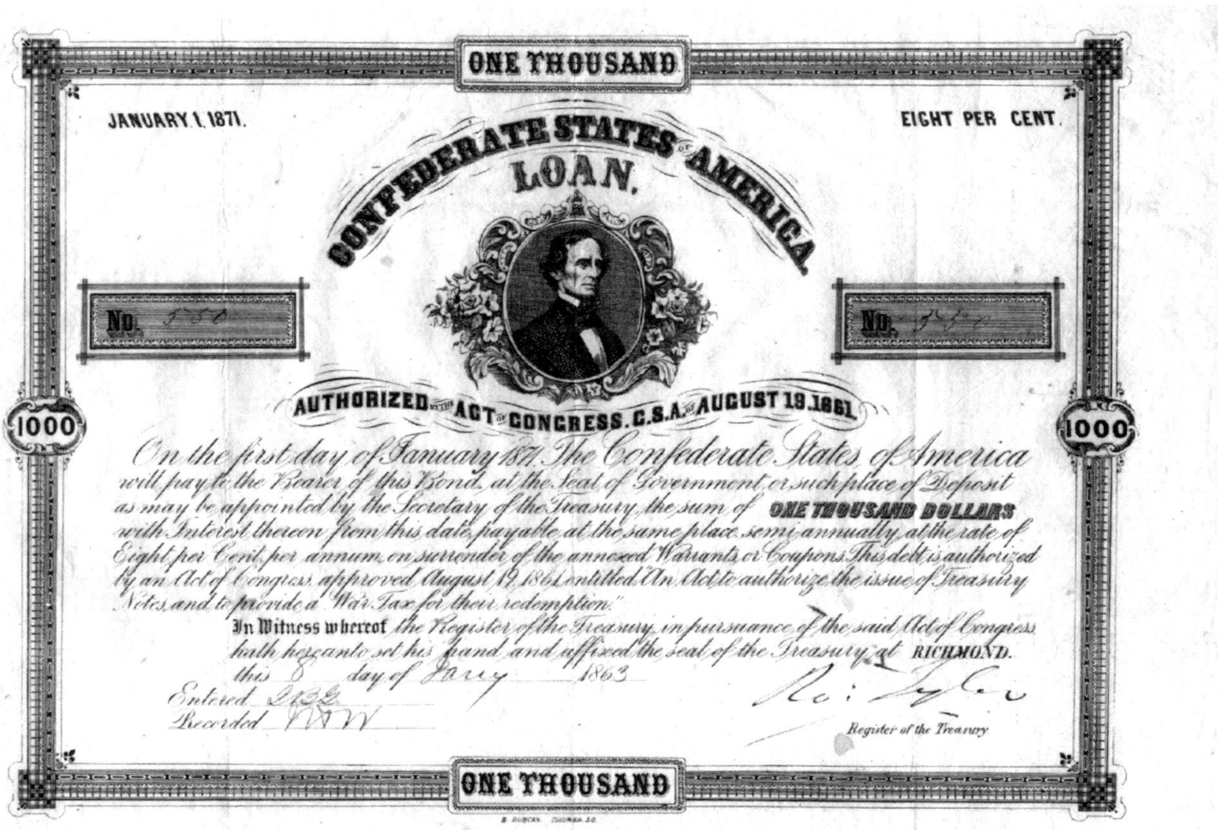

TYPE 53 **$1,000**

66.	$1,000	As above, but Davis portrait. Number issued: 1,600 (#1-1600) Signed by Tyler.	Rarity (4+)	$60	$80

L. 8% coupon bonds due July 1, 1871[42]
Imprint: "B. Duncan, Richmond, Va."

(Thomas Bragg)

(J.P. Benjamin)

(C.G. Memminger)

100 ONE HUNDRED 100

CONFEDERATE STATES OF AMERICA LOAN.

AUTHORIZED BY ACT CONGRESS. C.S.A. AUGUST 19.1861.

On the first day of July 1871. The Confederate States of America will pay to the Bearer of this Bond, at the Seat of Government or such place of Deposit as may be appointed by the Secretary of the Treasury, the sum of ONE HUNDRED DOLLARS with Interest thereon from this date payable at the same place semi annually, at the rate of Eight per Cent per annum on surrender of the annexed Warrants or Coupons. This debt is authorized by an Act of Congress approved August 19, 1861 entitled An Act to authorize the issue of Treasury Notes and to provide a War Tax for their redemption.

In Witness whereof the Register of the Treasury in pursuance of the said Act of Congress hath hereunto set his hand and affixed the seal of the Treasury at RICHMOND. this 23 day of July 1862

Entered

Recorded

Register of the Treasury

FOUR DOLLARS

FOUR DOLLARS

FOUR DOLLARS

FOUR DOLLARS

FOUR DOLLARS

TYPE 54 **$100**

				fine	very fine
67.	$100	Illustrated, printed on white paper. Number issued: 2,294 (#1-2294) Signed by Tyler and Jones (1990s).	Rarity (4)	$40	$50

TYPE 55 **$500**

				fine	very fine
68.	$500	Same as above, but J.P. Benjamin portrait. Number issued: 1,207 (#1-1207) Signed by Tyler (#1-1000; 1101-1207) and Jones (#1001-1100).	Rarity (4+)	$40	$60

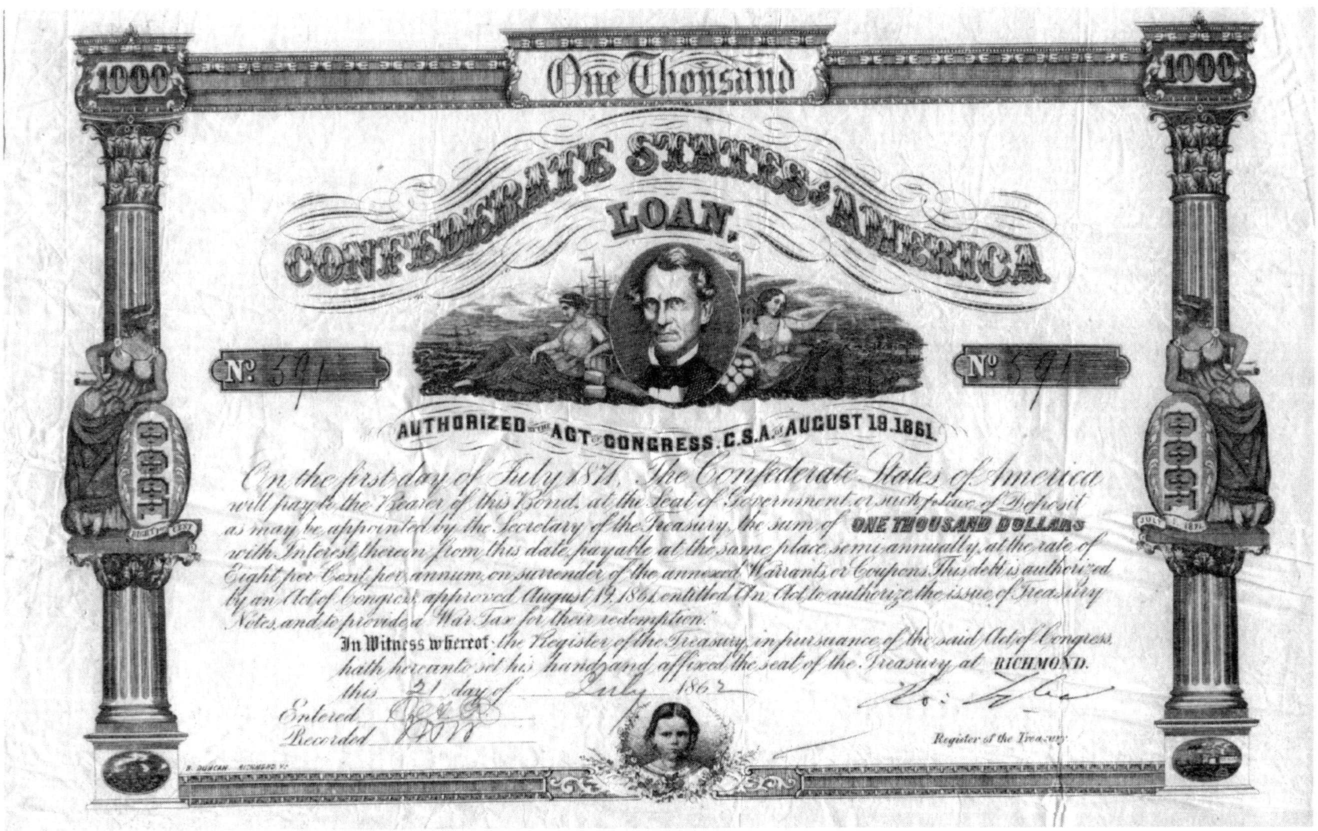

TYPE 56 **$1,000**

69.	$1,000	Same as above, but C.G. Memminger portrait. Number issued: c. 1,388 (#1-1000; 1101-1488) Signed by Tyler (c. #1-800; 1101-c. 1488) and Jones (c. #801-1000).	Rarity (4+)	$45	$60
70.	$1,000	Same, but reissued in the Trans-Mississippi by James Sorley at Houston, Texas on back in red ink. Number issued: c. 100 (#1001-1100) Dates of issue: December 1863 Signed by Tyler.	Rarity (6+)	$130	$200

M. 8% coupon bonds due July 1, 1872[43]
Imprint: "B. Duncan, Richmond, Va."

(J.H. Reagan)

(S.R. Mallory)

(J.P. Benjamin)

(C.G. Memminger)

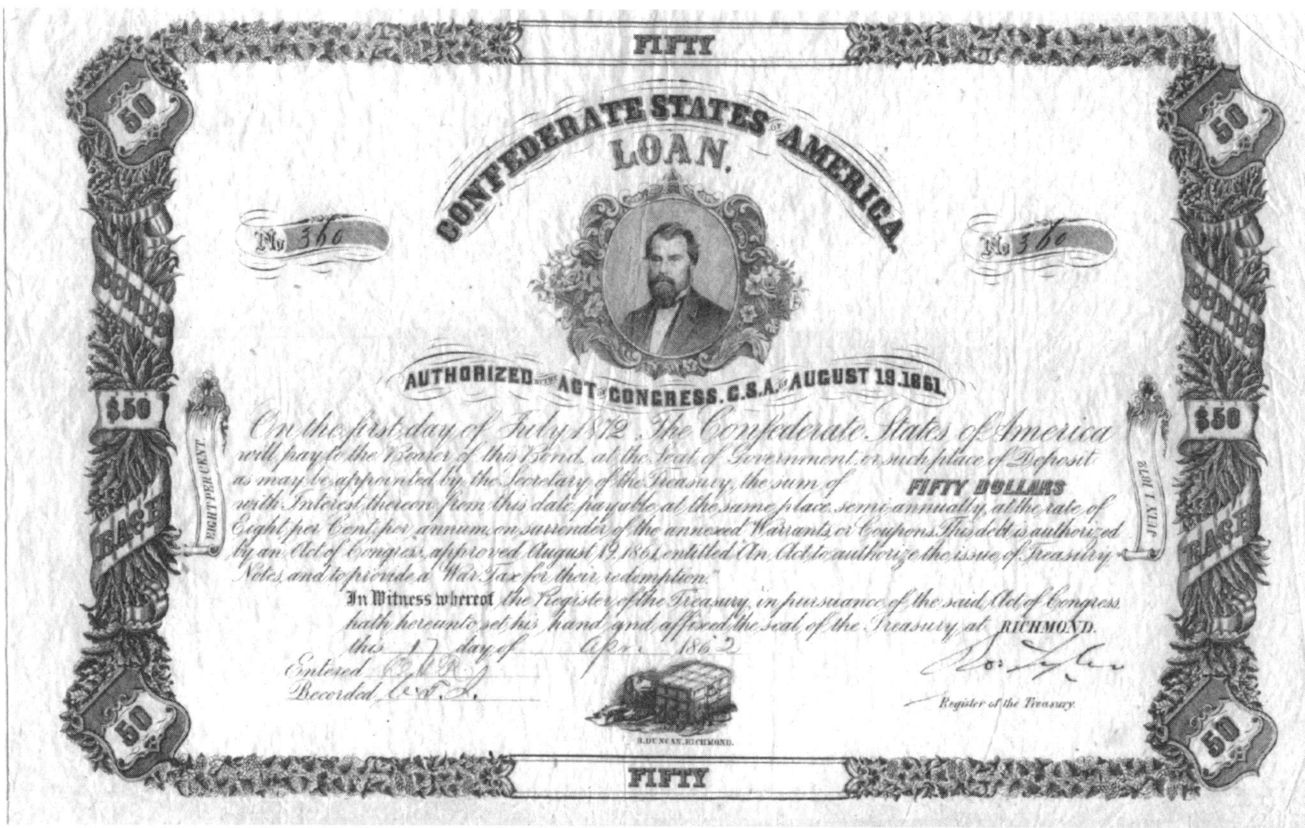
FIFTY
CONFEDERATE STATES OF AMERICA
LOAN.
No 360
No 360
AUTHORIZED BY ACT OF CONGRESS, C.S.A. AUGUST 19 1861.
On the first day of July 1872 The Confederate States of America will pay to the Bearer of this Bond, at the Seat of Government, or such place of Deposit as may be appointed by the Secretary of the Treasury, the sum of FIFTY DOLLARS with Interest thereon from this date payable at the same place semi-annually, at the rate of Eight per Cent per annum, on surrender of the annexed Warrants or Coupons. This debt is authorized by an Act of Congress, approved August 19, 1861, entitled "An Act to authorize the issue of Treasury Notes, and to provide a War Tax for their redemption."
In Witness whereof the Register of the Treasury, in pursuance of the said Act of Congress hath hereunto set his hand and affixed the Seal of the Treasury at RICHMOND.
this 17 day of Apr. 1862
Entered
Recorded
Register of the Treasury.
B. DUNCAN, RICHMOND.
EIGHT PER CENT.
JULY 1 1872
50 BONDS $50 EACH
FIFTY

TYPE 57 **$50**

				fine	very fine
71.	$50	Illustrated, printed on white paper.			
		Number issued: 1,110 (#1-1110)	Rarity (5-)	$90	$120
		Signed by Tyler (c. #1-600; 801-1110) and Jones (c. #601-800).			

TYPE 58 **$100**

				fine	very fine
72.	$100	Same as above, but S.R. Mallory portrait facing left. Number issued: c. 800 (#1-800) Signed by Tyler.	Rarity (5+)	$40	$60

TYPE 59 **$100**

73.	$100	Same, but Mallory facing right. Number issued: c. 1,212 (#801-2012) Signed by Tyler.	Rarity (5)	$40	$55

TYPE 60 **$500**

74.	$500	Same, but Benjamin portrait. Number issued: 1,307 (#1-1307) Signed by Tyler.	Rarity (4+)	$40	$55

ONE THOUSAND
CONFEDERATE STATES OF AMERICA
LOAN.
No 10
AUTHORIZED BY ACT CONGRESS. C.S.A. AUGUST 19 1861.
EIGHT PER CENT
JULY 1 1872
On the first day of July 1872 The Confederate States of America will pay to the Bearer of this Bond at the Seat of Government or such place of Deposit as may be appointed by the Secretary of the Treasury the sum of ONE THOUSAND DOLLARS with Interest thereon from this date payable at the same place semi annually at the rate of Eight per Cent per annum on surrender of the annexed Warrants or Coupons. This debt is authorized by an Act of Congress approved August 19, 1861 entitled "An Act to authorize the issue of Treasury Notes and to provide a War Tax for their redemption."
In Witness whereof the Register of the Treasury in pursuance of the said Act of Congress hath hereunto set his hand and affixed the seal of the Treasury at RICHMOND.
this 22 day of Mar. 1862
Register of the Treasury.
ONE THOUSAND
C.S. LOAN OF AUGT 19, 1861. THE CONFEDERATE STATES OF AMERICA Will pay to Bearer FORTY DOLLARS FOR SIX MONTHS INTEREST, DUE JULY 1, 1872. On Bond No 10 for $1000.

TYPE 61 **$1,000**

				fine	very fine
75.	$1,000	Same, but Memminger portrait. Number issued: 1,600 (#1-1600) Signed by Tyler.	Rarity (4+)	$35	$45

N.B. This bond bears the imprint of "Wagner & Co." Wagner was a Nashville, Tennessee printer picked up by Duncan on November 1, 1861 and brought to Richmond to work for Duncan. Wagner did most of Duncan's bonds, to judge by the comparative superiority of their workmanship *vis-a-vis* the notes.

Hot air balloons were used by both sides for observation of the enemy.

N. 8% coupon bonds due January 1, 1873[44]
Imprint: "B. Duncan, Columbia, S.C."

(R.M.T. Hunter, $100)

(J.H. Reagan, $500)

(S.R. Mallory, $1000)

TYPE 62 **$100**

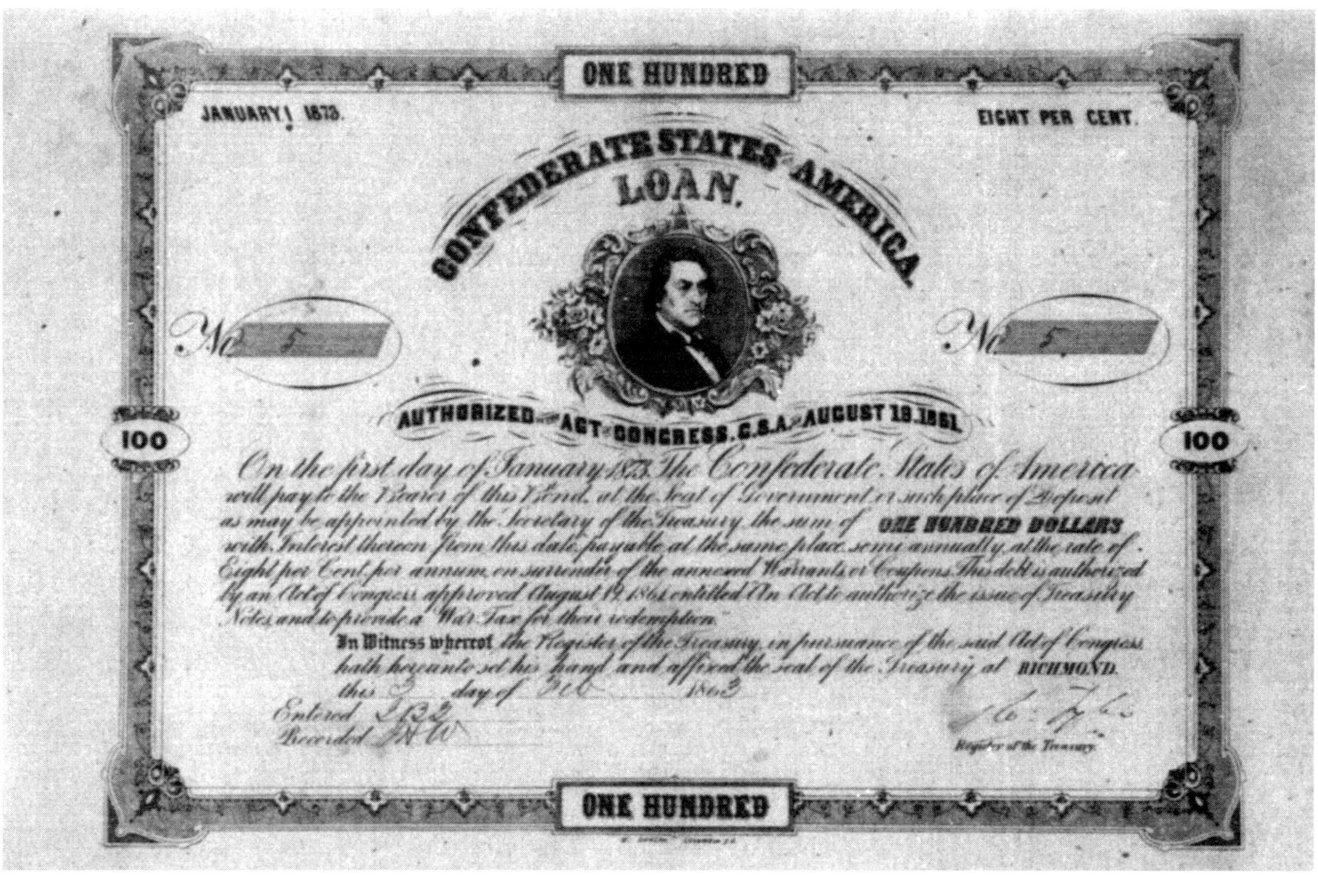

ONE HUNDRED

JANUARY 1 1873. EIGHT PER CENT.

CONFEDERATE STATES OF AMERICA
LOAN.

No 5 No 5

AUTHORIZED BY ACT CONGRESS, C.S.A. AUGUST 19, 1861.

100 100

On the first day of January 1873 The Confederate States of America will pay to the Bearer of this Bond, at the Seat of Government or such place of Deposit as may be appointed by the Secretary of the Treasury, the sum of ONE HUNDRED DOLLARS with Interest thereon from this date payable at the same place semi annually at the rate of Eight per Cent per annum on surrender of the annexed Warrants or Coupons. This debt is authorized by an Act of Congress approved August 19, 1861 entitled An Act to authorize the issue of Treasury Notes, and to provide a War Tax for their redemption.

In Witness whereof the Register of the Treasury in pursuance of the said Act of Congress hath hereunto set his hand and affixed the seal of the Treasury at RICHMOND. this 3 day of Dec 1863

Entered

Recorded

Register of the Treasury

ONE HUNDRED

76.	$100	Illustrated, printed on white paper.		fine	very fine
		Number issued: 846 (#1-846)	Rarity (5)	$50	$65
		Signed by Tyler.			

TYPE 63 **$500**

				fine	very fine
77.	$500	Same, but portrait of J.H. Reagan. Number issued: 1,338 (#1-225; 276-1388) Signed by Tyler.	Rarity (5)	$40	$55
78.	$500	Same, but printed in blue black ink. Number issued: c. 50 (#226-275) Signed by Tyler.	Rarity (7+)	$175	$250

TYPE 64 **$1,000**

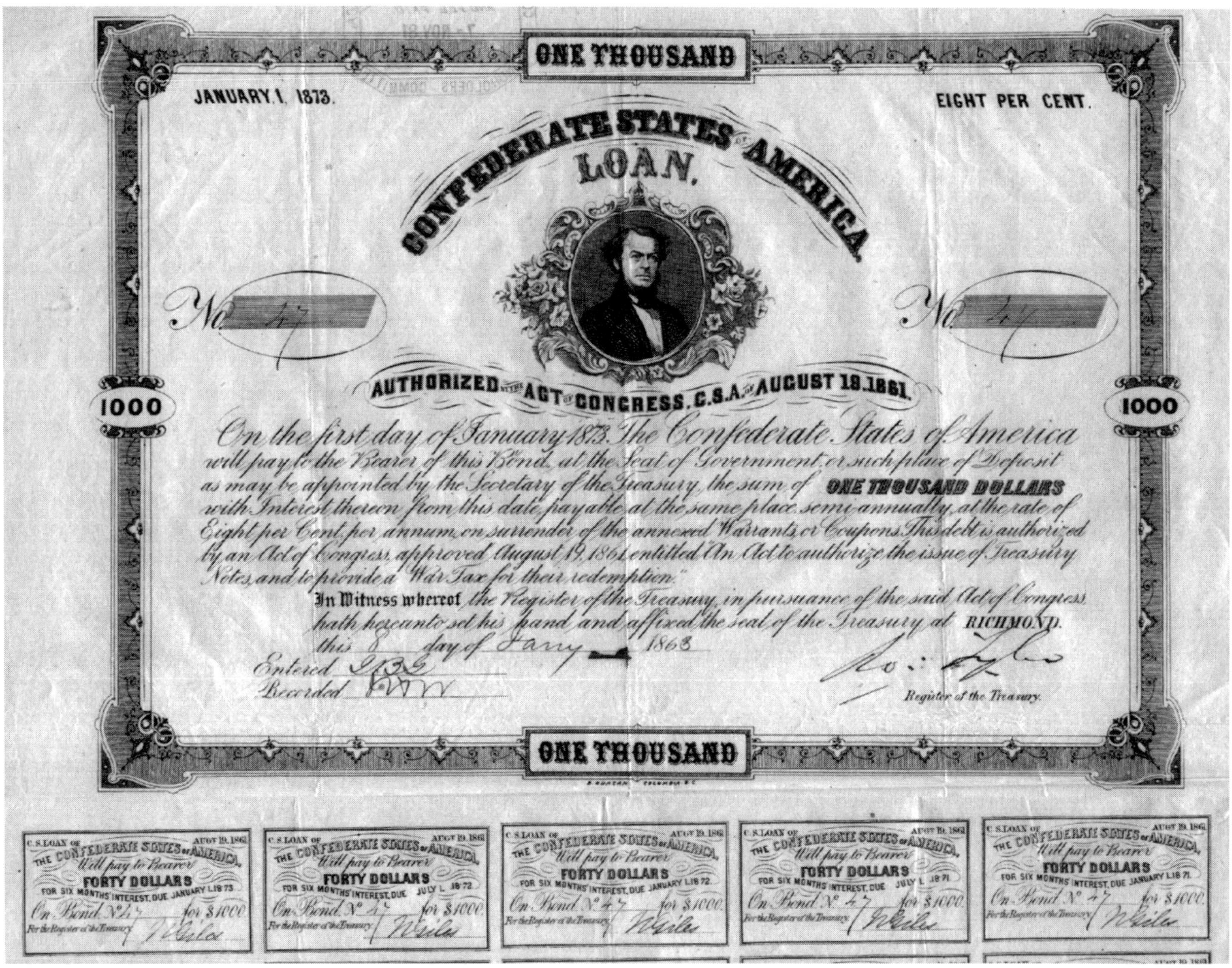

79.	$1,000	Same, but S.R. Mallory portrait. Number issued: 1,832 (#1-1832) Signed by Tyler.	Rarity (5-)	$65	$100

O. 8% coupon bonds due July 1, 1873[45]

$100 and $500 bonds printed by B. Duncan, Columbia, S.C.

(J.H. Reagan)

(S.R. Mallory)

TYPE 65 **$100**

				fine	very fine
80.	$100	Similar to illustration with Reagan, printed on white paper.			
		Number issued: 1,094 (#1-1094)	Rarity (5)	$75	$100
		Signed by Tyler.			

TYPE 66 **$500**

81.	$500	As illustrated			
		Number issued: 1,397 (#1-1397)	Rarity (5-)	$50	$65
		Signed by Tyler.			

TYPE 67 **$1,000**
Engraved and printed by Evans & Cogswell

(*The Confederacy*, with flag and ships)

				fine	very fine
82.	$1,000	Illustrated, printed on white paper.			
		Number issued: 1,901 (#1-1901)	Rarity (4+)	$75	$150
		Signed by Tyler, Jones (c. #801-900).			

P. 8% coupon bonds due July 1, 1874[46]
Printed by B. Duncan, Columbia, S.C.

(Burton Harrison
President Davis' Secretary)

(Robert Toombs)

(George W. Randolph)

(Lucy Pickens)

50 FIFTY 50

CONFEDERATE STATES OF AMERICA
LOAN.

AUTHORIZED BY THE ACT OF CONGRESS, C.S.A. AUGUST 19, 1861.

EIGHT PER CENT — JULY 1. 1874

On the first day of July 1874. The Confederate States of America will pay to the Bearer of this Bond, at the Seat of Government, or such place of Deposit as may be appointed by the Secretary of the Treasury, the sum of **FIFTY DOLLARS** *with Interest thereon, from this date, payable at the same place, semi annually, at the rate of Eight per Cent per annum, on surrender of the annexed Warrants or Coupons. This debt is authorized by an Act of Congress, approved August 19, 1861, entitled "An Act to authorize the issue of Treasury Notes, and to provide a War Tax for their redemption."*

In Witness whereof *the Register of the Treasury, in pursuance of the said Act of Congress, hath hereunto set his hand, and affixed the seal of the Treasury at* RICHMOND.
this 8 day of Oct 1862

Entered
Recorded

Register of the Treasury

50 FIFTY 50

TYPE 68 **$50**

83.	$50	Illustrated, printed on white paper.		fine	very fine
		Number issued: 998 (#1-998)	Rarity (5)	$160	$200
		Signed by Jones (c. #1-100) and Tyler (#101-998).			

TYPE 69 **$100** [47]

				fine	very fine
84.	$100	Same, but portrait of Robert Toombs. Number issued: 1,187 (#1-1187) Signed by Jones.	Rarity (5-)	$50	$70

TYPE 70 **$500**

85.	$500	Illustrated, but portrait of George W. Randolph. Number issued: 1,408 (#1-1408) Signed by Jones.	Rarity (4+)	$60	$85

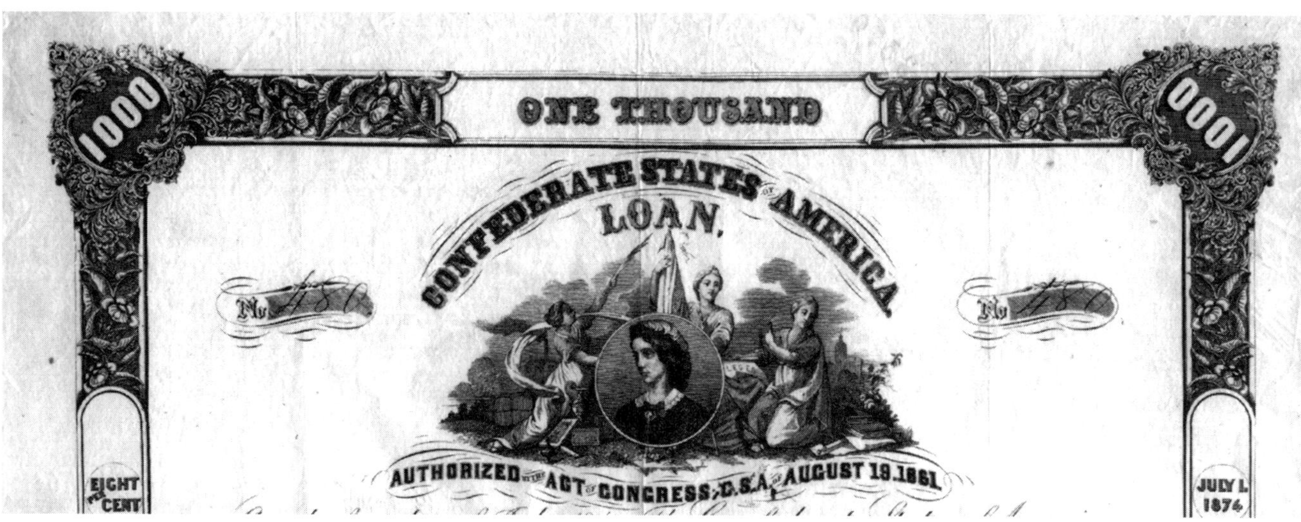

TYPE 71 **$1,000**

86.	$1,000	Illustrated, but portrait of Mrs. Lucy H. Pickins. Number issued: 2,064 (#1-2064) Signed by Jones.	Rarity (4)	$150	$200

Q. 8% coupon bonds due January 1, 1875[48]
Printed by B. Duncan, Columbia, S.C.)

(Thomas Bragg)

(R.M.T. Hunter)

(J.P. Benjamin)

(C.G. Memminger)

FIFTY

JANUARY 1, 1875. EIGHT PER CENT.

CONFEDERATE STATES OF AMERICA
LOAN.

No. 179 No. 179

50 AUTHORIZED BY ACT OF CONGRESS. C.S.A. AUGUST 19.1861. 50

On the first day of January 1875 The Confederate States of America will pay to the Bearer of this Bond, at the Seat of Government, or such place of Deposit as may be appointed by the Secretary of the Treasury, the sum of FIFTY DOLLARS with Interest thereon from this date, payable at the same place semi-annually, at the rate of Eight per Cent. per annum, on surrender of the annexed Warrants or Coupons. This debt is authorized by an Act of Congress, approved August 19, 1861, entitled "An Act to authorize the issue of Treasury Notes, and to provide a War Tax for their redemption."

In Witness whereof the Register of the Treasury, in pursuance of the said Act of Congress, hath hereunto set his hand and affixed the seal of the Treasury at RICHMOND, this 21 day of Jany 1863

Entered
Recorded

Register of the Treasury.

FIFTY

C.S. LOAN OF AUGT 19.1861. CONFEDERATE STATES OF AMERICA Will pay to Bearer TWO DOLLARS For six months Interest Due January 1 1875 On Bond No 179 for $50

C.S. LOAN OF AUGT 19.1861. CONFEDERATE STATES OF AMERICA Will pay to Bearer TWO DOLLARS For six months Interest Due July 1 1874 On Bond No 179 for $50

C.S. LOAN OF AUGT 19.1861. CONFEDERATE STATES OF AMERICA Will pay to Bearer TWO DOLLARS For six months Interest Due January 1 1874 On Bond No 179 for $50

C.S. LOAN OF AUGT 19.1861. CONFEDERATE STATES OF AMERICA Will pay to Bearer TWO DOLLARS For six months Interest Due July 1 1873 On Bond No 179 for $50

C.S. LOAN OF AUGT 19.1861. CONFEDERATE STATES OF AMERICA Will pay to Bearer TWO DOLLARS For six months Interest Due January 1 1873 On Bond No 179 for $50

C.S. LOAN OF AUGT 19.1861. CONFEDERATE STATES OF AMERICA Will pay to Bearer TWO DOLLARS For six months Interest Due July 1 1872 On Bond No 179 for $50

TYPE 72 **$50**

				fine	very fine
87.	$50	Illustrated, printed on white paper. Number issued: 3,614 (#1-3614) Signed by Tyler (c. #1-800), Jones (#801-3614).	Rarity (4+)	$45	$60

TYPE 73 **$100**

88.	$100	Same, but R.M.T. Hunter portrait.[49] Number issued: 934 (#1-500; 801-1234) Signed by Tyler (c. #1-1000), Jones (c. #1001-1234).	Rarity (5+)	$45	$60

TYPE 74 **$100**

89.	$100	Same as preceding, but in blue-black ink. Number issued: c. 300 (#501-800) Signed by Tyler.	Rarity (6+)	$80	$110

TYPE 75 **$500**

90.	$500	Same, but J.P. Benjamin portrait.[50] Number issued: 1,600 (#1-1600) Signed by Tyler (#1-800; 1250-1600), Jones (#801-1250).	Rarity (5-)	$40	$55

Union patriotic cover.

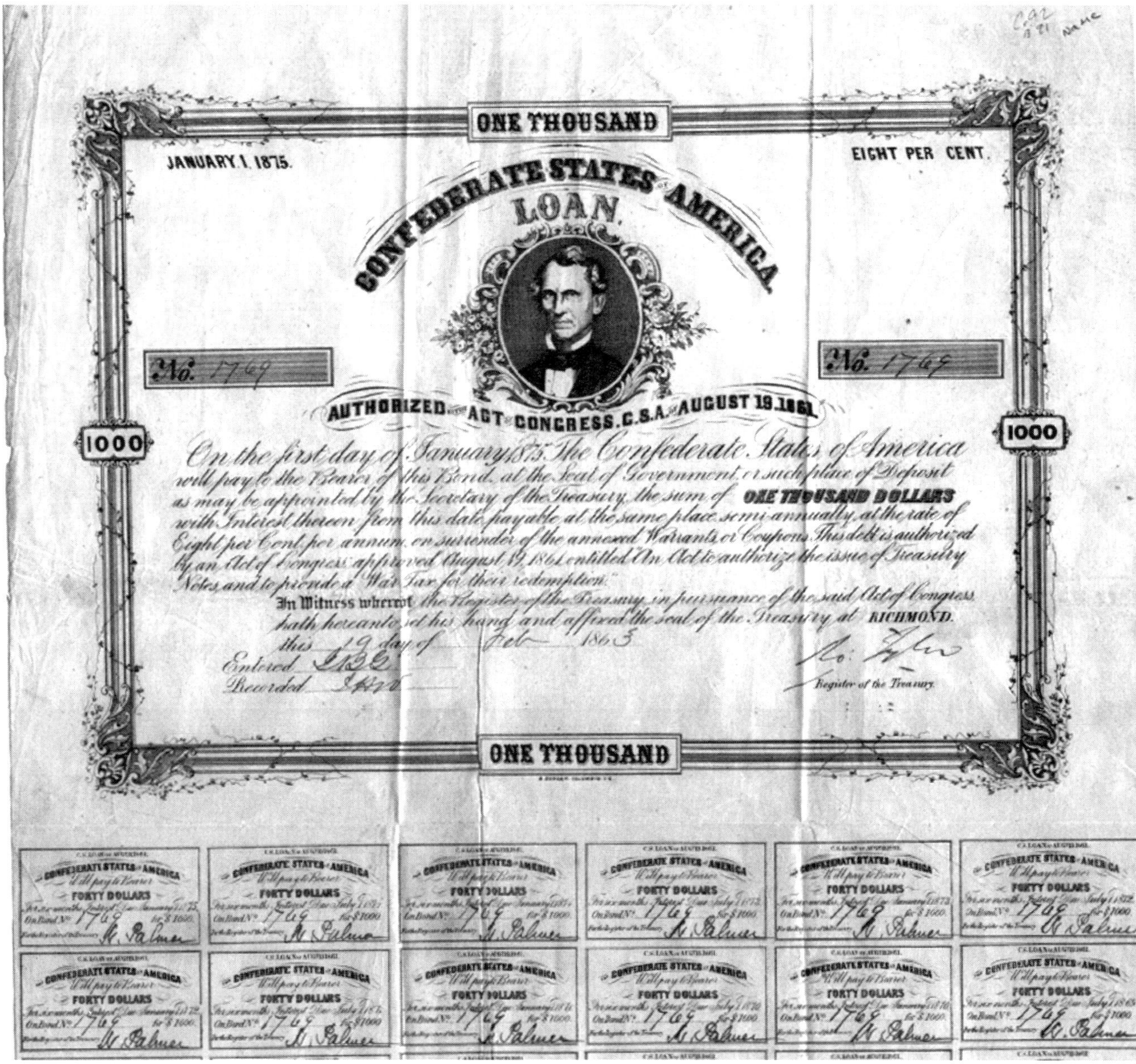

ONE THOUSAND

JANUARY 1. 1875.

EIGHT PER CENT.

CONFEDERATE STATES OF AMERICA

LOAN.

No. 1769

No. 1769

AUTHORIZED BY ACT OF CONGRESS, C.S.A. AUGUST 19, 1861.

1000

1000

On the first day of January 1875 The Confederate States of America will pay to the Bearer of this Bond, at the Seat of Government, or such place of Deposit as may be appointed by the Secretary of the Treasury, the sum of ONE THOUSAND DOLLARS with Interest thereon from this date payable at the same place semi-annually, at the rate of Eight per Cent. per annum, on surrender of the annexed Warrants or Coupons. This debt is authorized by an Act of Congress approved August 19, 1861 entitled "An Act to authorize the issue of Treasury Notes, and to provide a War Tax for their redemption."

In Witness whereof the Register of the Treasury in pursuance of the said Act of Congress hath hereunto set his hand and affixed the seal of the Treasury at RICHMOND this 19 day of Feb 1863

Entered

Recorded

Register of the Treasury.

ONE THOUSAND

CONFEDERATE STATES OF AMERICA Will pay to Bearer FORTY DOLLARS

On Bond No. 1769 for $1000.

TYPE 76 **$1,000**

91. $1,000 Same, but C.G. Memminger portrait.[51]

Number issued: 1,950 (#1-1950) Rarity (4) $45 $55

Signed by Tyler.

R. 8% coupon bonds due July 1, 1875[52]
Printed by B. Duncan, Columbia, S.C.

(R.M.T. Hunter)

(unknown man)

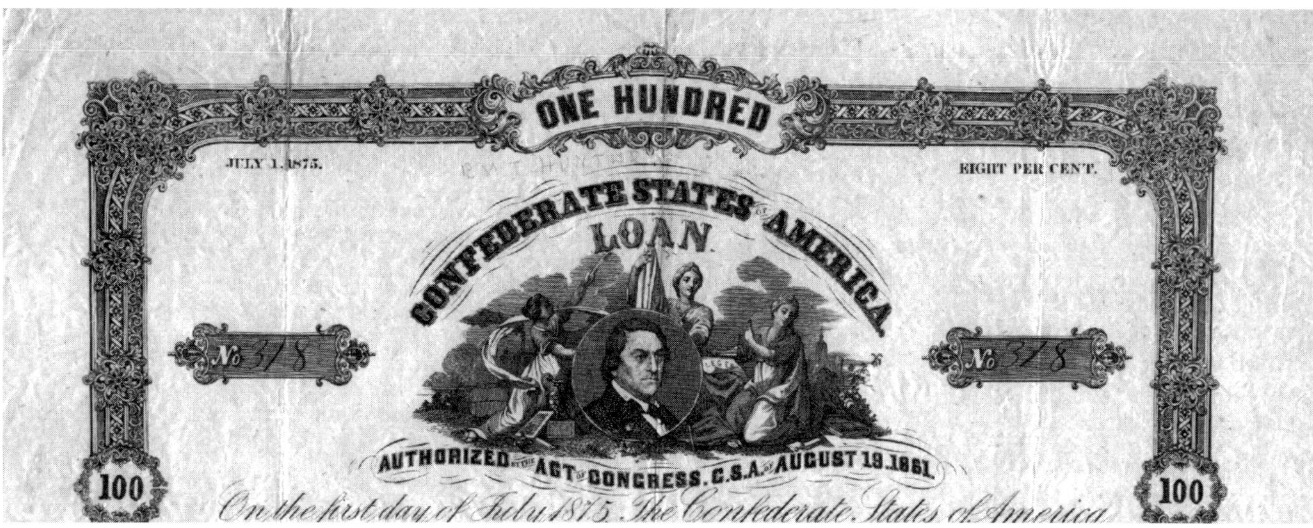

TYPE 77 **$100**

				fine	very fine
92.	$100	Illustrated, printed on white paper.[53]			
		Number issued: 1,752 (#1-1752)	Rarity (5)	$40	$55
		Signed by Tyler.			

TYPE 78 **$500**

93.	$500	Same, but unknown man's portrait.[54]			
		Number issued: 1,300 (#1-1300)	Rarity (5)	$45	$55
		Signed by Tyler.			

94.	$500	Same, but reissued in Houston, Texas by James Sorley, CSA depositary, handwritten on the back in red ink.		fine	very fine
		Number issued: c. 350 (#1301-1650)	Rarity (7-)	$100	$135
		Date of issue: January 1863			
		Signed by Tyler.			

TYPE 79 **$1,000**

Engraved by Evans & Cogswell, Charleston, S.C.; printed by B. Duncan, Columbia, S.C.

(*Confederacy,* with flag, shield and ships)

				fine	very fine
95.	$1,000	Illustrated, printed on white paper.			
		Number issued: 2,176 (#1-2176)	Rarity (4)	$90	$115
		Signed by Tyler.			

S. 8% coupon bonds due July 1, 1876[55]
Printed by B. Duncan, Columbia, S.C.

(S.R. Mallory)

(unknown man)

(General Winder)

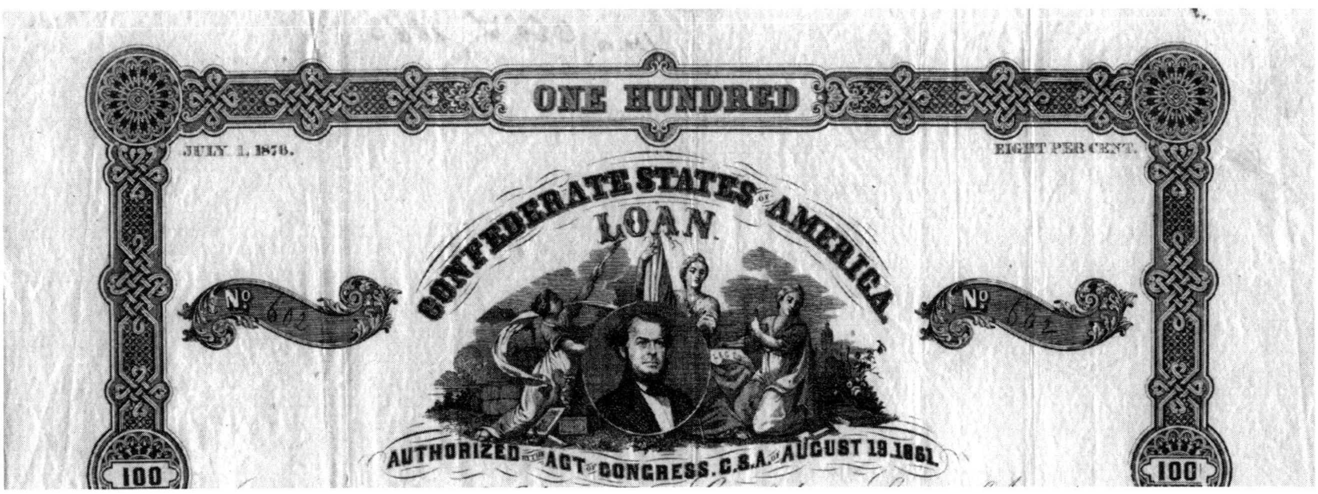

TYPE 80 **$100**

				fine	very fine
96.	$100	Illustrated, printed on white paper. Number issued: 1,564 (#1-870; 1721-2414) Signed by Tyler.	Rarity (4+)	$45	$55

TYPE 81 **$100**

97.	$100	Same, but reissued by James Sorley of Houston, Texas in red or black ink on the back. Number issued: c. 850 (#871-1720) Dates of issue: October 28, 1862 - January 23, 1863 Signed by Tyler.	Rarity (5+)	$125	$200

TYPE 82 **$500**

98.	$500	Same, but unknown man's portrait. Number issued: c. 1394 (#1-1794 less the #s for type 83) Signed by Jones (c.#1-100), Tyler (the residue).	Rarity (5)	$35	$45

TYPE 83 **$500**

99. $500 Same, but reissued by James Sorley of Houston, Texas in red ink on the back. — fine / very fine

Number issued: c. 400 (#1001-1400) Rarity (6) $100 $135

Dates of issue: October 27, 1862; December 15, 1862 - January 2, 1863

Signed by Tyler.

100. $500 Same, but issued by Wood & Power.

Number issued: c. 20 (c. #851-870) Rarity (8) -- $250

Dates of issue: October 1862.

Signed by Tyler.

TYPE 84 **$1,000**

101. $1,000 Same, but General Winder's portrait.[56]

Number issued: 2,302 (#1-2302) Rarity (5-) $55 $80

Signed by Tyler.

T. 8% coupon bonds due January 1, 1877[57]
Printed by B. Duncan, Columbia, S.C.

(Burton Harrison, Davis' Secretary)

(George W. Randolph)

(Jefferson Davis)

TYPE 85 **$100**

				fine	very fine
102.	$100	Illustrated, printed on white paper.[58] Number issued: 1,454 (#1-1454) Signed by Tyler.	Rarity (5)	$55	$150

TYPE 86 **$500**

103.	$500	Same, George W. Randolph portrait, no imprint.[59] Number issued: c. 350 (#1-50; 501-700; 901-1000) Signed by Tyler.	Rarity (6-)	$60	$85
104.	$500	Same, but B. Duncan imprint, bottom center. Number issued: c. 1,381 (#51-500; 701-900; 1001-1731) Signed by Tyler, Jones (a few in the 800 range).	Rarity (5)	$45	$65

TYPE 87 **$1,000**

				fine	very fine
105.	$1,000	Same, as above, but Jefferson Davis portrait and no imprint.[60]			
		Number issued: c. 1,000 (#1-1000)	Rarity (5)	$50	$65
		Signed by Tyler.			

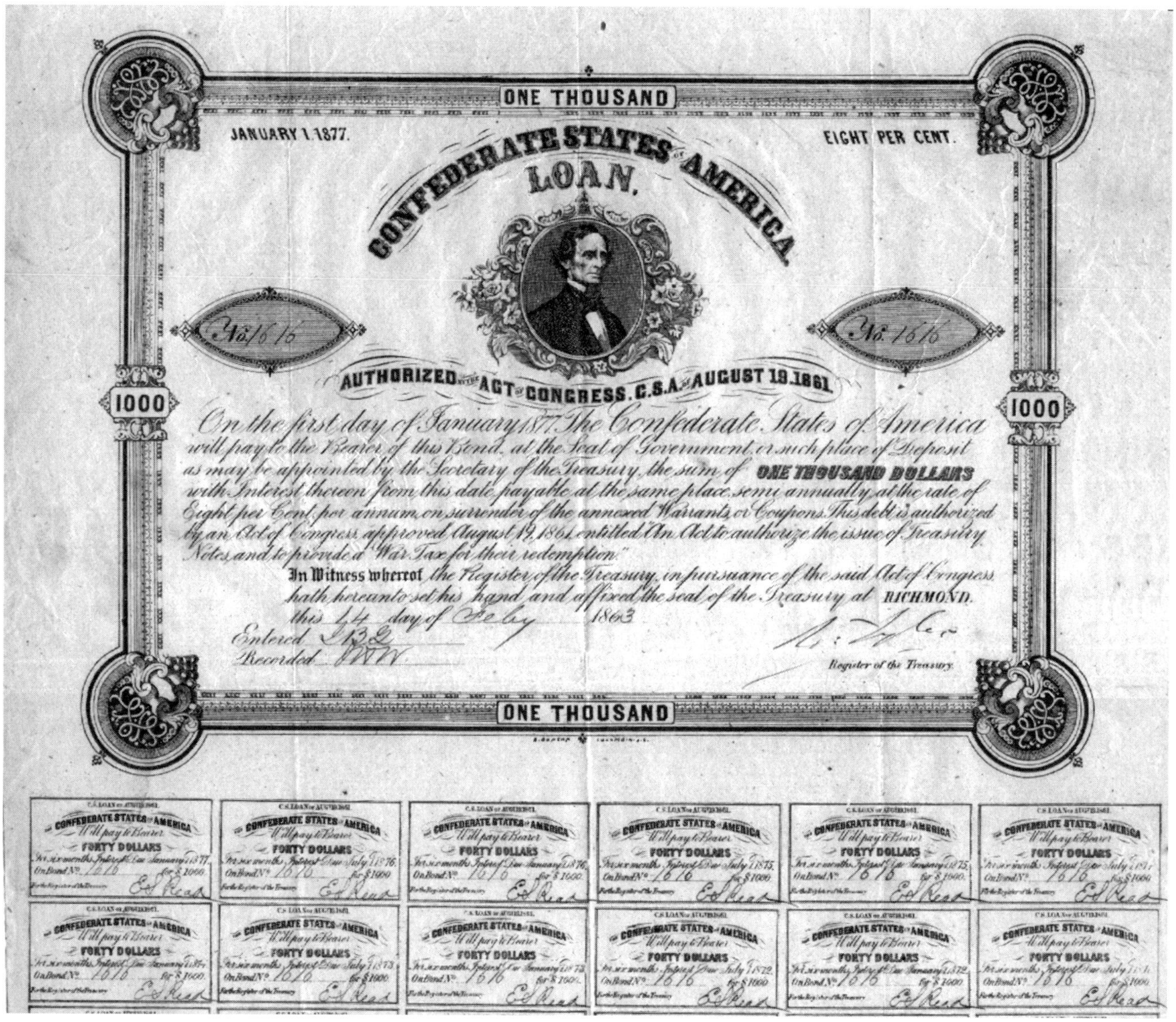

106.	$1,000	Same as preceding, but B. Duncan imprint.			
		Number issued: c. 1,512 (#1001-2512)	Rarity (5-)	$65	$85
		Signed by Tyler.			

U. 8% coupon bonds due July 1, 1877[61]
Printed by B. Duncan, Columbia, S.C.

(George W. Randolph)

(Robert Toombs)

(Burton Harrison)

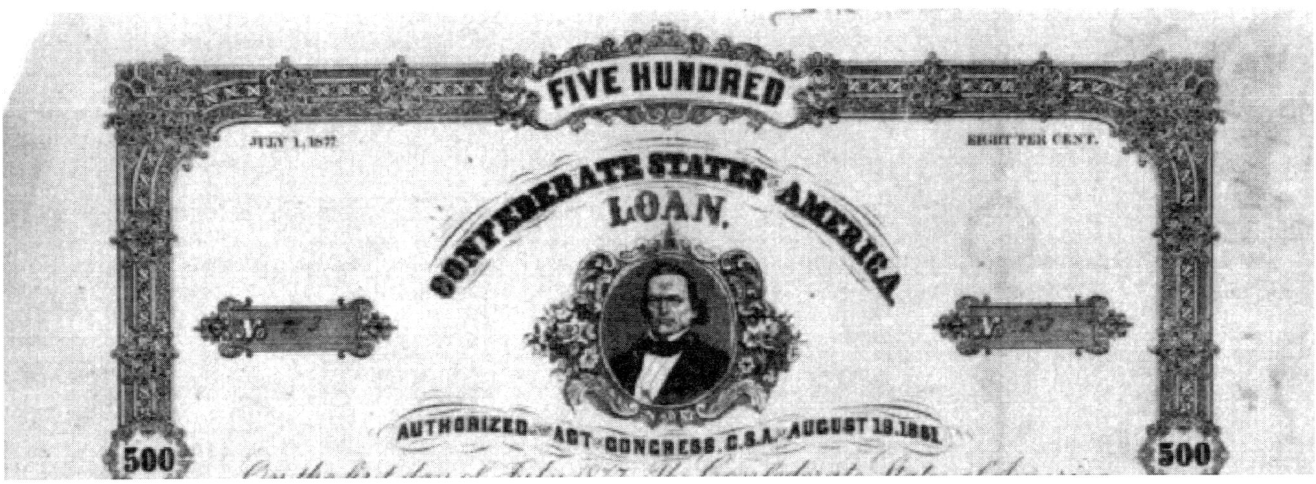

TYPE 88 **$100**

No.	Value	Description	Rarity	fine	very fine
107.	$100	Portrait of Randolph, on white paper.[62] Number issued: 1,513 (#1-1513) Signed by Tyler.	Rarity (5)	$50	$65

TYPE 89 **$500**

No.	Value	Description	Rarity	fine	very fine
108.	$500	Illustrated, on white paper. Number issued: 1,833 (#1-700; 801-1933) Signed by Tyler.	Rarity (5-)	$40	$55
109.	$500	Same but reissed by Edward Cross on the back. Number issued: c. 100 (701-800) Signed by Tyler.	Rarity (7)	$200	$300

TYPE 90 **$1,000**

No.	Value	Description	Rarity	fine	very fine
110.	$1,000	Same, portrait of Burton Harrison, on white paper. Number issued: 2,598 (#1-2598) Signed by Tyler.	Rarity (4+)	$35	$50

V. 8% coupon bonds due January 1, 1878[63]
Printed by B. Duncan, Columbia, S.C.

(J.P. Benjamin)

(A.H. Stephens)

(C.G. Memminger)

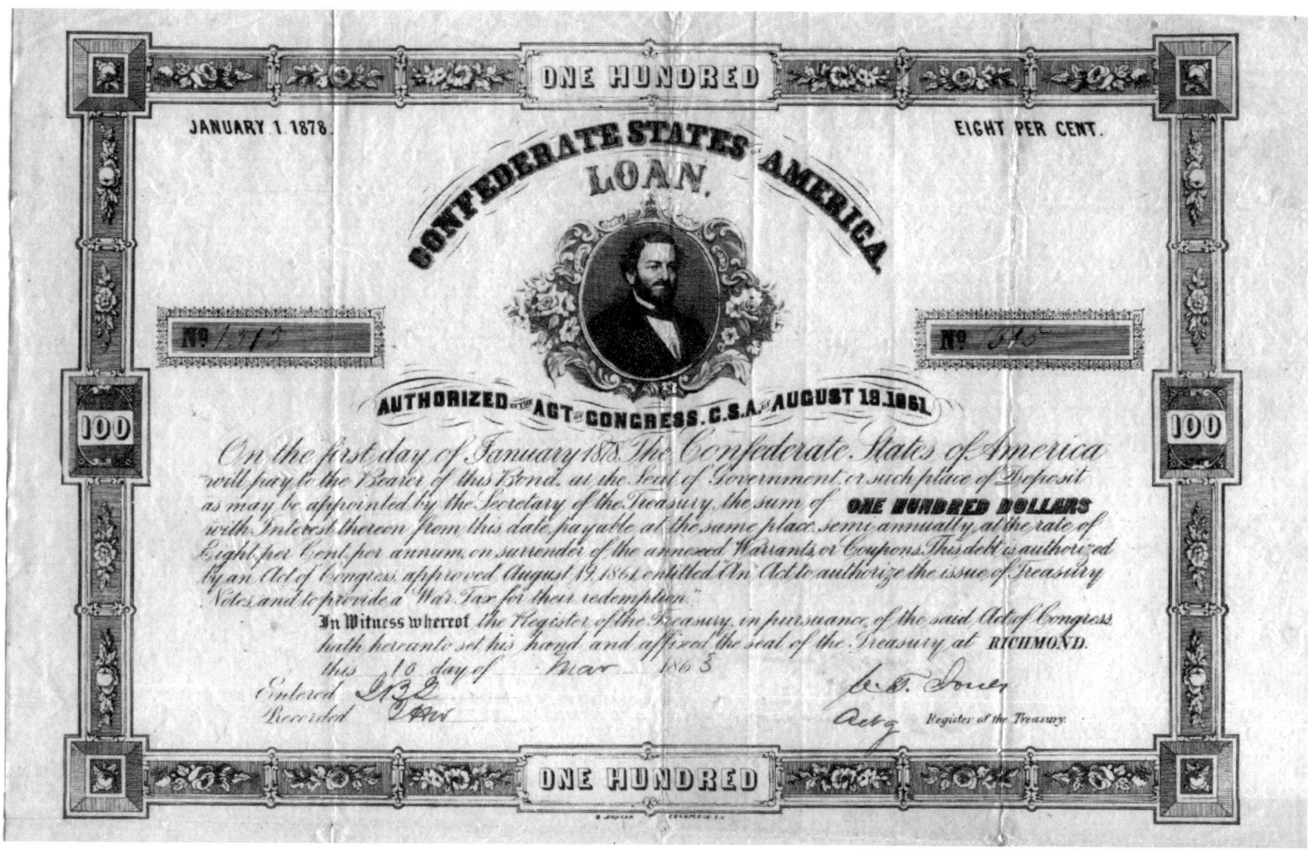

ONE HUNDRED

JANUARY 1 1878.

EIGHT PER CENT.

CONFEDERATE STATES OF AMERICA

LOAN.

No 1515

No 1515

100

100

AUTHORIZED BY THE ACT OF CONGRESS. C.S.A. OF AUGUST 19, 1861.

On the first day of January 1878 The Confederate States of America will pay to the Bearer of this Bond, at the Seat of Government, or such place of Deposit as may be appointed by the Secretary of the Treasury, the sum of ONE HUNDRED DOLLARS with Interest thereon from this date, payable at the same place, semi annually, at the rate of Eight per Cent, per annum, on surrender of the annexed Warrants or Coupons. This debt is authorized by an Act of Congress, approved August 19, 1861, entitled "An Act to authorize the issue of Treasury Notes, and to provide a War Tax for their redemption."

In Witness whereof the Register of the Treasury, in pursuance of the said Act of Congress hath hereunto set his hand and affixed the seal of the Treasury at RICHMOND.

this 10 day of Mar 1863

Entered

Recorded

Actg Register of the Treasury.

ONE HUNDRED

TYPE 91 **$100**

				fine	very fine
111.	$100	Illustrated, no imprint, printed on white paper. Number issued: c. 1200 (#1-1200) Signed by Jones.	Rarity (5)	$35	$65

				fine	very fine
112.	$100	Same as above, but B. Duncan imprint. Number issued: c. 559 (#1201-1759) Signed by Jones.	Rarity (5+)	$50	$75

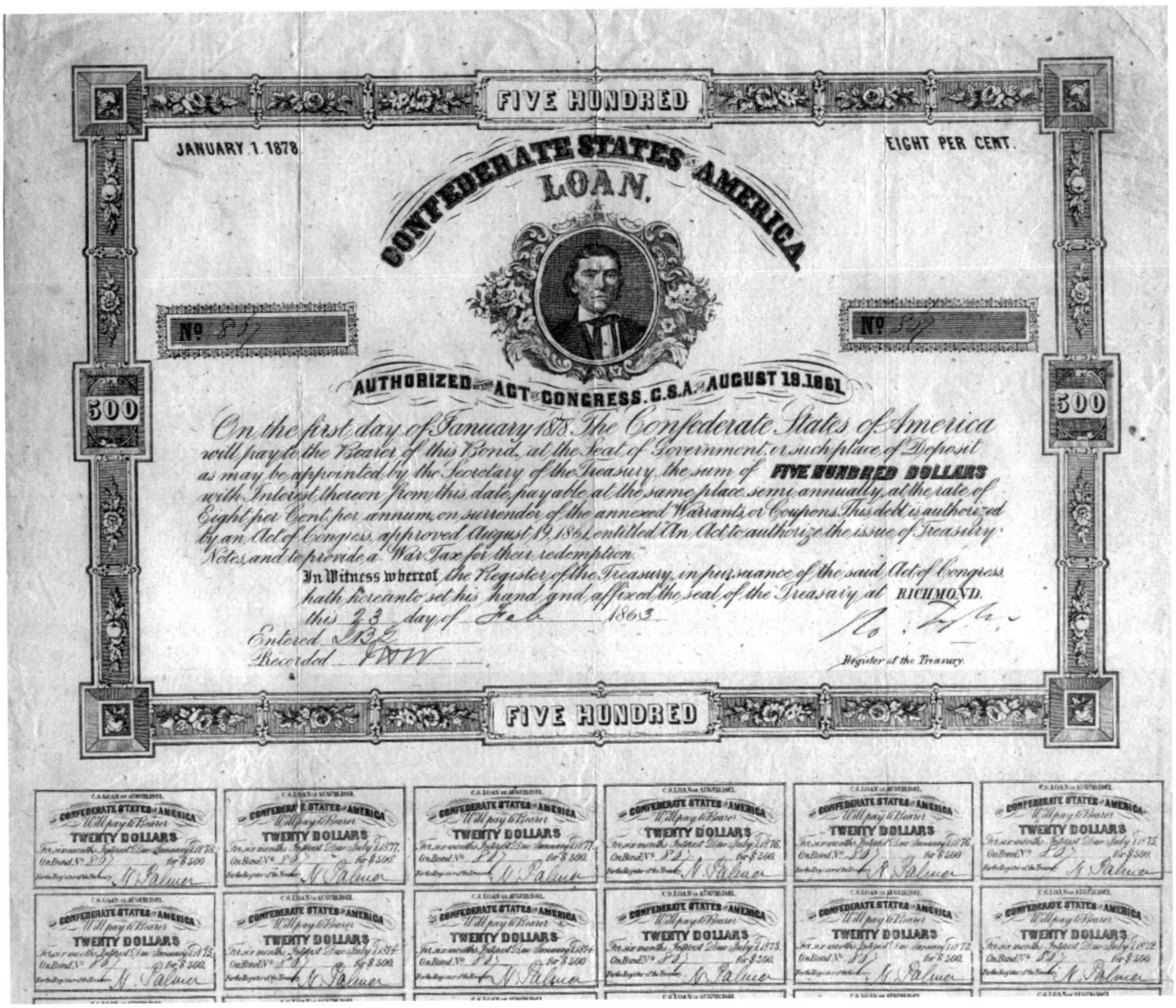
FIVE HUNDRED

JANUARY 1 1878

EIGHT PER CENT.

CONFEDERATE STATES OF AMERICA
LOAN.

№ 87

№ 87

500

500

AUTHORIZED BY ACT OF CONGRESS. C.S.A. AUGUST 19.1861.

On the first day of January 1878 The Confederate States of America will pay to the Bearer of this Bond, at the Seat of Government, or such place of Deposit as may be appointed by the Secretary of the Treasury, the sum of FIVE HUNDRED DOLLARS with Interest thereon from this date, payable at the same place semi-annually, at the rate of Eight per Cent. per annum, on surrender of the annexed Warrants or Coupons. This debt is authorized by an Act of Congress, approved August 19, 1861, entitled "An Act to authorize the issue of Treasury Notes, and to provide a War Tax for their redemption."

In Witness whereof the Register of the Treasury, in pursuance of the said Act of Congress, hath hereunto set his hand and affixed the seal of the Treasury at RICHMOND this 23 day of Feb 1863.

Entered

Recorded

Register of the Treasury.

FIVE HUNDRED

CONFEDERATE STATES OF AMERICA Will pay to Bearer TWENTY DOLLARS

TYPE 92 **$500**

113.	$500	Same, but portrait of A.H. Stephens, no imprint. Number issued: c. 1,671 (#1-1971 less #114 below) Signed by Tyler.	Rarity (5)	$50	$65
114.	$500	Same, blue-black ink on mottled paper. Number issued: c. 300 (c. #301-900) Signed by Tyler.	Rarity (6)	$165	$220

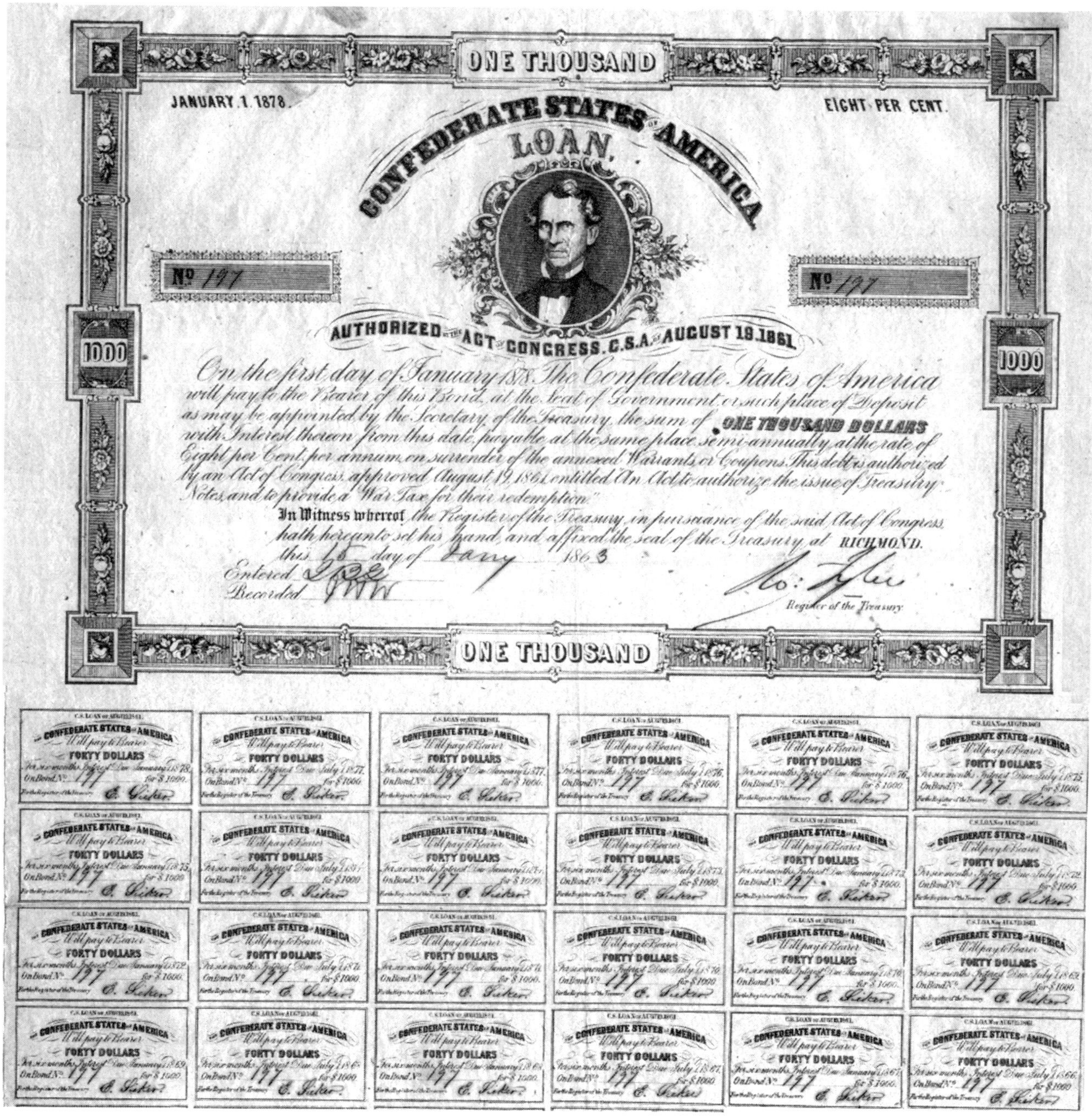
ONE THOUSAND

JANUARY 1 1878. EIGHT PER CENT.

CONFEDERATE STATES OF AMERICA

LOAN,

No 197 No 197

1000 1000

AUTHORIZED BY THE ACT OF CONGRESS, C.S.A. AUGUST 19.1861.

On the first day of January 1878 The Confederate States of America will pay to the Bearer of this Bond, at the Seat of Government or such place of Deposit as may be appointed by the Secretary of the Treasury, the sum of ONE THOUSAND DOLLARS with Interest thereon from this date, payable at the same place semi-annually, at the rate of Eight per Cent. per annum, on surrender of the annexed Warrants or Coupons. This debt is authorized by an Act of Congress, approved August 19, 1861, entitled "An Act to authorize the issue of Treasury Notes, and to provide a War Tax for their redemption."

In Witness whereof the Register of the Treasury, in pursuance of the said Act of Congress, hath hereunto set his hand, and affixed the seal of the Treasury at RICHMOND. this 15 day of Jany 1863

Entered

Recorded

Register of the Treasury

ONE THOUSAND

TYPE 93 **$1,000**

				fine	very fine
115.	$1,000	Same, no engraver's name, Memminger portrait. Number issued: 2,702 (#1-2702) Signed by Tyler.	Rarity (4+)	$40	$50

W. 8% coupon bonds due July 1, 1878[64]
Printed by B. Duncan, Columbia, S.C.

(Thomas Bragg)

(J.P. Benjamin)

(C.G. Memminger)

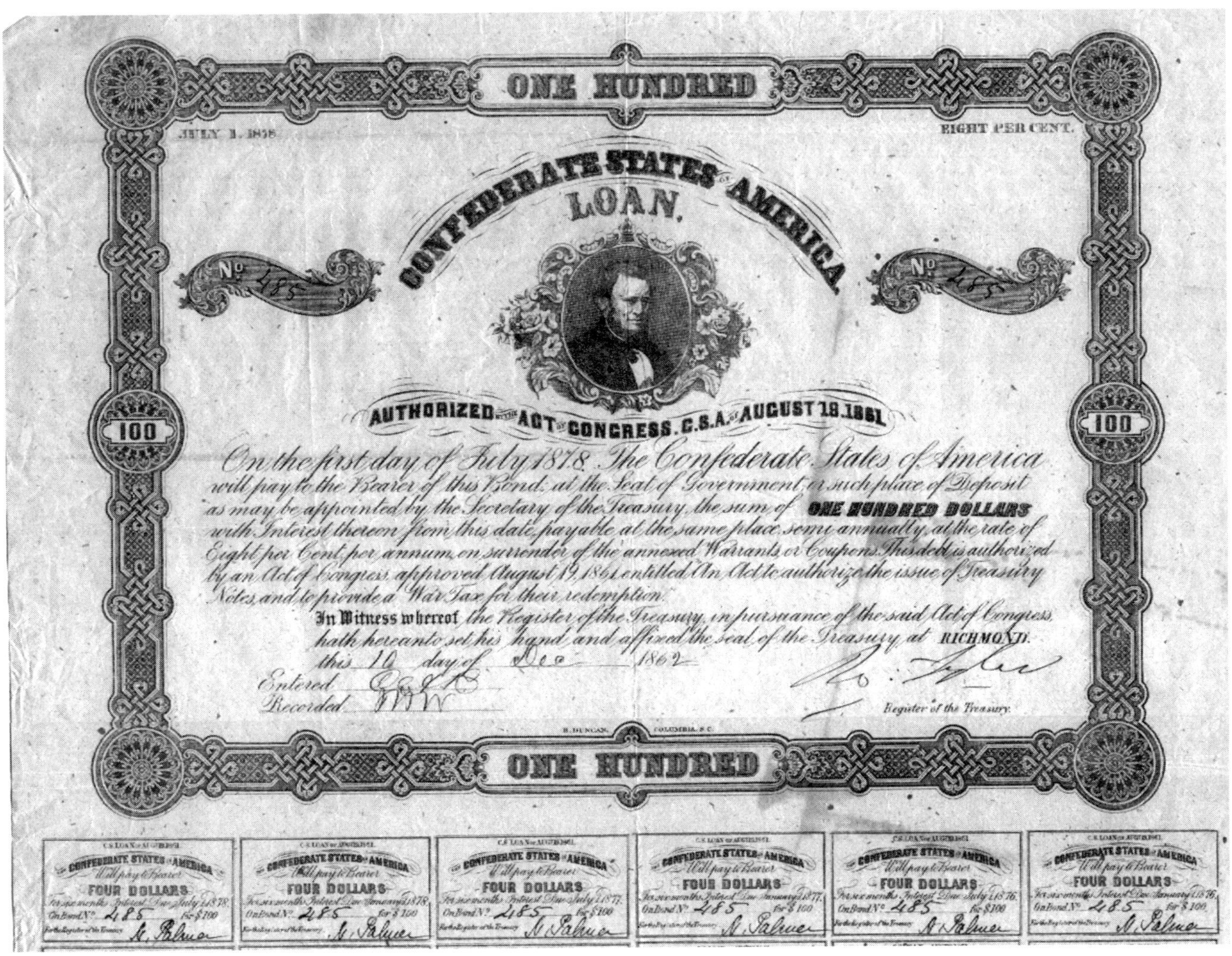

TYPE 94 **$100**

				fine	very fine
116.	$100	Illustrated, printed on white paper.[65] Number issued: 1,615 (#1-1615) Signed by Tyler.	Rarity (5)	$40	$60

TYPE 95 **$500**

117.	$500	Same, but Benjamin portrait. Number issued: 2,115 (#1-2115) Signed by Tyler.	Rarity (5-)	$40	$50

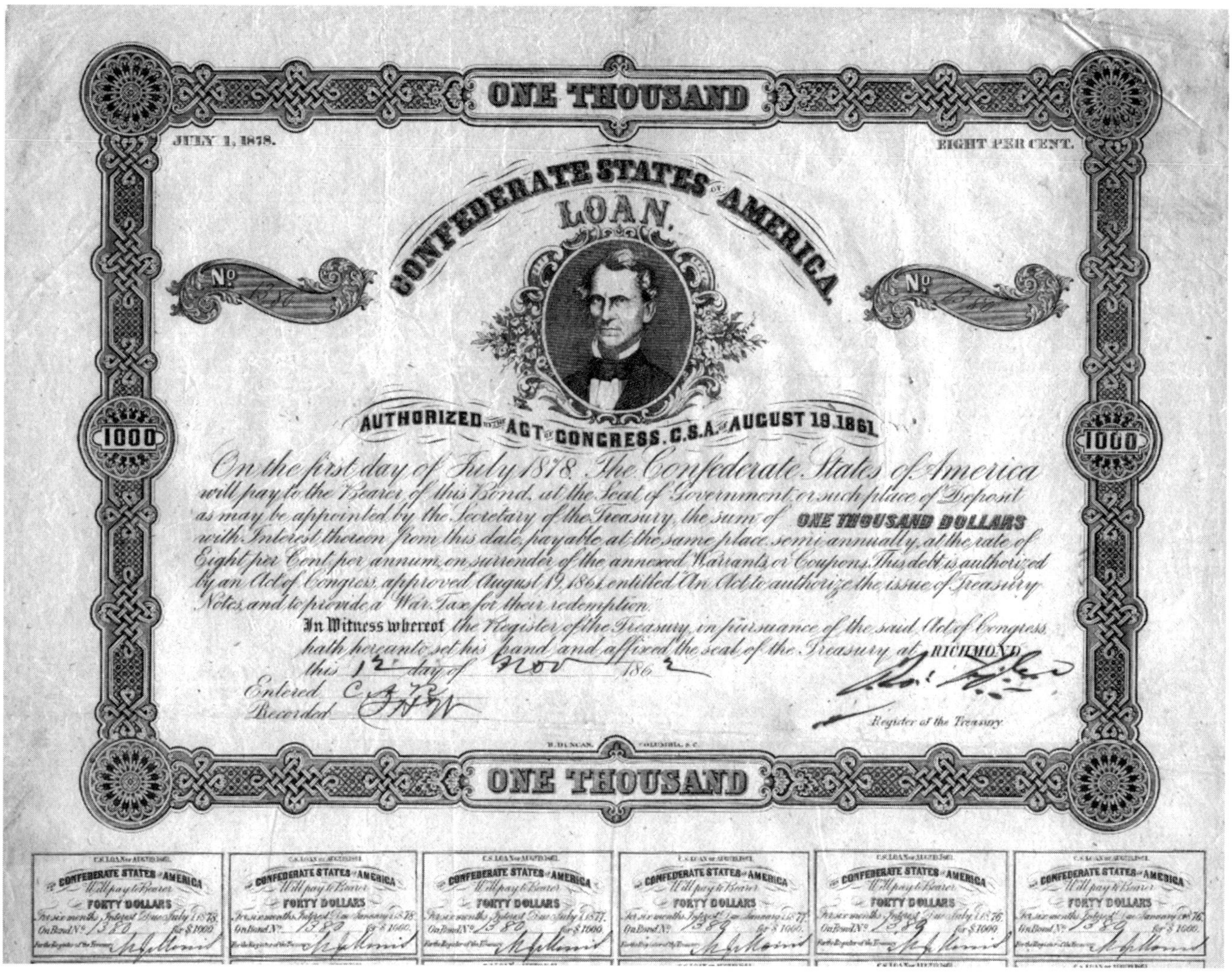
ONE THOUSAND

JULY 1, 1878. EIGHT PER CENT.

CONFEDERATE STATES OF AMERICA LOAN.

AUTHORIZED BY THE ACT OF CONGRESS, C.S.A. AUGUST 19, 1861.

On the first day of July 1878 The Confederate States of America will pay to the Bearer of this Bond, at the Seat of Government or such place of Deposit as may be appointed by the Secretary of the Treasury, the sum of ONE THOUSAND DOLLARS with Interest thereon from this date, payable at the same place semi-annually, at the rate of Eight per Cent per annum, on surrender of the annexed Warrants or Coupons. This debt is authorized by an Act of Congress approved August 19, 1861, entitled An Act to authorize the issue of Treasury Notes, and to provide a War Tax for their redemption.

In Witness whereof the Register of the Treasury, in pursuance of the said Act of Congress, hath hereunto set his hand and affixed the seal of the Treasury at RICHMOND this 12 day of Nov 1862

Entered C.

Recorded

Register of the Treasury

ONE THOUSAND

CONFEDERATE STATES of AMERICA Will pay to Bearer FORTY DOLLARS

TYPE 96 **$1,000**

118.	$1,000	Same, but Memminger portrait. Number issued: 2,800 (#1-2800) Signed by Tyler.	Rarity (4+)	$50	$60

X. 8% coupon bonds due July 1, 1879
Printed by B. Duncan, Columbia, S.C.

(R.M.T. Hunter)

(T.H. Watts)

TYPE 97 **$100**

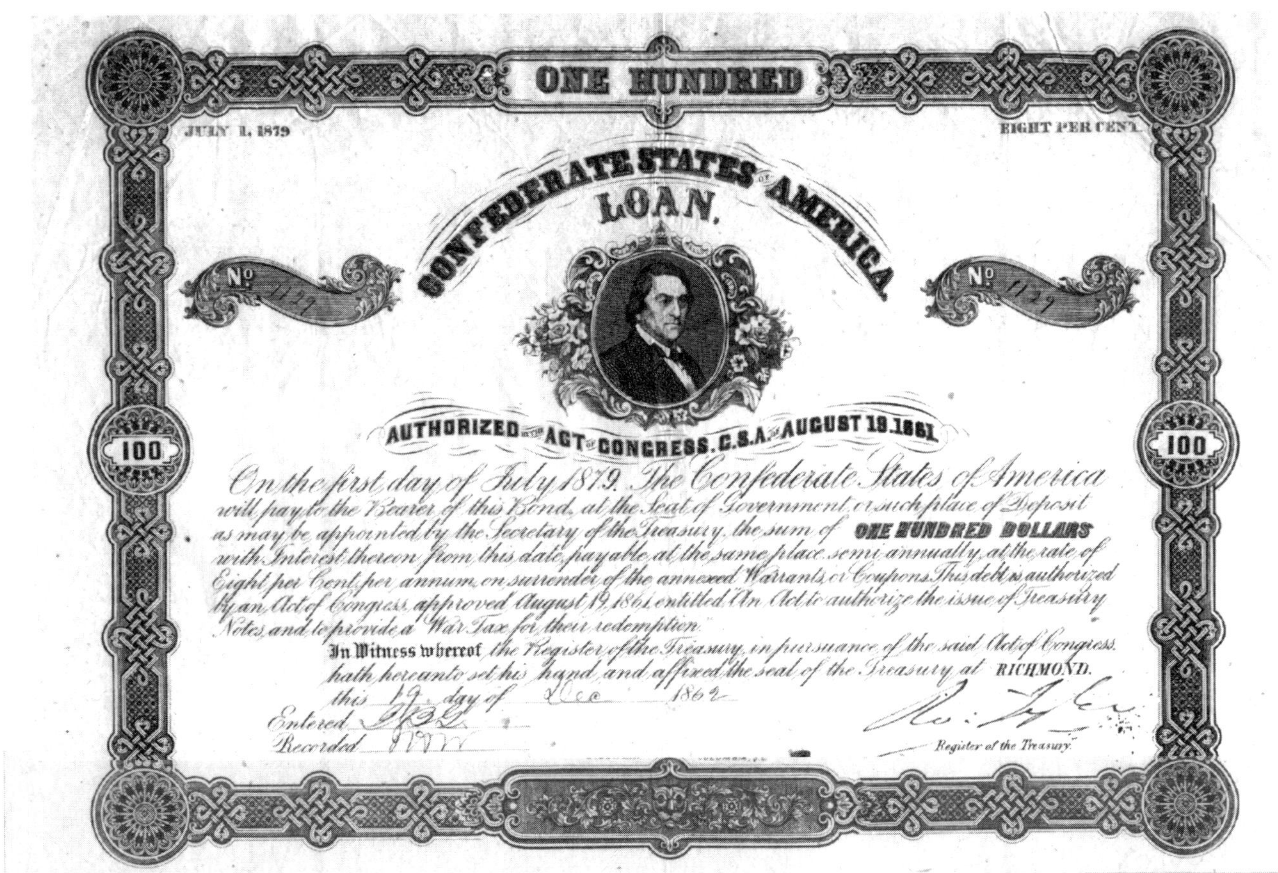

119. $100 Illustrated, printed on white paper.[66]
Number issued: 1,399 (#1-1399)
Signed by Tyler.

	fine	very fine
Rarity (5)	$50	$65

TYPE 98 **$500**

				fine	very fine
120.	$500	Same, but T.H. Watts portrait.[67] Number issued: 2,576 (#1-2576) Signed by Tyler.	Rarity (4+)	$40	$50

(*Industry* with cornucopia, etc., center)[68]

TYPE 99 **$1,000**

Imprint: "Hoyer & Ludwig, Richmond, Va."; lithographed.

121.	$1,000	Illustrated, printed on white paper. Number issued: 2,919 (#1-2919) Signed by Tyler.	Rarity (4)	$45	$65

Y. 8% coupon bonds due January 1, 1880[69]
Imprint: "B. Duncan, Columbia, S.C."

(Thomas Bragg)

(R.M.T. Hunter)

(J.P. Benjamin)

TYPE 100 **$100**

				fine	very fine
122.	$100	Portrait of Bragg, printed on white paper.[70] Number issued: 1,798 (#1-1798) Signed by Tyler.	Rarity (5)	$35	$50

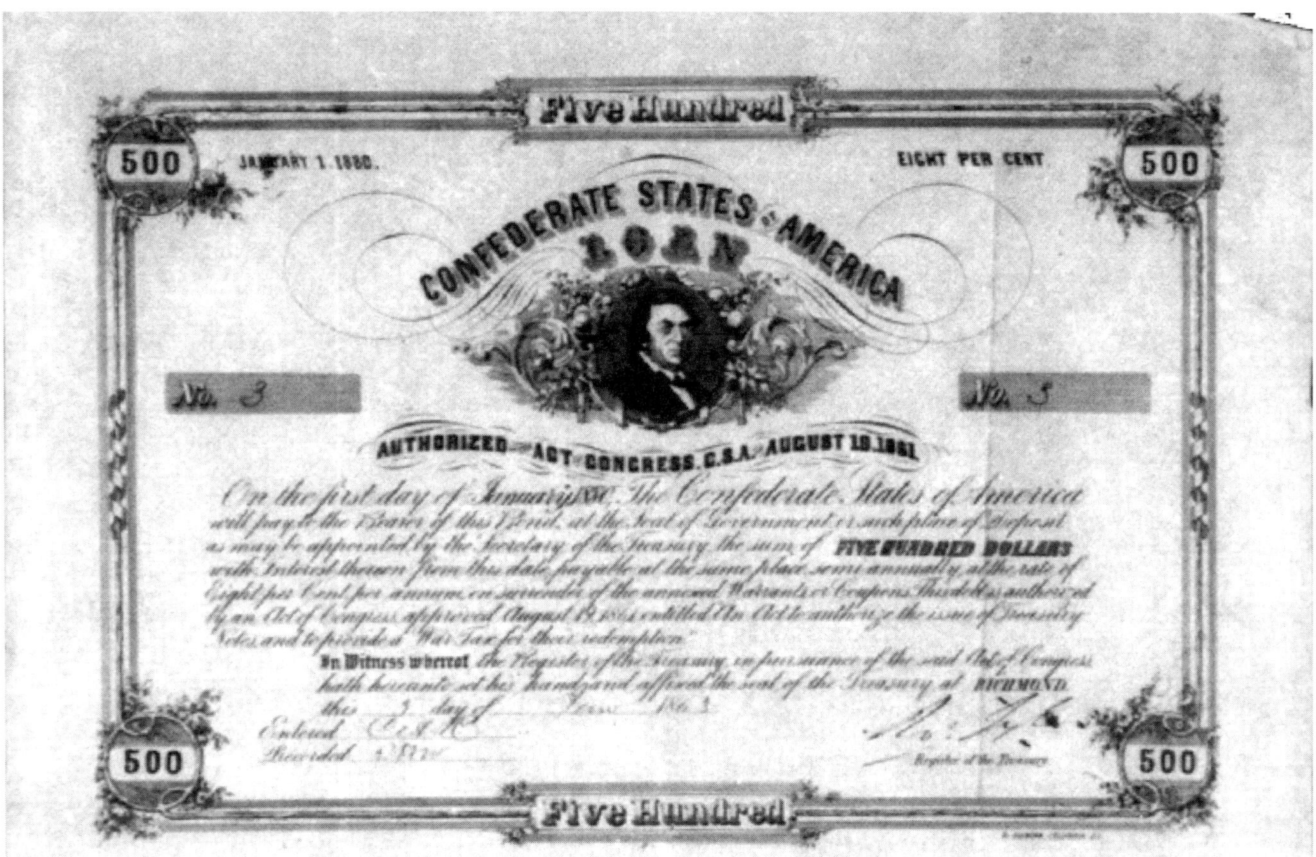

TYPE 101 **$500**

				fine	very fine
123.	$500	Illustrated, but portrait of Hunter.[71]			
		Number issued: 2,485 (#1-2485)	Rarity (5-)	$35	$50
		Signed by Tyler.			

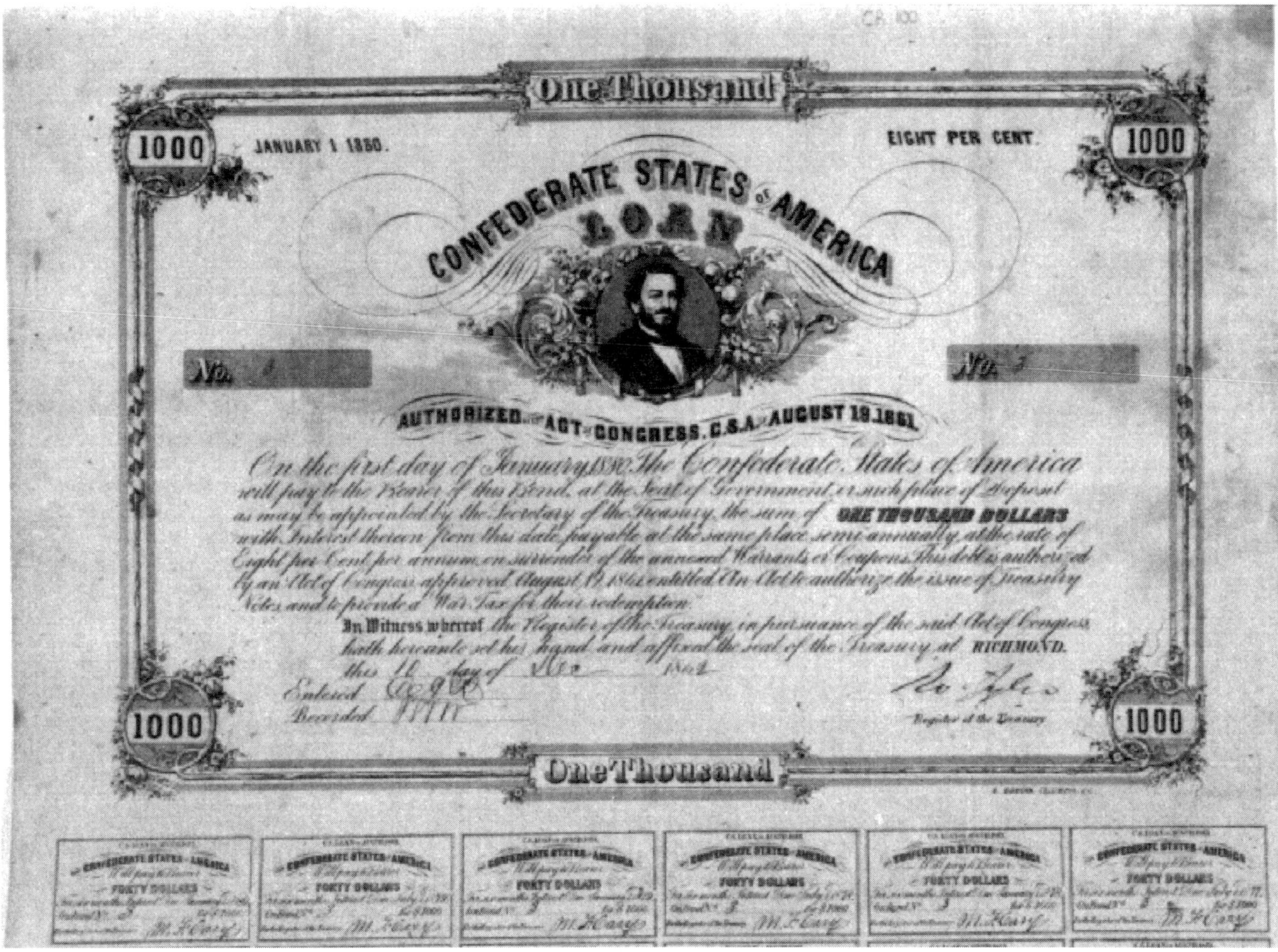

TYPE 102 **$1,000**

124.	$1,000	Illustrated, but portrait of Benjamin.[72]			
		Number issued: 3,099 (#1-3099)	Rarity (4+)	$40	$55
		Signed by Tyler.			

Z. 8% coupon bonds due July 1, 1880[73]
Imprint: "B. Duncan, Richmond, Va."

(R.M.T. Hunter)

(unidentified man)

(J.H. Reagan)

ONE HUNDRED
CONFEDERATE STATES OF AMERICA
LOAN.
No
AUTHORIZED BY THE ACT OF CONGRESS. C.S.A. OF AUGUST 19, 1861.
On the first day of July 1880. The Confederate States of America will pay to the Bearer of this Bond, at the Seat of Government or such place of Deposit as may be appointed by the Secretary of the Treasury, the sum of ONE HUNDRED DOLLARS with Interest thereon from this date, payable at the same place, semi-annually, at the rate of Eight per Cent. per annum, on surrender of the annexed Warrants or Coupons. This debt is authorized by an Act of Congress approved August 19, 1861, entitled "An Act to authorize the issue of Treasury Notes, and to provide a War Tax for their redemption."
In Witness whereof the Register of the Treasury, in pursuance of the said Act of Congress, hath hereunto set his hand, and affixed the seal of the Treasury at RICHMOND, this day of 1862
Entered
Recorded
Register of the Treasury
B. DUNCAN, RICHMOND.
EIGHT PER CENT
JULY 1 1880
100
$100
BONDS
EACH
ONE HUNDRED

TYPE 103 **$100**

				fine	very fine
125.	$100	Illustrated, printed on white paper[74].			
		Number issued: 1,401 (#501-1901)	Rarity (5)	$40	$55
		Date of issue: October 28, 1862			
		Signed by Tyler.			

				fine	very fine
126.	$100	Printed on white paper. Endorsed on the back in red ink and hand dated by James Sorley, CSA depositary at Houston, Texas.			
		Number issued: c. 500 (#1-500)	Rarity (5+)	$100	$135
		Dates of issue: December 1862 - February 1863 Signed by Tyler.			

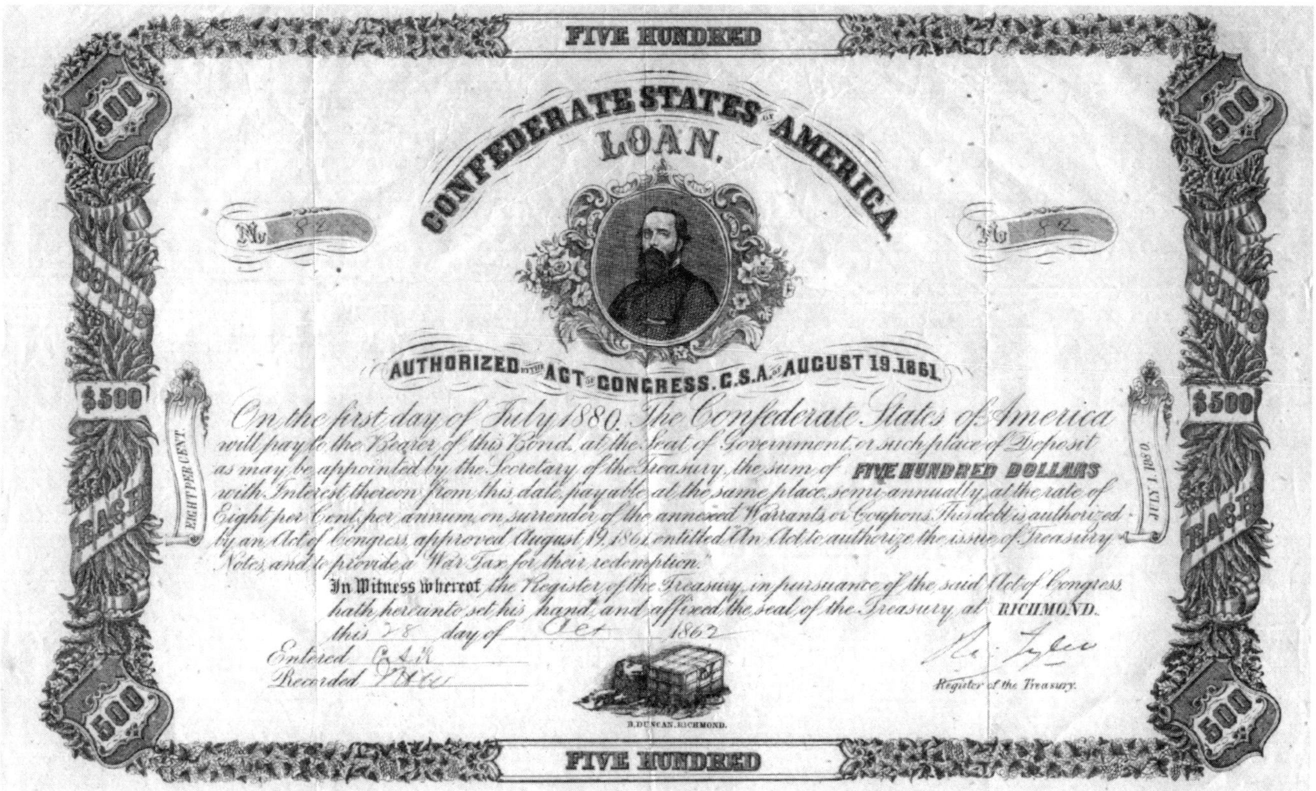

TYPE 104 **$500**

127.	$500	Same, but for portrait of an unidentified man.[75]			
		Number issued: 2,621 (#1-2621)	Rarity (4+)	$35	$45
		Signed by Tyler.			

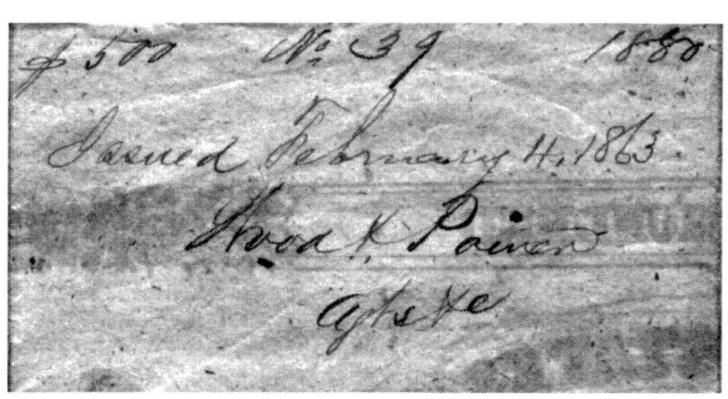

128.	$500	Same, printed on white paper. Endorsed on back by Wood and Power.			
		Number issued: c. 50 (#1-50)	Rarity (7)	$250	$350
		Signed by Tyler. Issued February 24, 1863.			

TYPE 105 **$1,000**

129. $1,000 Illustrated, Reagan portrait.[76] — fine / very fine
Number issued: 3,146 (#151-3296) — Rarity (4+) — $40 — $60
Signed by Tyler.

130. $1,000 Same, endorsed on the back in red ink
and hand dated by James Sorley, CSA depositary at Houston, Texas.
Number issued: c. 100 (#1-100) — Rarity (7-) — $80 — $120
Dates of issue: January - February 1863
Signed by Tyler.

131. $1,000 Same, printed on white paper. Endorsed on the back by Wood and Power.
Number issued: c. 50 (#101-150) — Rarity (7+) — $150 — $250
Date of issue: February 20, 1863
Signed by Tyler.

AA. 8% coupon bonds due July 1, 1881[77]
Imprint: "B. Duncan, Richmond, Va."

(unidentified man)

(Edward C. Elmore)

(J.P. Benjamin)

(C.G. Memminger)

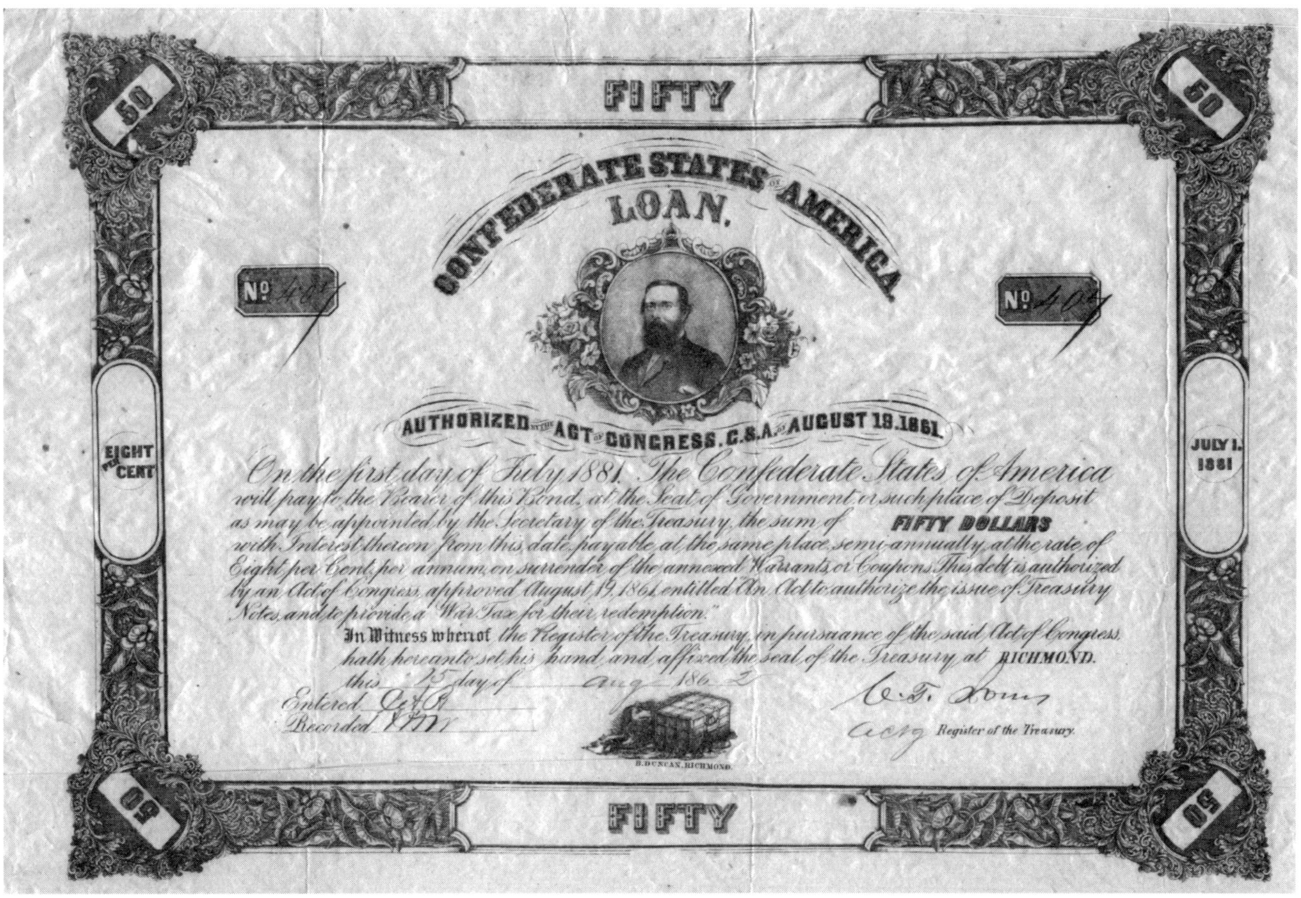

FIFTY

CONFEDERATE STATES OF AMERICA
LOAN.

AUTHORIZED BY THE ACT OF CONGRESS, C.S.A. AUGUST 19, 1861.

EIGHT PER CENT

JULY 1. 1881

On the first day of July 1881 The Confederate States of America will pay to the Bearer of this Bond, at the Seat of Government or such place of Deposit as may be appointed by the Secretary of the Treasury, the sum of FIFTY DOLLARS with Interest thereon from this date payable at the same place, semi-annually, at the rate of Eight per Cent per annum, on surrender of the annexed Warrants or Coupons. This debt is authorized by an Act of Congress, approved August 19, 1861, entitled "An Act to authorize the issue of Treasury Notes, and to provide a War Tax for their redemption."

In Witness whereof the Register of the Treasury in pursuance of the said Act of Congress hath hereunto set his hand and affixed the seal of the Treasury at RICHMOND.

this 15 day of Aug 1862

Entered

Recorded

Register of the Treasury

B. DUNCAN, RICHMOND.

FIFTY

TYPE 106 **$50**

					fine	very fine
132.	$50	Illustrated, printed on white paper.				
		Number issued: 2,059 (#1-2059)		Rarity (5-)	$50	$70
		Signed by Tyler, Jones (scattered, 400 range).				

TYPE 107 **$100**

				fine	very fine
133.	$100	Same, but E.C. Elmore portrait.			
		Number issued: 2,000 (#1-2000)	Rarity (5-)	$40	$55
		Signed by Tyler (c. #1-300; 1201-2000) and Jones (c. #301-1200).			

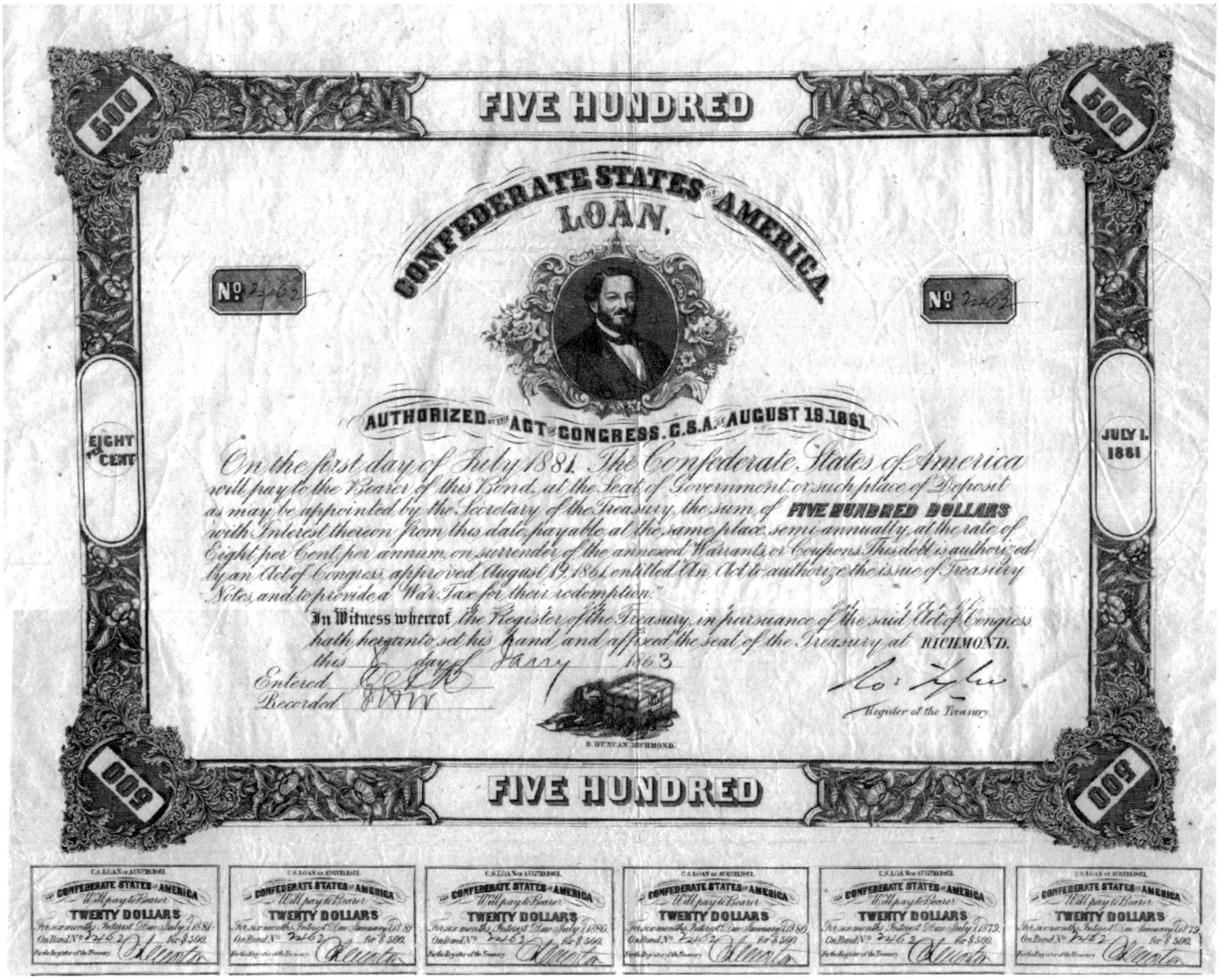

TYPE 108 **$500**

				fine	very fine
134.	$500	Illustrated, Benjamin portrait.			
		Number issued: 2,621 (#1-2621)	Rarity (4+)	$35	$55
		Signed by Tyler (c. #1-800; 1401-2621) and Jones (c. #801-1400).			

TYPE 109 **$1,000**

				fine	very fine
135.	$1,000	Same, but for Memminger portrait. Number issued: 3,457 (#1-3457) Signed by Tyler (c. #1-1000; 2001-3457) and Jones (c. #1001-2000).	Rarity (4+)	$35	$45

TYPE 110 written denominations

136.		All handwritten forms, usually on ruled, white woven paper. Number issued: Unknown, possibly c. 50. Dates of issue: October 1861 - April 1862, mostly January - February 1862. Signed by Tyler.	Rarity (7+)	$6,500

AB. Stock certificates (registered bonds)
Total amount issued: $35,389,450 (net - $25,147,850)

Because the Confederate records in this area are incomplete (some of the books being lost), it has not proved possible to do more than estimate the quantities of each of the four varieties of stock certificates used. From the records, it would appear that due dates were assigned and the numbering begun with a numeral one until the end of the sequence. While 13,360 (not 13,287 as reported in Thian) different certificates worth $35,389,450 were emitted, total transfers (*i.e.,* cancellation of old certificates and the substitution of new ones) amounted to $10,241,600 for a net issue of $25,147,850. The amounts of certificates given therefore are for the totals used, not the net amounts outstanding. In addition, the quantities of each type issued and the number of bonds thought to have been made due on any particular date are at best close approximations of the actual figures; no doubt new information requiring changes in some numbers will be forthcoming after collectors have had an opportunity to review the ranges shown and to examine their own bonds.

Issue of these certificates did not start until October 22, 1861 and continued (at least so far as the transfers were concerned) until March 23, 1865. The lowest known denomination was $50; the highest denomination was $550,000 (#1012), due January 1, 1876. The twenty-four highest denominations (to $50,000) amount to $4,868,200; the average value is $2,664 per certificate.

TYPE 111 various denominations
Imprint: "Hoyer & Ludwig, Richmond, Va."; lithographed.

(sailing ship, center)

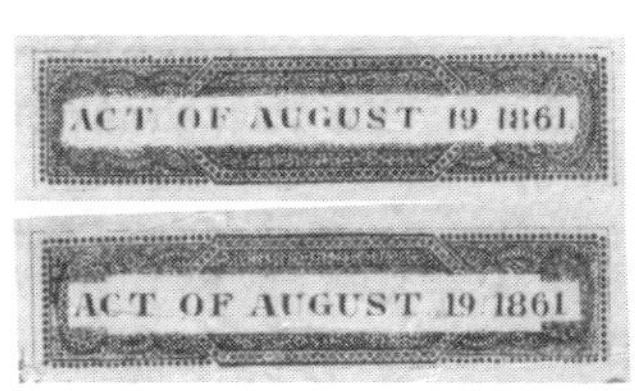

variety 1 top, variety 2 bottom

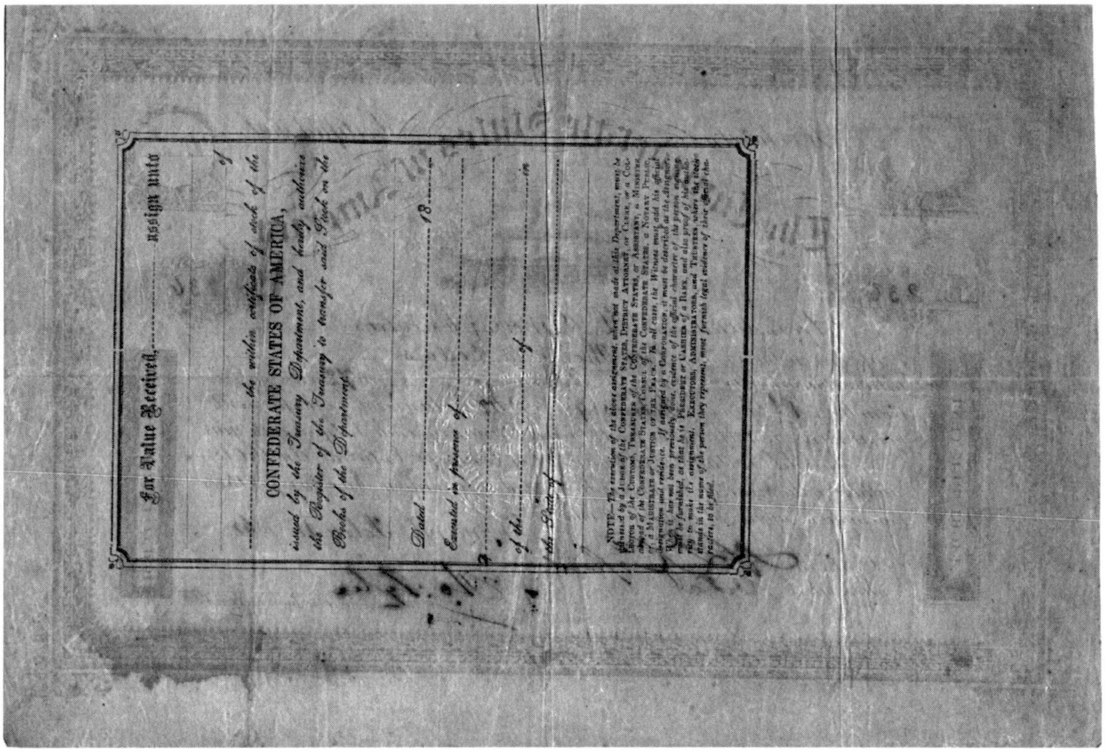

137.	Printed on white paper, varieties 1 and 2.		fine	very fine
	Number issued: c. 3,070 (various numbers as below)	Rarity (5)	$125	$200
	Dates of issue: c. October 22, 1861 - September 9, 1862			
	Signed by Tyler.			

Due date	Approximate number issued	Serial #s	Rarity
January 1, 1864	375	1-375	7-
July 1, 1864[78]	2	1-2	—
January 1, 1865	139	1-139	7
July 1, 1865	17	1-17	8
January 1, 1866	175	1-175	6+
January 1, 1867	90	1-90	8
January 1, 1868	54	1-54	8
January 1, 1869	64	1-64	8
January 1, 1870	58	1-58	8
January 1, 1872	1,063	1-1063	6-
January 1, 1874	190	1-190	7
January 1, 1876	20	1-20	—
January 1, 1878	88	1-88	8
January 1, 1879	55	1-55	7-
January 1, 1881	680	1-680	6-
	3,070		

Items without rarity numbers are not known to exist and may therefore not be collectable.

TYPE 112 various denominations
Imprint: "J.T. Paterson, Columbia, S.C."; lithographed.

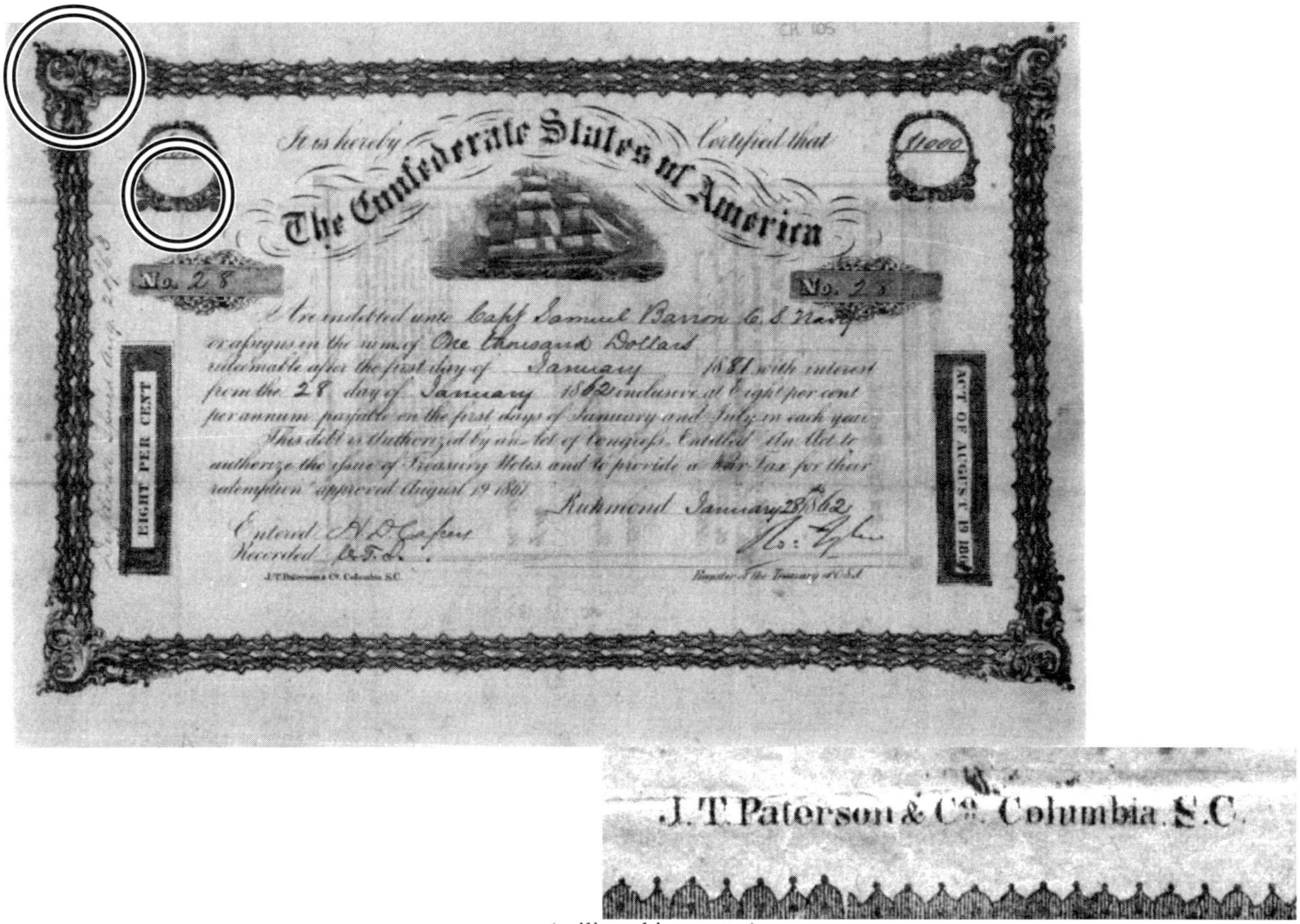

(sailing ship, center)

138. Printed on white paper.
Number issued: c. 3,343 (various numbers as below) — Rarity (4+) — fine $135 — very fine $210
Dates of issue: September 10 - December 10, 1862
Signed by Tyler, Jones.

Due date	Approximate number issued	Serial #s	Rarity
January 1, 1864	322	376-697	8
January 1, 1865	149	140-288	8
January 1, 1866	350	176-525	6+
January 1, 1869	62	65-126	8
January 1, 1870	98	59-156	8
January 1, 1872	454	1064-1517	7
January 1, 1874	104	191-294	8
January 1, 1876	274	21-337	7
January 1, 1879	382	56-437	7
January 1, 1881	1105	681-1785	7
	3,343		

TYPE 113 various denominations
Imprint: "J.T. Paterson & Co., Columbia, S.C."

(sailing ship, center)

139. Printed on white paper.
Number issued: c. 5,029 (various numbers as below)
Dates of issue: c. December 11, 1862 - August 1, 1863
Signed by Tyler, Jones.

	fine	very fine
Rarity (4+)	$125	$175

Due date	Approximate number issued	Serial #s	Rarity
January 1, 1864	93	698-790	8
January 1, 1865	4	289-292	—
January 1, 1866	387	526-912	6
January 1, 1867	6	91-96	—
January 1, 1868	3	55-57	—
January 1, 1869	593	127-719	6-
January 1, 1870	631	157-787	6-
July 1, 1870	1	1	—
January 1, 1872	152	1518-1669	7-
July 1, 1873[79]	7	1-7	—
January 1, 1874	925	295-1219	6
January 1, 1876	796	338-1133	6
January 1, 1879	1,060	438-1497	6-
January 1, 1881	369	1786-2154	7-
July 1, 1881[80]	2	1-2	8
	5,029		

Items without rarity numbers are not known to exist and may therefore not be collectable.

TYPE 114 various denominations
Imprint: "J.T. Paterson & Co., Columbia, S.C."

140. Printed on white paper.†
Number issued: c. 1,918 (various numbers as below) Rarity (5+)
Dates of issue: c. August 1, 1863 - March 23, 1865
Signed by Tyler, Jones.

fine	very fine
$200	$250

Due date	Approximate number issued	Serial #s	Rarity
January 1, 1864	31	791-821	—
January 1, 1865	15	293-307	—
January 1, 1866	137	913-1049	7
January 1, 1867	17	97-113	—
January 1, 1868	14	58-71	—
January 1, 1869	212	720-931	7
January 1, 1870	187	788-974	7-
January 1, 1872	259	1670-1928	7-
July 1, 1873	2	8-9	—
January 1, 1874	263	1220-1482	7
January 1, 1876	251	1134-1384	8
January 1, 1879	258	1498-1755	7
January 1, 1881	272	2155-2426	7
	1,918		

Items without rarity numbers are not known to exist and may therefore not be collectable.

† A "1" is missing on the later certificates in the act date at right, so that it reads "186_."

IV. LOAN OF OCTOBER 12 - NOVEMBER 5, 1861

Fall 1861 bank note loan

The slowness of Hoyer & Ludwig in filling the orders for currency and the fact that the treasury was falling ever further behind in meeting its obligations necessitated a stopgap bridge financing loan from the banks. This was also rendered necessary because the notes being printed were largely $100 and $50 notes that were not readily usable in day-to-day transactions. Thus the need for funds and notes in $5 to $20 denominations resulted in a loan of almost $10.5 million in bank notes to the Confederacy. Naturally, the banks wanted certificates to cover these loans, and another batch of manuscript bonds was prepared and distributed in anticipation of the secretary getting authority from the Congress for this unauthorized loan. In trying to make these look more official, the treasury retained the services of a Jewish Richmond scribe, Wilhelm Flagenheimer, who hand drew a number of large denomination bonds that were distributed among the lending banks. Later, this 5% loan was taken up with the call certificates authorized by the Act of December 24, 1861.

5% banknote loan certificates

Amount approved: $10,280,000[81]

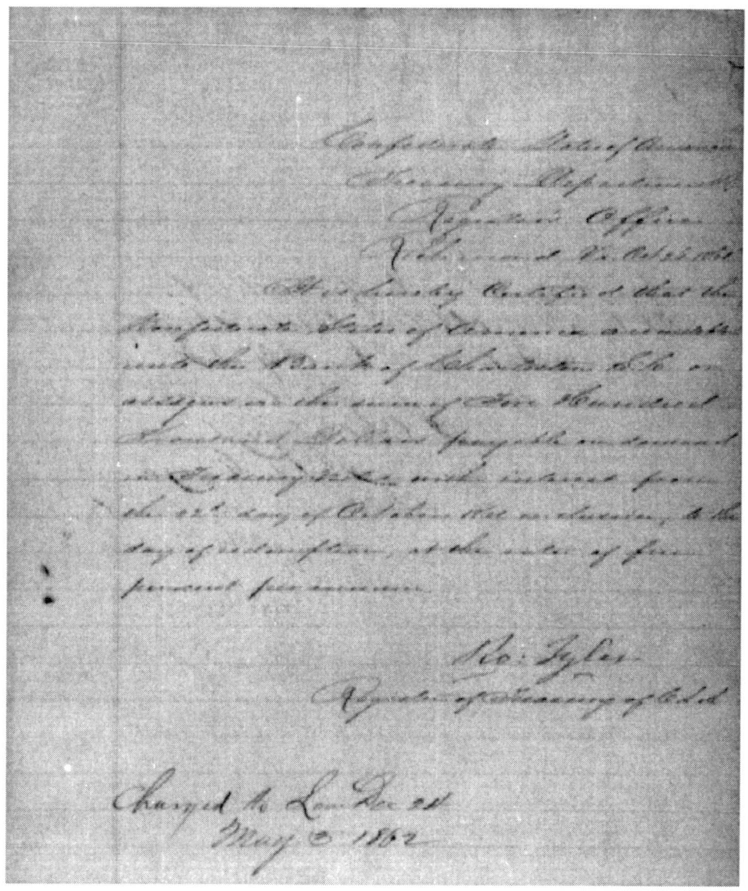

TYPE 115 various written denominations

			fine	very fine
141.	All handwritten, high-denomination bonds. Number issued: c. 80 Dates of issue: c. October 22 - November 3, 1861 Signed by Tyler.	Rarity (7)	$6,500	

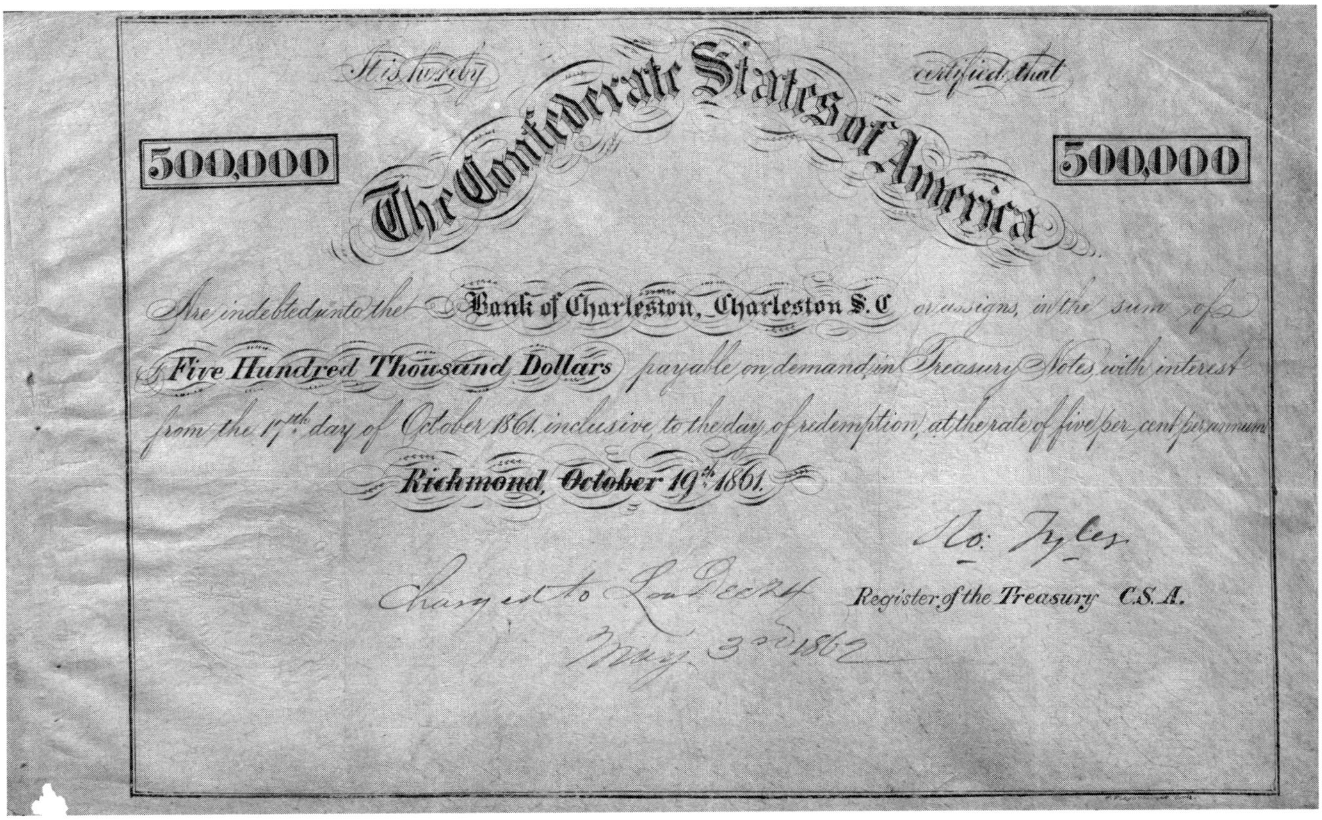
500,000 500,000

It is hereby certified that The Confederate States of America

Are indebted unto the Bank of Charleston, Charleston S.C or assigns, in the sum of Five Hundred Thousand Dollars payable on demand in Treasury Notes with interest from the 17th day of October 1861 inclusive to the day of redemption at the rate of five per cent per annum

Richmond, October 19th 1861.

Ro: Tyler
Register of the Treasury C.S.A.

May 3rd 1862

TYPE 116 hand-drawn
Imprint: "W. Flegenheimer, Scrib."

			fine	very fine
142.	Hand-drawn certificates on sheepskin. Number issued: unknown; five known to exist. Date of issue: October 17, 1861 Signed by Tyler.	Rarity (7+)	$7,500	

V. ACT OF DECEMBER 24, 1861

By the end of 1861 the amount of treasury notes accumulating in the banks was reaching new heights, while the treasury was in desperate need of cash. It was evident that most people were not willing to put their notes into long term investments, and even the May 16, 1861 notes, which were call certificates in effect, were not attracting a large group of investors. In any case, those having August 19, 1861 act notes (dated September 2, 1861) could not buy those securities. Thus Secretary Memminger requested that Congress authorize an issue of 6% call certificates for those notes. Later, by the Act of April 12(18), 1862 the amount authorized was raised to $80 million and of this over $70 million worth were outstanding when the authority to issue ceased in 1863. With the redemptions, the total issue nearly reached $82 million.

Here, as always, Hoyer & Ludwig started by printing certificates. Paterson then took over the work and the plates, and made a new bond that superficially resembles Ludwig's work, but the spacing of the border elements is markedly different. Toward the end of the run, in early 1863, the old plate gave out and a new plate was prepared. This plate has no imprint, but treasury records, confirmed by an examination of the workmanship, disclose a new design done by Paterson, the border being a perfect copy of Ball 19 (Cr. 10). Toward the end of the issue certificates were possibly illegally issued for purchases made with "December 2, 1862" notes. These are rarity 7+.

6% call certificates
Amount authorized: $30 million, later made unlimited by the Act of April 12(18), 1862.
Total amount issued (all types): $70,729,030[82]

$1000

It is hereby Certified that The Confederate States of America

No 2774

Are indebted unto and will pay to

or his order the sum of One Thousand Dollars

payable January 1 1872 with interest from the date of the first Indorsement of this Certificate at the rate of six per cent per annum payable on the first days of January and July in each year. This debt is authorized by an Act of Congress approved December 24 1861 and upon application of the holder or Indorsee of this Certificate redeemable in Treasury Notes issued under the provisions of said Act. The faith of the Confederate States is pledged to provide and establish sufficient revenues for the regular payment of the interest and for the redemption of the principal.

Richmond

Entered

Recorded

Register of the Treasury

Six per Cent

Act of Decr 24th 1861

TYPE 117 various denominations

			fine	very fine
143.	Printed by Hoyer & Ludwig on plain white paper, border variety 1.			
	Number issued: c. 3,800 (#1-3800)	Rarity (5+)	$150	$200
	Dates of issue: c. January 1862 - August 4, 1862			
	Signed by Tyler, Jones.			

TYPE 118 various denominations

144.	Similar to the preceding, but with the imprint of "J.T. Paterson & Co., Columbia, S.C."; border variety 2.			
	Number issued: c. 1,950 (#3801-7699, odd numbers only)	Rarity (6-)	$200	$250
	Dates of issue: c. August 4, 1862 - December 1, 1862			
	Signed mostly by Tyler, a few by Jones.			

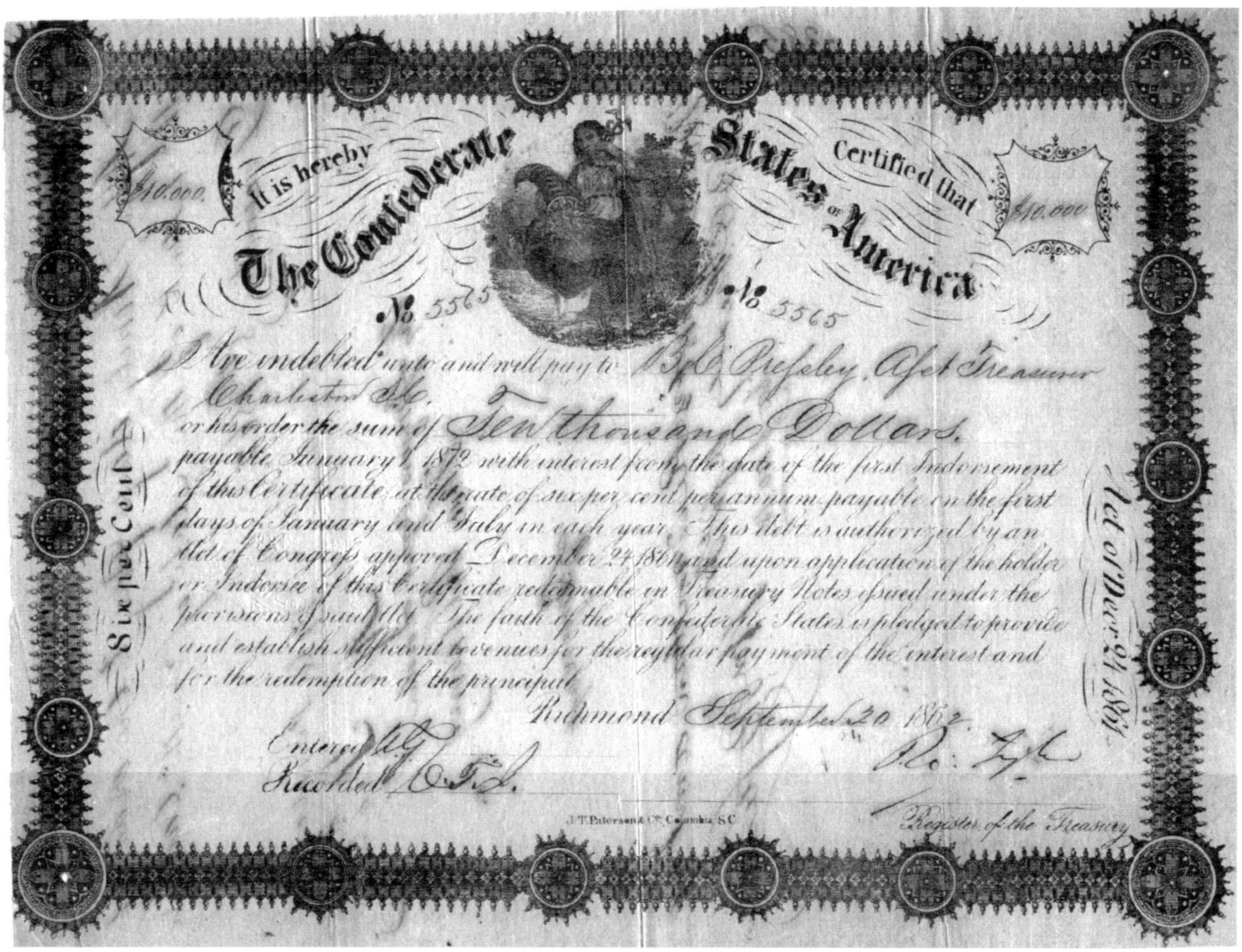

(*Commerce,* with cornucopia, center)
TYPE 119 various written denominations
Imprint: none, but by J.T. Paterson & Co.

			fine	very fine
145.	Similar to the preceding, including the Paterson imprint, except bottom border has differently spaced elements; border variety 3.			
	Number issued: 1,950 (#3802-7700, even numbers only)	Rarity (6-)	$180	$240
	Dates of issue: December 2, 1862 - March 23, 1863			
	Signed mostly by Tyler, a few by Jones.			

It is hereby Certified that The Confederate States of America
№ 7786 № 7786
Are indebted unto and will pay to
Charleston S.C.
or his order the sum of One Thousand Dollars
payable January 1st 1872 with interest from the date of the first Indorsement of this Certificate at the rate of six per cent per annum payable on the first days of January and July in each year. This debt is authorized by an Act of Congress approved December 24 1861 and upon application of the holder or Indorsee of this Certificate redeemable in Treasury Notes issued under the provisions of said Act. The faith of the Confederate States is pledged to provide and establish sufficient revenues for the regular payment of the interest and for the redemption of the principal.
Richmond January 1st 1863
Entered
Recorded
Register of the Treasury
Six per Cent
Act of Decr 24 1861
$1,000

(Commerce with cornucopia at center)

TYPE 119 (R)
H3 Various written denominations
Imprint: None, but by J. T. Paterson & Co.

146.	Printed on plain white paper.			
	Number issued: c. 900 (#7701-8600, plus remainders†)	Rarity (6)	$200	$250
	Dates of issue: c. December 2, 1862 - March 23, 1863			
	Signed mostly by Tyler, a few by Jones.			

†The unissued remainder certificates are rarity 6- and are worth only $200. The issued bonds are mostly in the National Archives. Denominations range from $500 to $25,000. Denominations under $100 are rare.

			fine	very fine
146.a	Similar to the preceding, but made payable in notes dated "December 2, 1862."†			
	Number issued: c. 10 (scattered)	Rarity (7+)	$200	$500
	Dates of issue: c. December 2, 1862 - March 23, 1863			
	Signed mostly by Tyler, a few by Jones.			

†After the notes dated "December 2, 1862" began to be issued, note holders began to find them at 6%. The act authorizing such notes did not state the interest to be carried by such call certificates and depositaries and assistant treasurers gave Act of December 24, 1861 certificates in exchange for such notes. This dubiously legal practice ceased when the Act of March 23, 1863, limited the rate to 4%.

President Lincoln visits Union troops.

VI. ACT OF APRIL 12, 1862

The end of the Provisional Government and the arrival of the first Confederate Congress led to extensive reports and a need for new legislation to meet the escalating costs of conducting the war. At Secretary Memminger's behest, Congress authorized an issue of $165 million of bonds. Recognizing the lack of enthusiasm for funding notes into bonds, Memminger suggested and the Congress allowed the substitution of 7.30% treasury notes for the 10-30 year 8% bonds. Since the notes could be used as cash, it is not surprising that the sale of the bonds came to a paltry $3.2 million. For some reason, unknown, only the $500 and $100 denominations were used for the coupon bonds and only 132 registered bonds were prepared.

No evidence has yet surfaced telling why the printing order was split. George Dunn handled the $100 coupon bonds and the registered bonds. These reflected his Richmond background, the first with a view of Richmond from the west (later used on the Ball 201 (Cr. 125) bonds) and the latter with a view of the Confederate defenses at Drury's Bluff, south of Richmond. Since the fortifications were not completed until early 1863, we can date the design of this bond without the added information that the first bond was issued February 2, 1863.

The $500 bond, much the commonest of the bonds of this act, was produced at Columbia by Blanton Duncan. Its central theme was the Battle of Shiloh, which had taken place on April 6-7, 1862. Since this engagement is now generally considered to have been a Union victory, it may well be wondered why a Confederate bond should commemorate such an event. However, at the time, and particularly in view of the South's successes on April 6, 1862, many in the South thought of this battle as a victory. Evidently, it was hoped to sell many more of these bonds than in fact occurred, and there are a fair number of remainders into the 7000 number range.

Congress did not make any specific provision for call certificates under this act as it had just increased the authorization for the December 24, 1861 6% call certificates.

Richmond in ruins.

A. 8% coupon bonds
Amount authorized: $165 million
Total amount issued: $3,189,550

(C.G. Memminger, center, with view of Richmond, Virginia from the west)
TYPE 120 **$100**
Imprint: "Engraved by Geo. Dunn & Compy. Richmond, Va."
Printed by Hoyer & Ludwig

				fine	very fine
147.	$100	Printed on plain white paper. Number issued: 380 (#1-380)[83] Dates of issue: September 5, 1862 - January 12, 1865 Signed by Rose.[84]	Rarity (6-)	$450	$800

TYPE 121 **$500**

Imprint: "B. Duncan, Columbia, S.C."

148. $500 Printed on white paper.

Number issued: 5,541 (#1-5541)[85] Rarity (4-) $100 $150

Dates of issue: June 12, 1862 - January 12, 1865

Signed by Rose.

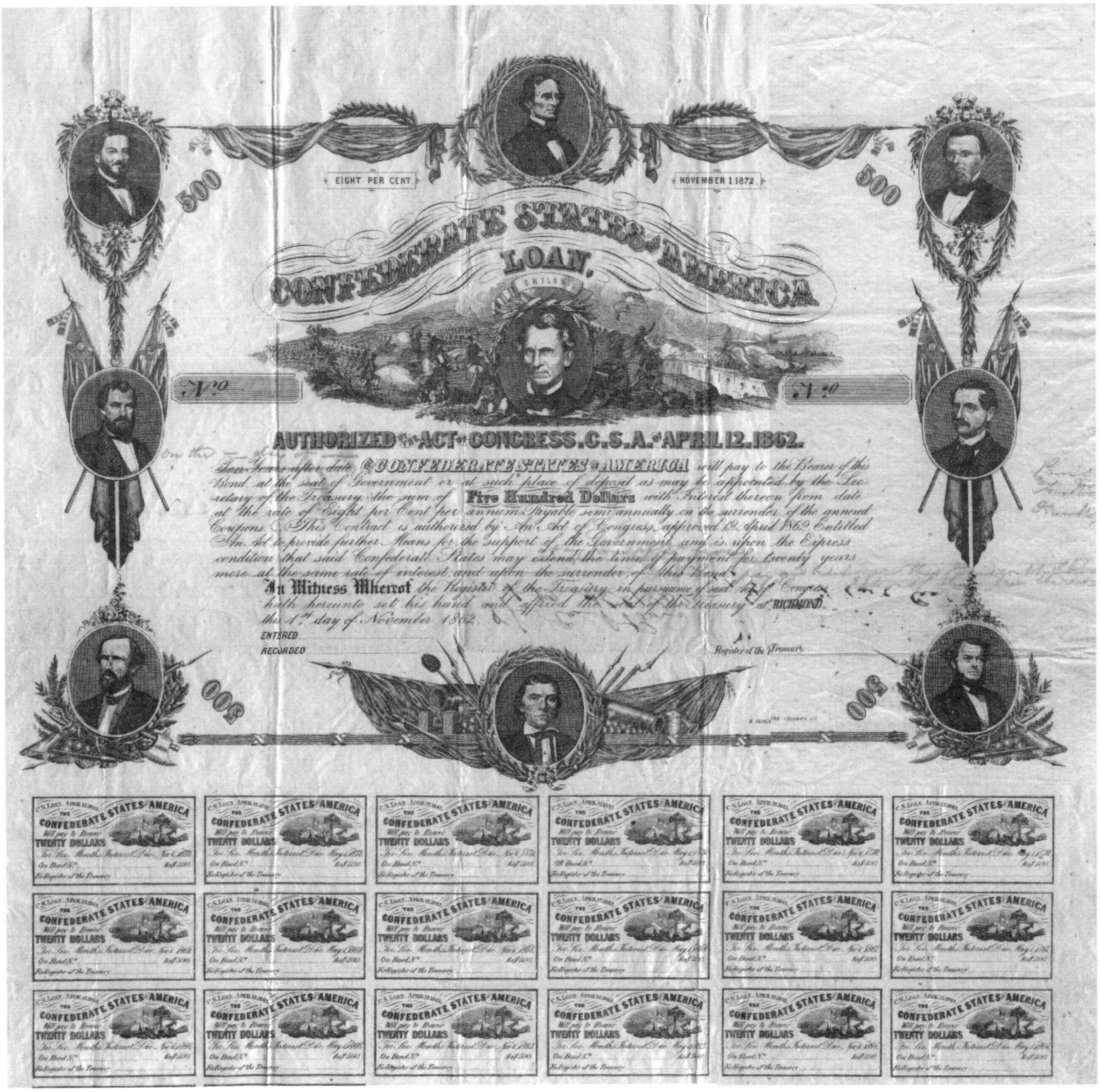

TYPE 122 **$500**

				fine	very fine
149.	$500	Essay by B. Duncan (never used), on plain white paper.			
		Number prepared: ? (1 known)	Rarity (8)	$22,275[86]	
		Dates of issue: May - June 1862			

B. Stock certificates
Total amount issued: $431,050, less $26,600 transfers

No. 66 No. 66
$100 $100
ACT OF CONGRESS. APRIL 12th 1862.
It is hereby Certified that the Confederate States of America are indebted unto Marx E Cohen Trustee of Mrs C De L Harby or Assigns in the sum of One Hundred Dollars, redeemable after the first day of May 1872 with interest from the 13th day of February 1863 inclusive at eight per Cent per annum payable on the first days of May and November in each year. This debt is authorized by an Act of Congress entitled "An Act to provide further means for the support of the Government" Approved April 12th 1862 and is upon the express condition that said Confederate States may extend the time of payment for twenty years more, at the same rate of interest, upon the surrender of this Certificate.
Entered
Recorded
8 per cent
RICHMOND, May 1st 1862
Register of the Treasury

(Confederate defenses at Drury's Bluff, including stakes and a sunken ship)

TYPE 123 written denominations

150.	Printed on white paper. Number issued: 181 (#1-181)[87] Dates of issue: August 20, 1863 - February 21, 1865 Signed by Tyler.	Rarity (7)	fine $10,000	very fine $12,500

Denomination	Qty issued
$100	4
$150	1
$200	3
$250	50
$300	2
$400	1
$500	6
$550	1
$600	2
$700	2
$750	1
$1,000	20
$1,200	2
$1,300	3
$1,500	3
$1,550	1
$1,800	1
$5,100	1
$5,500	1
$6,000	1
$6,500	1
$6,800	3
$7,000	2
$7,500	2

Denomination	Qty issued
$1,850	1
$2,000	16
$2,100	2
$2,200	3
$2,250	1
$2,500	7
$2,600	1
$2,900	1
$3,000	4
$3,400	1
$3,500	1
$4,000	6
$4,200	2
$4,350	1
$4,400	1
$4,800	1
$5,000	5
$7,950	1
$8,100	1
$9,000	3
$10,000	1
$11,000	3
$11,500	2
$12,000	1
$14,550	1

VII. ACT OF APRIL 21, 1862

Cotton certificates
Amount authorized: $1,500,000
Total amount issued (all types): None

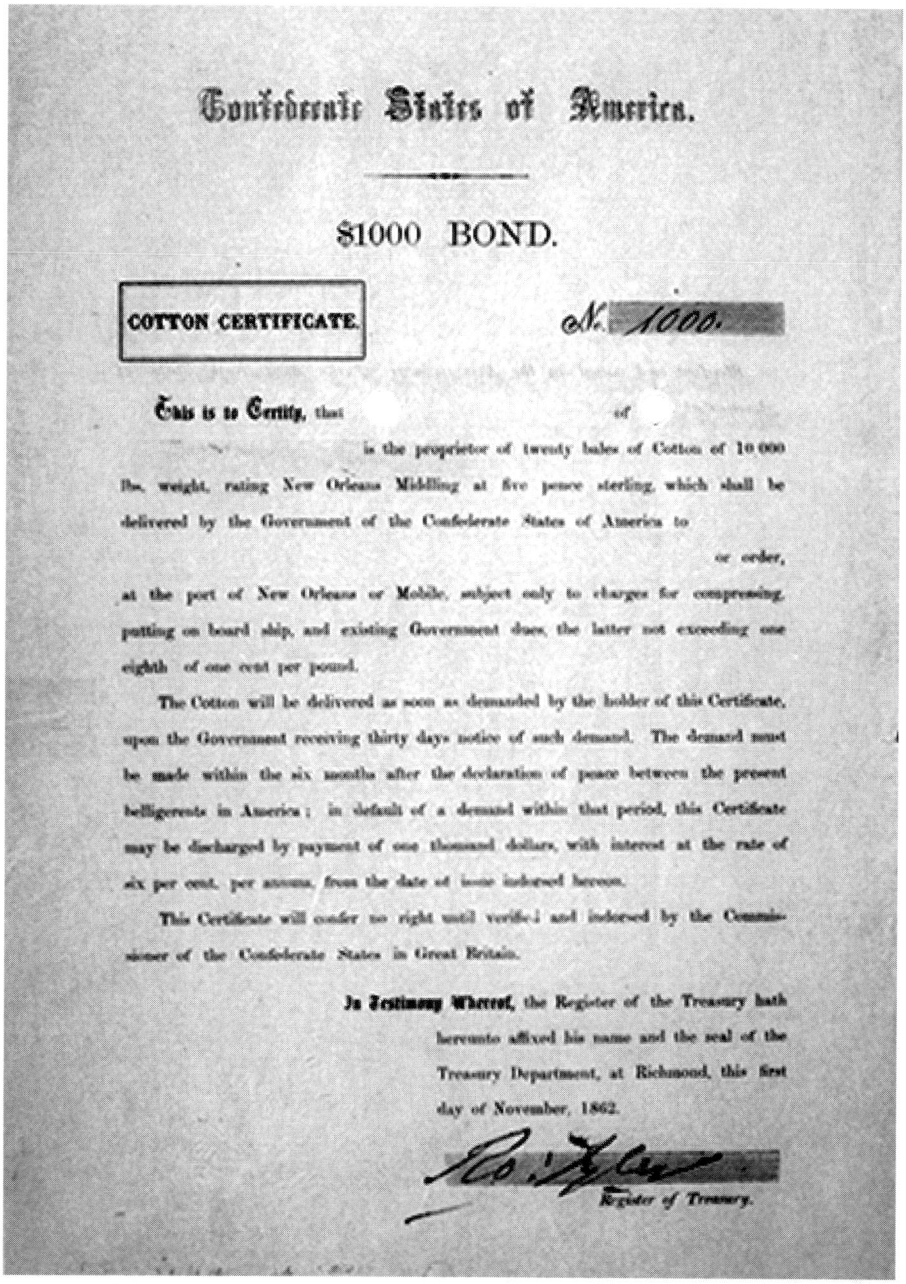

Confederate States of America.

$1000 BOND.

COTTON CERTIFICATE.

No. 1000.

This is to Certify, that of is the proprietor of twenty bales of Cotton of 10,000 lbs. weight, rating New Orleans Middling at five pence sterling, which shall be delivered by the Government of the Confederate States of America to or order, at the port of New Orleans or Mobile, subject only to charges for compressing, putting on board ship, and existing Government dues, the latter not exceeding one eighth of one cent per pound.

The Cotton will be delivered as soon as demanded by the holder of this Certificate, upon the Government receiving thirty days notice of such demand. The demand must be made within the six months after the declaration of peace between the present belligerents in America; in default of a demand within that period, this Certificate may be discharged by payment of one thousand dollars, with interest at the rate of six per cent. per annum, from the date of issue indorsed hereon.

This Certificate will confer no right until verified and indorsed by the Commissioner of the Confederate States in Great Britain.

In Testimony Whereof, the Register of the Treasury hath hereunto affixed his name and the seal of the Treasury Department, at Richmond, this first day of November, 1862.

Register of Treasury.

TYPE 124 **$1,000**
Payable at New Orleans or Mobile

				fine	very fine
151.	$1,000	Printed on white paper. Number issued: 1,000 (#1-1000) Dates of issue: Nov. 1, 1862 (shipped to Europe Dec. 14, 1862) Signed by Tyler.	Rarity (7+)[88]	$7,500	

TYPE 125 **$1,000**
Payable at Charleston or Savannah

152.	$1,000	Printed on white paper. Number issued: 500 (#1001-1500) Date of issue: November 1, 1862 (shipped to Europe December 14, 1862)[89] Signed by Tyler.	Rarity (7+)	$10,000	

TYPE 126 **$1,000**
Payable at any port

153.	$1,000	Printed on white, floral watermarked paper, red printed numbers. "Original." None seen to date; may no longer exist.		(—)	
154.	$1,000	Printed on white, floral watermarked paper, red printed numbers. "Duplicate." None seen to date; may no longer exist.		(—)	

Essay

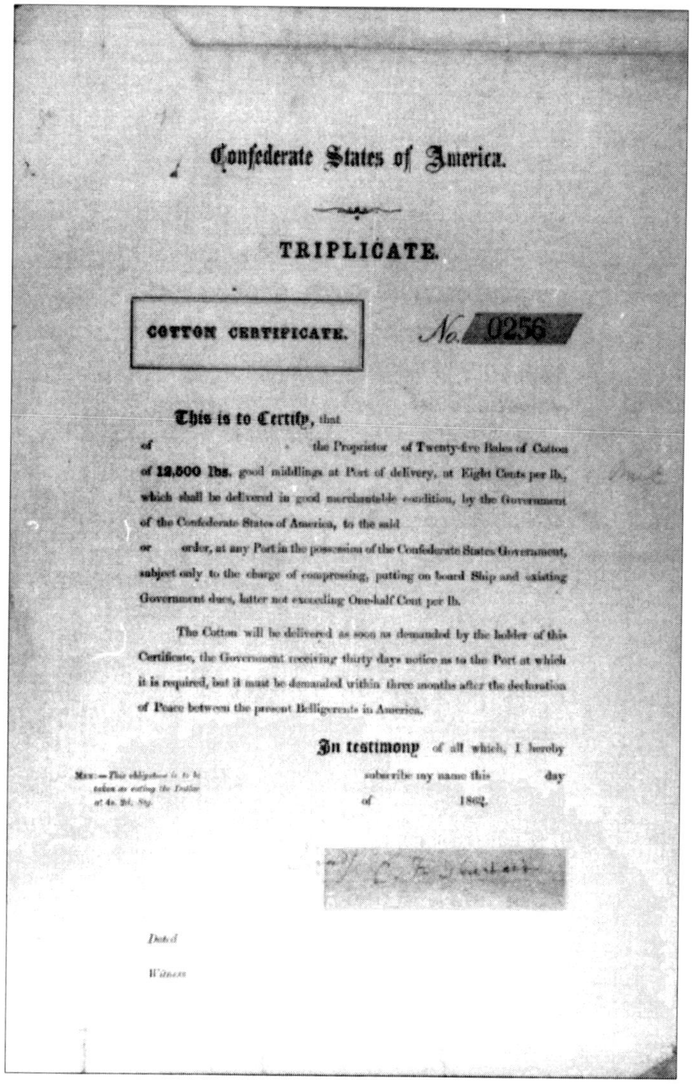

Confederate States of America.

TRIPLICATE.

COTTON CERTIFICATE.

No. 0256

This is to Certify, that

of the Proprietor of Twenty-five Bales of Cotton of 12,500 lbs. good middlings at Port of delivery, at Eight Cents per lb, which shall be delivered in good merchantable condition, by the Government of the Confederate States of America, to the said or order, at any Port in the possession of the Confederate States Government, subject only to the charge of compressing, putting on board Ship and existing Government dues, latter not exceeding One-half Cent per lb.

The Cotton will be delivered as soon as demanded by the holder of this Certificate, the Government receiving thirty days notice as to the Port at which it is required, but it must be demanded within three months after the declaration of Peace between the present Belligerents in America.

In testimony of all which, I hereby subscribe my name this day of 1862.

Dated

Witness

(alternate form)

155. $1,000 Printed on white, floral watermarked paper, red printed numbers. “Triplicate.”
Number issued: 1,500; only 1, #256, left. Rarity (8) (—)[90]
Date of issue: November 1, 1862

Signed in pencil by C. F. Sinclair, Confederate diplomat and procurement agent in Europe.

VIII. ACT OF JANUARY 29, 1863

(Erlanger loan)

The history of the South's cotton warrants and cotton bonds is fairly straightforward. The South was the world's major cotton producer. To damage the Confederate economy, President Lincoln proclaimed a blockade of the southern coast after the outbreak of fighting on April 12, 1861. The Confederates were unable to pursue any consistent policy, being hopelessly divided between those who favored an embargo of cotton shipments to Europe with a view to forcing France and Britain to intervene on their behalf, and those who saw the need for exports to pay for vital imports and to keep the economy liquid. In addition, the fatal doctrine of *laissez-faire* resulted in opposition to government efforts to foster cotton exports. As a result, the opportunity to export cotton in the first year of the war was largely allowed to lapse. Not until late 1863 did the government get itself organized to run the blockade and get its cotton sold abroad.

At the same time, the Congress had authorized a produce loan, allowing planters to subscribe to the loans of May 16, 1861 and August 19, 1861 by pledging the proceeds of the sales of produce. In addition to the cotton received under the second act, there was also the Act of April 14, 1862, which allowed the government to purchase cotton and other produce. Finally, the tax in kind called for payments in cotton, but this cotton would not help the government to meet its needs at home or abroad unless it could be reduced to cash, or unless lenders would furnish money in exchange for a pledge of cotton. In sum, how could the government secure cash for its cotton?

In the fall of 1862, confronted by a payments crisis in Europe, Secretary Memminger authorized the printing of certificates of $1000 each, a thousand promising to deliver cotton at New Orleans or Mobile and another 500 at Charleston or Savannah, at the rate of 5 pence sterling for each of the 10,000 pounds of promised cotton, worth $1,012.50. These certificates were then printed by a local printer, signed by Robert Tyler, the register, and shipped to Europe. These were substitutes for an earlier original, duplicate, and triplicate form (one each for the treasury, the purchaser and the Confederate agents abroad), promising to pay 12,500 pounds of cotton for $1000, or at a rate of 8¢ per pound as against the 10¢ per pound rate on the warrants sent to Europe.

In both cases, the price being received by the government, 8¢ or 10¢ per pound, was well under the 30¢ per pound that cotton was bringing in the open market. This windfall profit was not offered as a means of selling the cotton warrants at a premium or inducing speculators to buy them, but merely because the 8¢ to 10¢ rate was the price being paid in inflated Confederate dollars for cotton.

In any case, the warrants reached London but were not sold because the merchant bank, run by Baron Emile Erlanger, had offered to float a £3 million loan whose nominal $15 million proceeds offered ten times as much money as the warrants. Ultimately, a contract was agreed to and the Erlanger loan floated, but the loan, thanks to Confederate defeats, mismanagement, and other problems, produced only about $8 million.

The bonds of this issue were emitted in £100, £200, £500 and £1000 denominations, with amounts in francs at 25:1, which somewhat overstated the value of the franc. It is not known who printed these beautiful certificates, but we may safely assume a London source because the bulk of the bonds were sold there and every bond has an embossed British tax stamp for 2 shillings 6 pence, 5 shillings, 12 shillings 6 pence or 25 shillings, depending upon the denomination. They may well have been ordered by Henry Schroeder and Company, which firm managed the offering in London.

In preparing the bonds, the printers, who evidently started with the £1000 denomination, seem to have had no instructions as to whether the signatures on the coupons should be printed or not. The first fifty or so of the £1000 bonds were run off without signatures. Then it was decided to print all the signatures except for the last one next to the lower right corner. This coupon is actually signed on each bond, as a comparison of its brown ink with the black ink used on the rest of the coupons will readily disclose.

The history of the cotton warrants and the Erlanger loan bonds is a tragic one. The cotton warrants were handed over to Erlanger, who placed them in his archives. The issued bonds, with the exception of the 2.5% of the total face value drawn every six months, remained in the hands of the public, steadily losing value until the March 1, 1865 interest and drawing payments, after which further payments ceased and the bonds became practically worthless. They continued to be quoted from time to time at a fraction of 1% of their value, except during the 1879-1884 period during which they sometimes fetched as much as 2% of face.

Between 1880 and 1940, the Erlanger family gradually severed its connection with the continent, closing the Frankfurt and Paris offices and moving their entire operation to London. This was just as well, because while the family converted from Judaism to Roman Catholicism, after the marriage of Matilda Slidell with Erlanger's son, that would not have saved the family from the murderous attentions of the Nazis.

A considerable amount of Erlanger bonds, possibly a third of them, remained in the Erlanger family's hands, these being the remnants of the bonds bought back in 1863 as part of an unsuccessful market support operation. So did all, or almost all, of the cotton warrants. These survived the vicissitudes of World War II and were still on hand, with the exception of a single Ball 151 (Cr. 114) that had leaked out somehow.

In the late 1950s John J. Ford, of New Netherlands Coin Company, found himself in London and went to the Erlanger Bank to make inquiries regarding the Erlanger bonds. Not only was he able to buy some of those (then steeply priced at about $600 a set), but his attention was drawn to the existence of the cotton warrants. After some negotiations, Ford was able to buy four sets of bonds numbered 997 to 1004, with the changeover of types occurring at numbers 1000 and 1001. These, with the exception of some leftovers that remained in America and were used for official correspondence with the Confederate Congress, represent most of the extant supply.

In 1964, Mr. Leo Erlanger, owner of the bank, found himself without a family heir for the firm and with a favorable offer to buy out his business. Accordingly, he sold out and moved himself into a modest office where he had a secretary and could continue to do such business as he wished without the strain of running a full-time operation.

On October 1, 1966 my father, George W. Ball, having completed nearly six years as Under Secretary of State for Economic Affairs and then as Under Secretary (now styled the Deputy Secretary), decided that his physical exhaustion, plus the need to recoup his sorely depleted financial resources, necessitated his resignation from the government. On doing so he promptly flew off to Italy, where he began work on what was to be his first book, *The Discipline of Power*. I later joined my parents in Rome.

On the way back to the United States in December 1966, we stopped off in London. I used some of our time there to go down to Maidstone, Kent, and out to Wookey Hole Mill in Somerset to visit some of the places that had made paper used by the Confederates. The succeeding Saturday, my father and I went to Mr. Erlanger's home, where we had an excellent lunch with the banker and his intelligent and attractive daughter. We then left for Erlanger's office, where his secretary was waiting for us. She got out the family papers relating to John Slidell, and I spent a happy hour taking notes for my doctoral thesis, which later became a book, *Financial Failure and Confederate Defeat*.

Keeping in mind Ford's story and wanting to see if by using my father's good offices I might be able to buy some Erlanger bonds for resale in America, I asked about these bonds. I also inquired, with the hope of acquiring a pair of cotton warrants for my collection, about those bonds. Neither Mr. Erlanger nor his secretary knew where they were, but his nephew, his sister's son, so we were told, had packed up the Erlanger family papers for the move to the new office. Mr. Erlanger asked what I thought the bonds might be worth. I told him that sold slowly they might produce as much as $100,000. He then left us and went into his adjacent office to call his nephew, who was taking the weekend in Hampshire.

In due course he got his nephew on the phone and asked about where the bonds were. There was a silence for a short time while the nephew was speaking. Then I heard Mr. Erlanger say, "You did what!? How could you be so stupid!? I have troubles enough without your burning up $100,000 of my money." At that point the secretary tactfully closed the door between Mr. Erlanger's office and the office where we were.

When he returned, Mr. Erlanger looked flushed and deeply agitated. He explained that none of the bonds were left, his nephew having not bothered, in his zeal to discard what he considered to be trash, to save even samples of the loan bonds or cotton warrants. My father, tactfully realizing the unexpected problem that had arisen and knowing that I had finished my research, claimed an early dinner engagement prior to our going to the theater, made his excuses, and we left the scene of the crime. By such misfortunes are great rarities created.

7% coupon bonds
Total amount issued (all types): £3,000,000 (75,000,000 francs)
All dated January 1, 1863 (actually March-April 1863)[91]

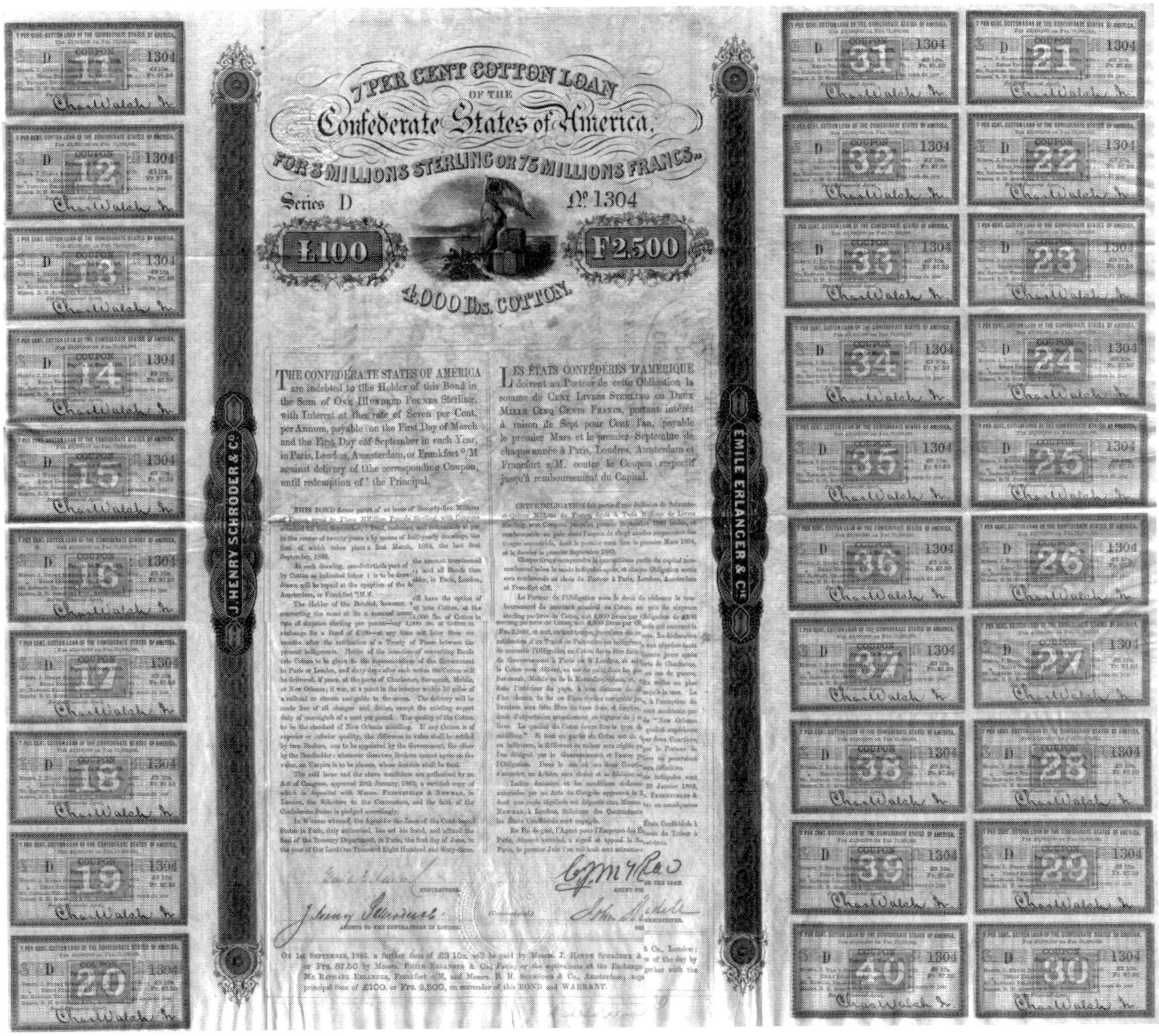

(*Confederacy* with flag, bales, etc.)
European printer unknown. Three of four rows of coupons shown.

TYPE 127 **£100** (2,500 francs)

				fine
156.	£100	Orange-brown tint on white watermarked paper with each coupon watermarked with its due date.[92] Number issued: c. 3,000 (#1-3000)	Rarity (5-)	$500

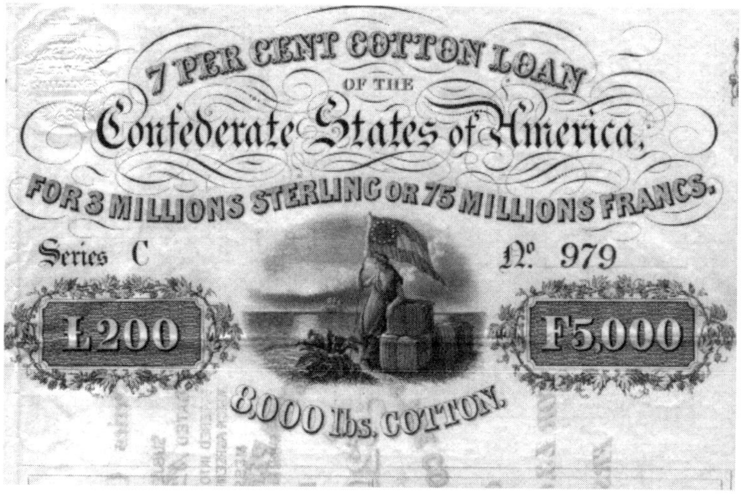

TYPE 128 **£200** (5,000 francs)

157.	£200	Similar to preceding, but for denomination and beige tint.[93] Number issued: c. 1,500 (#1-1500)	Rarity (5+)	$600

TYPE 129 **£500** (12,500 francs)

158.	£500	Similar to the preceding, but for the denomination and grayish-brown tint.[94] Number issued: c. 1,600 (#1-1600)	Rarity (5)	$500

TYPE 130 **£1,000** (25,000 francs)

159.	£1,000	Same, but all coupons are hand signed.		
		Number issued: c. 60 (#1-60)[96]	Rarity (7+)	$3,000
160.	£1,000	Same, but for denomination and orange tint.[95]		fine
		Number issued: c. 1,540 (#61-1600)	Rarity (5+)	$1,300

TYPE 131

161.		CSA commissioner's form (original). Duplicate, triplicate, and quadruplicate certificates also existed.		
		Typeset on white paper watermarked "Joynson, 1863."		
		Number issued: unknown[97]	Rarity (8)	(—)
		Dates of issue: fall of 1863 to spring of 1865		

IX. ACT OF FEBRUARY 20, 1863

The forced funding act passed on October 13, 1862 created a number of problems. Under the terms of this act, all notes dated September 2, 1861 (part of the August 19, 1861 act as amended) were required to be funded into 8% bonds not later than April 22, 1863. Those notes and those dated December 2, 1862 could be funded into 7% bonds until August 1, 1863. After that time, the December 2, 1862 notes would be fundable only into bonds bearing 4% interest. These arrangements were confirmed, as regards the old currency, by the Act of March 23, 1863.

The obvious problem with these laws was that the supply of unissued 8% bonds under the Act of August 19, 1861 was manifestly inadequate to fund all the outstanding notes into bonds. Nor had any legal provision been made for the issue of 7% bonds. Accordingly, Congress passed the Act of February 20, 1863 calling for the issue of an unlimited amount of 8% and 7% bonds to carry out the funding act. It must also be noted that, in contrast to the August 19, 1861 bonds, these were 5-30 bonds. That is, the bonds were to run for five years (hence the small number of coupons) but could be extended at five-year intervals as the Congress elected, up to thirty years. This would allow the treasury to execute a refunding operation at any one of the five-year intervals, thereby permitting the saving of large amounts of interest. Moreover, it was thought that by 1868, when the bonds fell due, it would be possible to get the extension bonds done in a better style by more skilled workmen.

By this time, Duncan was on the way out and the large quantity of bonds needed to cover $290 million of September 2, 1861 notes and over $140 million of December 2, 1862 notes could not possibly be produced by the printers in Columbia. Accordingly, the order was split. Since the 8% bonds were needed first, Evans & Cogswell was put to work on that project. They produced $100, $500 and $1000 coupon bonds and the registered bond certificate.

This issue has many anomalies. Evans & Cogswell had hired a Polish lithographer by the name of George Wojciechowski to do their work for them. Wojciechowski got started with three bonds that were materially different from those that followed. The $100 had Evans & Cogswell's name only, for the first bonds. The $500 bond started out with a rectangular box to hold the word "loan," which then had its corners clipped, creating an octagonal shape.

In the case of the $1000, Wojciechowski put his name in the lower right corner, just inside the outer border line. The portrait of President Davis on the $1000 bond Ball 200 (Cr. 125B) is markedly different from the succeeding varieties. The same is true of Ball 192 (Cr. 124A), which is on a tan paper quite unlike the thin English paper used for the succeeding bonds. Basically, these early bonds were confined to one plate, whereas the common bonds were the products of many plates. The appearance of various engraver names in various forms at the bottoms of the bonds proves this conclusively. Moreover, some of the paper imported earlier in 1862 became mixed with the 1863 paper, creating the various watermarked varieties.

A real effort was made to make these bonds counterfeit-proof. One can see traces of Duncan's work in these efforts. The portrait of Vice President Stephens echoes the T-20 Confederate bill; the $500 bond is covered with vignette work. Similarly, the $1000 bond borrows a figure of *Liberty* used on Georgia bank notes to fill the bottom. The operation was not a success, as the figure looks remarkably dejected. The Davis portrait is surrounded by a view of Richmond from the west that echoes the Ball 147 (Cr. 110) bond's central vignette.

Memminger contracted with Archer & Daly in Richmond to prepare the 7% coupon bonds. This series commemorates the Confederate army, with its scenes of an officer overlooking the Rappahannock River, a soldier warming his hands by a campfire, and the memorial portrait of General Jackson. These bonds, moreover, were not lithographed as stated in the Kerksis-Criswell book. They were printed from copper plates, as an examination of their workmanship will readily disclose.

We can also reasonably guess in what order these bonds were prepared. The plates were engraved for the $500, $1000, and $100 bonds in the order indicated. The first printings were on a soft white paper. However, with a view to making counterfeiting this issue more difficult, the special pink paper used for the December 2, 1862 treasury notes was also used for this series. Quite a number of $500 bonds were printed on white paper. Only a tiny number of $1000 bonds were printed on white paper, and all of the $100 bonds were done on the new paper. It has already been noted that the July 1, 1863 coupon was deleted and that the coupons for most of the bonds began on January 1, 1864.

For reasons unknown, probably as an afterthought, the registered bond certificate contract was given to J. T. Paterson & Co. This bond shows a mounted slave owner or overseer supervising the work of slaves, not in a cotton field, as had been true on the southern bank notes, but instead in a wheat field, a vignette much used in the North. Why Paterson's workmen chose to copy this northern vignette is unknown.

A. 8% coupon bonds
Total amount issued (all types): $81,668,100

The bonds of this series appear in two forms: those with coupons commencing July 1, 1863 and those with coupons commencing January 1, 1864. That is, the last row of coupons had either three or two coupons. In either case the first coupon was so composed as to have the date of issue and the amount of interest to be paid to be hand written.

The reason for this change lay in the fact that the July coupon became useless after July 1, 1863. Since under the forced funding act, the 7% bonds would not be issued in any quantity until after that date, a change was needed.

Based on the limited information available, the author believes that the initial variety of each denomination bore the July 1, 1863 coupon. Some of the more common second variety bonds also had three coupons. The conversion to a first coupon maturing on January 1, 1864 occurred somewhere between bond numbers 8,000 and 15,000 for each denomination. The varieties with two coupons on the last line represent practically all the surviving complete bonds.

An additional item relating solely to the bonds issued under this act, is the presence on several varieties of bonds of two red stamps; one of two lines reading "This BOND NOT TO BE VALID until indorsed/by the Depositary who issues it" or the other in three lines which reads "This Bond not to be valid until/endorsed by the Depositary by whom it is to be issued." These stamps were made by Frederick Baumgartner in Richmond, while the stamping was done by Wynne & Company in Richmond.

The reason for stamping the bonds lay in the fact that the Confederacy had been cut off from the Trans-Mississippi Department after the Union's capture of Vicksburg and Port Hudson in July 1863. Shipments of mail, money, or bonds would only take place on small packets by couriers crossing Union dominated territory along the Mississippi River or by running the blockade.

In point of fact, most of the bonds seem to have run the blockade. The $15 million of these bonds in the custody of Clarence Thayer left Wilmington on October 19th and ended their voyage at Matamorros on November 6, 1863. There they narrowly eluded capture, when a complaisant Briton claimed that the unopened case filled with notes and bonds were his.

Thayer then deposited the bonds with Paticio Milmo, son-in-law of Governor Vidaurri, both men being involved in the Confederate cotton trade. Milmo impounded the cases and demanded a past due payment of $200,000. After some Byzantine machinations on both sides, an agreement was struck and the bonds reached Houston, Texas on April 2, 1864. From that point, some of the bonds were distributed to various depositories in Louisiana and Arkansas where they were issued.

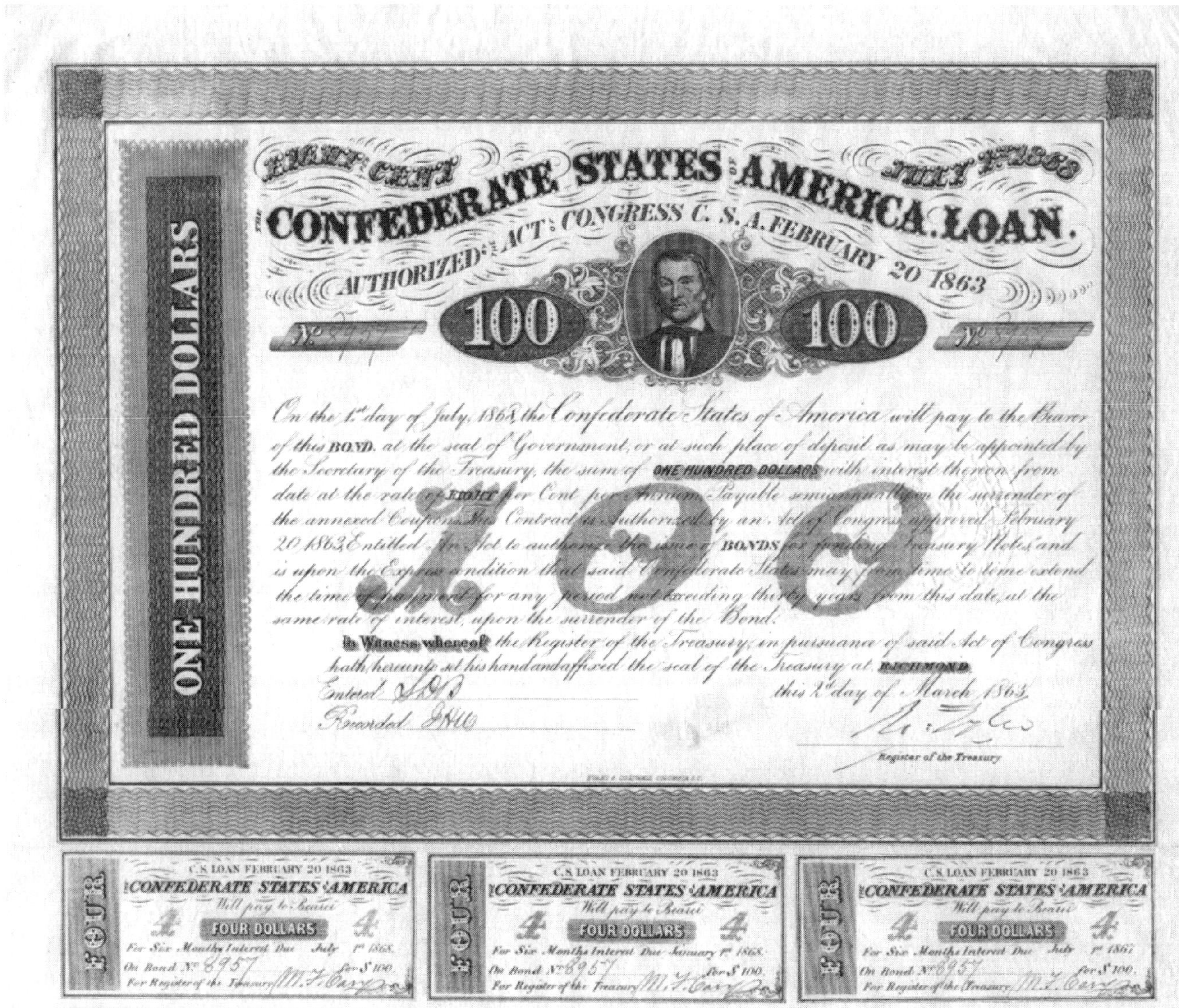

(Vice President Alexander H. Stephens)

TYPE 132 **$100**
Imprint: "Evans & Cogswell, Columbia, S.C."
Total issued: 28,636

				fine	very fine
165.	$100	Printed on bluish banknote paper.[98]			
		Number issued: c. 10,000 (#1-10000)	Rarity (3+)	$45	$55
		Dates of issue: c. May 29, 1863 - September 30, 1863			
		Signed by Rose.			

166. $100 Same, but "G(eorge) Wojciechowski, Litho." in lower right-hand corner. fine very fine
Number issued: c. 17,936 (#10001-28636 less Ball 170-188)[99] Rarity (3) $45 $50
Dates of issue: c. October 1, 1863 - January 27, 1864
Signed by Rose, Tyler.

172. $100 As last, two line red overprint on face "This Bond...who issues it."
Endorsed on back by H.S.G. Battle, CSA depositary at Shreveport, LA.
Number issued: 100 (#20401-20500) Rarity (7+) $75 $150
Dates of issue: April 1864
Signed by Rose.

177. $100 As last, two line red overprint on face "This Bond...who issues it."
Endorsed on back by Samuel T. Moseley, CSA depositary at Jefferson, Texas.
Number issued: 40 (#24661-24700) Rarity (7+) $150 $250
Date of issue: April 1864
Signed by Rose.

178. $100 Plain paper, but three line red overprint "This Bond...to be issued."
Signed by Alphonse Desmore, CSA depositary at Opelousas, La.
Number issued: c. 90 (#24801-24901 less pieces at #185, 186) Rarity (7) $125 $200
Dates of issue: December 1863
Signed by Rose.

179. $100 Three line red surcharge, endorsed on the back by H.S.G. Battle,
CSA depositary at Shreveport, La.
Number issued: c. 199 (#24701-24800; 24902-25000) Rarity (7) $100 $175
Dates of issue: December 1863
Signed by Rose.

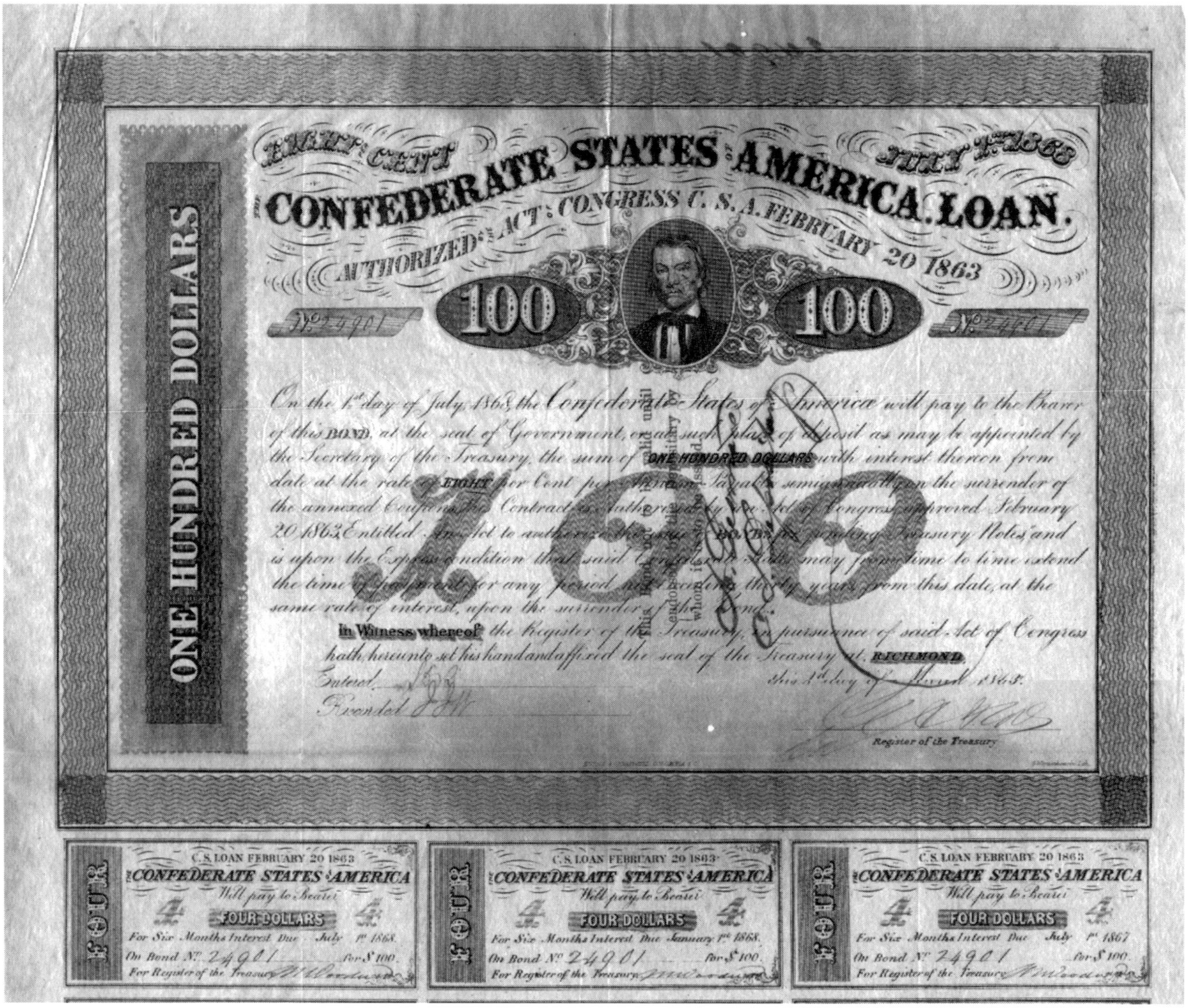

				fine	very fine
181.	$100	Three line red overprint, "This bond...to be issued."; "Issued at Houston, Texas." Depositary (Sorley) signature. Number issued: c. 260 (#24401-660) Dates of issue: December 1863 Signed by Rose.	Rarity (7-)	$75	$125
187.	$100	Three line red overprint, Opelousas, La; printed on paper watermarked "CSA" in block letters. Number issued: only 1 known (#24851) Date of issue: December 1863 Signed by Rose.	Rarity (8)	--	$3,000

				fine	very fine
188.	$100	Three line red overprint, but printed on bluish banknote paper, watermarked "J. Green & Son, 1862."			
		Number issued: c. 10 (#24850-24860, less above)*	Rarity (7)	$1,200	--
		Date of issue: c. December 1863			
		Signed by Rose.			
		*all are stained at the lower right			

TYPE 133 **$500**
Imprint: "Evans & Cogswell, Columbia, S.C."
Total issued: 58,917

(Secretary Christopher G. Memminger)

				fine	very fine
191.	$500	Printed on tan paper, different from the rest of this bond issue. The "loan" medallion is rectangular. Number issued: c. 1,500 (#1-1400; 1601-1700) Dates of issue: c. March 2-9, 1863 Signed by Rose.	Rarity (5)	$60	$80

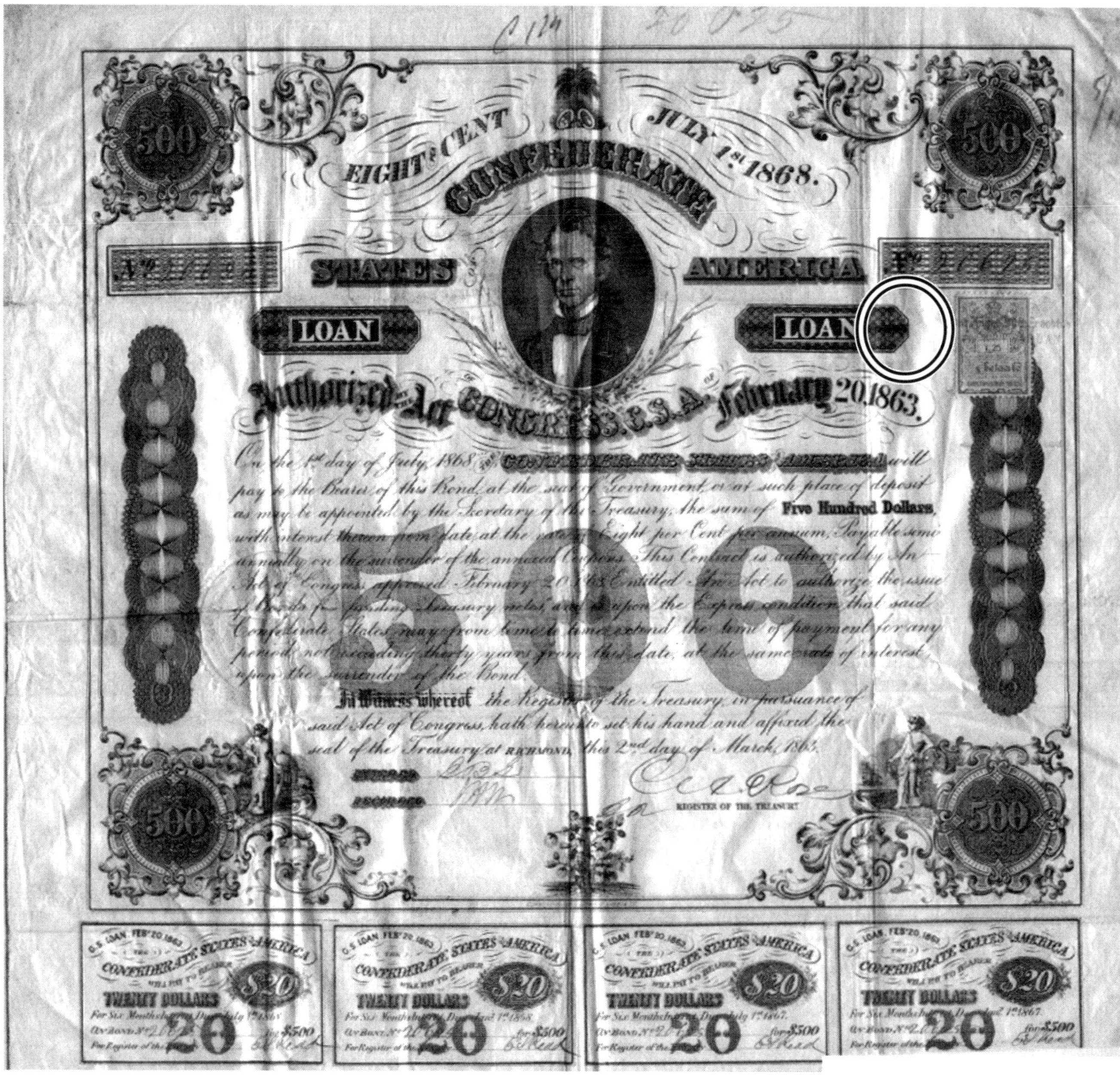

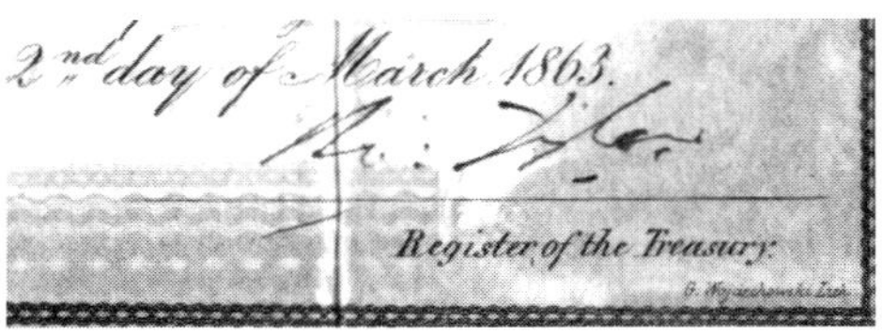

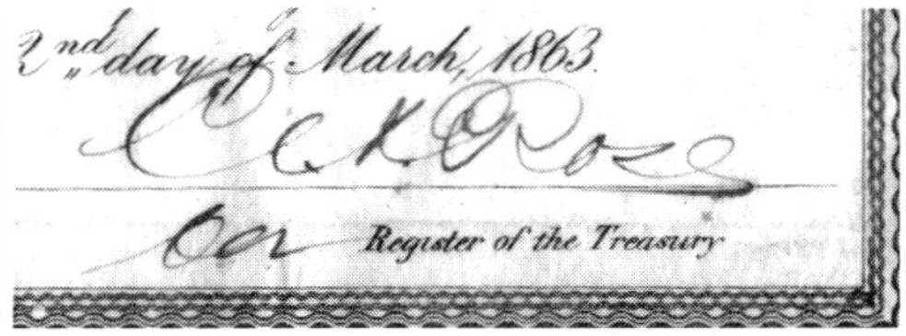

No.	Value	Description	Rarity	fine	very fine
192.	$500	Printed on bluish banknote paper; the "loan" medallion is octagonal because the corners are clipped off.[100] Number issued: c. 56,417 (#1401-1600; 1701-51900; 52901-58917) Dates of issue: c. March 9, 1863 - February 5, 1864 Signed by Rose, Tyler.	Rarity (2+)	$40	$50
195.	$500	Same, but a two line red overprint "This bond...who issues it." Endorsed on back by H.S.G. Battle, CSA depositary at Shreveport, La. Number issued: c. 100 (#51901-52000) Date of issue: February 5, 1864 Signed by Rose.	Rarity (7+)	$100	$125
196.	$500	Same, two line red overprint. Endorsed on the face by hand by James Sorley, depositary at Houston, Texas. Number issued: c. 400 (#52201-52700 scattered) Date of issue: February 5, 1864 Signed by Rose.	Rarity (7)	$125	$300
199.	$500	Same, three line red overprint "This bond...to be issued." Also, "Issued at Houston, Texas, Depositary" in black. Endorsed on face by James Sorley, CSA depositary at Houston. Number issued: c. 400 (#52001-52600 scattered) Date of issue: February 5, 1864 Signed by Rose.	Rarity (7+)	$150	$250

(President Jefferson Davis;
view of Richmond from the west)

TYPE 134 **$1,000**
Imprint: "Evans & Cogswell, Columbia, S.C."
Total issued: 49,650

200.	$1,000	Wojciechowski imprint at lower right near the outer border; printed on bluish-white banknote paper.[101]			
		Number issued: c. 1,200 (#1-1500, less scattered)	Rarity (6)	$200	$350
		Dates of issue: c. March 8-10, 1863			
		Signed by Rose.			

One Thousand Dollars.

No

EIGHT PER CENT JULY 1st 1868

THE CONFEDERATE STATES OF AMERICA LOAN.

AUTHORIZED BY ACT OF CONGRESS, C.S.A. February 20 1863

1000

On the 1st day of July 1868, the Confederate States of America will pay to the Bearer of this BOND at the seat of Government, or at such place of Deposit as may be appointed by the Secretary of the Treasury, the sum of ONE THOUSAND DOLLARS with interest thereon from date, at the rate of Eight per Cent per annum, payable semi annually on the surrender of the annexed Coupons. This Contract is authorized by An Act of Congress approved February 20 1863, Entitled An Act to authorize the issue of BONDS for funding Treasury notes and upon the Express condition that said Confederate States may from time to time extend the time of payment for any period not exceeding thirty years from this date, at the same rate of interest upon the surrender of the Bond.

In Witness whereof the Register of the Treasury, in pursuance of said Act of Congress hath hereunto set his hand and affixed the seal of the Treasury at RICHMOND, this 2nd day of March 1863.

Entered

Recorded

Register of the Treasury.

C.S. LOAN FEB 20 1863 40 CONFEDERATE STATES of AMERICA Will pay FORTY DOLLARS to Bearer For Six Months Interest Due July 1st 1868. ON BOND No 19801 for $1000 For Register of the Treasury

$ C.S. LOAN FEB 20 1863 40 CONFEDERATE STATES of AMERICA Will pay FORTY DOLLARS to Bearer For Six Months Interest Due Jan 1st 1868. ON BOND No 19801 for $1000 For Register of the Treasury

$ C.S. LOAN FEB 20 1863 40 CONFEDERATE STATES of AMERICA Will pay FORTY DOLLARS to Bearer For Six Months Interest Due July 1st 1867. ON BOND No 19801 for $1000 For Register of the Treasury

$ C.S. LOAN FEB 20 1863 40 CONFEDERATE STATES of AMERICA Will pay FORTY DOLLARS to Bearer For Six Months Interest Due Jan 1st 1867. ON BOND No 19801 for $1000 For Register of the Treasury

201. $1,000 Wojciechowski imprint near the inside border; printed on bluish white paper.[102] <u>fine</u> <u>very fine</u>

Number issued: c. 36,550 (#1001-1800; 2201-3300; 9601-10500; 13201-13600; 15501-16000; 16401-18000; 18201-19100; 19301-30000; 30201-42800; 43300-45401; scattered to 49,650)[103]

Rarity (3-) $75 $100

Dates of issue: March 10, 1863 - February 5, 1864

Signed by Rose, Tyler.

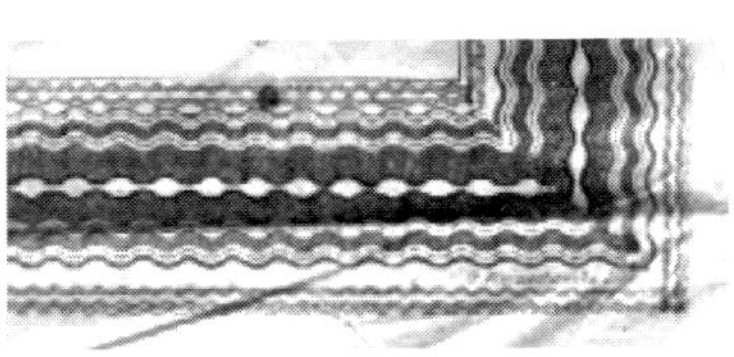

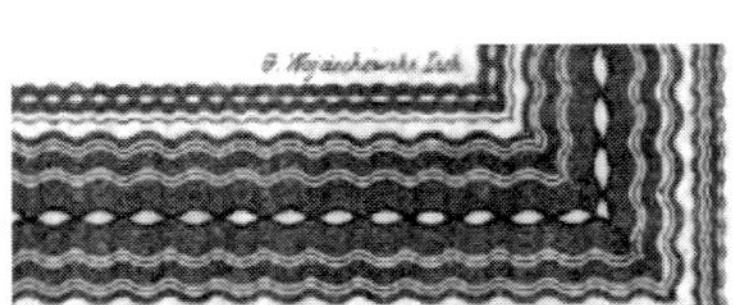

corner from 201, far left from Ball 200.

203. $1,000 Same as #199, but two line red overprint "This bond...who issues it" on face with handwritten endorsement by H.B.G. Battle, CSA depositary at Shreveport, La. on back. — fine / very fine
Number issued: c. 300 (#42001-42700 scattered) — Rarity (5+) — $175 — $250
Dates of issue: February 1864
Signed by Rose.

204. $1,000 Same as #199, but two line red overprint "This bond... who issues it" on face with all hand-written endorsement by James Sorley, CSA depositary at Houston, Texas.
Number issued: c. 400 (#42101-42700 scattered) — Rarity (6-) — $175 — $250
Date of issue: February 1864
Signed by Rose.

205. $1,000 Same, but issued at Alexandria, La.
Number issued: c. 50 (#45301-45400 scattered) — Rarity (7+) — $250 — $350
Dates of issue: February 1864
Signed by Rose.

				fine	very fine
206.	$1,000	Same, but three line red overprint; endorsed by Alphonse Desmare, CSA depositary at Opelousas, La. Number issued: c. 100 (#43301-43400) Date of issue: February 1864 Signed by Rose.	Rarity (7-)	$200	$300
207.	$1,000	Same, but three line red overprint, endorsed by H.B.G. Battle, CSA depositary at Shreveport, La. on back. Number issued: c.50 (#45301-45400 scattered) Dates of issue: February 1865 Signed by Rose.	Rarity (7+)	$250	$350

208. $1,000 Same, but three line red overprint on the face "This Bond...to be issued." "Houston, Texas, Depositary" in black. Signed by James Sorley.

	fine	very fine
Number issued: c. 600 (#42701-43500 scattered) — Rarity (5+)	$175	$250

Date of issue: February 1864

Signed by Rose.

210. $1,000 Similar to 201, but on paper watermarked "C. Ansell 1863."[104]

Number issued: c. 12,200 (1801-2200; 3301-9600; 10501-13200; 13601-15500; 16001-16400; 18001-18200; 19101-19300; 30101-30200) Rarity (3) $100 $150

Dates of issue: c. March 10 - September 20, 1863

Signed by Tyler.

B. Stock certificates
Total amount issued (all types): $21,372,100

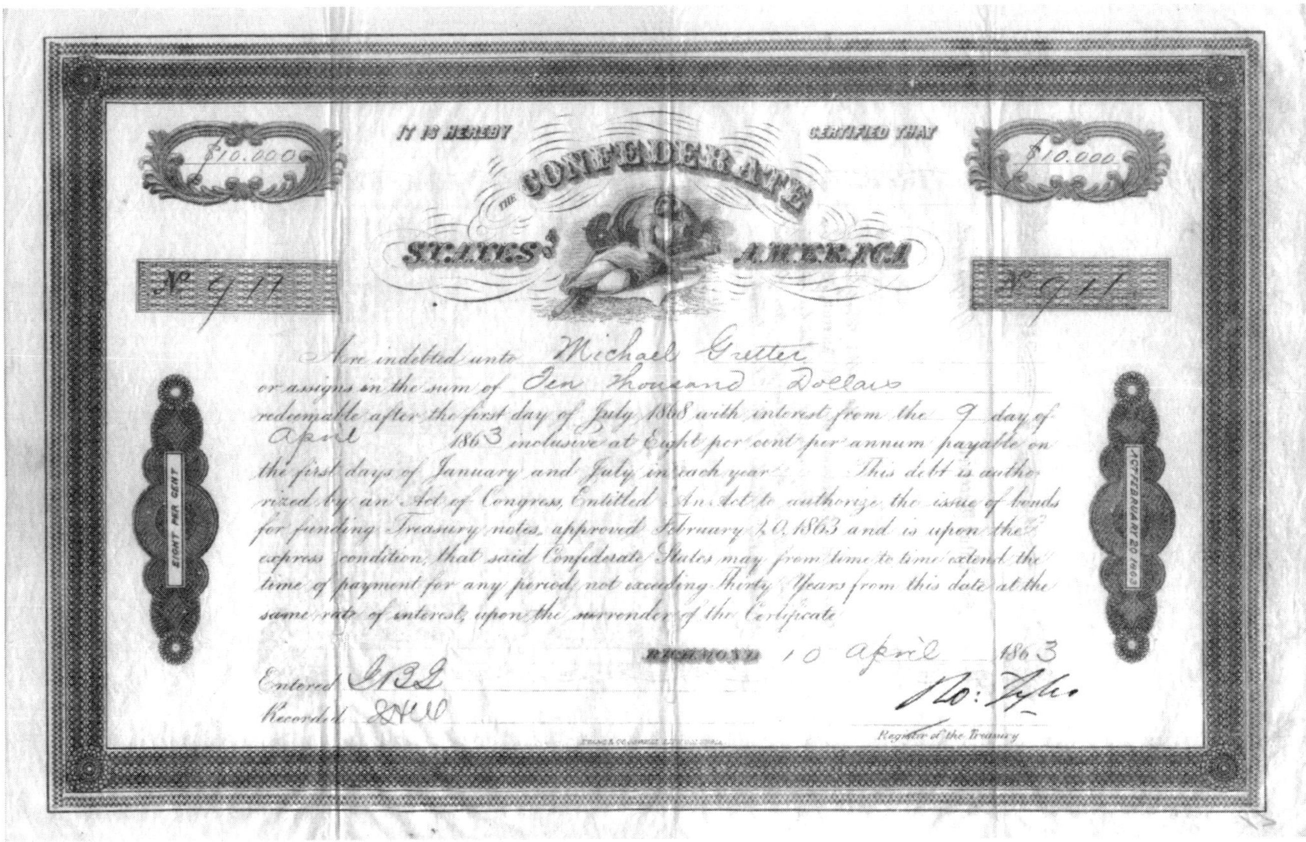

(*Science,* center)

TYPE 135 various denominations
Imprint: "Evans & Cogswell, Lith. Columbia."

			fine	very fine
211.	Printed on thin, bluish-white banknote paper. Number issued: 6,388 (#1-6386, plus #s 5878 $^{1}/_{2}$, 6078 $^{1}/_{2}$) Dates of issue: March 25, 1863 - April 1, 1865 Signed by Tyler.	Rarity (5-)	$150	$200

Denomination	Number issued	Rarity	Denomination	Number issued	Rarity
$50	10	—	$1,250	4	—
$100	308	7	$1,300	76	8
$150	2	—	$1,350	2	—
$200	285	7	$1,400	59	8
$250	10	—	$1,450	4	8
$300	260	7	$1,500	143	7-
$350	5	—	$1,550	3	—
$400	230	7	$1,600	45	8
$450	7	—	$1,700	36	8
$500	720	6-	$1,750	1	—
$550	2	—	$1,800	49	8
$600	225	7	$1,850	1	—
$650	5	—	$1,900	16	—
$700	162	7-	$1,950	2	—
$750	4	—	$2,000	404	7-
$800	139	7-	$2,100	32	8
$850	3	—	$2,150	2	—
$900	81	8	$2,200	33	8
$950	3	—	$2,250	2	—
$1,000	883	6	$2,300	20	8
$1,050	2	—	$2,350	1	—
$1,100	91	8	$2,400	30	8
$1,150	1	—	$2,450	1	—
$1,200	153	7-	$2,500	131	7-

Items without rarity numbers are not known to exist and may therefore not be collectable.

Contemporary Jefferson Davis vignettes.

Denomination	Number issued	Rarity	Denomination	Number issued	Rarity
$2,600	33	8	$6,700	4	—
$2,700	23	8	$6,800	2	—
$2,800	21	8	$6,900	2	—
$2,900	16	8	$7,000	40	8
$3,000	231	7	$7,100	2	—
$3,100	16	8	$7,300	2	—
$3,150	3	—	$7,350	1	—
$3,200	18	8	$7,500	7	—
$3,300	10	—	$7,550	1	—
$3,350	1	—	$7,600	1	—
$3,400	8	—	$7,700	2	—
$3,500	43	8	$7,850	1	—
$3,550	1	—	$7,900	3	—
$3,600	14	—	$8,000	30	—
$3,700	8	—	$8,100	1	8
$3,800	5	—	$8,200	2	—
$3,850	1	—	$8,300	1	—
$3,900	5	—	$8,400	2	—
$4,000	123	7-	$8,500	2	—
$4,050	1	—	$8,700	3	—
$4,100	11	—	$8,750	1	—
$4,200	11	—	$8,800	2	—
$4,300	9	—	$9,000	20	8
$4,400	13	—	$9,100	1	—
$4,500	29	8	$9,150	1	—
$4,550	1	—	$9,200	2	—
$4,600	5	—	$9,300	3	—
$4,650	1	—	$9,400	4	—
$4,700	8	8	$9,700	1	—
$4,800	5	—	$9,900	1	—
$4,900	2	—	$10,000	166	7
$5,000	307	7-	$10,500	3	—
$5,100	4	—	$10,600	4	—
$5,200	6	—	$11,000	9	—
$5,250	1	—	$11,400	1	—
$5,300	7	—	$11,500	3	—
$5,400	6	—	$11,700	1	—
$5,500	17	8	$11,900	1	—
$5,600	5	—	$12,000	13	—
$5,650	1	—	$12,200	1	—
$5,700	4	—	$12,300	1	—
$5,800	3	—	$12,400	1	—
$5,900	1	—	$12,500	2	—
$6,000	67	8	$12,750	1	—
$6,100	5	—	$13,000	3	—
$6,200	5	—	$13,300	1	—
$6,300	4	—	$13,400	2	—
$6,400	3	—	$13,500	3	—
$6,500	12	—	$14,000	9	—
$6,550	1	—	$14,200	2	—
$6,600	2	—	$14,300	1	

Items without rarity numbers are not known to exist and may therefore not be collectable.

Denomination	Number issued	Rarity
$14,500	3	—
$14,700	1	—
$14,800	1	—
$14,850	1	—
$14,900	1	—
$15,000	20	8
$15,100	1	—
$15,400	2	—
$15,500	1	—
$15,700	1	—
$16,000	5	—
$16,100	1	—
$16,500	3	—
$17,000	2	—
$17,100	1	—
$17,300	1	—
$17,500	1	—
$17,600	1	—
$18,000	4	—
$18,100	1	—
$18,500	1	—
$19,000	5	—
$19,300	1	—
$20,000	30	8
$20,500	3	—
$21,000	1	—
$21,250	2	—
$22,000	2	—
$23,000	3	—
$25,000	10	—
$26,500	1	—
$29,000	1	—
$30,000	4	—
$30,500	1	—

Denomination	Number issued	Rarity
$31,800	1	—
$32,000	4	—
$34,000	4	—
$35,000	2	—
$35,800	1	—
$36,900	1	—
$37,000	1	—
$40,000	7	8
$40,700	1	—
$43,000	1	—
$45,000	2	—
$46,000	1	—
$49,000	1	—
$50,000	11	—
$55,000	1	—
$59,400	1	—
$61,000	1	—
$63,000	1	—
$67,100	1	—
$78,000	1	—
$81,000	1	—
$82,700	1	—
$85,000	1	—
$87,400	1	—
$90,400	1	—
$95,400	1	—
$100,000	9	—
$109,000	1	—
$147,000	1	—
$150,000	2	—
$166,200	1	—
$173,000	1	—
$200,000	6	—
$300,000	1	—
$500,000	1	8

Items without rarity numbers are not known to exist and may therefore not be collectable.

C. 7% coupon bonds

Total amount issued (all types): $54,183,100

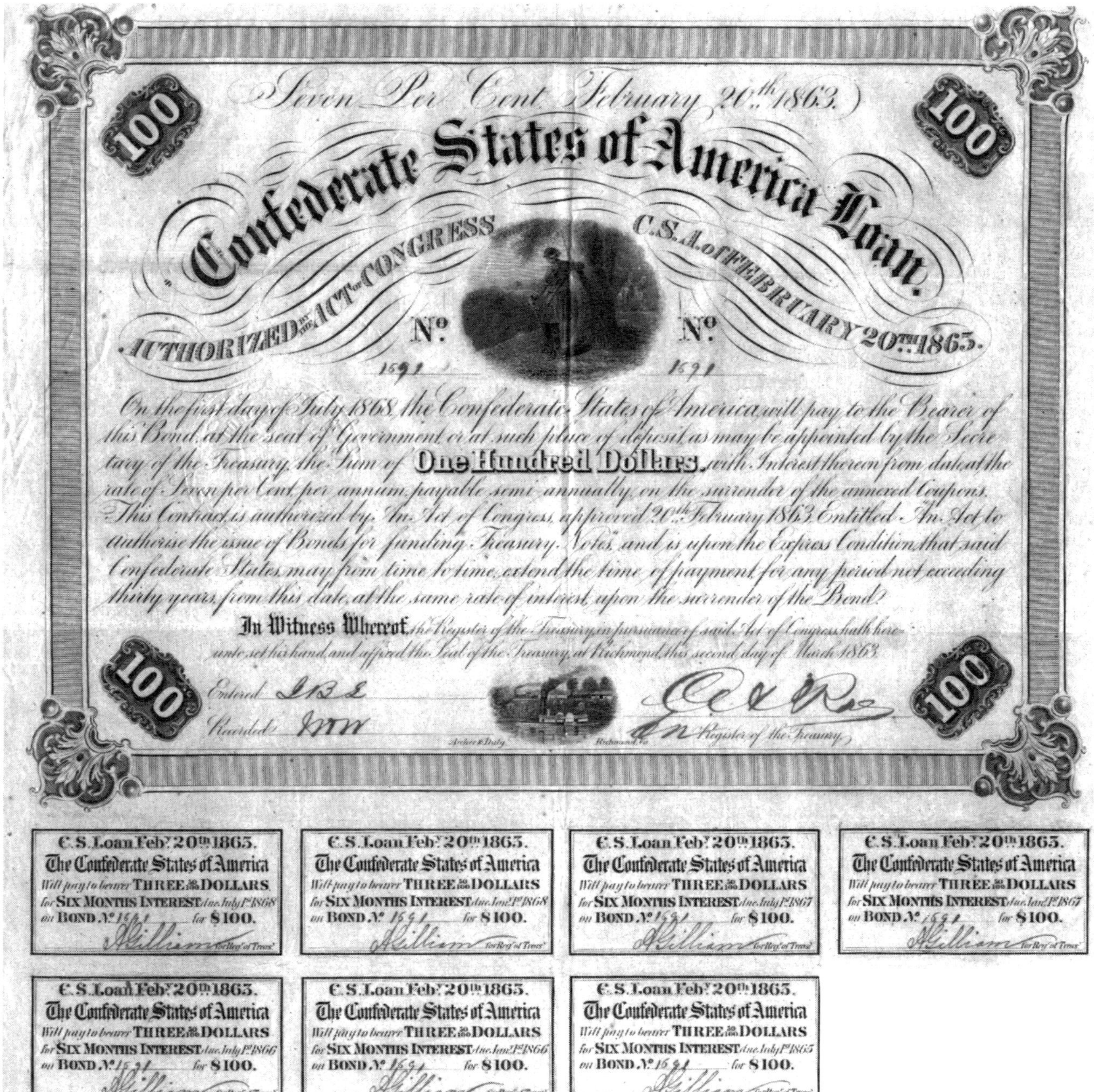

100 Seven Per Cent February 20th 1863. 100

Confederate States of America Loan.

Authorized by the Act of Congress C.S.A. of February 20th 1863.

No. 1591 No. 1591

On the first day of July 1868 the Confederate States of America will pay to the Bearer of this Bond at the seat of Government or at such place of deposit as may be appointed by the Secretary of the Treasury the Sum of One Hundred Dollars, with Interest thereon from date at the rate of Seven per Cent per annum payable semi-annually on the surrender of the annexed Coupons. This Contract is authorized by An Act of Congress approved 20th February 1863 Entitled An Act to authorise the issue of Bonds for funding Treasury Notes, and is upon the Express Condition that said Confederate States may from time to time extend the time of payment for any period not exceeding thirty years from this date at the same rate of interest upon the surrender of the Bond.

In Witness Whereof, the Register of the Treasury in pursuance of said Act of Congress hath hereunto set his hand and affixed the Seal of the Treasury at Richmond this second day of March 1863.

Entered

Recorded

Archer & Daly, Richmond, Va.

Register of the Treasury.

100 100

C.S. Loan Feb. 20th 1863. The Confederate States of America Will pay to bearer THREE 50/100 DOLLARS for SIX MONTHS INTEREST due July 1st 1868 on BOND No. 1591 for $100. for Reg. of Treas.

C.S. Loan Feb. 20th 1863. The Confederate States of America Will pay to bearer THREE 50/100 DOLLARS for SIX MONTHS INTEREST due Jan. 1st 1868 on BOND No. 1591 for $100. for Reg. of Treas.

C.S. Loan Feb. 20th 1863. The Confederate States of America Will pay to bearer THREE 50/100 DOLLARS for SIX MONTHS INTEREST due July 1st 1867 on BOND No. 1591 for $100. for Reg. of Treas.

C.S. Loan Feb. 20th 1863. The Confederate States of America Will pay to bearer THREE 50/100 DOLLARS for SIX MONTHS INTEREST due Jan. 1st 1867 on BOND No. 1591 for $100. for Reg. of Treas.

C.S. Loan Feb. 20th 1863. The Confederate States of America Will pay to bearer THREE 50/100 DOLLARS for SIX MONTHS INTEREST due July 1st 1866 on BOND No. 1591 for $100. for Reg. of Treas.

C.S. Loan Feb. 20th 1863. The Confederate States of America Will pay to bearer THREE 50/100 DOLLARS for SIX MONTHS INTEREST due Jan. 1st 1866 on BOND No. 1591 for $100. for Reg. of Treas.

C.S. Loan Feb. 20th 1863. The Confederate States of America Will pay to bearer THREE 50/100 DOLLARS for SIX MONTHS INTEREST due July 1st 1865 on BOND No. 1591 for $100. for Reg. of Treas.

(Confederate officer overlooking the Rappahannock River west of Fredericksburg)

TYPE 136 **$100**
Imprint: "Archer & Daly, Richmond, Va"

No.	Value	Description	Rarity	fine	very fine
212.	$100	Printed on dark pink paper. Number issued: c. 31,066 (#1-25801; 27801-33066) Dates of issue: June 9, 1863 - Jan. 17, 1864 Signed by Rose.	Rarity (3)	$45	$60
214.	$100	Same as #212, but three line red overprint "This Bond...to be issued." Endorsed by Edward Cross on the back at Washington, Arkansas. Number issued: c. 200 (#26801-27000) Dates of issue: February 1864 Signed by Rose.	Rarity (7)	$200	$300
216.	$100	Same, three line red overprint, bond endorsed on the face by Alphonse Desmore, depositary at Opelousas, La. Number issued: c. 200 (#27601-27800) Dates of issue: February 1864 Signed by Rose.	Rarity (3)	$180	$250
217.	$100	Same, three line red overprint, hand issued on the back by H.J.G. Battle, CSA depositary at Shreveport, La. Number issued: c. 600 (#27001-27600) Dates of issue: February 1864 Signed by Rose.	Rarity (5)	$150	$200
218.	$100	Same, but issued with a three line red overprint, "This Bond...to be issued" and a black "Houston, Texas Depositary" stamp; signed by James Sorley, CSA depositary at Houston. Number issued: c. 800 (#25801-26600) Dates of issue: c. February 1864 Signed by Rose.	Rarity (7-)	$180	$250
219.	$100	Same, three line red overprint, endorsed by M. Hall, Principal Depositary, Trans-Mississippi, Marshal, Texas. Number issued: c. 200 (#26,601-26,800) Dates of issue: early 1864. Signed by Rose.	Rarity (7+)	$250	$300

TYPE 137 **$500**

Imprint: "Archer & Daly, Richmond, Va"; lithographed.

				fine	very fine
220.	$500	Printed on white paper. Number issued: c. 3,800 (#1-3900, less scattered) Dates of issue: May 1 - c. December 1863) Signed by Rose.	Rarity (3+)	$50	$90

Seven Per Cent February 20th 1863.

$500 $500

Confederate States of America Loan.

Authorized by an Act of Congress C.S.A. of February 20th 1863.

No. 1309 No. 1309

On the first day of July 1868 the Confederate States of America will pay to the Bearer of this Bond at the seat of Government or at such place of deposit as may be appointed by the Secretary of the Treasury the Sum of Five Hundred Dollars with Interest thereon from date at the rate of Seven per Cent per annum payable semi-annually on the surrender of the annexed Coupons. This Contract is authorized by An Act of Congress approved 20th February 1863, Entitled "An Act to authorise the issue of Bonds for funding Treasury Notes," and is upon the Express Condition that said Confederate States may from time to time extend the time of payment for any period not exceeding thirty years from this date at the same rate of interest upon the surrender of the Bond.

In Witness Whereof the Register of the Treasury in pursuance of said Act of Congress hath hereunto set his hand and affixed the Seal of the Treasury at Richmond this second day of March 1863.

Entered

Recorded

Register of the Treasury

$500 $500

C.S. LOAN FEB. 20th 1863. The Confederate States of America Will pay to bearer SEVENTEEN 50/100 DOLLS for SIX MONTHS INTEREST due July 1st 1868 on BOND No. 1309 for $500. for Reg. of Treas.

C.S. LOAN FEB. 20th 1863. The Confederate States of America Will pay to bearer SEVENTEEN 50/100 DOLLS for SIX MONTHS INTEREST due Jan. 1st 1868 on BOND No. 1309 for $500. for Reg. of Treas.

C.S. LOAN FEB. 20th 1863. The Confederate States of America Will pay to bearer SEVENTEEN 50/100 DOLLS for SIX MONTHS INTEREST due July 1st 1867 on BOND No. 1309 for $500. for Reg. of Treas.

C.S. LOAN FEB. 20th 1863. The Confederate States of America Will pay to bearer SEVENTEEN 50/100 DOLLS for SIX MONTHS INTEREST due Jan. 1st 1867 on BOND No. 1309 for $500. for Reg. of Treas.

(Soldier warming hands over camp fire, center)

221. $500 Printed on dark pink paper. fine very fine
Number issued: c. 26,249 (#3601-33549, less scattered) Rarity (3-) $40 $55
Dates of issue: c. May to December 16, 1864
Signed by Rose, Tyler.

221. $500 As last, two line red overprint written for Alexandria, La. General Arbuckle.
Number issued: c. 100 (#32801-32900) Rarity (7+) $200 $250
Dates of issue: unknown, undated.
Signed by Rose.

224. $500 As last, two line red overprint on face, "This Bond...who issues it," endorsed by Alphonse Desmare, CSA depositary, Opelousas, Louisiana.
Number issued: c. 200 (#26201-26400 scattered) Rarity (7-) $150 $200
Dates of issue: February 1864
Signed by Rose.

225. $500 Two line red overprint, issued from Shreveport, LA by H.J.G. Battle, CSA depositary.
Number issued: c. 400 (#23901-24300) Rarity (5) $125 $175
Dates of issue: February 1864
Signed by Rose.

227. $500 Two line red overprint, but issued from Jefferson, Texas by Samuel Moseley, CSA depositary.
Number issued: c. 300 (#23601-23900) Rarity (7) $200 $250
Dates of issue: February 1864
Signed by Tyler.

232. $500 Three line red overprint on face, "This Bond...to be issued." Issued at Shreveport, La. on back.
Number issued: c. 800 (#26401-27200 scattered) Rarity (5-) $65 $100
Dates of issue: February 1864
Signed by Rose.

233. $500 Three line red overprint, "This Bond...to be issued." Back endorsement of J.W. Smith, depositary at Dallas, Texas (no date). Very rare (only one piece has been seen to date).
Number issued: c. 50 (#28850-28900) Rarity (8) $1,000 $2,000
Dates of issue: probably February 1864
Signed by Rose.

234. $500 Three line red overprint, "This Bond...to be issued" on face, "Houston, Texas Depositary" black stamp, signed by James Sorley, CSA depositary.
Number issued: c. 1650 (#27201-28850 scattered) Rarity (4+) $100 $150
Dates of issue: February 1864
Signed by Rose.

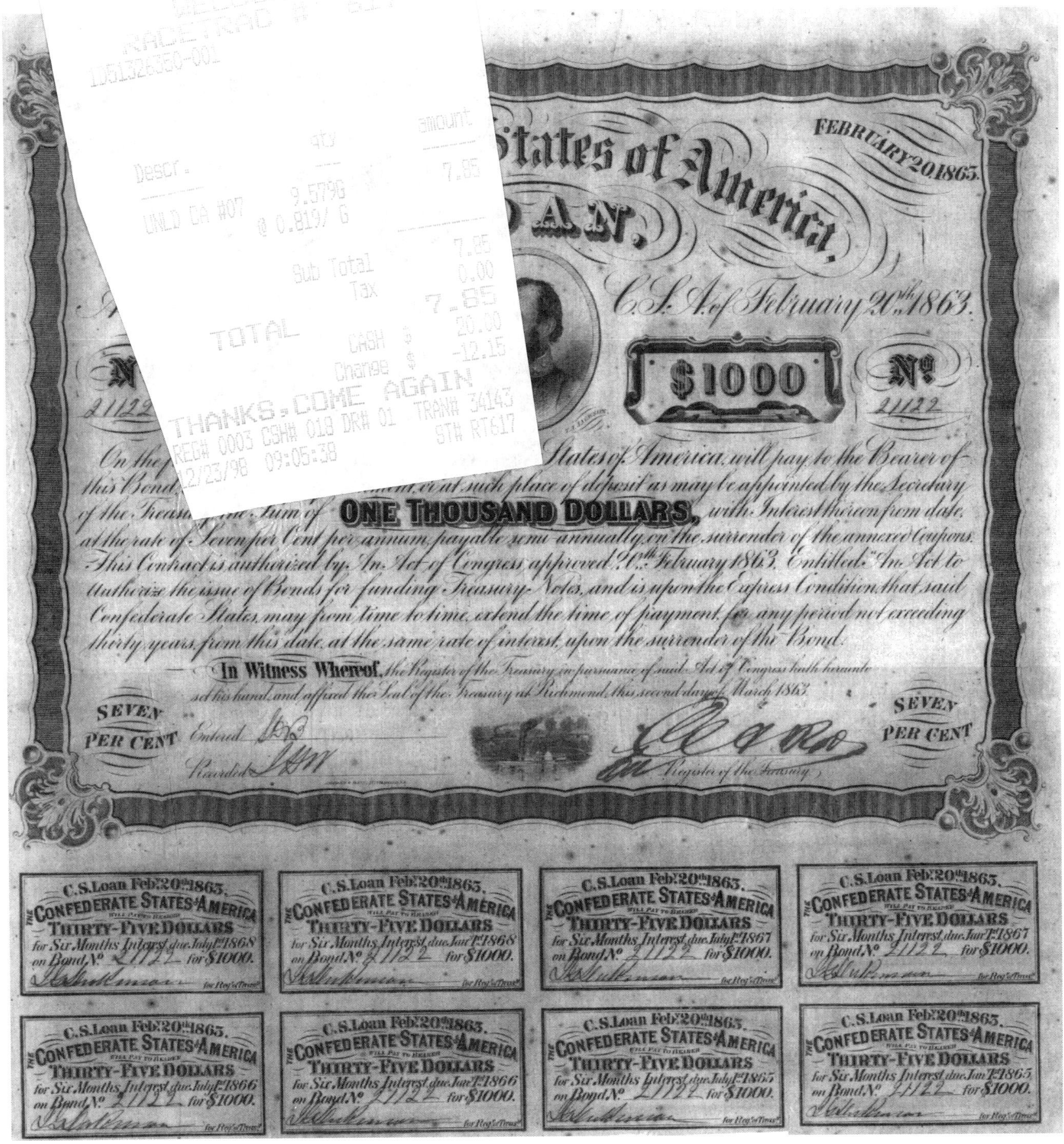

States of America
LOAN.
FEBRUARY 20, 1863.
C. S. A. of February 20th 1863.
$1000
No 21122
On the ... States of America, will pay to the Bearer of this Bond, ... or at such place of deposit as may be appointed by the Secretary of the Treasury, the Sum of ONE THOUSAND DOLLARS, with Interest thereon from date, at the rate of Seven per Cent per annum, payable semi-annually, on the surrender of the annexed Coupons. This Contract is authorized by An Act of Congress approved 20th February 1863. Entitled "An Act to authorize the issue of Bonds for funding Treasury Notes, and is upon the Express Condition that said Confederate States, may from time to time, extend the time of payment, for any period not exceeding thirty years from this date, at the same rate of interest, upon the surrender of the Bond.
In Witness Whereof, the Register of the Treasury in pursuance of said Act of Congress hath hereunto set his hand, and affixed the Seal of the Treasury at Richmond, this second day of March 1863.
SEVEN PER CENT
Entered
Recorded
Register of the Treasury
SEVEN PER CENT

C. S. Loan Feby 20th 1863. The Confederate States of America will pay to bearer Thirty-Five Dollars for Six Months Interest due July 1st 1868 on Bond No 21122 for $1000.
C. S. Loan Feby 20th 1863. The Confederate States of America will pay to bearer Thirty-Five Dollars for Six Months Interest due Jany 1st 1868 on Bond No 21122 for $1000.
C. S. Loan Feby 20th 1863. The Confederate States of America will pay to bearer Thirty-Five Dollars for Six Months Interest due July 1st 1867 on Bond No 21122 for $1000.
C. S. Loan Feby 20th 1863. The Confederate States of America will pay to bearer Thirty-Five Dollars for Six Months Interest due Jany 1st 1867 on Bond No 21122 for $1000.
C. S. Loan Feby 20th 1863. The Confederate States of America will pay to bearer Thirty-Five Dollars for Six Months Interest due July 1st 1866 on Bond No 21122 for $1000.
C. S. Loan Feby 20th 1863. The Confederate States of America will pay to bearer Thirty-Five Dollars for Six Months Interest due Jany 1st 1866 on Bond No 21122 for $1000.
C. S. Loan Feby 20th 1863. The Confederate States of America will pay to bearer Thirty-Five Dollars for Six Months Interest due July 1st 1865 on Bond No 21122 for $1000.
C. S. Loan Feby 20th 1863. The Confederate States of America will pay to bearer Thirty-Five Dollars for Six Months Interest due Jany 1st 1865 on Bond No 21122 for $1000.

(Lt. General Thomas R. "Stonewall" Jackson, center)

TYPE 138 **$1,000**
Imprint: "Archer & Daly, Richmond, Va"; lithographed.

240. $1,000 Printed on white paper, no series[105] fine very fine
Number issued: c. 70 (#1-70, remainders) Rarity (7+) $6,000 $7,500
Date of issue: July 28, 1863
Signed by Rose.

241. $1,000 Printed on dark pink paper, no series.
Number issued: 34,891 (#71-39361, less B245-256) Rarity (2+) $125 $175
Dates of issue: July 28, 1863 - January 1, 1864
Signed by Rose, Tyler.

245. $1,000 As last, but two line red overprint on the face, "This Bond...who issues it."
Issued from and endorsed by H.J.G. Battle, CSA depositary, Shreveport, La.
Number issued: c. 700 (#23701-24400) Rarity (5+) $200 $250
Dates of issue: May to September 1864
Signed by Tyler.

248. $1,000 Three line red overprint on the face, "This Bond...to be issued." Issued
at Camden, Ark., by Edward Cross, erstwhile CSA depositary at Little Rock.
Number issued: c. 100 (#24801-24900) Rarity (7) $250 $350
Dates of issue: spring 1864
Signed by Rose.

249. $1,000 Three line red overprint, issued at Washington, Ark. by Edward Cross.
Number issued: 100 (#24701-24800) Rarity (7) $250 $350
Dates of issue: spring 1864
Signed by Rose.

250. $1,000 Same, three line red overprint, endorsed by depositary at Alexandria, La.
Number issued: c. 200 (#34001-34200) Rarity (7) $220 $300
Dates of issue: spring and summer, 1864
Signed by Tyler.

251. $1,000 Same, three line red overprint, endorsed by Alphonse Desmare, CSA depositary at Opelousas, La. on face.
Number issued: c. 260 (#25341-25400; #29801-30000) Rarity (7-) $259 $300
Dates of issue: September 1864 - February 1865
Signed by Tyler.

252. $1,000 As last, three line face overprint, issued on back at Shreveport, La. by H.J.G. Battle, CSA depositary.
Number issued: c. 2,100 (#27701-29800) Rarity (4+) $150 $200
Dates of issue: September 1864 - February 1865
Signed by Tyler, Rose.

255. $1,000 Three line red overprint on face, "This Bond...to be issued,"
black stamp, "Houston, Texas Depositary," signed by James Sorley.
Number issued: c. 900 (24401-25300) Rarity (6-) $200 $250
Dates of issue: spring 1864
Signed by Rose.

256. $1,000 Same as the preceding, but issued by Kellogg.
Number issued: c. 40 (c. #25301-25340) Rarity (7+) $400 $500
Dates of issue: probably spring 1864
Signed by Tyler.

D. 7% stock certificates
Total amount issued (all types): $12,758,100

IT IS HEREBY CERTIFIED THAT THE CONFEDERATE STATES OF AMERICA

$200 $200

No 3723 No 3723

Are indebted unto E L Tompkins Trustee for J H Cheney or assigns in the sum of Two Hundred Dollars redeemable after the first day of July 1868 with interest from the 28 day of July 1863 inclusive at SEVEN per cent per annum payable on the first days of January and July in each year. This debt is authorized by an Act of Congress, Entitled "An Act to authorize the issue of bonds for funding Treasury notes, approved February 20 1863, and is upon the express condition, that said Confederate States may from time to time extend the time of payment for any period not exceeding Thirty Years from this date at the same rate of interest, upon the surrender of the Certificate.

SEVEN PER CENT

ACT 20th FEBRUARY 1863

RICHMOND 13 Aug 1863

Entered

Recorded

J.T. Paterson & Co. Columbia, S.C.

Register of the Treasury

(Overseer with slaves in wheat field)

TYPE 139 various denominations
Imprint: "J.T. Paterson & Co., Columbia, S.C."; lithographed.

			fine	very fine
258.	Printed on thin, waxy white paper. Number issued: 6,311 (#1-6309, 143 $^1/_2$, 1360 $^1/_2$) Dates of issue: April 1, 1863 - March 23, 1865 Signed by Jones (c. #1-50) and Tyler (the residue).	Rarity (4+)	$200	$250

Denomination	Number issued	Rarity
$100	363	7-
$200	365	7-
$300	337	7-
$400	298	7
$500	819	6
$600	282	7
$700	216	7
$800	169	7-
$900	100	7-
$1,000	942	6
$1,050	1	—
$1,100	105	7-
$1,200	136	7-
$1,300	62	8
$1,350	1	—
$1,400	77	8
$1,500	173	7
$1,550	1	—
$1,600	52	8
$1,700	46	8
$1,800	38	8
$1,850	1	—
$1,900	20	8
$2,000	327	7-
$2,050	1	—
$2,100	26	8
$2,200	37	8
$2,250	1	—
$2,300	20	8
$2,400	25	8
$2,500	85	7-
$2,600	22	8
$2,650	1	—
$2,700	18	8
$2,800	19	8
$2,900	11	—
$3,000	130	7-
$3,100	11	—
$3,150	1	—
$3,200	15	8
$3,300	16	8
$3,400	21	8
$3,500	38	8
$3,600	7	—
$3,700	10	—
$3,800	10	—
$3,850	1	—
$3,900	13	8

Items without rarity numbers are not known to exist and may therefore not be collectable.

Denomination	Number issued	Rarity	Denomination	Number issued	Rarity
$4,000	98	7+	$9,900	1	—
$4,100	5	—	$10,000	76	7+
$4,200	6	—	$10,100	1	—
$4,250	1	—	$10,250	1	—
$4,300	4	—	$10,300	2	—
$4,400	4	—	$10,400	2	—
$4,500	24	8	$10,500	2	—
$4,600	4	—	$10,700	1	—
$4,700	4	—	$10,800	1	—
$4,800	4	—	$10,900	1	—
$4,900	5	—	$11,000	6	—
$5,000	154	7	$11,400	2	—
$5,200	4	—	$11,500	1	—
$5,250	1	—	$11,700	1	—
$5,300	5	—	$11,900	1	—
$5,400	3	—	$12,000	9	—
$5,500	9	—	$12,500	4	—
$5,600	6	—	$12,800	1	—
$5,700	4	—	$13,000	3	—
$5,800	3	—	$13,100	2	—
$5,900	2	—	$13,200	1	—
$6,000	45	8	$13,300	1	—
$6,050	1	—	$13,400	2	—
$6,100	2	—	$13,800	2	—
$6,200	3	—	$14,000	1	—
$6,300	1	—	$14,200	1	—
$6,400	1	—	$14,300	2	—
$6,500	9	—	$14,400	1	—
$6,600	4	—	$14,700	1	—
$6,700	3	—	$15,000	8	8
$6,800	3	—	$16,200	1	—
$7,000	22	8	$16,500	1	—
$7,100	3	—	$17,300	1	—
$7,200	1	—	$17,500	1	—
$7,300	2	—	$18,000	1	—
$7,400	1	—	$18,300	1	—
$7,500	5	—	$18,800	1	—
$7,600	1	—	$19,000	1	—
$7,700	3	—	$19,400	1	—
$7,900	1	—	$19,900	1	—
$8,000	27	8	$20,000	25	8
$8,100	2	—	$20,200	1	—
$8,300	4	—	$20,300	1	—
$8,500	3	—	$20,500	2	—
$8,600	3	—	$21,000	1	—
$9,000	11	—	$22,000	1	—
$9,300	1	—	$22,300	1	—
$9,500	3	—	$22,700	3	—
$9,550	1	—	$23,000	5	—
$9,600	1	—	$23,300	1	—
$9,800	3	—	$23,800	1	—

Items without rarity numbers are not known to exist and may therefore not be collectable.

Denomination	Number issued	Rarity
$24,000	1	—
$24,400	1	—
$24,500	1	—
$25,000	16	7+
$25,500	1	—
$25,900	1	—
$26,500	2	—
$27,000	2	—
$27,700	1	—
$29,000	1	—
$29,100	1	—
$30,000	3	—
$30,100	4	—
$32,000	1	—
$33,000	1	—
$33,200	1	—
$34,000	1	—
$35,000	3	—
$35,200	1	—
$36,000	1	—
$36,900	1	—
$39,200	1	—
$40,000	3	—
$42,000	1	—
$49,800	1	—
$50,000	23	7+
$51,000	1	—
$54,400	1	—
$55,000	1	—
$59,400	1	—
$60,000	1	—
$61,900	1	—
$64,500	1	—
$64,700	1	—
$65,000	1	—
$70,000	2	—
$75,100	1	—
$79,600	1	—
$80,000	1	—
$83,800	1	—
$85,400	1	—
$100,000	16	7+
$101,900	1	—
$110,400	1	—
$115,200	1	—
$130,000	1	—
$180,000	1	—
$200,000	1	—
$300,000	1	—

Items without rarity numbers are not known to exist and may therefore not be collectable.

Note: eighteen additional pieces are not listed in the table.

X. ACT OF MARCH 23, 1863

The bonds and call certificates of the Act of March 23, 1863 had their origins in two pieces of legislation: the Act of October 13, 1862 and the March act itself. Under the terms of the second act, the secretary was authorized to issue $50 million a month in notes. To fund these, he was authorized to issue 6% coupon or registered bonds together with an issue of 5% call certificates. Given the immense amount of treasury note printing that had to be attended to in Columbia, with Keatinge and Ball preparing the plates and printing the $100 and $50 notes and Evans & Cogswell and Paterson dividing the printing of the lower denominations between them, there was precious little time to do any bonds there. Indeed, as noted, some of the $1 and $2 notes had to be subcontracted to Hoyer & Ludwig.

Given the fact that Archer & Daly (or Archer and Halpin) was tied up producing stamps for the post office at this time, this left the task of designing the new bonds to George Dunn. Dunn produced three 6% coupon bonds modeled on the old customs house, which was then the treasury and the executive office building, where Davis had an office in addition to the one he used in his own home. The bonds with the word "Engraved" came first, followed by those with the abbreviation "Engd." At least some of the $1000s were done by Evans & Cogswell at the end of the run in early 1864, as their imprint will testify.

Similarly, the 6% cotton press registered bond was engraved by Dunn and printed by Evans & Cogswell in Columbia, from Dunn's plate. Dunn also engraved the 5% call certificate, with sailing ship, but handled the printing himself. All these bonds were a cut above what had heretofore been done by the other printers, and this despite the fact that Dunn was not a copper or steel plate engraver, but only a very skilled lithographer.

The next piece of business was undertaken because of the need to prepare the 4% coupon and registered bonds for the funding of the December 2, 1862 notes after August 1, 1863, together with the accompanying 4% call certificates. It was apparently decided that the demand for registered bonds would not be great enough to warrant the preparation of a plate, and plans for the issue of such a security were scrapped. Dunn, according to the books listing the warrants issued by the treasury, was paid for engraving the coupon bonds, although they do not bear any imprint. The bonds, with the equestrian statue of George Washington to the west of the capitol building in Richmond, were actually printed by Hoyer & Ludwig, who had excess capacity and could therefore be given this work without delaying more vital matters. Two thousand-seven hundred to twenty-nine hundred bonds of each denomination were manufactured in a first printing: later 1700 more were done of the $100 and $500. A further 1900 were made of the $1000. The vignette on these bonds had been used before and would be used again on the $100, $500, and $1,000 6% coupon bonds of February 17, 1864

That left only the 4% call certificates to be supplied. Again, Dunn engraved and printed these. The $1000 showed a James River scene with the old church tower at Jamestown in the background. Since Federal troops had overrun that portion of Virginia in early 1862, perhaps Dunn worked from a photograph. Similarly, the $5000, the only other call certificate denomination employed, showed a pre-bombardment picture of Fort Sumter, outside Charleston harbor, but from the sea side. This vignette was reused by Dunn in late 1864 to make the last issue of treasury warrants. All of these call certificates were redeemed in early 1864 and destroyed; hence their existence only as remainders, with two proof $5000s. There are precious few survivors, even as remainders.

Based on the recent discover of an uncut pair of B276 call certificates in a junk box during an auction in Southside Virginia, it is now known with certainty that B276 and 277 were printed two to a sheet. The $1000 call certificates have such a narrow margin between the certificates that a well margined specimen is practically impossible to secure.

A. 6% coupon bonds [106]

Total amount issued (all types): $15,941,300

For the further issue of bonds of varieties 258, 260, 265, see numbers 369-371.

ONE HUNDRED DOLLARS

Confederate STATES OF AMERICA.

No 131 — No 131

LOAN AUTHORIZED BY Act of Congress. C.S.A. OF MARCH 23rd 1863.

SIX PER CENT — ACT MARCH 23rd 1863

On the first day of April 1893 The Confederate States of America will pay to the Bearer of this Bond at the Seat of Government, or at such place of Deposit as may be appointed by the Secretary of the Treasury, the sum of ONE HUNDRED DOLLARS with interest from date at the rate of Six per cent per annum payable semi-annually, on the surrender of the annexed Coupons. This contract is authorized by an Act of Congress approved March 23rd 1863, Entitled "An Act to provide for the funding and further issue of Treasury Notes," and is upon the express condition that it shall be redeemable five years after date at the pleasure of the Government.

Semi-annual Coupons are hereunto attached for the said period of five years, after which should this Bond not be redeemed, another Bond for the same amount with semi-annual Coupons at the same rate of interest for the remainder of the thirty years, will be delivered to the holder, upon the surrender of this Bond.

In Witness Whereof, the Register of the Treasury in pursuance of the said Act of Congress hath hereunto set his hand and affixed the seal of the Treasury at Richmond, this first day of April 1863.

Entered — Recorded —

Register of the Treasury

C.S. Loan of March 23rd 1863. The Confederate States of America Will pay to Bearer the sum of THREE DOLLARS, For Six Months Interest due ... On Bond No 131 For $100. For Register of the Treasury B.B. Jones (seven coupons)

(Vignette of old U.S. customs house [now post office], then the CSA executive offices and Treasury Department)

TYPE 140 **$100**

Engraved and printed by George Dunn & Co., Richmond, Va.

				fine	very fine
259.	$100	"Engraved by Geo. Dunn & Compy. Richmond, Va" at lower left corner; printed on white paper. Number issued: c. 1,900 (#1-1900) Dates of issue: c. October 2, 1863 - February 29, 1864 Signed by Jones (c. #1-400) and Rose (c. #401-1900).	Rarity (4+)	$45	$50

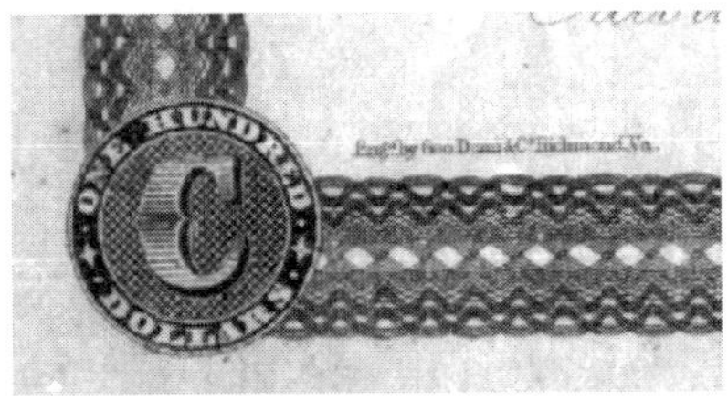

260.	$100	"Engd. by Geo. Dunn & Co., Richmond, Va."; printed on white paper. Number issued: c. 2,968 (#1901-4868) Dates of issue: March 1, 1864 - February 6, 1865 Signed by Tyler (c. #1901-2200) and Rose (#2201-4868) less a few Apperson (± 4726).	Rarity (4-)	$40	$50

TYPE 141 **$500**

Engraved and printed by George Dunn & Co., Richmond, Virginia

261.	$500	Design as preceding, except for denomination. "Engraved by Geo. Dunn & Compy. Richmond, Va"; on white paper. Number issued: c. 1,900 (#1-1900) Dates of issue: September 23, 1863 - February 29, 1864 Signed by Rose, a few by Tyler.	Rarity (4+)	$45	$50
262.	$500	As last, but "Engd. by Geo. Dunn & Co. Richmond, Va"; on white paper. Number issued: c. 451 (#1901-2351) Dates of issue: c. March 1, 1864 - February 6, 1865 Signed by Rose.	Rarity (5+)	$125	$200

TYPE 142 **$1,000**

ONE THOUSAND DOLLARS

Confederate STATES OF AMERICA.

No 88

LOAN AUTHORIZED BY Act of Congress C.S.A. MARCH 23rd 1863.

SIX PER CENT

ACT MARCH 23rd 1863

On the first day of April 1893 The Confederate States of America will pay to the Bearer of this Bond, at the Seat of Government, or at such place of Deposit as may be appointed by the Secretary of the Treasury, the sum of ONE THOUSAND DOLLARS with interest from date, at the rate of Six per cent per annum, payable semi-annually, on the surrender of the annexed Coupons. This contract is authorized by an Act of Congress approved March 23rd 1863, Entitled "An Act to provide for the funding and further issue of Treasury Notes" and is upon the express condition that it shall be redeemable five years after date, at the pleasure of the Government.

Semi annual Coupons are hereunto attached for the said period of five years, after which, should this Bond not be redeemed, another Bond for the same amount, with semi-annual Coupons, at the same rate of interest for the remainder of the thirty years, will be delivered to the holder, upon the surrender of this Bond.

In Witness Whereof, the Register of the Treasury, in pursuance of the said Act of Congress, hath hereunto set his hand, and affixed the seal of the Treasury, at Richmond, this first day of April 1863.

Entered
Recorded

Register of the Treasury

C.S. Loan of March 23rd 1863. The Confederate States of America Will pay to Bearer the sum of THIRTY DOLLARS. For Six Months Interest due April 1st 1868 On Bond No 88 For $1,000 For Register of the Treasury

C.S. Loan of March 23rd 1863. The Confederate States of America Will pay to Bearer the sum of THIRTY DOLLARS. For Six Months Interest due Oct. 1st 186 On Bond No 88 For $1,000 For Register of the Treasury

C.S. Loan of March 23rd 1863. The Confederate States of America Will pay to Bearer the sum of THIRTY DOLLARS. For Six Months Interest due April 1st 1867 On Bond No 88 For $1,000 For Register of the Treasury

C.S. Loan of March 23rd 1863. The Confederate States of America Will pay to Bearer the sum of THIRTY DOLLARS. For Six Months Interest due Oct. 1st 1866 On Bond No 88 For $1,000 For Register of the Treasury

Engraved and printed by George Dunn & Co., Richmond, Virginia

263. $1,000 Design as preceding, except for denomination. "Engraved by Geo. Dunn & Compy. Richmond, Va," at lower left corner; printed on white paper. Some coupons for October 1, 1867 missing the "7" (handwritten).

	fine	very fine
Number issued: c. 1,800 (#1-1800) — Rarity (5-)	$45	$60

Dates of issue: October 5 - 20, 1863

Signed by Rose, a few by Jones.

				fine	very fine
264.	$1,000	"Geo. Dunn & Co., Richmond, Va" at bottom center; printed on white paper.			
		Number issued: c. 2,000 (#1801-3800)	Rarity (4+)	$45	$60
		Dates of issue: October 5, 1863 - February 6, 1864			
		Signed by Rose.			

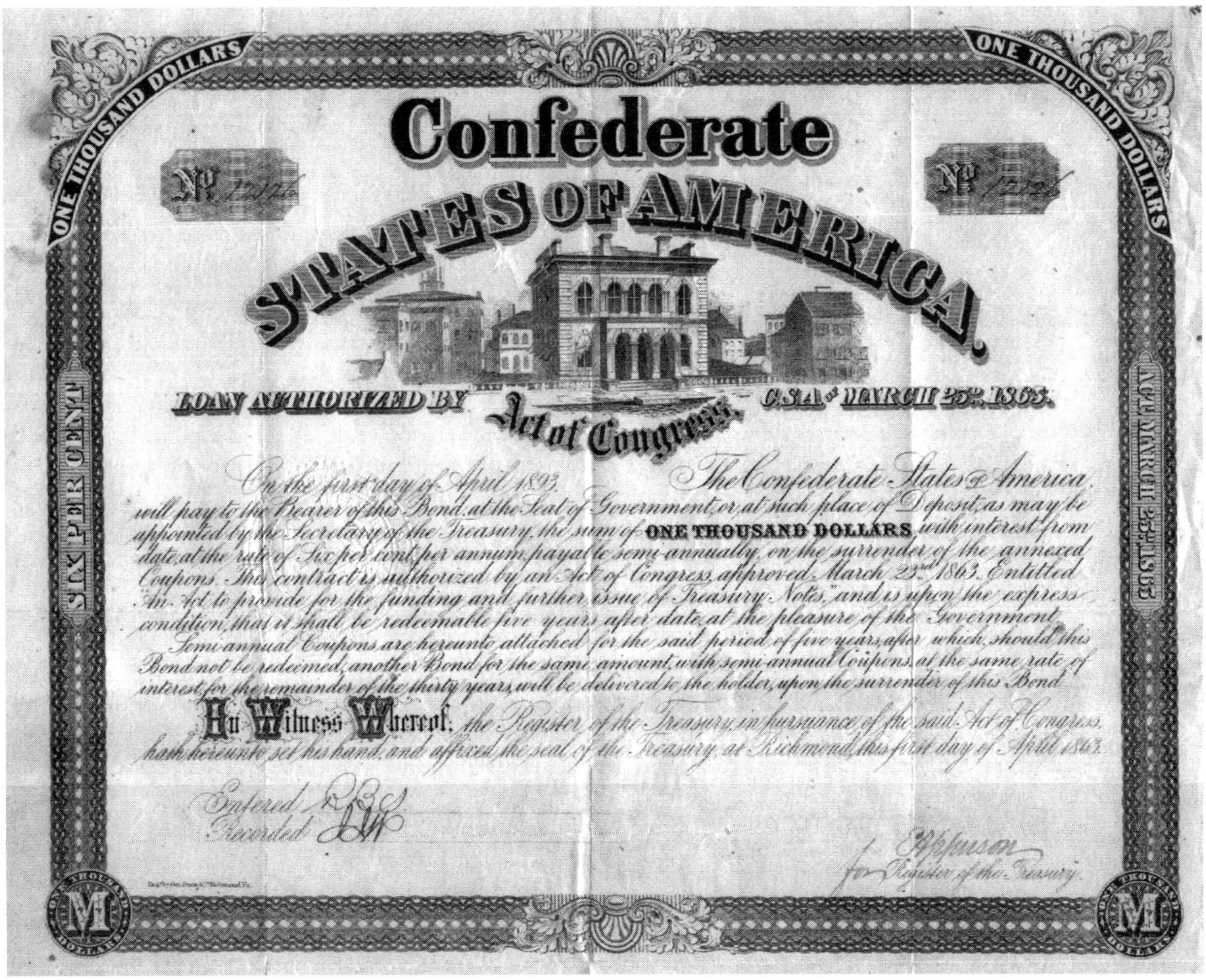
ONE THOUSAND DOLLARS

Confederate STATES OF AMERICA.

LOAN AUTHORIZED BY Act of Congress C.S.A. OF MARCH 23rd 1863.

SIX PER CENT

ACT OF MARCH 23rd 1863

On the first day of April 1893 The Confederate States of America will pay to the Bearer of this Bond at the Seat of Government, or at such place of Deposit as may be appointed by the Secretary of the Treasury, the sum of ONE THOUSAND DOLLARS with interest from date at the rate of Six per cent per annum payable semi-annually, on the surrender of the annexed Coupons. This contract is authorized by an Act of Congress approved March 23rd 1863. Entitled "An Act to provide for the funding and further issue of Treasury Notes," and is upon the express condition, that it shall be redeemable five years after date at the pleasure of the Government.

Semi-annual Coupons are hereunto attached for the said period of five years, after which, should this Bond not be redeemed, another Bond for the same amount, with semi-annual Coupons at the same rate of interest for the remainder of the thirty years, will be delivered to the holder, upon the surrender of this Bond.

In Witness Whereof, the Register of the Treasury in pursuance of the said Act of Congress, hath hereunto set his hand and affixed the seal of the Treasury at Richmond this first day of April 1863.

Entered

Recorded

Apperson

for Register of the Treasury

				fine	very fine
265.	$1,000	"Engd. by Geo. Dunn & Co., Richmond, Va."; name 12 mm from left border. Printed on white paper.			
		Number issued: c. 2,300 (#3801-5800; 8701-8800; 9800-10000)	Rarity (3+)	$50	$65
		Dates of issue: October 20 - November 13, 1863			
		Signed by Rose, Apperson, a few by Tyler.			

ONE THOUSAND DOLLARS — ONE THOUSAND DOLLARS

No 7800 — No 7800

Confederate
STATES OF AMERICA.

LOAN AUTHORIZED BY Act of Congress C.S.A. MARCH 23rd 1863.

SIX PER CENT — ACT MARCH 23rd 1863

On the first day of April 1893 The Confederate States of America will pay to the Bearer of this Bond at the Seat of Government or at such place of Deposit as may be appointed by the Secretary of the Treasury, the sum of ONE THOUSAND DOLLARS with interest from date at the rate of Six per cent per annum, payable semi-annually, on the surrender of the annexed Coupons. This contract is authorized by an Act of Congress approved March 23rd 1863, Entitled "An Act to provide for the funding and further issue of Treasury Notes," and is upon the express condition that it shall be redeemable five years after date, at the pleasure of the Government.
Semi-annual Coupons are hereunto attached for the said period of five years, after which should this Bond not be redeemed, another Bond for the same amount, with semi-annual Coupons, at the same rate of interest for the remainder of the thirty years, will be delivered to the holder, upon the surrender of this Bond.

In Witness Whereof, the Register of the Treasury, in pursuance of the said Act of Congress, hath hereunto set his hand and affixed the seal of the Treasury, at Richmond, this first day of April 1863.

Entered / Recorded

Register of the Treasury

M — ONE THOUSAND DOLLARS — M

C.S. Loan of March 23rd 1863.
The Confederate States of America
Will pay to Bearer the sum of THIRTY DOLLARS.
For Six Months Interest due April 1st 1868.
On Bond No 7800 For $1,000
For Register of the Treasury

C.S. Loan of March 23rd 1863.
The Confederate States of America
Will pay to Bearer the sum of THIRTY DOLLARS.
For Six Months Interest due Oct 1st 1867.
On Bond No 7800 For $1,000
For Register of the Treasury

C.S. Loan of March 23rd 1863.
The Confederate States of America
Will pay to Bearer the sum of THIRTY DOLLARS.
For Six Months Interest due April 1st 1867.
On Bond No 7800 For $1,000
For Register of the Treasury

C.S. Loan of March 23rd 1863.
The Confederate States of America
Will pay to Bearer the sum of THIRTY DOLLARS.
For Six Months Interest due Oct 1st 1866.
On Bond No 7800 For $1,000
For Register of the Treasury

C.S. Loan of March 23rd 1863.
The Confederate States of America
Will pay to Bearer the sum of THIRTY DOLLARS.
For Six Months Interest due April 1st 1866.
On Bond No 7800 For $1,000
For Register of the Treasury

C.S. Loan of March 23rd 1863.
The Confederate States of America
Will pay to Bearer the sum of THIRTY DOLLARS.
For Six Months Interest due Oct 1st 1865.
On Bond No 7800 For $1,000
For Register of the Treasury

C.S. Loan of March 23rd 1863.
The Confederate States of America
Will pay to Bearer the sum of THIRTY DOLLARS.
For Six Months Interest due April 1st 1865.
On Bond No 7800 For $1,000
For Register of the Treasury

			fine	very fine
266.	$1,000	Same, but name 22 mm from left border; printed on white paper.		
		Number issued: c. 6,400 (#5801-8700; 8801-9800; 10001-12500) Rarity (3)	$35	$50
		Dates of issue: November 6, 1863 - January 22, 1864		
		Signed by Rose.		

ONE THOUSAND DOLLARS ONE THOUSAND DOLLARS

Confederate STATES OF AMERICA.

No 14773 No 14773

LOAN AUTHORIZED BY Act of Congress C.S.A. of MARCH 23rd 1863.

SIX PER CENT ACT MARCH 23rd 1863

On the first day of April 1893, The Confederate States of America will pay to the Bearer of this Bond at the Seat of Government, or at such place of Deposit as may be appointed by the Secretary of the Treasury, the sum of ONE THOUSAND DOLLARS with interest from date at the rate of Six per cent per annum payable semi-annually, on the surrender of the annexed Coupons. This contract is authorized by an Act of Congress approved March 23rd 1863, Entitled "An Act to provide for the funding and further issue of Treasury Notes," and is upon the express condition that it shall be redeemable five years after date, at the pleasure of the Government.

Semi annual Coupons are hereunto attached for the said period of five years after which, should this Bond not be redeemed, another Bond for the same amount with semi annual Coupons, at the same rate of interest for the remainder of the thirty years, will be delivered to the holder, upon the surrender of this Bond.

In Witness Whereof, the Register of the Treasury, in pursuance of the said Act of Congress, hath hereunto set his hand and affixed the seal of the Treasury at Richmond this first day of April 1863.

Entered

Recorded

Register of the Treasury.

PRINTED BY EVANS & COGSWELL, COLUMBIA, S.C.

C.S. Loan of March 23rd 1863 The Confederate States of America Will pay to Bearer the sum of THIRTY DOLLARS. For Six Months Interest due April 1st 1868. On Bond No 14773 For $1,000 For Register of the Treasury

C.S. Loan of March 23rd 1863. The Confederate States of America Will pay to Bearer the sum of THIRTY DOLLARS. For Six Months Interest due Oct. 1st 1867 On Bond No 14773 For $1,000. For Register of the Treasury

C.S. Loan of March 23rd 1863. The Confederate States of America Will pay to Bearer the sum of THIRTY DOLLARS. For Six Months Interest due April 1st 1867. On Bond No 14773 For $1,000 For Register of the Treasury

C.S. Loan of March 23rd 1863 The Confederate States of America Will pay to Bearer the sum of THIRTY DOLLARS. For Six Months Interest due Oct. 1st 1866. On Bond No 14773 For $1,000 For Register of the Treasury

				fine	very fine
267.	$1,000	"Printed by Evans & Cogswell, Columbia, S.C." at bottom center; printed on white paper.			
		Number issued: c. 1779 (#12501-14279)	Rarity (4)	$45	$65
		Dates of issue: January 22 - February 6, 1864			
		Signed by Rose, a few by Apperson.			

B. 6% stock certificates
Total amount issued (all types): $5,023,800

SIX PER CENT.

ACT 23. MARCH 1863.

It is hereby Certified, that the

No. 154 No. 154

$ 500 CONFEDERATE STATES OF AMERICA, $ 500

are indebted unto or Assigns in the sum of Dollars redeemable on the first day of April 1893 with interest from the 1st day of Sept 1863, inclusive at SIX PER CENT PER ANNUM, Payable on the first days of January and July in each Year.

This Contract is Authorized by an Act of Congress approved 23rd March 1863, entitled "An Act to provide for the funding and further issue of Treasury Notes" and is upon the express condition, that it shall be redeemable five years after date at the pleasure of the Government.

Entered

Recorded

RICHMOND, 7 Nov 1863

Register of the Treasury.

Lithogd by Evans & Cogswell

(cotton gin and cotton press)

TYPE 143 various denominations
Imprint: Engd. by Geo. Dunn & Co., Richmond Va. Lithgd. by Evans & Cogswell

			fine	very fine
268.	Printed on white paper.			
	Number issued: 1,620 (#1-1620, plus remainders)	Rarity (5+)	$900	$1,250
	Dates of issue: October 15, 1863 - March 25, 1865			
	Signed by Tyler.			

Denomination	Number issued	Rarity
$100	75	7
$200	71	7
$300	65	7
$400	60	7
$500	175	7
$600	71	7
$700	34	8
$800	39	8
$900	17	8
$1,000	240	7
$1,100	21	8
$1,200	37	8
$1,300	21	8
$1,400	12	—
$1,500	70	7
$1,600	14	—
$1,700	16	8
$1,800	10	—
$1,900	6	—
$2,000	78	7
$2,100	6	—
$2,200	14	8

Denomination	Number issued	Rarity
$2,300	9	—
$2,400	5	—
$2,500	29	8
$2,600	2	—
$2,700	11	8
$2,800	9	—
$2,900	3	—
$3,000	53	8
$3,100	2	—
$3,200	2	—
$3,300	3	—
$3,400	4	—
$3,500	10	—
$3,600	3	—
$3,700	3	—
$3,800	1	—
$3,900	1	—
$4,000	32	8
$4,100	2	—
$4,200	5	—
$4,300	1	—
$4,400	3	—

Items without rarity numbers are not known to exist and may therefore not be collectable.

Denomination	Number issued	Rarity
$4,500	19	8
$4,600	2	—
$4,700	2	—
$4,800	3	—
$5,000	43	8
$5,100	2	—
$5,200	3	—
$5,300	1	—
$5,400	2	—
$5,500	5	—
$5,600	1	—
$5,800	2	—
$6,000	19	8
$6,200	1	—
$6,300	2	—
$6,400	2	—
$6,500	4	—
$6,600	4	—
$6,700	2	—
$6,900	1	—
$7,000	9	—
$7,200	1	—
$7,600	1	—
$7,700	1	—
$8,000	9	—
$8,300	1	—
$8,500	2	—
$8,900	1	—
$9,000	8	—
$9,300	1	—
$9,500	4	—
$9,700	1	—
$10,000	23	8
$10,700	1	—
$11,000	5	—
$11,300	2	—
$11,600	1	—
$11,800	2	—
$12,000	7	—
$13,000	4	—
$13,400	1	—
$15,000	1	—
$16,000	2	—
$17,500	1	—
$19,000	1	—
$20,000	29	8
$22,500	1	—
$23,000	1	—
$23,500	1	—
$24,500	1	—
$22,000	3	—
$25,000	4	—
$26,000	1	—
$27,000	1	—
$30,000	4	—
$30,300	1	—
$33,100	1	—
$34,500	1	—
$35,000	1	—
$36,400	1	—
$39,000	1	—
$40,000	2	—
$42,600	1	—
$45,700	1	—
$46,200	1	—
$50,000	3	—
$70,800	1	—
$74,000	1	—
$100,000	1	—
$124,500	1	—
$300,000	1	—

Items without rarity numbers are not known to exist and may therefore not be collectable.

C. 4% coupon bonds[107]

Total amount issued (all types): $22,300[108]

4 PER CENT CSA INTEREST

ONE HUNDRED DOLLARS ONE HUNDRED DOLLARS

Confederate

No 9 No 9

STATES OF AMERICA.

LOAN AUTHORIZED BY Act of Congress, C.S.A. MARCH 23rd 1863.

FOUR PER CENT ACT MARCH 23, 1863

On the first day of April 1893 The Confederate States of America will pay to the Bearer of this Bond at the Seat of Government, or at such place of Deposit as may be appointed by the Secretary of the Treasury, the sum of ONE HUNDRED DOLLARS with interest from date at the rate of FOUR PER CENT per annum payable semi-annually, on the surrender of the annexed Coupons. This contract is authorized by an Act of Congress approved March 23rd 1863 Entitled "An Act to provide for the funding and further issue of Treasury Notes" and is upon the express condition that it shall be redeemable five years after date at the pleasure of the Government.

Semi annual Coupons are hereunto attached for the said period of five years, after which should this Bond not be redeemed, another Bond for the same amount with semi annual Coupons at the same rate of interest for the remainder of the thirty years, will be delivered to the holder, upon the surrender of this Bond.

In Witness Whereof, the Register of the Treasury in pursuance of the said Act of Congress hath hereunto set his hand and affixed the seal of the Treasury at Richmond this first day of April 1863.

Entered 37173

Recorded WCC

C. A. Rose

for Register of the Treasury

C.S. Loan of March 23rd 1863 — The Confederate States of America — Will pay to Bearer the sum of TWO DOLLARS — for Six Months Interest due — On Bond No 9 — For $ 100 — M. E. Bronaugh

(Washington equestrian monument [used in Confederate coat of arms] west of the Virginia capitol in Richmond. Photo by Katherine Wetzel from Eleanor S. Brockenbrough Library, The Museum of the Confederacy, Richmond, Virginia)

TYPE 144 **$100**

Engraved by George Dunn; printed by Hoyer & Ludwig.

				fine	very fine
269.	$100	Printed on white paper. Number issued: 13 (#1-13) Dates of issue: January 1, 1863 - August 9, 1864 Signed by Rose.	Rarity (8)[109]	$7,500	(-)
270.	$100	Same as the preceding, unissued. Number printed: c. 2,700 Unsigned.	Rarity (7-)	$1,500	(-)

TYPE 145 **$500**

Engraved by George Dunn; printed by Hoyer & Ludwig.

271.	$500	Design as preceding, except for denomination; printed on white paper. Number issued: 6 (#1-6)[110] Dates of issue: March 15 - December 21, 1864 Signed by Rose.	Rarity (7+)	$4,500	(-)
272.	$500	Same, unissued. Number printed: c. 2,700 Unsigned.	Rarity (6+)	$1,250	(-)

Table of rarities

8	=	1-3
7+	=	4-10
7	=	11-20
7-	=	21-35
6+	=	36-50
6	=	51-75
6-	=	76-100
5+	=	101-200
5	=	201-350
5-	=	351-500
4+	=	501-750
4	=	751-1000
4-	=	1001-1500
3+	=	1501-2500
3	=	2501-5000
3-	=	5001-7500
2+	=	7501-10,000
2	=	10,001-20,000
2-	=	20,001-35,000
1+	=	35,001-50,000
1	=	50,001-100,000
1-	=	100,000+

TYPE 146 **$1,000**

Engraved by George Dunn; printed by Hoyer & Ludwig.

				fine	very fine
273.	$1,000	Design as preceding, except for denomination; printed on white paper.			
		Number issued: 18 (#1-18)[111]	Rarity (7-)	$3,500	(-)
		Dates of issue: July 27 - August 9, 1864			
		Signed by Rose.			
274.	$1,000	Same, but unissued.			
		Number printed: c. 2,900	Rarity (6)	$500	(-)
		Unsigned.			

D. 5% call certificates
Total amount issued (all types): $70,729,030

$100000 Call Certificate Authorized by $100000
Act of Congress, March 23d 1863.
No. 4578 No. 4578
It is Hereby Certified that One Hundred Thousand Dollars in Treasury Notes, issued in the Month of January 1864 have been deposited in the Treasury at Charleston S.C. by the person to whom this Certificate is endorsed by the Treasurer, Assistant Treasurer, or Depositary at said place of Deposit, and that like Notes will be delivered to said person or his Order at the said place, or at the Treasury at Richmond at any time within Six Months from the first day of the said Month with Interest from the date of said indorsement at the rate of five per cent. per Annum, and if not so converted this Certificate shall be exchanged for Bonds, or Registered Stock of the Confederate States bearing Interest at the rate of six per cent. per Annum payable thirty years after date, redeemable at the pleasure of the Government any time after five years.
This Contract is authorized by an Act of Congress approved March 23d 1863.
Richmond January 1st 1864.
Entered
Recorded
Register of the Treasury.
Engd & Lithogd by Geo. Dunn & Compy.

(sailing ship, center)

TYPE 147 various denominations
Imprint: "Engraved & Lithographed by Geo. Dunn & Compy."

			fine	very fine
275.	Printed on white paper.			
	Number issued: c. 3,200 (#1-3200)[112]	Rarity (5+)	$220	$300
	Dates of issue: September 11, 1863 - February 16, 1864			
	Signed by Tyler.			

E. 4% call certificates
Total amount issued (all types): $1,825,000

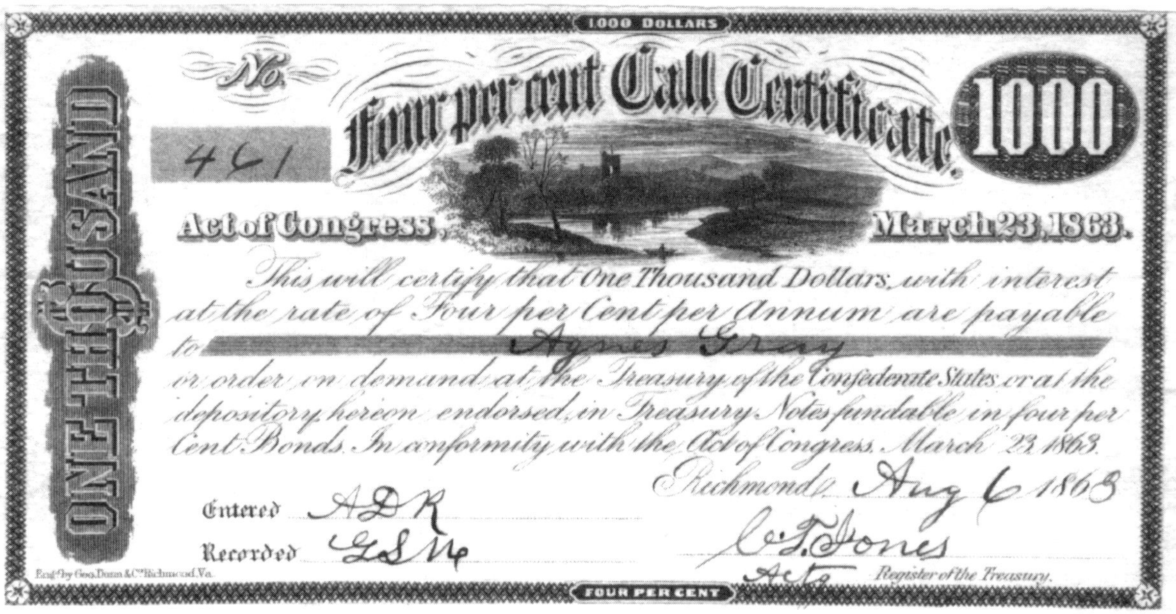

(ruins of Jamestown, Va., center)

TYPE 148 **$1,000**
Imprint: "Engd. by Geo. Dunn & Co. Richmond, Va."

276.	$1,000	Printed on white paper.		<u>fine-very fine</u>
		Number issued: 25 (#1-25, plus remainders)*	Rarity (7)[113]	$3,500
		Dates of issue: August 11 - November 3, 1863		
		Signed by: unknown[114]		

*all issued pieces redeemed and destroyed

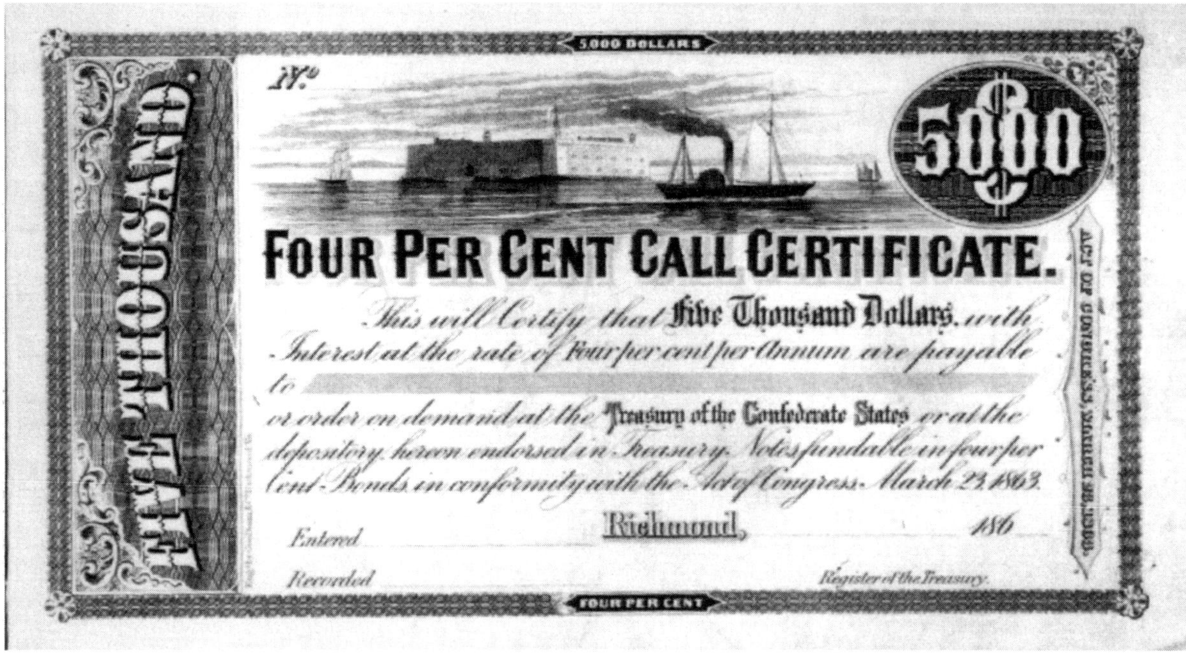

5,000 DOLLARS

No

5000

FIVE THOUSAND

FOUR PER CENT CALL CERTIFICATE.

This will Certify that Five Thousand Dollars, with Interest at the rate of Four per cent per Annum are payable to

or order on demand at the Treasury of the Confederate States or at the depository hereon endorsed in Treasury Notes fundable in four per cent Bonds in conformity with the Act of Congress March 23, 1863.

Entered Richmond, 186

Recorded Register of the Treasury.

ACT OF CONGRESS MARCH 23, 1863.

FOUR PER CENT

(Fort Sumter, center)

TYPE 149 **$5,000**

				<u>fine-very fine</u>
277.	$5,000	Printed on white paper. Number issued: 360 (#1-360, plus remainders)* Dates of issue: August 14 - December 9, 1863 Signed by: unknown	Rarity (7+)[115]	$10,000

*all issued pieces redeemed and destroyed

XI. ACT OF APRIL 27, 1863

(amendatory to the Act of April 12, 1862)

8% coupon bonds
Total amount authorized: $9,100.
Total amount issued: $9,100.

TYPE 150 **$100**
Imprint: "B. Duncan, Columbia, S.C."

278. $100 Similar to Ball 145 (type 120) but issued under this act. — fine / very fine
Number issued: 1 (#381)[116] — Rarity (8) — $1,200
Dates of issue: January 1865
Signed by Rose.

TYPE 151 **$500**
Imprint: "B. Duncan, Columbia, S.C."

279. $500 Similar to Ball 148 (type 121) but issued for the purposes of this act. — fine / very fine
Number issued: 18 (#5543-5560)[117] — Rarity (7) — $150
Dates of issue: January 1865
Signed by Rose.

XII. ACT OF APRIL 30, 1863

While the March 23, 1863 act was under consideration the congress added section 8 to that law providing for the issue of $100 million of 6% twenty year bonds to be sold to the highest bidder, after July 1, 1863, the bonds to be payable in currency or in cotton certificates payable in cotton of the quality of New Orleans middlings, the cotton to be valued at eight pence per pound and to be delivered at five designated ports (New Orleans, Mobile, Savannah, Charleston, or Wilmington.) Subsequently, according to the bonds themselves, congress passed an act on April 30, 1863 clarifying these points, deleting Wilmington from the list of ports. The bonds were to be sold to reduce the circulation and the coupons were payable in coin or cotton at the election of the government. For some reason the April 30, 1863 act does not appear in any of the volumes of the statutes at large, but is found only in handwritten form in the National Archives. It was either not sent to the publishers through an oversight or was regarded as a secret act. In any case, occupied as he was preparing the March 23rd Act bonds, George Dunn had to pass this job onto Evans and Cogswell.

Several plates were prepared and over 10,000 bonds printed before the order to cease production came from Richmond. The public reaction had not been as expected. Memminger had insisted upon selling the bonds at a 50% premium. The defeats in mid-1863 caused a collapse in confidence in the financial community, which suspected that the government would either renege on its promise to pay cotton in April 1864 (it did) or that it would soon cease to exist (it did). This bond was therefore a monument to the failure to put the treasury on a cotton basis as well as to the bad faith of a regime that had cotton to spare but that refused to pay what was promised, either in cotton or in coin.

Cotton interest bonds
Amount authorized: $200 million
Total amount issued (all types): $8,372,000 ($12,558,000 including premium)

TYPE 152 **$1,000**

Engraved by George Wojciechowski; printed by "Evans & Cogswell, Columbia, S.C."

(James A. Seddon of Va., CSA Secretary of War)

280. $1,000 Printed on white paper.[118]

	fine	very fine
Number issued: 8,372 (#1-8372) Rarity (3)	$50	$70

Dates of issue: July 28, 1863 - November 21, 1864

Signed by Tyler (c.#1-7000) and Jones (c. #7001-8372).

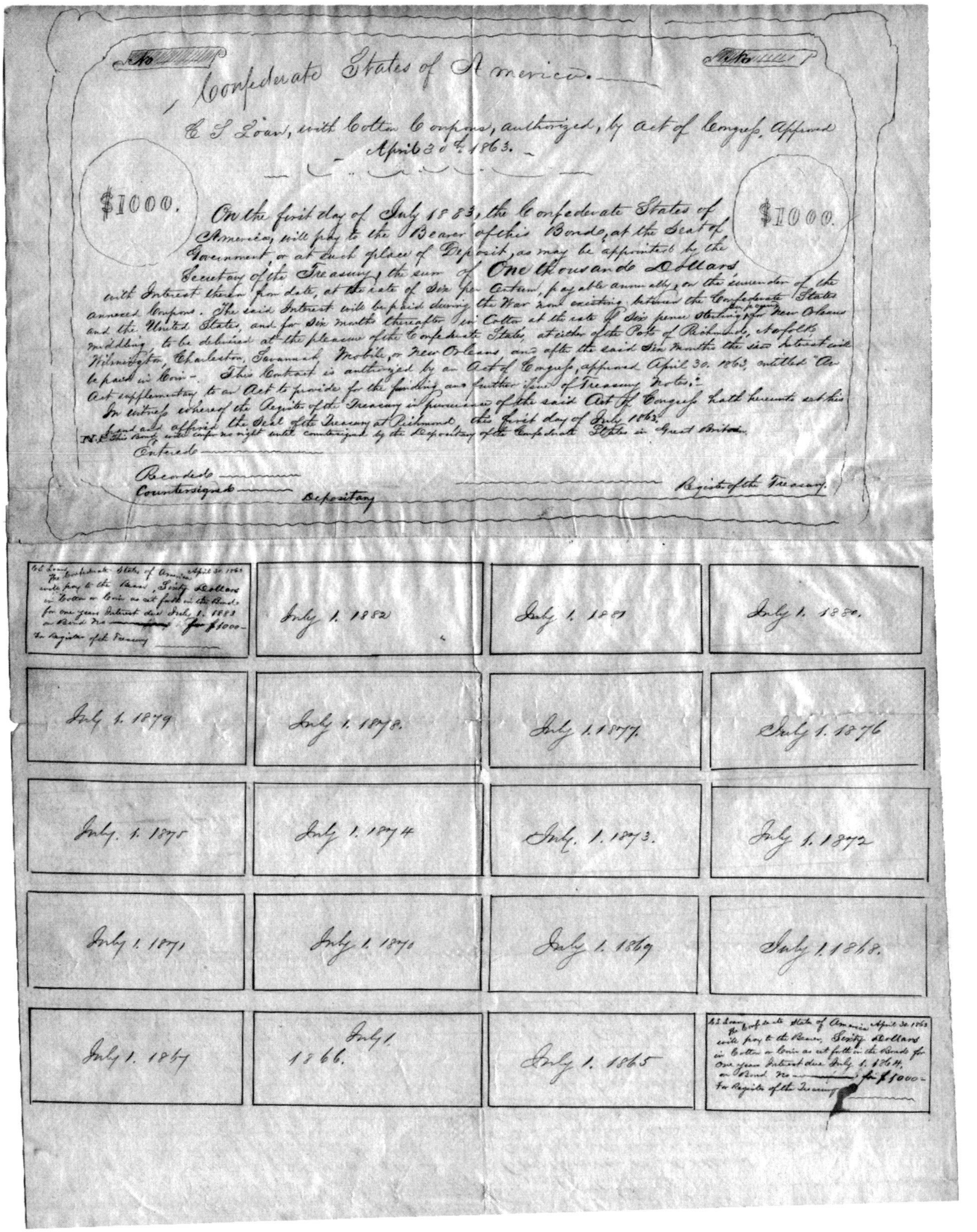

280. $1,000 Handwritten draft for the Act of April 30, 1863 on blue wove paper, pieces glued together; with hand-drawn coupons. Note the clause at the bottom, "This bond will confer no rights until countersigned by the Depositary of the Confederate States in Great Britain."[119]

Unique.	Rarity (8)	very fine $5,750

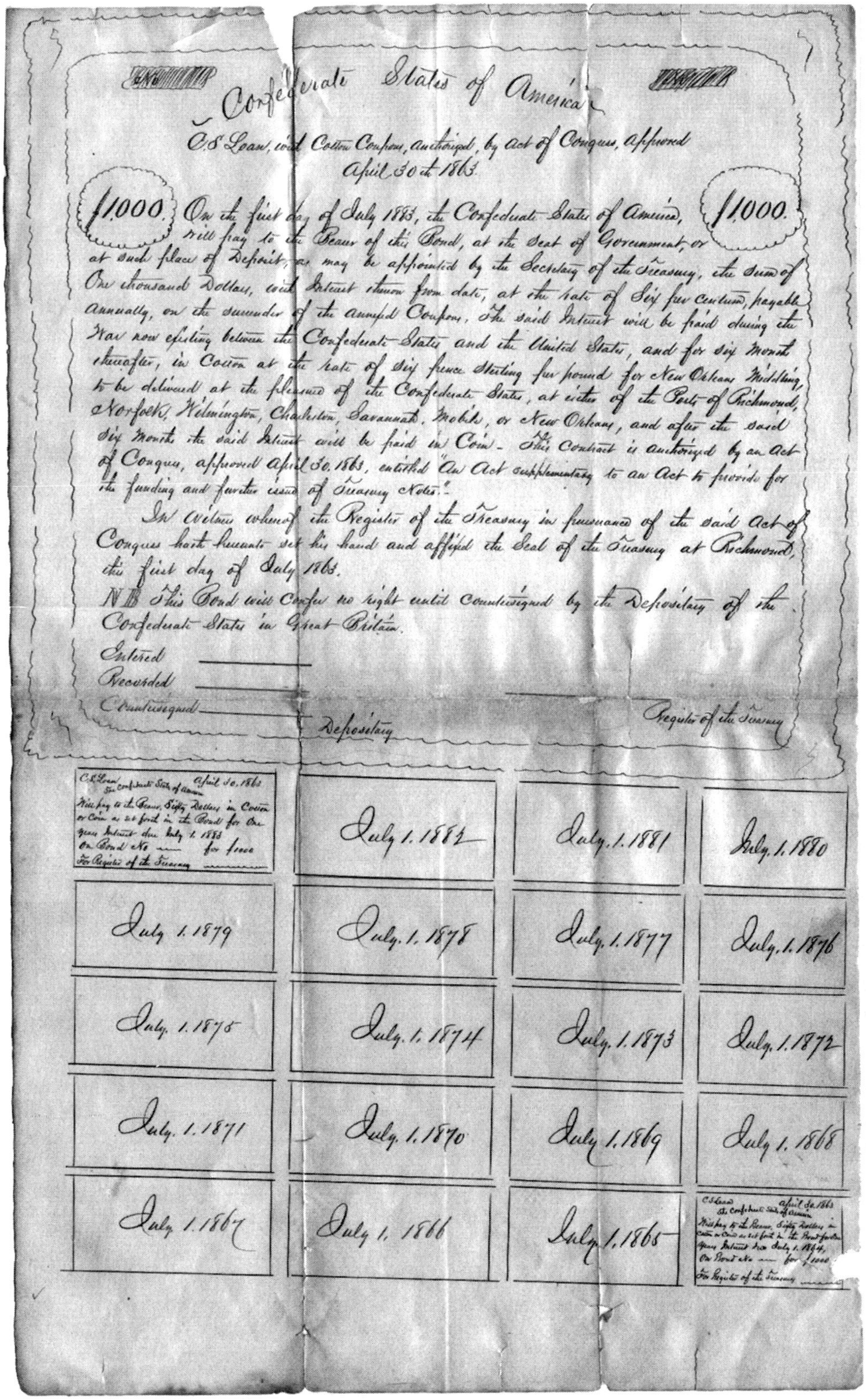

Confederate States of America

C.S. Loan, with Cotton Coupons, authorized, by Act of Congress, approved April 30th 1863.

$1000 On the first day of July 1883, the Confederate States of America, will pay to the Bearer of this Bond, at the Seat of Government, or at such place of Deposit, as may be appointed by the Secretary of the Treasury, the Sum of One thousand Dollars, with Interest thereon from date, at the rate of Six per centum, payable annually, on the surrender of the annexed Coupons. The said Interest will be paid during the War now existing between the Confederate States and the United States, and for six months thereafter, in Cotton at the rate of Six pence Sterling per pound for New Orleans Middling, to be delivered at the pleasure of the Confederate States, at either of the Ports of Richmond, Norfolk, Wilmington, Charleston, Savannah, Mobile, or New Orleans, and after the said Six Months the said Interest will be paid in Coin. This Contract is authorized by an Act of Congress, approved April 30, 1863, entitled "An Act supplementary to an Act to provide for the funding and further issue of Treasury Notes." $1000

In Witness whereof the Register of the Treasury in pursuance of the said Act of Congress hath hereunto set his hand and affixed the Seal of the Treasury at Richmond, this first day of July 1863.

N.B. This Bond will confer no right until countersigned by the Depository of the Confederate States in Great Britain.

Entered
Recorded
Countersigned
Depository
Register of the Treasury

C.S. Loan April 30, 1863 The Confederate States of America Will pay to the Bearer, Sixty Dollars in Cotton or Coin as set forth in the Bond for One years Interest due July 1, 1883 On Bond No ___ for $1000 For Register of the Treasury

July 1, 1882 | July 1, 1881 | July 1, 1880
July 1, 1879 | July 1, 1878 | July 1, 1877 | July 1, 1876
July 1, 1875 | July 1, 1874 | July 1, 1873 | July 1, 1872
July 1, 1871 | July 1, 1870 | July 1, 1869 | July 1, 1868
July 1, 1867 | July 1, 1866 | July 1, 1865

C.S. Loan April 30, 1863 The Confederate States of America Will pay to the Bearer, Sixty Dollars in Cotton or Coin as set forth in the Bond for One years Interest due July 1, 1864. On Bond No ___ for $1000 For Register of the Treasury

281. $1,000 Handwritten draft for the Act of April 30, 1863 on blue laid paper watermarked "T & FH Superfine 1862." Unique.

		<u>fine</u>	<u>very fine</u>
Unique.	Rarity (8)	$6,600	

XIII. ACT OF FEBRUARY 11, 1864

(amendatory to the Act of February 28, 1861)

When the Congress came back into session in December 1863, the Confederacy's financial affairs were in practically hopeless disorder. The country was overrun with Yankees, disgruntled and defeated Congressmen, deserters, and paper money; taxes were not coming in quickly and steps had to be taken to get the currency and debt reduced and in order. While these weighty matters were being taken in hand, Secretary Memminger passed on to the Congress a modest request relating to the registered bond holders of the February 28, 1861 issue.

Under the terms of the original act, the coupons of the coupon bonds of the February 28, 1861 act were made receivable for customs dues and export duties. So long as the bond interest was paid in coin (up to July 1, 1862), this distinction had little meaning, but once coin payments went into default, the coupon bonds became more desirable than the registered bonds. Secretary Memminger therefore asked the Congress to put the registered bonds on a par with the coupon bonds by allowing the government to issue special certificates for the amount of interest due, which could be presented for payment of import and export dues.

The secretary had hoped that this request would be routinely disposed of, and ordered George Dunn to prepare a plate with a payment date of January 1, 1864. Dunn did in fact prepare a plate with that date, but Congress dawdled and the payment day came and went. Only with the Congress ready to expire within a week did the members at last get around to authorizing the desired certificates in February 1864.

New plates were prepared for July 1, 1864 and January 1, 1865. Certificates were printed four to a sheet, those in 1864 on plain paper and those in 1865 on paper watermarked "CSA" in block letters and with a wavy border line. This paper was surplus, as it was no longer being used for currency printing. One certificate was prepared for each bond outstanding. Efforts to find out if the customs officers were obliged to make change, in the form of a new certificate less the amount of duty paid, have not been successful. We do know, however, that with General Sherman's invasion disrupting communications in central Georgia in late 1864, many of the certificates for 1865 could not be distributed to their owners and remained with the Treasury Department. They passed into the "rebel archives" when those were captured later in the year.

Stock certificate interest forms
Total amount issued (all types): c. $348,252 (regular amounts due)

These certificates were issued to pay interest on the stock (registered bonds) of the February 28, 1861 act and were usable for the payment of customs dues.

TYPE 153 various denominations
Imprint: "Eng. by Geo. Dunn & Co. Richmond, Va."

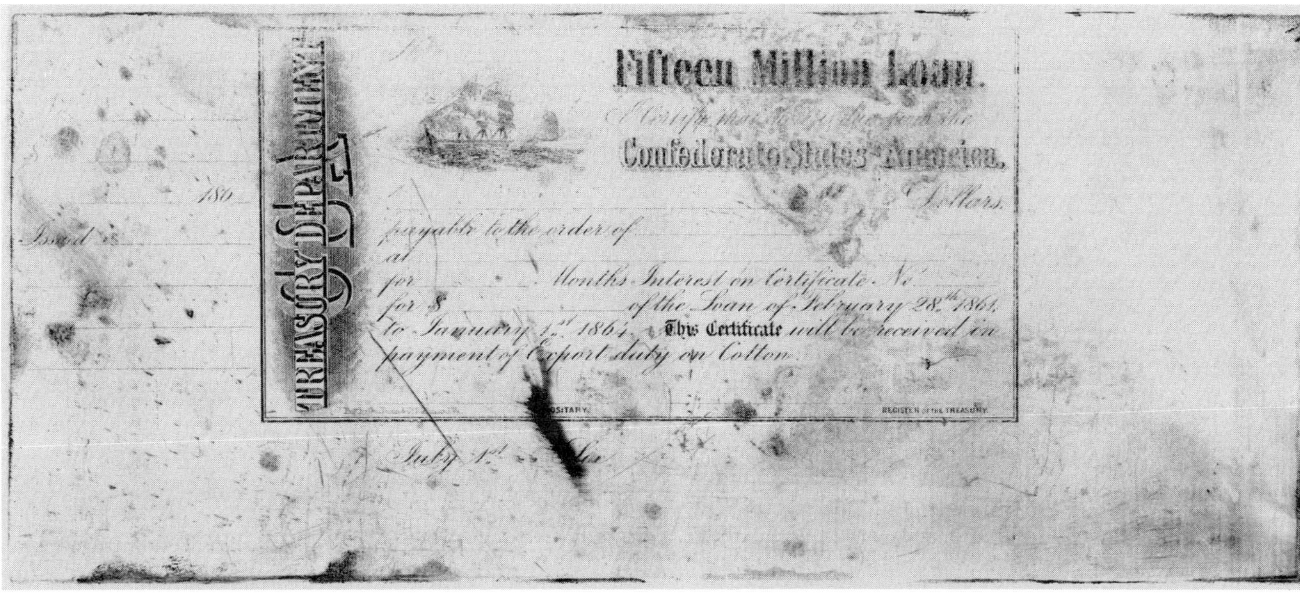

TREASURY DEPARTMENT C S

Fifteen Million Loan.

I Certify that there is due from the Confederate States of America

Dollars,

payable to the order of
at
for Months Interest on Certificate No.
for $ of the Loan of February 28th 1861,
to January 1st 1864. This Certificate will be received in
payment of Export duty on Cotton.

DEPOSITARY. REGISTER OF THE TREASURY.

283.	Printed on white paper.		unc
	Number issued: 10 (specimens only)	Rarity (7)	$500
	Dated January 1, 1864; unissued[120]		

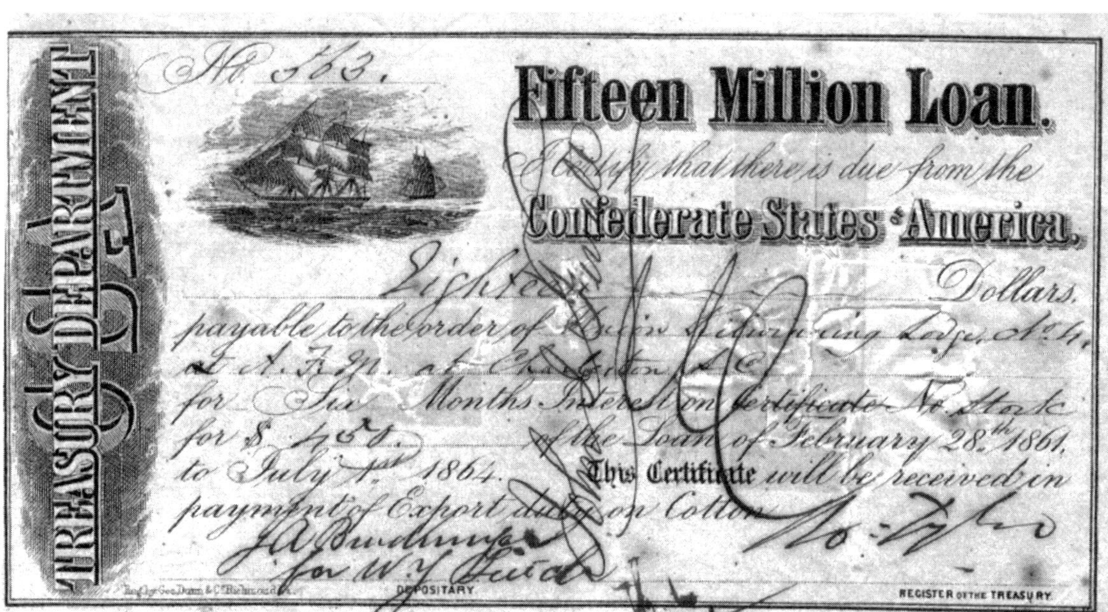

TREASURY DEPARTMENT C S

No. 563.

Fifteen Million Loan.

I Certify that there is due from the Confederate States of America

Dollars,

payable to the order of
at
for Six Months Interest on Certificate No.
for $ of the Loan of February 28th 1861,
to July 1st 1864. This Certificate will be received in
payment of Export duty on Cotton.

Eng. by Geo. Dunn & Co. Richmond Va. DEPOSITARY. REGISTER OF THE TREASURY.

(ship at top left)

TYPE 154 various denominations
Imprint: "Eng. by Geo. Dunn & Co. Richmond, Va."

			fine	ex fine
284.	Printed on white paper. Number issued: c. 2,760 Dates of issue: July - August 1864 Signed by Tyler.	Rarity (6+)	$350	$600

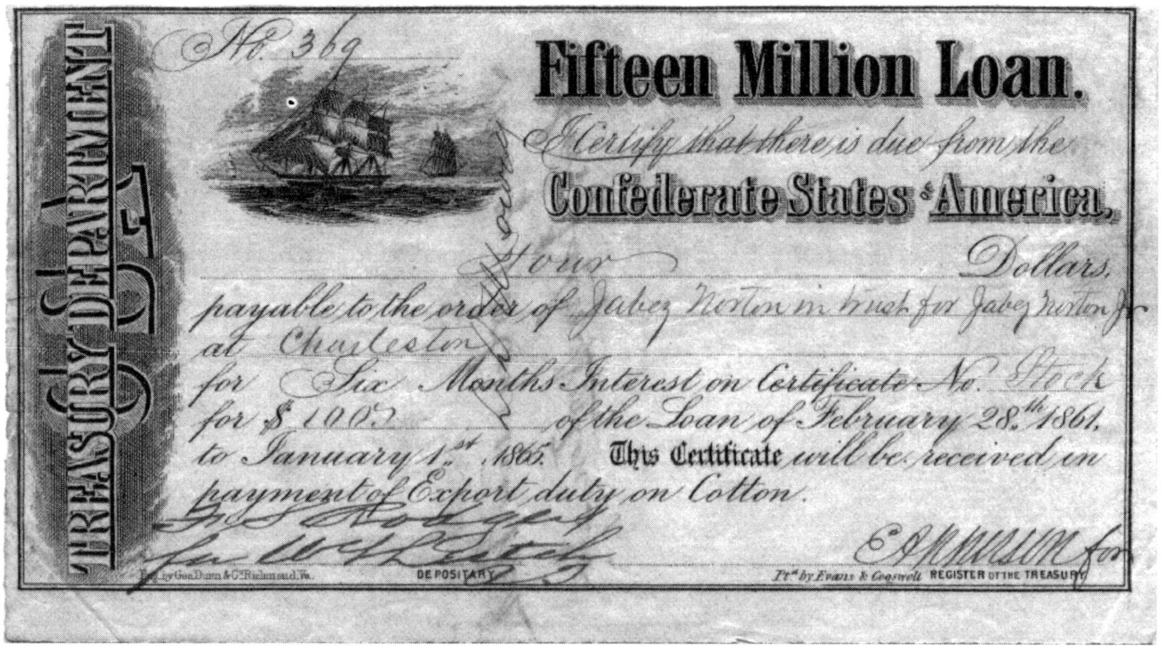
TREASURY DEPARTMENT
CSA
No. 369
Fifteen Million Loan.
I Certify that there is due from the
Confederate States of America,
Four Dollars,
payable to the order of Jabez Norton in trust for Jabez Norton Jr
at Charleston
for Six Months Interest on Certificate No. Stock
for $1003 of the Loan of February 28th 1861,
to January 1st 1865. This Certificate will be received in
payment of Export duty on Cotton.
Eng. by Geo. Dunn & Co. Richmond, Va. DEPOSITARY
Ptd. by Evans & Cogswell REGISTER OF THE TREASURY

(ship at top left)

TYPE 155 various denominations
Imprint: "Eng. by Geo. Dunn & Co., Richmond, Va. Ptd. by Evans & Cogswell"

			fine	very fine
285.	Printed on paper watermarked CSA in block letters with wavy border line. Number issued: c. 2,760 Dates of issue: January - March 1865[121] Signed by Tyler.	Rarity (7-)	$300	$550

XIV. ACT OF FEBRUARY 17, 1864

The Act of February 17, 1864, passed just before midnight when the First Congress's mandate expired, involved several series of bonds, certificates of indebtedness, and call certificates. These were directed towards efforts to fund notes into bonds, sell new debt to meet the 1864 appropriations, and for other purposes. And as might have been expected, there was a considerable amount of confusion, helped along by Thian figures that sometimes obfuscate as much as they elucidate.

The first problem was to clear off nearly $700 million of treasury notes by funding them into bonds. The act required in section two that these should be funded into 4% registered bonds with the intent of preventing their easy movement from hand to hand. Yet by the end of the Confederacy on April 1, 1865, only $10 million of such bonds had been issued, amounting to 16,746 certificates. The issue of these was doubtless slowed by the need to write in the names, numbers, denominations, the date, and the series. It clearly would have expedited getting these bonds produced and issued if the denominations and series had been printed, rather than written.

The next problem was to deal with the complaints of the states about being compelled to yield their Confederate treasury notes in exchange for the 4% registered bonds. Thian reports quite a number of bonds were issued under the section twelve of this act for that purpose, both in 4% and 6% bonds. So far as the 4% bonds were concerned, Ball numbers 384 and 385 (Cr. 166-167), with their memorial picture of the steam frigate *Alabama,* were issued after an amendatory act was passed June 14, 1864. Moreover, several hundred $1000 March 23, 1863 bonds, left over from the earlier issue, were also pressed into service and used for such payments. They could be used because they were due in 20 years and were ready, whereas the other bonds had to be engraved by Evans & Cogswell. It should also be noted that the new bonds show signs of haste, inasmuch as they do not have any space specifically prepared for the writing of a number.

The 6% bonds are reasonably well known. They have the portrait of a sergeant standing before the door of a tent. All three denominations were engraved by Archer and Halpin, but say "Printed by Evans & Cogswell," a sure sign that they were printing from copper or steel plates and not from lithograph stones.

These bonds are surrounded by mystery. The $1000 bonds, clearly issued as fully signed pieces, are readily available, but the actually issued bonds in no case equal the 4,000 bonds supposedly issued. Moreover, despite reported issue figures of 2,500 and 3,500 for the $100 and $500 bonds, no one has ever seen a properly issued bond in those denominations. The extant bonds are only numbered, not properly signed or registered. What happened to the issued bonds? Or were they never actually issued, and was Thian merely reporting bonds that had been partially prepared or printed?

While preoccupied with the need to clear the books of old treasury notes to prepare the way for new issues, there was an urgent need to sell a variety of new debt instruments. Since the April 1863 tax law had finally inaugurated a system of real fiscal revenues, the avoidance of taxation was becoming ever more attractive. Under section six of the Act of February 17, 1864, the Congress authorized the sale of up to $500 million of 6% nontaxable coupon bonds and registered "stock." Secretary Memminger arbitrarily set the price of these at 135% of face, thereby reducing the actual yield to around 4%. He then ordered the preparation of the bonds.

The contract for this order was given to Archer in Richmond, and involved the printing of bonds with 60 or 61 coupons using the great seal of the Confederacy as the main vignette and covering the whole bond with a bright red tint. Denominations were to range from $100 up to $10,000. Demand for the $100 bond, which was almost worthless, was modest, and the two high denomination pieces enjoyed but small acceptance. The overwhelming production of bonds was of the $500 and $1000 denominations. Evidently, Archer was slow in getting these bonds finished and commencing the printing process, or perhaps it had always been planned that Evans & Cogswell would do the printing. In any case, every bond bears that firm's imprint.

Each of these bonds was made from a black bond plate, each with its own number. The same was truc of the red tints, which also had plate numbers assigned to them. As was the case with some of the other 1864 bond issues, the issue figures reported in Thian are highly deceptive. The $100s. seem to have been printed and issued pretty much as Thian said they were, and the same is true of the $5,000 and $10,000. But the $500 and $1000 bonds are another matter.

Each of these has numbers reported by Thian, all pretty much in the 9,000 to 10,000 number range. There is the odd number of 4,876 assigned to series three of the $500, and Thian overlooked the report of 3,900 prepared for the series twelve $1000 bonds. From this we may assume that the printers were still working on these two series and that the others were ready for signature and issue. But what was prepared and what is available are two different matters.

The $500 bonds were not actually issued past the third series and not nearly to the number range indicated. Indeed, quite a few bonds of that series above the early range appear with forged, fictitious signatures, a clear sign that they were prepared with the late 1870s British market in view. All the other series are quite rare, and some may well be all but extinct, having been bought, turned over, and Greenville and Columbia Railroad bills of lading printed on the back. The same seems to be true of the $1000 bonds, especially series seven, only one complete remainder specimen having turned up in the forty years I have been in this hobby. All the rest appear on backs of railroad paper. However, first through sixth series $1000 bonds are readily available, which has apparently not previously been appreciated.

The higher denomination bonds, the $5000 and $10,000, were first offered at auction in Charleston, but were later actually sold in Columbia. One might have thought that many of these would have turned up in the London hoard, but only a few were found there. There are rumors that an old time Charleston dealer has a number of them, but if so, they have yet to come to light.

In keeping with the general practices of an earlier day, the Congress also provided for registered bonds. These bonds, Ball 341 (Cr. 161), had until recently been presumed to have never been filled in or properly issued. However, two pieces (numbers 3 and 4) have now turned up, indicating that some purchases were made of this sort of security.

In addition to the section six bonds, there were nontaxable "certificates of indebtedness" issued under section fourteen of the act. These were issued to appeal to the short term investor, since they were payable two years after peace. Over $57 million were nominally issued, but their issue is associated with a great deal of confusion.

Many, if not most, of these bonds were never properly issued. Bonds would be completed with the exception of the name of the purchaser and the place of issue and sent out to the depositary who was to issue them. Not many were sold and quite a few were left over, hence the quantities available today. Bonds in less than fully issued condition are much more common than fully issued ones.

Another variety arises from the fact that George Dunn had prepared quite a few of these bonds and had printed the transfer form on the back, when orders came down changing the transfer form to conform with the authorizing law. As a result, quite a few incomplete bonds without back transfer forms, or with the old form, exist, with and without stubs at the left. The new transfer form can be readily distinguished from the old because it has red and black ink and is much smaller than the original layout (which contained spaces for six transfers).

Under section eighteen of the Act of February 17, 1864, there was to be an issue of 4% and 6% coupon bonds and stock certificates. Thian reports the issue of over 15,061 $1000 4% bonds and 2,405 $500 bonds. He also indicates that 6% bonds were issued of the March 23, 1863 act types totalling 767 $1000, 53 $500, and 55 $100. In addition, he reports 1,602 $20,000 registered bonds, in that denomination only. None of these bonds has been seen to date, except the surplus issue of the March 23, 1863 bonds (Ball 374-376). What happened to them is one of the mysteries of Confederate finance. In any case, places have been left for them in the event they surface.

The February 17, 1864 Act did not make specific provision for call certificates as such, but by a rather liberal interpretation of section seven, Secretary George A. Trenholm did sell quite a quantity of these ($135 million), nominally denominated from $100 to $100,000. One says nominally because the $100 denomination, by then being of little value, was scarcely issued, although there were plenty of other denominations prepared and sold.

Apparently, orders were given to Evans & Cogswell to prepare a call certificate form (Ball 352, Cr. 160), but this was delayed and very few were printed before orders for its production were cancelled. Instead, Secretary Trenholm had Ritchie & Dunnavant, the Virginia state printers, prepare a simple, typeset form on leftover pink paper, prepared two to a sheet and bound into books with stubs. Due to a typesetting mistake, the two forms are not identical, but they represent the only certificate form actually issued for this purpose. Again, because of the discrepancy between those fully issued and those not issued, the numbers reportedly issued in Thian are not an accurate indicator of what was really emitted.

A. 4% registered stock certificates, Section 2
Total amount issued (all types): $10,198,800

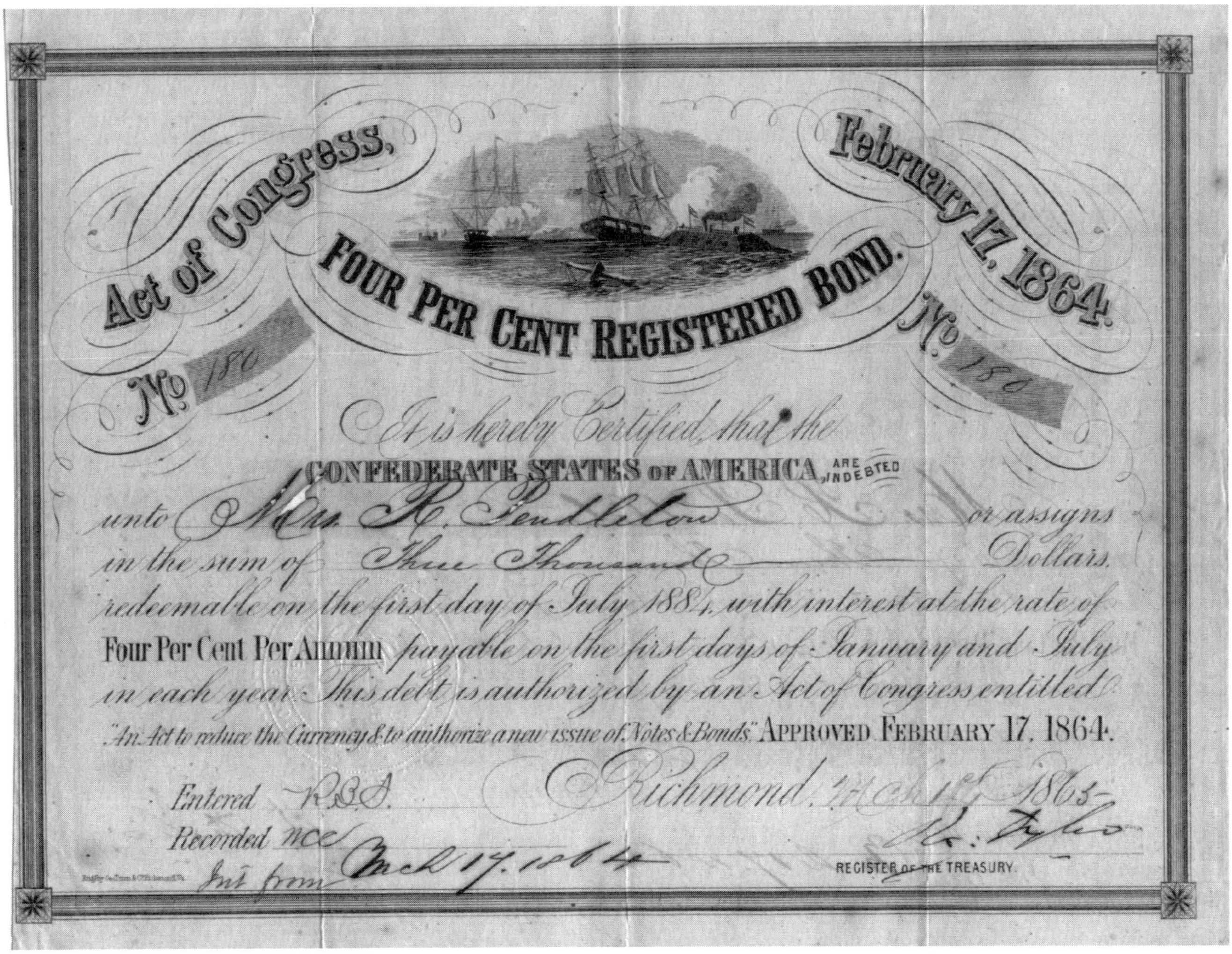
Act of Congress, February 17, 1864.
FOUR PER CENT REGISTERED BOND.
No. 180 No. 180
It is hereby Certified, that the CONFEDERATE STATES OF AMERICA, are indebted unto Mrs. R. Pendleton or assigns in the sum of Three Thousand Dollars, redeemable on the first day of July 1884, with interest at the rate of Four Per Cent Per Annum payable on the first days of January and July in each year. This debt is authorized by an Act of Congress entitled "An Act to reduce the Currency & to authorize a new issue of Notes & Bonds." APPROVED FEBRUARY 17, 1864.
Richmond,
Entered
Recorded
Int from Mch 17. 1864
REGISTER OF THE TREASURY.

(CSS *Virginia* sinking USS *Cumberland*, March 8, 1862)

TYPE 156[122]
Imprint: "Engd. by Geo. Dunn & Co. Richmond, Va."

$100

No.	Denomination	Description	Rarity	fine	very fine
286.	$100	No series (actually first series); printed on plain white paper. Number issued: 8,842 (#1-8842) Dates of issue: May 3, 1864 - Feb. 28, 1865 Signed by Tyler.	Rarity (4+)	$140	$175
287.	$100	"2nd Series" at top left; printed on plain white paper. Number issued: c. 1,250 (#1-1250; #1235 known) Dates of issue: March 1-31, 1864 Signed by Tyler.	Rarity (5)	$150	$250

$500

No.	Denomination	Description	Rarity	fine	very fine
288.	$500	No series (actually first series); printed on plain white paper. Number issued: 2,890 (#1-2890) Dates of issue: May 3, 1864 - February 28, 1865 Signed by Tyler.	Rarity (5-)	$150	$250
289.	$500	"2nd Series" at top left; printed on plain white paper. Number issued: 256 (#1-256) Dates of issue: March 1-31, 1865 Signed by Tyler.	Rarity (7)	$900	$1,250

$1,000

No.	Denomination	Description	Rarity	fine	very fine
290.	$1,000	No series (actually first series); printed on plain white paper. Number issued: 2,269 (#1-2269) Dates of issue: May 3, 1864 - February 28, 1865 Signed by Tyler.	Rarity (5-)	$150	$225
291.	$1,000	"2nd Series" written at upper left; printed on plain white paper. Number issued: c. 256 (#1-256) Dates of issue: March 1-31, 1865 Signed by Tyler.	Rarity (7)	$900	$1,250

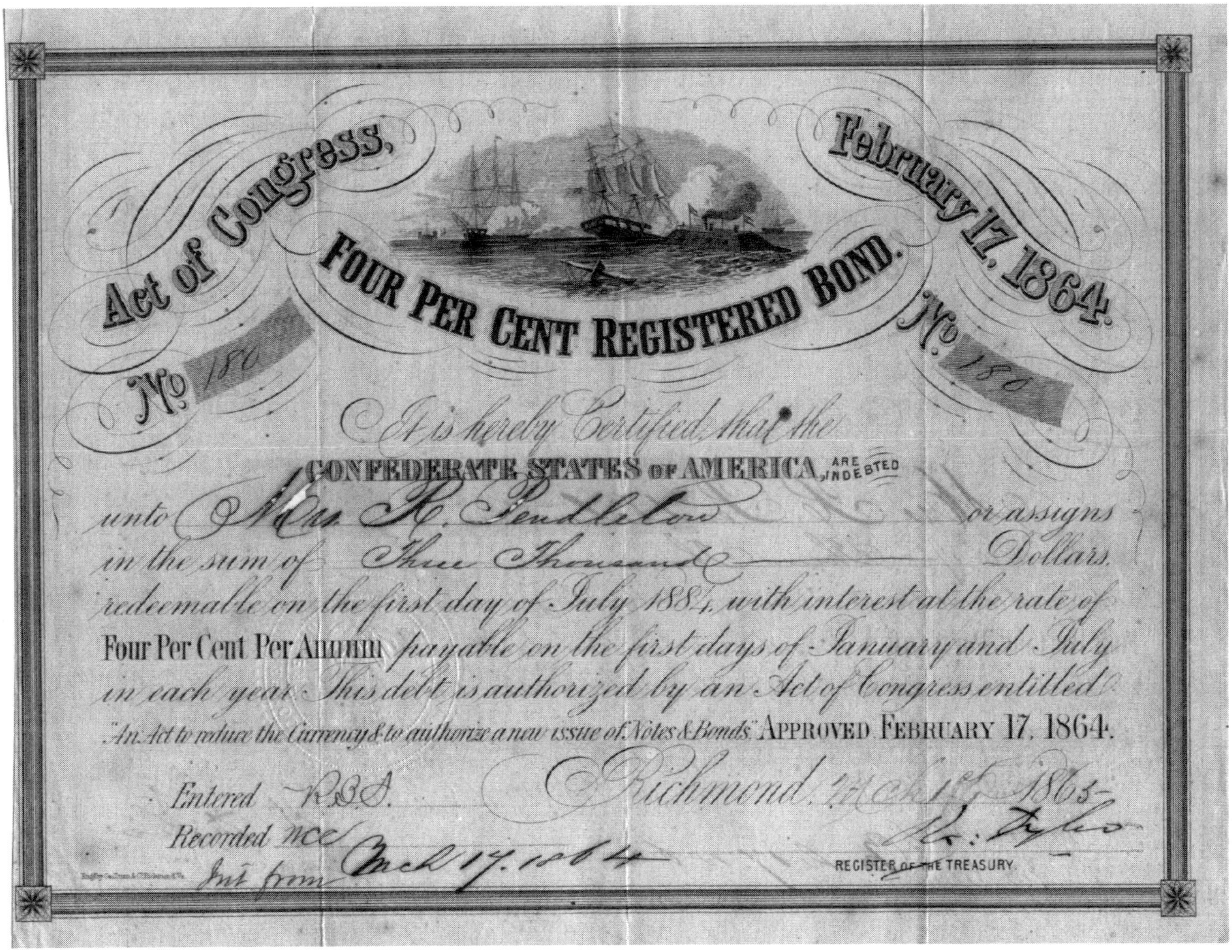

Act of Congress, February 17, 1864.
FOUR PER CENT REGISTERED BOND.
No 180 No 180
It is hereby Certified that the CONFEDERATE STATES OF AMERICA, ARE INDEBTED
unto Mrs R. Pendleton or assigns
in the sum of Three Thousand Dollars,
redeemable on the first day of July 1884, with interest at the rate of
Four Per Cent Per Annum payable on the first days of January and July
in each year. This debt is authorized by an Act of Congress entitled
"An Act to reduce the Currency & to authorize a new issue of Notes & Bonds." APPROVED FEBRUARY 17, 1864.
Richmond, 1865.
Entered R.B.S.
Recorded WCE
Int from Mch 17. 1864
REGISTER OF THE TREASURY.

$3,000

				fine	very fine
292.	$3,000	No series (actually first series); printed on plain white paper. Number issued: 190 (#1-190) Dates of issue: May 3, 1864 - February 28, 1865 Signed by Tyler.	Rarity (7-)	$500	$650
293.	$3,000	"2nd Series" written at upper left; printed on plain white paper. Number issued: c. 50 (#1-50) Dates of issue: March 1-31, 1865 Signed by Tyler.	Rarity (8)	$800	$1,000

Act of Congress; February 17, 1864.

FOUR PER CENT REGISTERED BOND.

No. No.

It is hereby Certified that the CONFEDERATE STATES OF AMERICA, ARE INDEBTED unto or assigns in the sum of Five Thousand Dollars, redeemable on the first day of July 1884, with interest at the rate of Four Per Cent Per Annum payable on the first days of January and July in each year. This debt is authorized by an Act of Congress entitled "An Act to reduce the Currency & to authorize a new issue of Notes & Bonds." APPROVED. FEBRUARY 17, 1864.

Entered

Recorded

Richmond, 186

REGISTER OF THE TREASURY

$5,000

				fine	very fine
294.	$5,000	No series (actually first series); printed on white paper. Number issued: 815 (#1-815) Dates of issue: May 3, 1864 - February 28, 1865 Signed by Tyler.	Rarity (6)	$350	$450
295.	$5,000	"2nd Series" written at top left; printed on white paper. Number issued: c. 62 (#1-62) Dates of issue: c. March 1-31, 1865 Signed by Tyler.	Rarity (7+)	$750	$1,250

B. 6% coupon bonds, Sections 6 and 8

Total printed: $145,755,000
Total actually issued: c. $80,702,600

Bonds of this series are printed on a thin bluish and a thick, soft, white paper. Whereas the early series of each bond see a ratio of about 60% or 70% thin paper to thick paper (40-30%), the later series reverse these ratios. Both papers apparently came from the Belvidere paper works in Richmond. No separate listing is furnished for each kind of paper because of the absence of interest in collecting by such a minor variety.

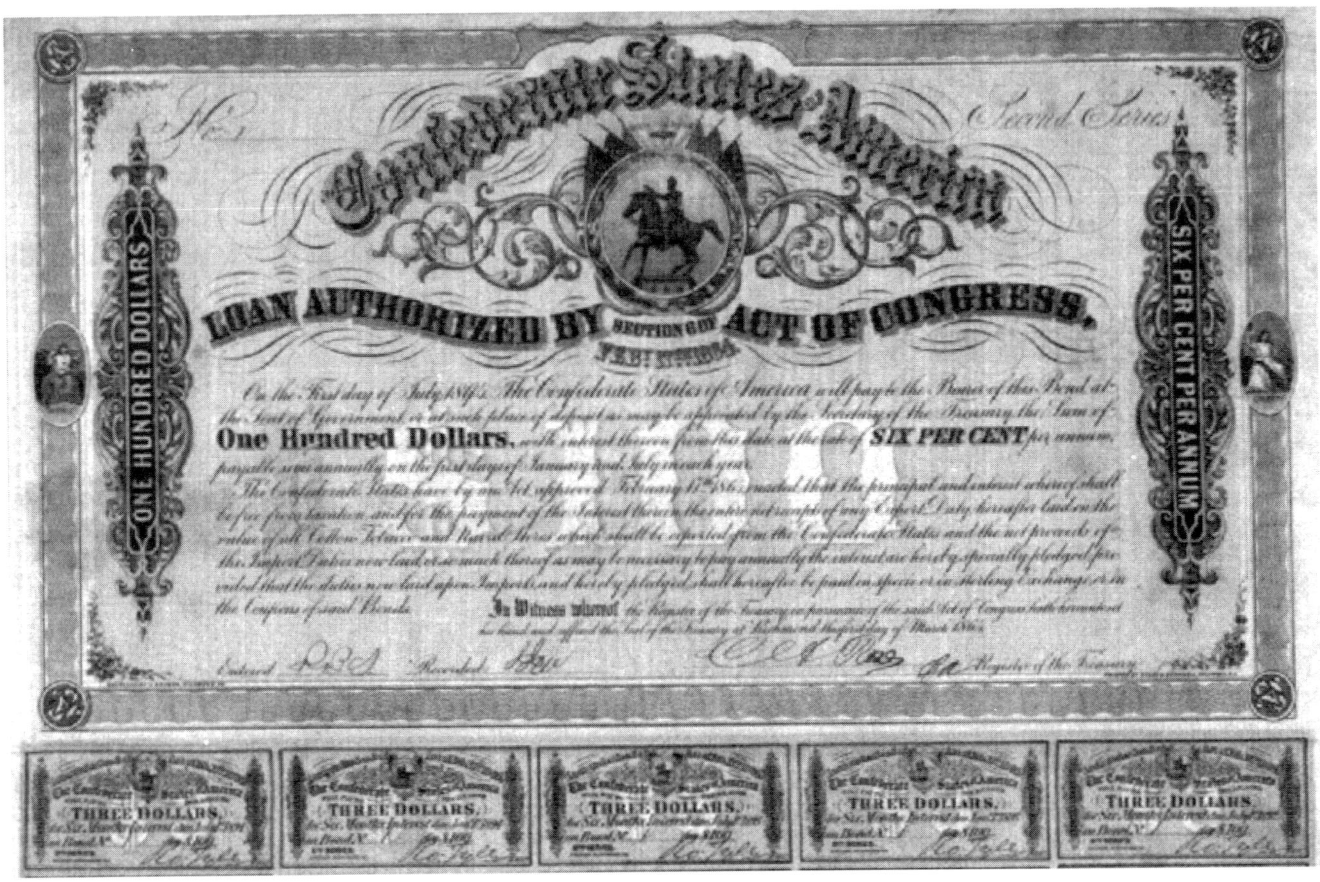

(Confederate seal, center. Black over a pink to dark red tint plate.)

TYPE 157 **$100**

Imprint: "Engraved by J. Archer, Richmond, Va." and "Printed by Evans & Cogswell, Columbia, S.C."

				fine	very fine
296.	$100	First series; printed on thick white or thin bluish paper; a July 1, 1864 coupon is or was present. Number issued: 6,200 (#1-3900; 4201-6500) Dates of issue: c. June 7, 1864 - August 1864 Signed by Rose.	Rarity (3+)	$45	$60

				fine	very fine
297.	$100	Same as preceding, hand reissued at Houston, Texas by James Sorley, CSA depositary. Number issued: c. 200 (#4001-4200) Dates of issue: c. March 1865 Signed by Rose.	Rarity (7+)	$125	$250
298.	$100	Same, but hand endorsed by M.J. Hall, CSA depositary at Marshall, Texas. Number issued: c. 100 (#3901-4000) Dates of issue: March 1865 Signed by Rose.	Rarity (7+)	$150	$300
299.	$100	Same as the preceding, coupons start January 1, 1865. Number issued: c. 3,000 (#6501-9500) Dates of issue: c. August - September 9, 1864 Signed by Apperson.	Rarity (4)	$55	$75
303.	$100	Second series. Printed on thick white or thin bluish paper. Number Prepared: 9,400[123] (#1-9400) Dates of issue: September 10, 1864 - December 20, 1864 Signed by Rose.	Rarity (4-)	$75	$110

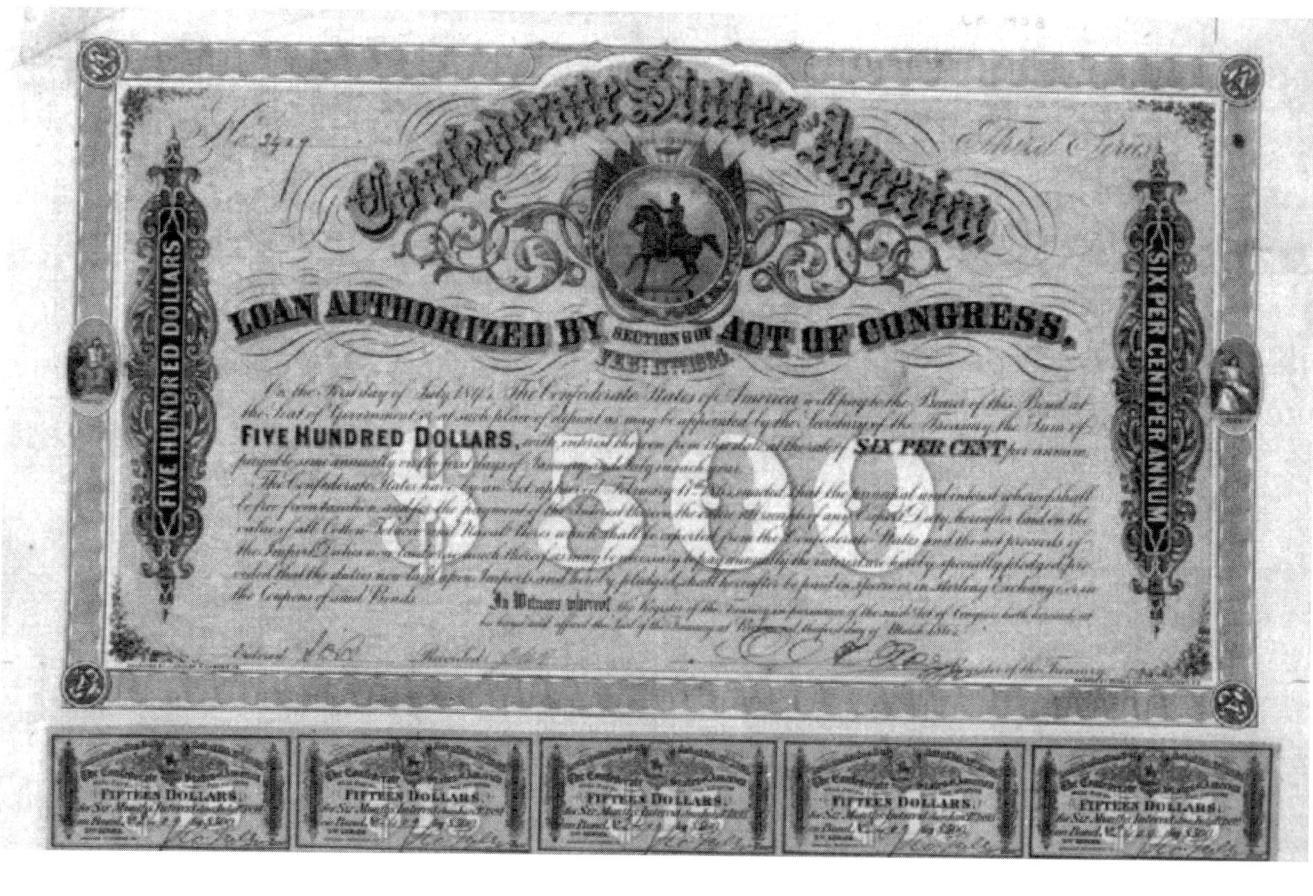

(Confederate seal, center; black over pink to dark red tint plate)

TYPE 158 **$500**

Imprint: "Engraved by J. Archer, Richmond, Va." and "Printed by Evans & Cogswell, Columbia, S.C."

No.	Value	Description	Rarity	fine	very fine
304.	$500	First series; printed on thick white or thin bluish paper; coupons from 1 July 1864. Number issued: 8,000 (#1-5200; 5401-8200) Dates of issue: June 7 - July 31, 1864 Signed by Tyler (#1-400); Rose (#401-800); Apperson the residue.	Rarity (3)	$40	$50
305.	$500	Same, but reissued on the back by James Sorley, CSA depositary at Houston, Texas. Number issued: c. 200 (#5201-5400) Dates of issue: December 1864 Signed by Apperson.	Rarity (6)	$125	$200
307.	$500	Same, but coupons from 1 January 1865. Number issued: c. 1,300 (#8201-9500) Dates of issue: c. August 1-20, 1864 Signed by Apperson.	Rarity (4+)	$60	$85
308.	$500	Second series; printed on thick white or thin bluish paper; coupons from 1 July 1864. Number issued: c. 150 (#1-150) Dates of issue: c. August 20-31, 1864 Signed by Apperson.	Rarity (6)	$100	$140
309.	$500	Second series; coupons from 1 January 1865. Number issued: 8,700 (#701-2100; 2701-10000) Dates of issue: September 1 - November 8, 1864 Signed by Apperson, Rose.	Rarity (4-)	$50	$75
311.	$500	Same as last, red and black stamp on back for Marshall, Texas, and endorsed by M.J. Hall, the CSA depositary. Number issued: c. 1,150 (#150-700; 2101-2700) Dates of issue: c. September 1864 - May 1865 Signed by Apperson, Rose.	Rarity (5-)	$100	$175
312.	$500	Third series; printed on thick white or thin bluish paper. Dates of issue: November 8, 1864 - March 31, 1865 Number issued: c. 5,200[124] (#1-5200) Signed by Rose.	Rarity (5-)	$75	$115
313.	$500	Fourth series; printed on thick white or thin bluish paper. Number prepared: 10,700[125] (#1-10700) Dates of issue: received to March 18, 1865	Rarity (4+)	$85	$125
314.	$500	Fifth series; printed on thick white or thin bluish paper. Number prepared: 10,700[126] (#1-10700) Dates of issue: received to March 18, 1865	Rarity (8)	(—)	(—)
315.	$500	Sixth series; printed on thick white or thin bluish paper. Number prepared: 8,000[127] (#1-8000) Dates of issue: received to March 18, 1865	Rarity (7+)	$500	(—)

				fine	very fine
316.	$500	Seventh series; printed on thick white or thin bluish paper. Number prepared: 9,200[128] (#1-9200) Dates of issue: received to March 18, 1865	Rarity (8)	$500	(—)

(Confederate seal, center; black over pink to dark red tint plate)

TYPE 159 **$1,000**

Imprint: "Engraved by J. Archer, Richmond, Va." and "Printed by Evans and Cogswell, Columbia, S.C."

317.	$1,000	First series; printed on thick white or thin bluish paper; coupons from 1 July 1864. Number issued: c. 8,200 (#1-3700; 4101-7400; 7601-7800; 8301-9300) Dates of issue: June 7 - July 23, 1863 Signed by Apperson.	Rarity (4-)	$45	$55

No.	Value	Description	Rarity	fine	very fine
318.	$1,000	First series, as last, endorsed and issued on back by James Sorley, CSA depositary in Houston, Texas. Number issued: c. 500 (#7801-8300) Dates of issue: December 1864 Signed by Apperson.	Rarity (5)	$90	$125
319.	$1,000	Same, but hand issued by M.J. Hall, CSA depositary at Marshall, Texas. Number issued: c. 200 (#7401-7600) Dates of issue: November 1864 Signed by Apperson.	Rarity (6)	$120	$150
320.	$1,000	As last, January 1, 1865 coupons; red and black issue stamp on back of M.J. Hall, CSA depositary at Marshall, Texas. Number issued: c. 400 (#3700-4100) Dates of issue: December 1864 Signed by Apperson.	Rarity (5+)	$100	$130
322.	$1,000	Second series; coupons printed from July 1, 1864 on, (usually on thin paper). Number issued: c. 1,100 (#401-650; 1001-1150; 9501-10200) Dates of issue: unknown Signed by Apperson.	Rarity (4+)	$75	$100
323.	$1,000	Second series; printed on thick white or thin bluish paper; coupons start January 1, 1865. Number issued: c. 9,450 (#1-300; 801-1000; 1151-6100; 6201-9500; 10201-10900) Dates of issue: July 23 - September 8, 1864 Signed by Apperson.	Rarity (3+)	$45	$55
324.	$1,000	Same, but tint plate is for July 1, 1864 coupons; the bond plate is for 1 January 1865 coupons.[129] Number issued: c. 350 (#301-400; 651-800; 6101-6200) Dates of issue: July 25 - August 11, 1864 Signed by Apperson.	Rarity (6-)	$100	$135
325.	$1,000	Third series; printed on thick white or thin bluish paper. Number issued: 10,700 (#1-5700; 5801-10800) Dates of issue: August 31 - September 30, 1864 Signed by Apperson.	Rarity (3)	$45	$55

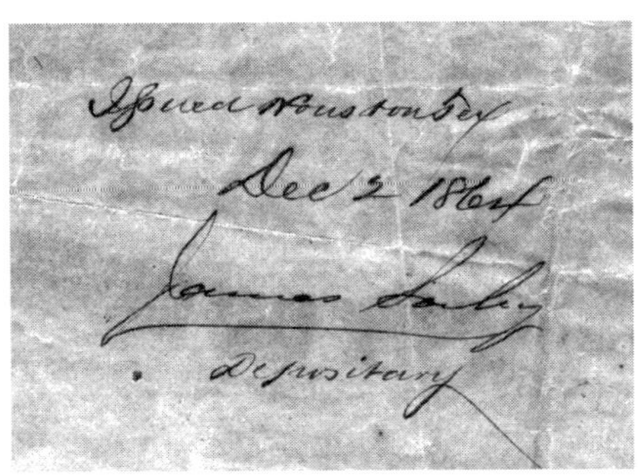

No.	Value	Description	Rarity	fine	very fine
326.	$1,000	Third series; hand issued on back by James Sorley, CSA depositary, Houston, Texas. Number issued: c. 100 (#5701-5800) Dates of issue: December 1864 Signed by Apperson.	Rarity (7+)	$200	$250

				fine	very fine
327.	$1,000	Fourth series; printed on thick white or thin bluish paper. Number issued: 8,000 (#1-700; 2801-10100) Dates of issue: September 30 - December 6, 1864 Signed by Apperson.	Rarity (3+)	$45	$50

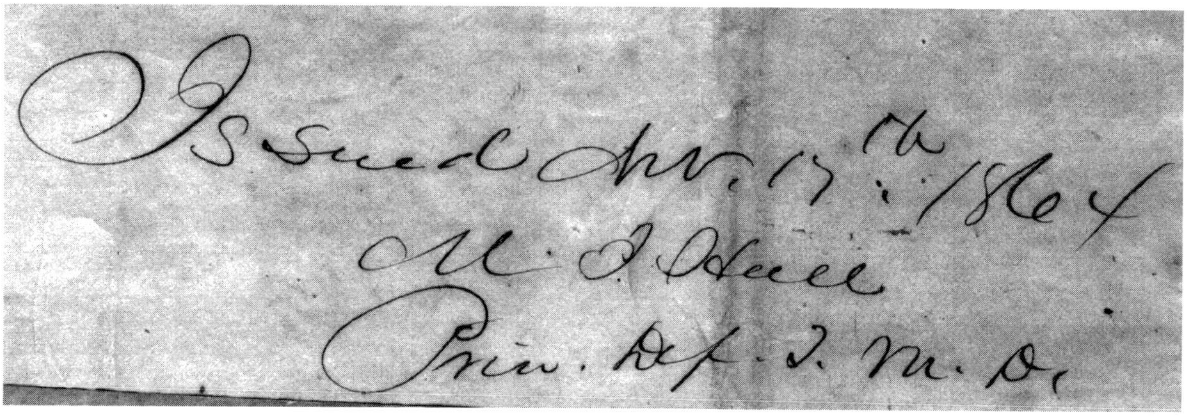

328.	$1,000	Fourth series; reissued on the back by M.J. Hall, CSA depositary in Marshall, Texas, in black script type with endorsement. Number issued: c. 2,100 (#701-2800) Dates of issue: unknown Signed by Apperson.	Rarity (4)	$90	$125
329.	$1,000	Fifth series; printed on thick white or thin bluish paper. Number issued: 11,200 (#1-11200) Dates of issue: September 30 - December 28, 1864 Signed by Apperson, Rose.	Rarity (3)	$45	$55
330.	$1,000	Sixth series; printed on thick white or thin bluish paper. Number issued: c. 10,050 (#1-10050)[130] Dates of issue: December 20, 1864 - March 1, 1865 Signed by Apperson.	Rarity (3)	$45	$55
331.	$1,000	Seventh series; printed on thick white or thin bluish paper. Number issued: c. 7,100 (#1-7100)*	Rarity (8)	$1,000	(-)
332.	$1,000	Eighth series; printed on thick white or thin bluish paper. Number issued: c. 10,200 (#1-10200)*	Rarity (7-)	$250	(-)
333.	$1,000	Ninth series; printed on white paper. Number issued: 9,800 (#1-9800)*	Rarity (5)	$150	(-)

				fine	very fine
334.	$1,000	Tenth series Number issued: 1,200 (#1-1200)*	Rarity (7-)	$250	(-)
335.	$1,000	Eleventh series Number issued: 12,200 (#1-12200)*	Rarity (7-)	$250	(-)
336.	$1,000	Twelfth series Number issued: c. 7,500 (#1-7500)*[131]	Rarity (7+)	$300	(-)

---

*Number delivered by printers. Most of these bonds were destroyed or used by various groups as scrap paper. Only one Seventh series bond has been seen intact to date; another has been reported.

TYPE 160 **$5,000**

Imprint: "Engraved by J. Archer, Richmond, Va." and "Printed by Evans and Cogswell, Columbia, S.C."

No.	Denom.	Description	Rarity	fine	very fine
337.	$5,000	First series; printed on white paper. Number issued: 200 (#1-200)[132] Date of issue: June 7, 1864 Signed by Tyler.	Rarity (7-)	$1,500	$2,500
338.	$5,000	Same, but a remainder. Number printed: 300 (#201-500)	Rarity (6+)	$1,000	$1,500

TYPE 161 **$10,000**

Imprint: "Engraved by J. Archer, Richmond, Va." and "Printed by Evans and Cogswell, Columbia, S.C."

No.	Denom.	Description	Rarity	fine	very fine
339.	$10,000	First series; printed on white paper. Number issued: c. 100 (#1-100) Date of issue: June 7, 1864 Signed by Tyler.	Rarity (7)	$2,500	$3,000
340.	$10,000	Same, but a remainder. Number printed: 400 (#101-500)	Rarity (7-)	$2,000	$2,500

No. 301.—RAILROAD MORTAR AT PETERSBURG, VA., July 25, 1864.

C. 6% registered bonds, Sections 6 and 8
Total prepared: unknown
Total actually issued: c. 15

IT IS HEREBY CERTIFIED THAT

THE Confederate States OF AMERICA

$10,000 $10,000

No 3 No 3

Are indebted unto D. H. Gregg or Assigns, in the sum of Ten Thousand Dollars payable on the First day of July 1894 with interest at the rate of Six per Cent per Annum payable on the first day of January and July of each year. Interest from July 1. 1864

The Confederate States of America, have by an Act approved February 17th 1864, enacted that the principal and interest thereof shall be free from taxation and for the payment of the interest thereon the entire net receipts of any export duty hereafter laid on the value of all Cotton, Tobacco and Naval Stores which shall be exported from the Confederate States and the net proceeds of the import duties now laid or so much thereof as may be necessary to pay annually the interest, are hereby specially pledged provided that the duties now laid upon imports and hereby pledged shall hereafter be paid in Specie, or in Sterling Exchange, or in the Coupons of the Bonds of this Loan.

Richmond Sept 6 1864

Entered

Recorded

Register of the Treasury

Evans & Cogswell Columbia S.C.

(farmer plowing, center)

TYPE 162 written denominations
Imprint: "Evans & Cogswell, Columbia, S.C."

341.	Printed on white paper.		fine-very fine
	Number issued: c. 15†	Rarity (8)[133]	$1,100
	Dates of issue: August 29 - December 8, 1864		
	Signed by Tyler.		

†of the two known at present, one is in an institution.

Denomination		Approximate number issued	Serial #(s)	Rarity
A	$500	3	—	—
B	$700	1	—	—
C	$1000	4	—	—
D	$1,300	1	—	—
E	$1,400	1	—	—
F	$1,500	1	4	8
G	$3,500	1	—	—
H	$7,200	1	—	—
I	$8,000	1	—	—
J	$10,000	1	3	8
		15		

Items without rarity numbers are not known to exist and may therefore not be collectable. Serial numbers are known only for observed pieces.

			fine	very fine
342.	Printed on white paper, remainder, unissued. Number printed: unknown (incomplete remainders) Dates of issue: n/a	Rarity (5-)	$220	$300

D. Call certificates, Section 7
All printed by Ritchie & Dunnavant of Richmond, Va.

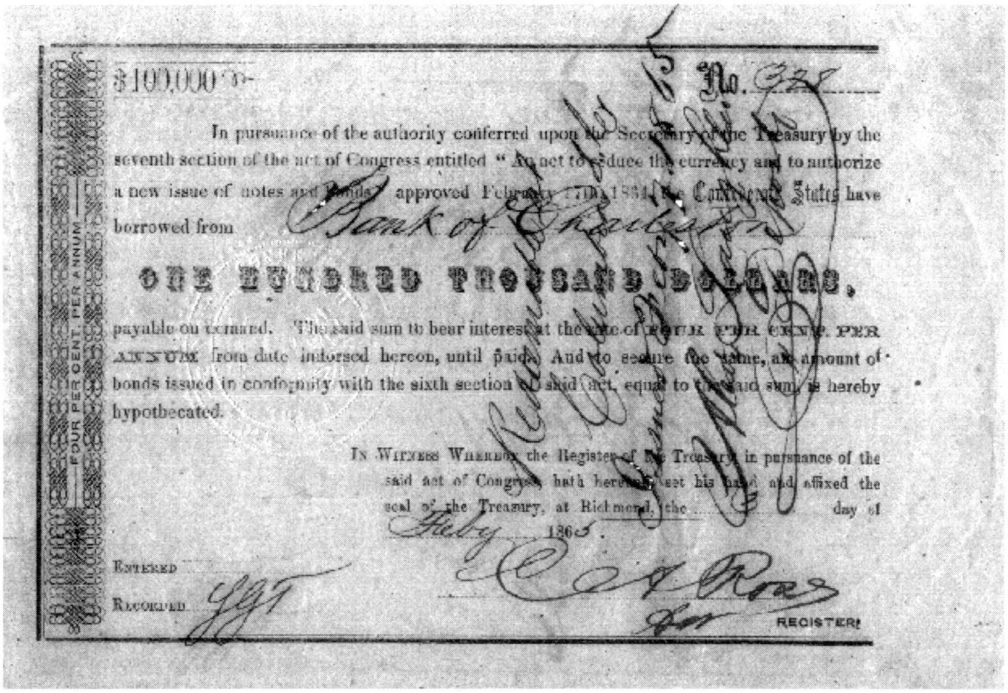

$100,000 No.

In pursuance of the authority conferred upon the Secretary of the Treasury by the seventh section of the act of Congress entitled "An act to reduce the currency and to authorize a new issue of notes and bonds," approved February 17th, 1864, the Confederate States have borrowed from Bank of Charleston

ONE HUNDRED THOUSAND DOLLARS,

payable on demand. The said sum to bear interest at the rate of FOUR PER CENT. PER ANNUM from date indorsed hereon, until paid. And to secure the same, an amount of bonds issued in conformity with the sixth section of said act, equal to the said sum, is hereby hypothecated.

IN WITNESS WHEREOF, the Register of the Treasury, in pursuance of the said act of Congress, hath hereunto set his hand and affixed the seal of the Treasury, at Richmond, the day of Feby 1865.

ENTERED

RECORDED

REGISTER

FOUR PER CENT. PER ANNUM

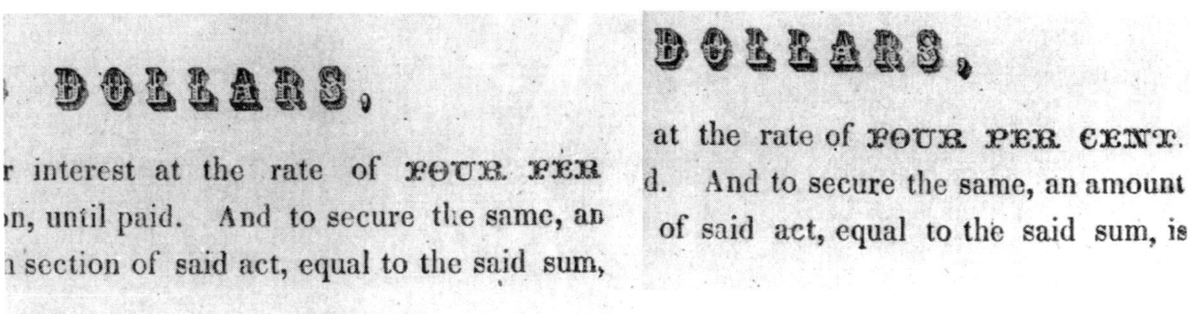

DOLLARS,
r interest at the rate of FOUR PER
on, until paid. And to secure the same, an
section of said act, equal to the said sum,

DOLLARS,
at the rate of FOUR PER CENT.
d. And to secure the same, an amount
of said act, equal to the said sum, is

Certificates from $500 to $10,000 were printed two to a sheet and come in the two varieties depending upon whether they are from position one or two.

TYPE 163 **$100**

				fine	very fine
343.	$100	Letterpress on pink paper. Number issued: c. 114[134] Dates of issue: August - December 20, 1864 signed by Tyler	Rarity (8)	$3,800	
343a.	$100	Letterpress on pink paper. Number printed: 200 less issued (86) Unissued remainders	Rarity (7+)	$600	$750

TYPE 164 **$500**

344.	$500	Letterpress on pink paper. Number issued: c. 1,427 (#1-1427)[135] Dates of issue: August 31, 1864 - March 31, 1865 Signed by Rose.	Rarity (5+)	$75	$110
344a.	$500	Letterpress on pink paper. Number printed: unknown Unissued or partially filled in remainders	Rarity (5)	$60	$80

TYPE 165 **$1,000**

345.	$1,000	Letterpress on pink paper. Number issued: c. 2,211 (#1-2211)[136] Dates of issue: August 11, 1864 - March 31, 1865 Signed by Rose.	Rarity (5+)	$90	$125
345a.	$1000	Letterpress on pink paper. Number printed: unknown Unissued or partially filled in remainders	Rarity (4)	$50	$65

TYPE 166 **$2,000**

346.	$2,000	Letterpressed on pink paper. Number issued: c. 1,292 (#1-1292)[137] Dates of issue: c. August 11, 1864 - March 27, 1865 Signed by Rose.	Rarity (6-)	$85	$120
346a.	$2000	Letterpress on pink paper. Number printed: unknown Unissued or partially filled in remainders	Rarity (5-)	$50	$65

TYPE 167 **$3,000**

No.	Denomination	Description	Rarity	fine	very fine
347.	$3,000	Letterpressed on pink paper. Number issued: c. 2,000 (#1-2000) Dates of issue: c. August 31, 1864 - March 27, 1865 Signed by Rose.	Rarity (6-)	$75	$100
347a.	$3000	Letterpress on pink paper. Number printed: unknown Unissued or partially filled in remainders	Rarity (5-)	$65	$80

TYPE 168 **$5,000**

No.	Denomination	Description	Rarity	fine	very fine
348.	$5,000	Letterpressed on pink paper. Number issued: c. 1,627 (#1-1627) Dates of issue: August 14, 1864 - March 31, 1865 Signed by Rose.	Rarity (5-)	$80	$115
348a.	$5000	Letterpress on pink paper. Number printed: unknown Unissued or partially filled in remainders	Rarity (5-)	$65	$80

TYPE 169 **$10,000**

No.	Denomination	Description	Rarity	fine	very fine
349.	$10,000	Letterpressed on pink paper. Number issued: c. 354 (#1-354) Dates of issue: August 8, 1864 - March 3, 1865 Signed by Rose.	Rarity (6)	$125	$200
349a.	$10000	Letterpress on pink paper. Number printed: unknown Unissued or partially filled in remainders	Rarity (5-)	$65	$80

TYPE 170 **$20,000**

No.	Denomination	Description	Rarity	fine	very fine
350.	$20,000	Letterpressed on pink paper. Number issued: c. 398 (#1-398)[138] Dates of issue: August 26, 1864 - March 31, 1865 Signed by Rose.	Rarity (6+)	$150	$200

TYPE 171 **$50,000**

No.	Denomination	Description	Rarity	fine	very fine
351.	$50,000	Letterpressed on pink paper. Number issued: 435 (#1-435) Dates of issue: c. August 26, 1864 - March 31, 1865 Signed by Rose.	Rarity (7-)	$200	$300

TYPE 172 **$100,000**

			fine	very fine
352. $100,000	Letterpressed on pink paper. Denomination 120mm at center Number issued: 246 (#1-491 odd numbers only)[139] Dates of issue: August 30, 1864 - March 31, 1865 Signed by Rose.	Rarity (7-)	$750	
353. $100,000	Letterpressed on pink paper. Denomination 145mm at center Number issued: c. 246 (#2-492 even numbers only)[139] Dates of issue: August 30, 1864 - March 31, 1865 Signed by Rose.	Rarity (7-)	$750	

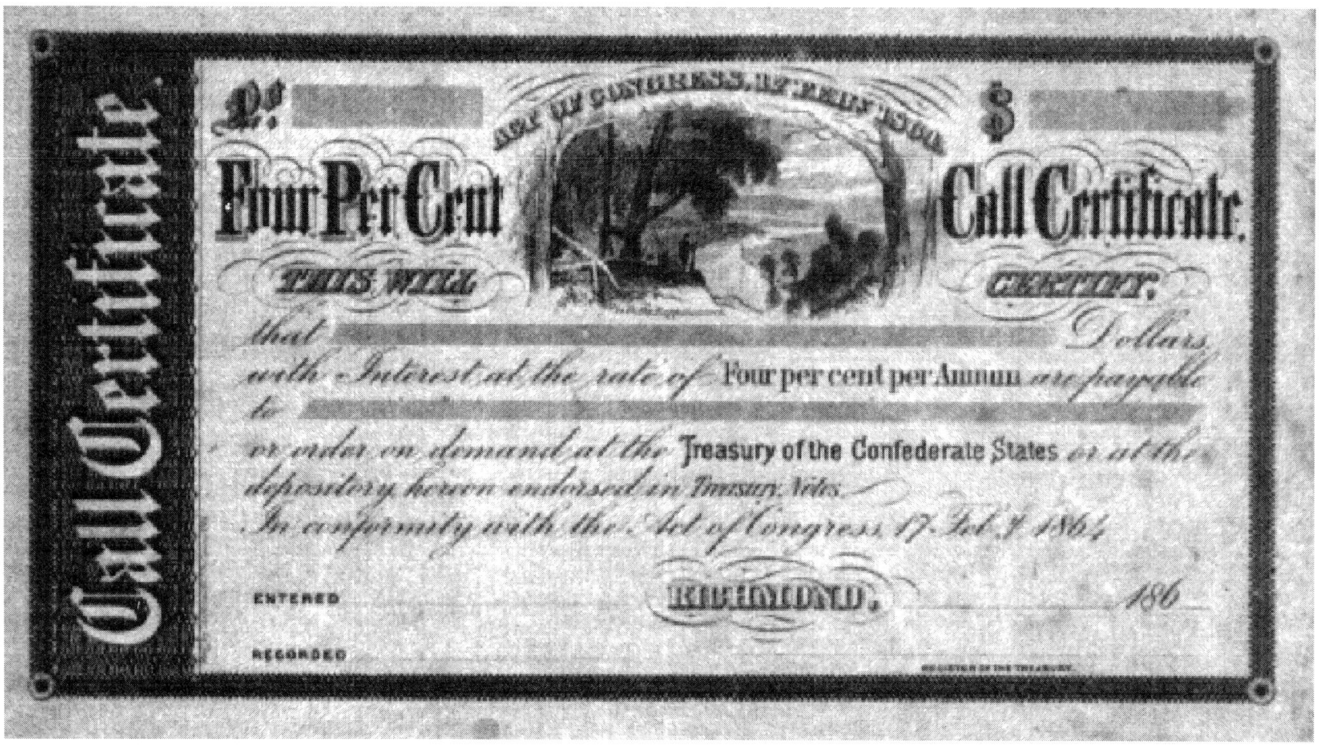

(Rappahannock River scene west of Fredericksburg)

TYPE 173 no denomination (incomplete remainders)
Imprint: "Eng. by Geo. Dunn & Co. Richmond, Va"

354.	Printed on white paper.[140] Number issued: none Dates of issue: n/a	Rarity (5)	$85	$125

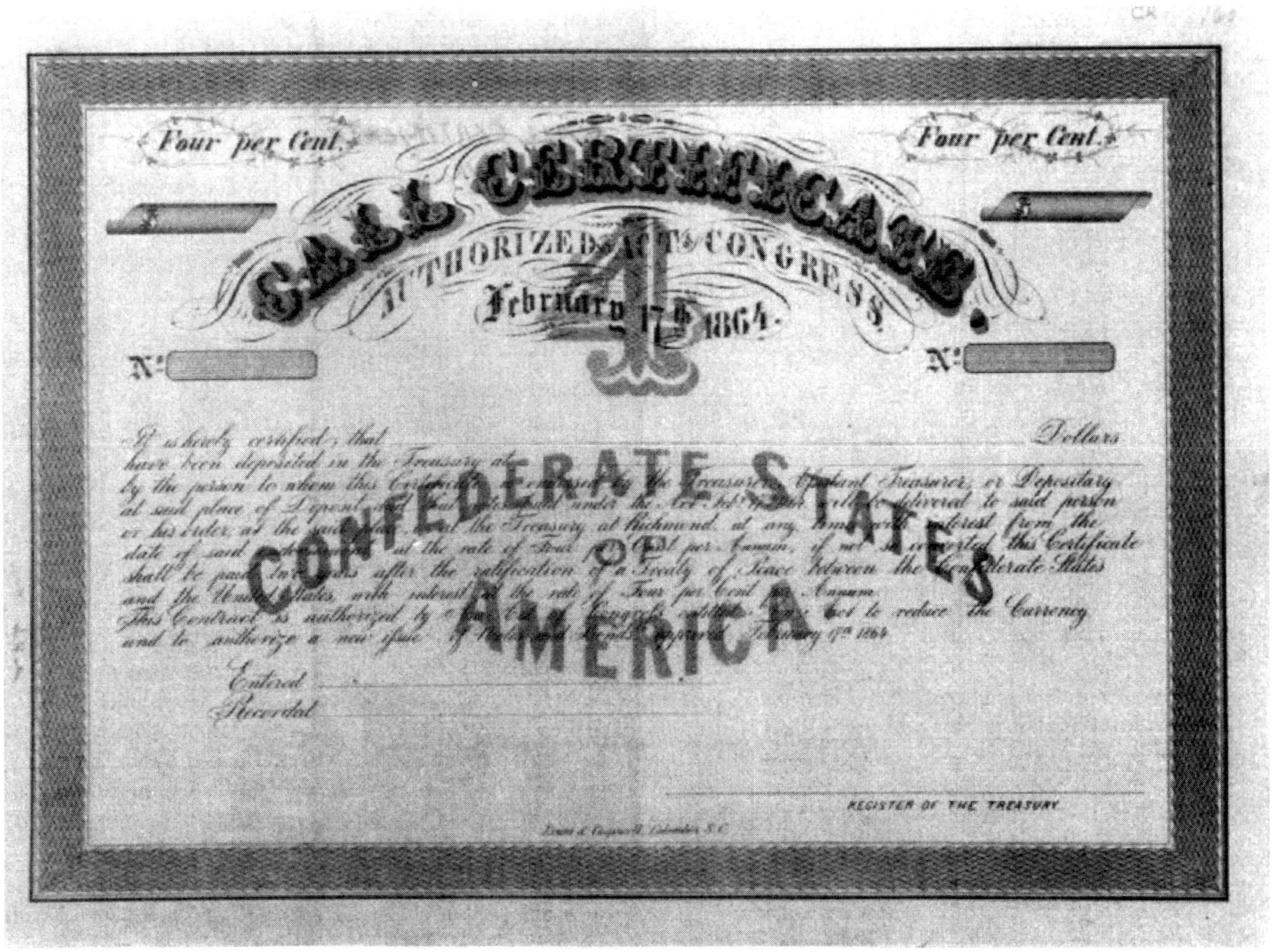

(big "4" at center)

TYPE 174 no denomination (incomplete remainders)
Imprint: "Evans & Cogswell, Columbia, S.C."

			fine	very fine
355.	Printed on white paper.			
	Number issued: none	Rarity (7)	$2000	$2800
	Number printed: unknown.			
	Dates of issue: n/a			

E. 6% coupon bonds, Section 12

(Confederate sergeant in front of tent)

TYPE 175 **$100**

Imprint: "Engraved by Archer & Halpin, Richmond, Va"; "Printed by Evans & Cogswell, Columbia, S.C."

				fine	very fine
357a.	$100	Printed on white paper. Remainders. Number issued: 2,500 (#1-2500) Dates of issue: no mention in records as actually issued.	Rarity (7-)	$575	$750

TYPE 176 **$500**

Printers and design similar to 354

				fine	very fine
359a.	$500	Printed on white paper. Remainders. Number issued: none, printed 3,500 Dates of issue: no record of issue.	Rarity (7-)	$575	$750

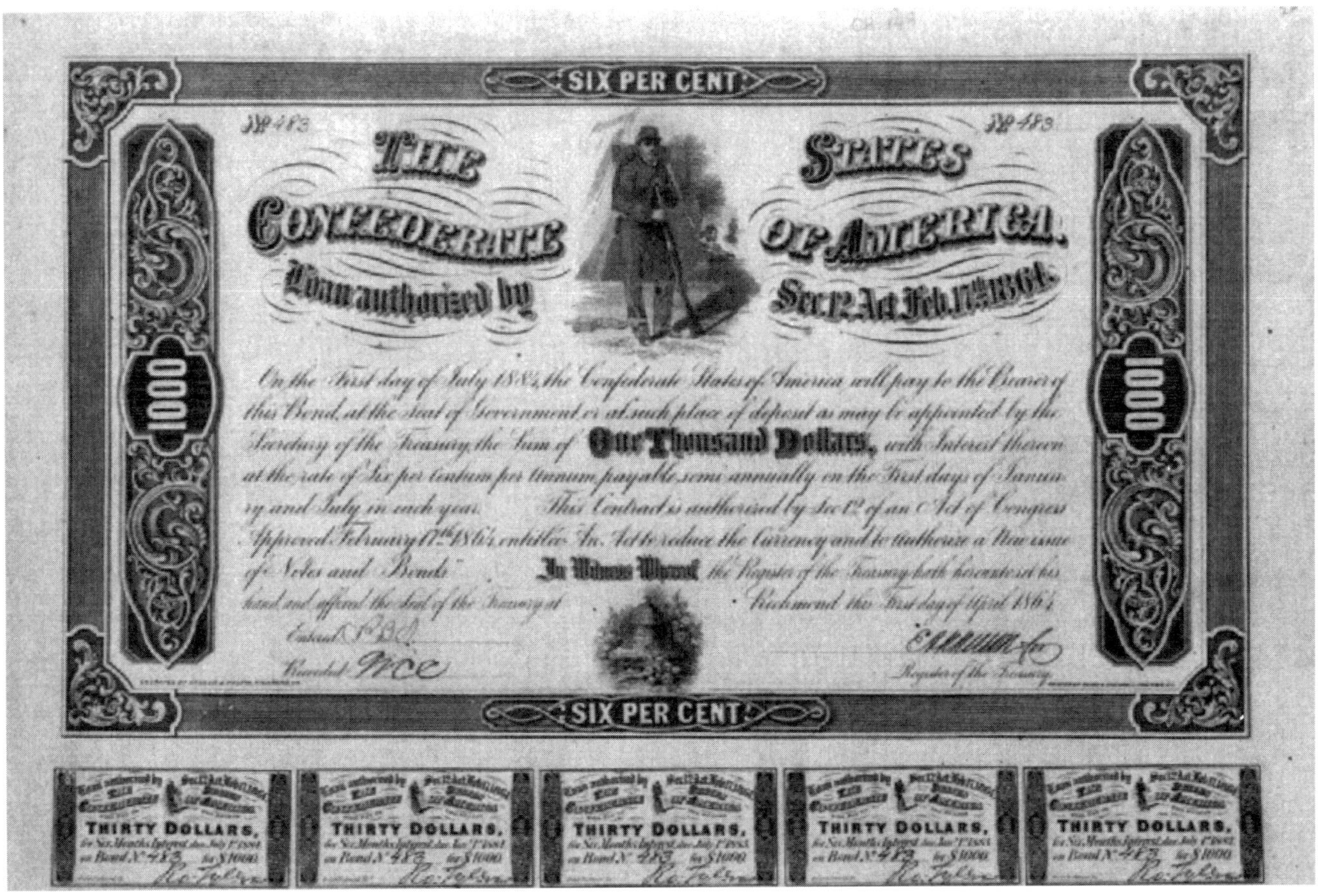

TYPE 177 **$1,000**[141]

Printers and design similar to 354

360.	$1,000	Printed on white paper. Number issued: #1-1100 Dates of issue: unknown Signed by Apperson.	Rarity (5-)	$125	$250
361.	$1,000	Printed on white paper. Remainders. Number printed: c. 2900 (#1101-4000) Dates of issue: n/a	Rarity (5)	$100	$150

F. 6% nontaxable certificates, Section 14

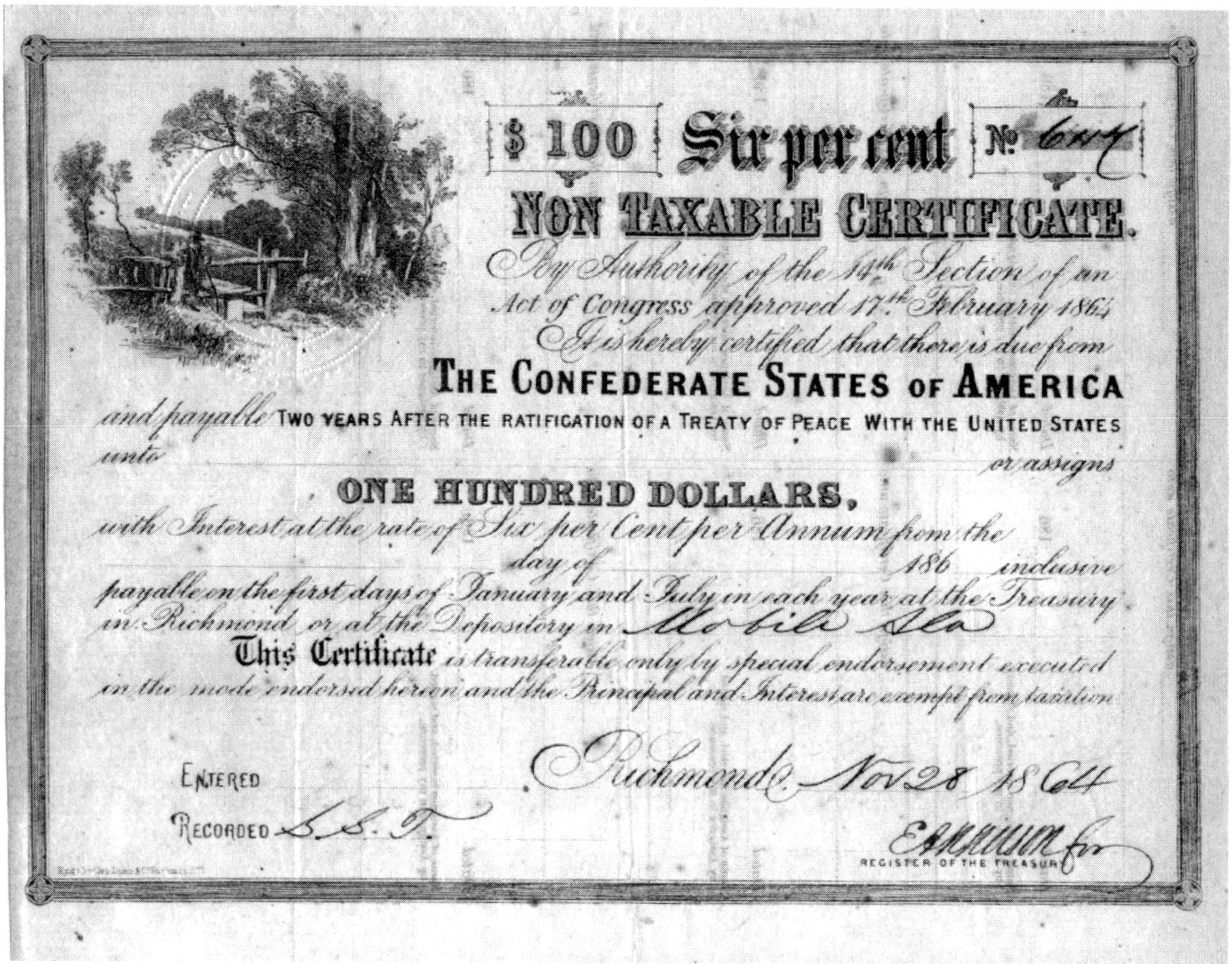

$100 Six per cent № 6447

NON TAXABLE CERTIFICATE.

By Authority of the 14th Section of an Act of Congress approved 17th February 1864

It is hereby certified that there is due from

THE CONFEDERATE STATES OF AMERICA

and payable TWO YEARS AFTER THE RATIFICATION OF A TREATY OF PEACE WITH THE UNITED STATES

unto or assigns

ONE HUNDRED DOLLARS,

with Interest at the rate of Six per Cent per Annum from the day of 186 inclusive payable on the first days of January and July in each year at the Treasury in Richmond or at the Depository in Mobile Ala

This Certificate is transferable only by special endorsement executed in the mode endorsed hereon and the Principal and Interest are exempt from taxation

Richmond Nov 28 1864

ENTERED

RECORDED S. S. T.

REGISTER OF THE TREASURY

(man and stile at top left)

The nontaxable certificates of indebtedness besides falling into denomination and transfer form varieties are also marked by a considerable quantity of partially issued or unissued remainders. A certificate is only completely issued when a payee's name is inserted over the written denomination at the center. Remainders or partially issued remainders arose from the changeover from long to short transfer forms, all the printed long forms became obsolete and are found with and without stub, and totally blank. Quite a few forms were sent to the pay depositaries and assistant treasurers partially made up. Many of these remained unsold at the end of the war. Prices of the fully issued certificates are those given; unissued or partially issued forms run between 50% up to 75% of those quoted. Moreover, items issued west of the Mississippi River command premiums of 200% to 300%.

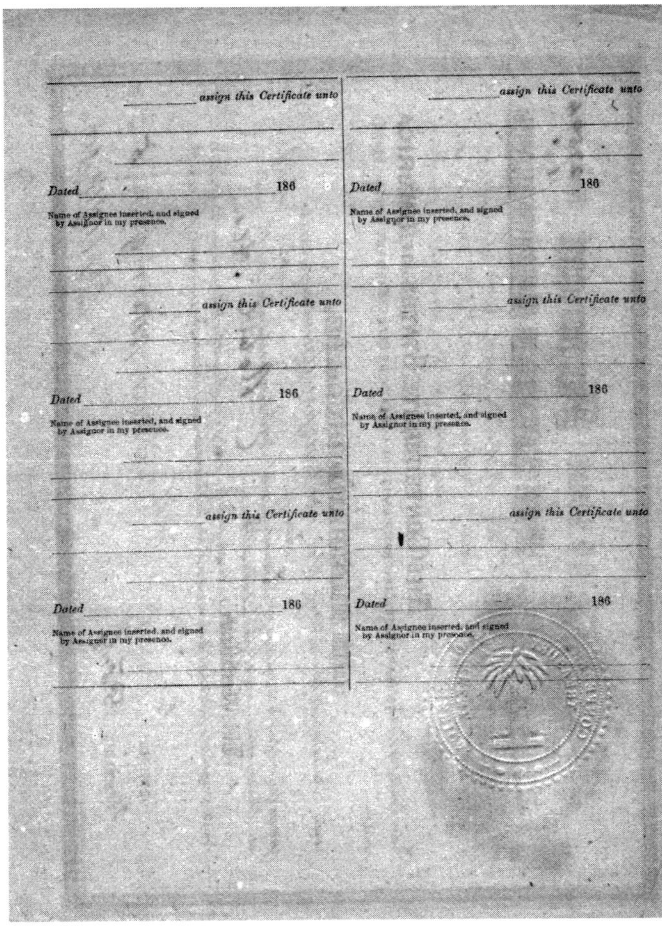

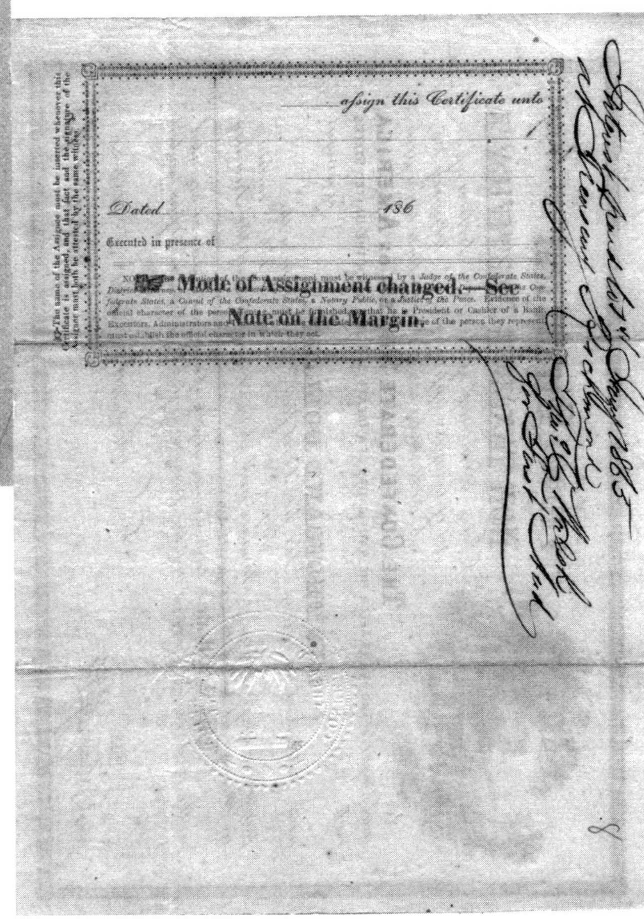

(long transfer form—spaces for six transfers) (short transfer form—the large two-line overprint is red)

TYPE 178 **$100**

Imprint: "Engd. by Geo. Dunn & Co. Richmond, Va"

				fine	very fine
362.	$100	Printed on white paper, long transfer form on back. Number issued: c. 12,500 (#1-12500)[142] Dates of issue: c. August 1864 - March 10, 1865 Signed by Apperson, Rose, Tyler.	Rarity (3+)	$50	$100
363.	$100	Printed as above, short transfer form on back. Number issued: c. 1,311 (#12501-13811)[143] Dates of issue: March 11 - April 1, 1865 Signed by Apperson, Rose.	Rarity (6-)	$125	$200

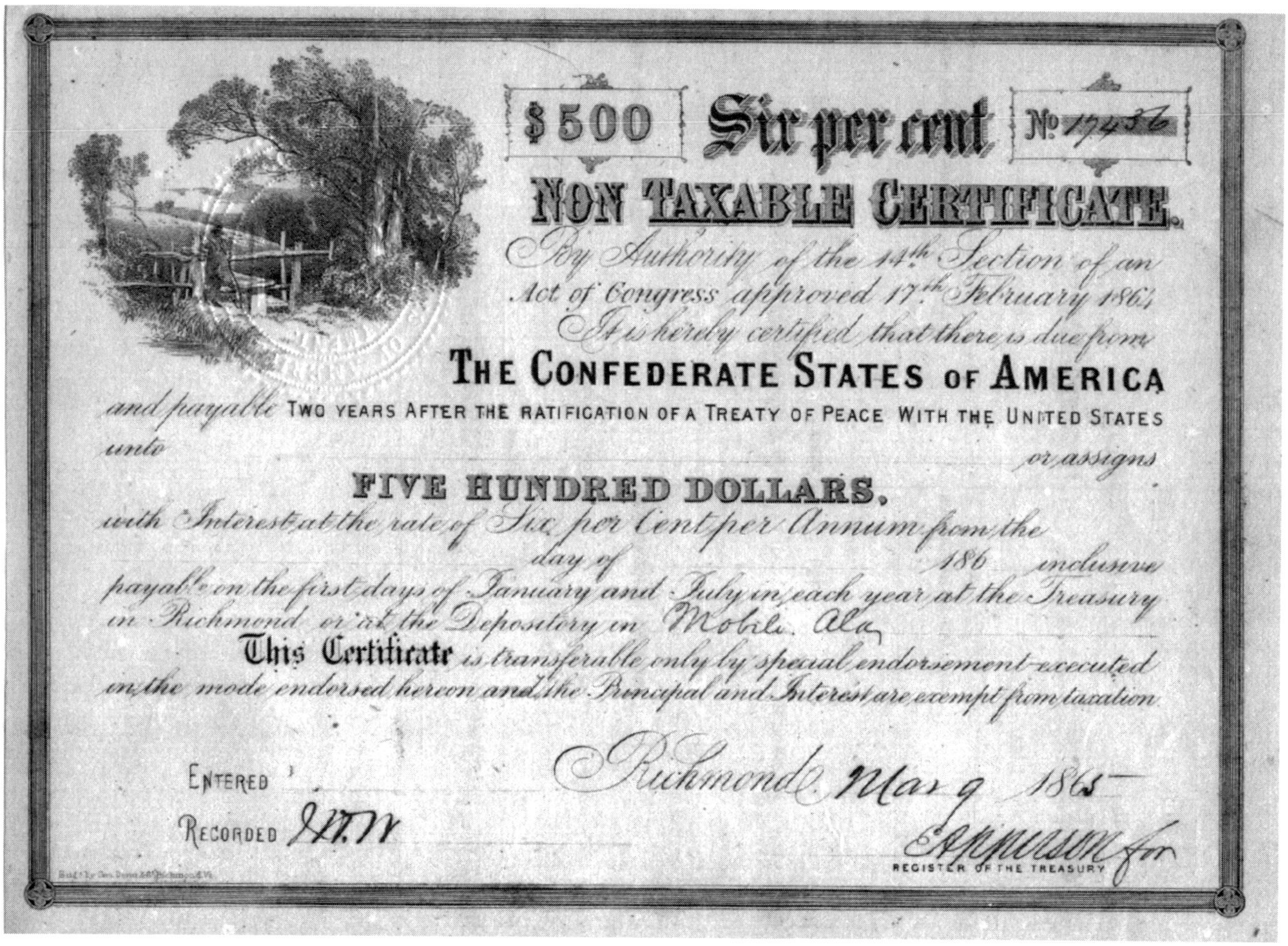
$500 Six per cent No 17436
NON TAXABLE CERTIFICATE.
By Authority of the 14th Section of an Act of Congress approved 17th February 1864
It is hereby certified that there is due from
THE CONFEDERATE STATES OF AMERICA
and payable TWO YEARS AFTER THE RATIFICATION OF A TREATY OF PEACE WITH THE UNITED STATES
unto or assigns
FIVE HUNDRED DOLLARS,
with Interest at the rate of Six per Cent per Annum from the day of 186 inclusive
payable on the first days of January and July in each year at the Treasury in Richmond or at the Depository in Mobile Ala
This Certificate is transferable only by special endorsement executed in the mode endorsed hereon and the Principal and Interest are exempt from taxation
Richmond May 9 1865
ENTERED
RECORDED
REGISTER OF THE TREASURY

TYPE 179 **$500**

Engraver and description similar to the preceding, except for the denomination.

364.	$500	Printed on white paper, long transfer form on back. Number issued: c. 20,000 (#1-20000)[144] Dates of issue: c. August 1864 - March 1, 1865 Signed by Rose, Apperson.	Rarity (3-)	$50	$100

				fine	very fine
365.	$500	Printed as above, with short transfer form on back. Number issued: c. 4,650 (#20001-24650) Dates of issue: c. March 2 - April 1, 1865 Signed by Rose, Apperson.	Rarity (4)	$90	$150

$1000 Six per cent № 6139
NON TAXABLE CERTIFICATE.
By Authority of the 14th Section of an Act of Congress approved 17th February 1864,
It is hereby certified that there is due from
THE CONFEDERATE STATES OF AMERICA
and payable TWO YEARS AFTER THE RATIFICATION OF A TREATY OF PEACE WITH THE UNITED STATES
unto Sampson Lee & Co or assigns
ONE THOUSAND DOLLARS,
with Interest at the rate of Six per Cent per Annum from the fifth day of Sept 1864 inclusive
payable on the first days of January and July in each year at the Treasury in Richmond ~~or at the Depository in~~
This Certificate is transferable only by special endorsement executed in the mode endorsed hereon and the Principal and Interest are exempt from taxation.
Richmond, Sept 5 1864
ENTERED
RECORDED
E Apperson for
REGISTER OF THE TREASURY

TYPE 180 **$1,000**

Engraver and design similar to the preceding.

366.	$1,000	Printed on white paper, long transfer form on back. Number issued: c. 25,000 (#1-25000)[145] Dates of issue: c. August 1864 - March 1, 1865 Signed by Rose, Apperson.	Rarity (3)	$50	$100
367.	$1,000	Same, but short transfer form on back. Number issued: 6,460 (#25001-31460) Dates of issue: March 2 - 31, 1865 Signed by Rose, Apperson.	Rarity (4)	$75	$125

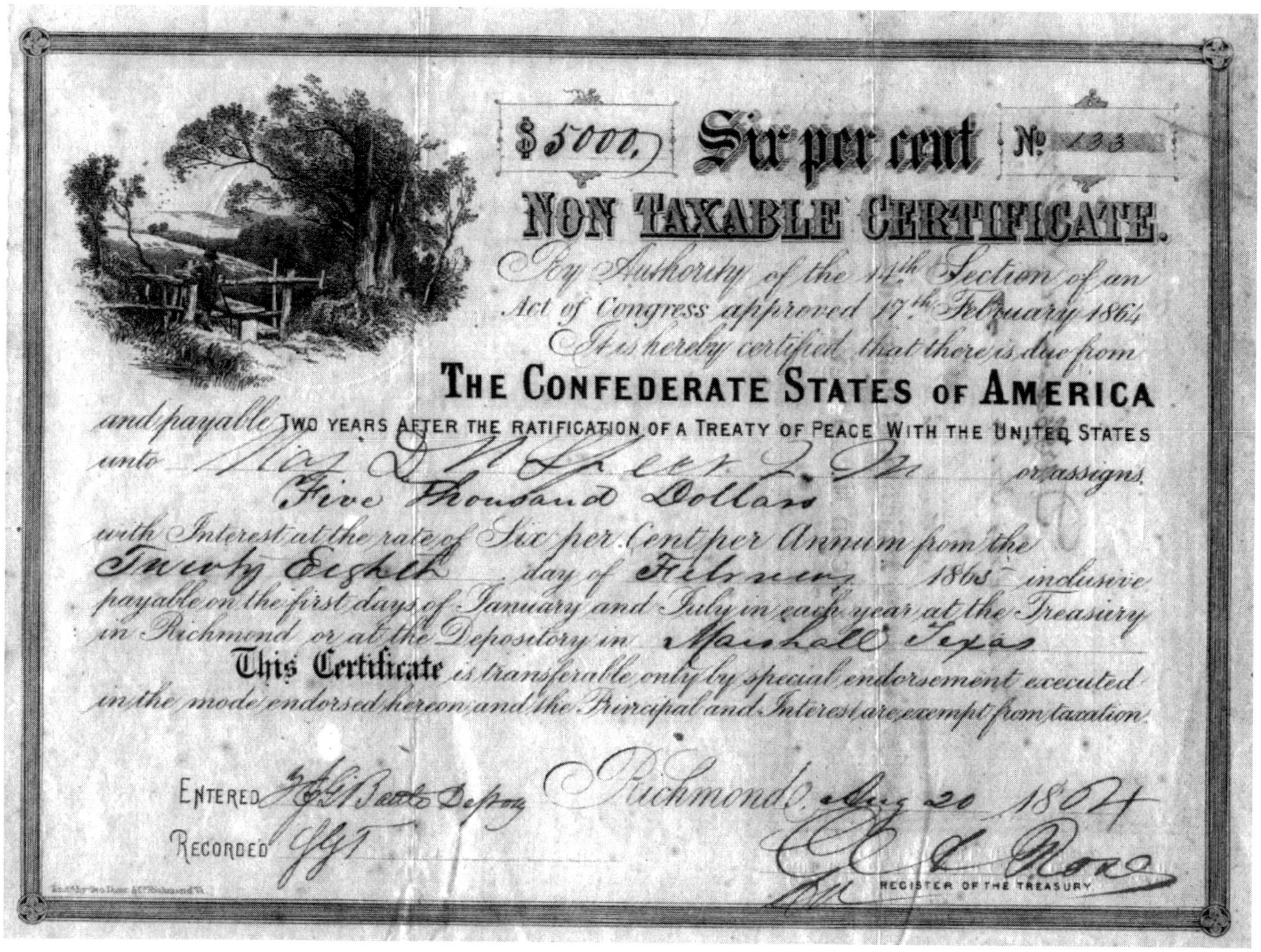
$5000, Six per cent №
NON TAXABLE CERTIFICATE.
By Authority of the 14th Section of an Act of Congress approved 17th February 1864
It is hereby certified that there is due from
THE CONFEDERATE STATES OF AMERICA
and payable TWO YEARS AFTER THE RATIFICATION OF A TREATY OF PEACE WITH THE UNITED STATES
unto or assigns
Five Thousand Dollars
with Interest at the rate of Six per Cent per Annum from the Twenty Eighth day of February 1865 inclusive
payable on the first days of January and July in each year at the Treasury
in Richmond or at the Depository in Marshall Texas
This Certificate is transferable only by special endorsement executed in the mode endorsed hereon and the Principal and Interest are exempt from taxation.
ENTERED Richmond, Aug 20 1864
RECORDED
REGISTER OF THE TREASURY

(man and stile, top left)

TYPE 181 **$5,000**
Imprint: "Engd. by Geo. Dunn & Co., Richmond, Va"

				fine	very fine
368.	$5,000	Printed on white paper, long transfer form on back. Number issued: 850 (#1-850) Dates of issue: August 1864 - March 1, 1865 Signed by Rose, Apperson.	Rarity (7-)	$300	$500
369.	$5,000	Same, short transfer form on back. Number issued: c. 91 (#851-941) Dates of issue: March 2-22, 1865 Signed by Rose, Apperson.	Rarity (7+)	$500	$750

TYPE 182 **$10,000**

				fine	very fine
370.	$10,000	Printed on white paper, long transfer form on back.			
		Number issued: c. 130 (#1-130)	Rarity (7)	$750	$1500
		Dates of issue: c. August 1864 - Feb. 23, 1865			
		Signed by Tyler, Rose.			
371.	$10,000	Printed on white paper, on short transfer form on back.			
		Number issued: c. 60 (#131-190)	Rarity (7+)	$1,250	
		Dates of issue: c. February 24 - March 29, 1865			
		Signed by Rose.			

G. 4% coupon bonds, Section 14

The six bonds that follow were issued to the states under Section 14 of the Act of February 17, 1864 as amended. The purpose was to furnish coupon bonds in lieu of registered bonds, which the states would have more trouble selling. The supply of bonds number 375-377 being limited, others were issued, see items 384-386.

4 PER CENT CSA INTEREST

ONE THOUSAND DOLLARS ONE THOUSAND DOLLARS

Confederate STATES OF AMERICA.

No 1461 No 1461

LOAN AUTHORIZED BY Act of Congress C.S.A. of MARCH 23rd 1863.

FOUR PER CENT ACT MARCH 23.1863

On the first day of April 1893. The Confederate States of America will pay to the Bearer of this Bond at the Seat of Government, or at such place of Deposit as may be appointed by the Secretary of the Treasury, the sum of ONE THOUSAND DOLLARS with interest from date at the rate of FOUR PER CENT, per annum payable semi-annually, on the surrender of the annexed Coupons. This contract is authorized by an Act of Congress, approved March 23rd 1863, Entitled "An Act to provide for the funding and further issue of Treasury Notes," and is upon the express condition, that it shall be redeemable five years after date at the pleasure of the Government.

Semi annual Coupons are hereunto attached for the said period of five years, after which should this Bond not be redeemed, another Bond for the same amount, with semi annual Coupons, at the same rate of interest for the remainder of the thirty years, will be delivered to the holder, upon the surrender of this Bond.

In Witness Whereof, the Register of the Treasury in pursuance of the said Act of Congress, hath hereunto set his hand and affixed the seal of the Treasury, at Richmond, this first day of April 1863.

Entered
Recorded WCC

C. T. Jones for
Register of the Treasury.

C. S. Loan of March 23rd 1863.	C. S. Loan of March 23rd 1863.	C. S. Loan of March 23rd 1863.	C. S. Loan of March 23rd 1863.
The Confederate States of America	The Confederate States of America	The Confederate States of America	The Confederate States of America
Will pay to Bearer the sum of TWENTY DOLLARS, For Six Months Interest due April 1st 1868.	Will pay to Bearer the sum of TWENTY DOLLARS, For Six Months Interest due Oct 1st 1867.	Will pay to Bearer the sum of TWENTY DOLLARS, For Six Months Interest due April 1st 1867.	Will pay to Bearer the sum of TWENTY DOLLARS, For Six Months Interest due Oct 1st 1866.
On Bond No 1460 For $1,000	On Bond No 1460 For $1,000	On Bond No 1460 For $1,000	On Bond No 1460 For $1,000
For Register of the Treasury	For Register of the Treasury	For Register of the Treasury	For Register of the Treasury

(Equestrian statue of George Washington near the capitol in Richmond, Virginia)

TYPE 183 **$100**

No.	Value	Description	Rarity	fine	very fine
372.	$100	Printed on white paper. March 23, 1863 bonds converted for Act of February 17, 1864 use.[146] Number issued: c. 55 (#14-68) Dates of issue: up to February 8, 1865	Rarity (—)	(—)	(—)

TYPE 184 **$500**

No.	Value	Description	Rarity	fine	very fine
373.	$500	As last, printed on white paper.[147] Number issued: 53 (#7-59) Dates of issue: up to February 8, 1865	Rarity (—)	(—)	(—)

TYPE 185 **$1,000**

No.	Value	Description	Rarity	fine	very fine
374.	$1,000	As last, printed on white paper.[148] Number issued: c. 813 (#19-831) Dates of issue: up to March 1865 Signed by Rose.	Rarity (7-)	$1,000	(—)

H. 6% coupon bonds, Section 18

ONE THOUSAND DOLLARS

Confederate States of America.

No 14774

Loan authorized by Act of Congress, C.S.A. of March 23rd 1863.

SIX PER CENT

On the first day of April 1893 The Confederate States of America will pay to the Bearer of this Bond at the Seat of Government, or at such place of Deposit as may be appointed by the Secretary of the Treasury, the sum of ONE THOUSAND DOLLARS with interest from date at the rate of Six per cent per annum, payable semi-annually, on the surrender of the annexed Coupons. This contract is authorized by an Act of Congress approved March 23rd 1863 Entitled "An Act to provide for the funding and further issue of Treasury Notes," and is upon the express condition that it shall be redeemable five years after date at the pleasure of the Government.

Semi annual Coupons are hereunto attached for the said period of five years, after which, should this Bond not be redeemed, another Bond for the same amount, with semi annual Coupons, at the same rate of interest for the remainder of the thirty years, will be delivered to the holder, upon the surrender of this Bond.

In Witness Whereof, the Register of the Treasury, in pursuance of the said Act of Congress hath hereunto set his hand, and affixed the seal of the Treasury, at Richmond, this first day of April, 1863.

Entered
Recorded

Register of the Treasury.

C.S. Loan of March 23rd 1863. The Confederate States of America Will pay to Bearer the sum of THIRTY DOLLARS. For Six Months Interest due ... On Bond No 14774 For $1,000

(Old Customs House in Richmond, Virginia)

TYPE 186 **$100**

Imprint: "Eng'd. by Geo. Dunn & Co., Richmond, Va"

				fine	very fine
375.	$100	Printed on white paper. March 23, 1863 bonds converted for Act of February 17, 1864 use.[149]			
		Number issued: 55 (#4869-4923)	Rarity (7+)	$700	$1000
		Dates of issue: unknown			
		Signed by Apperson.			

TYPE 187 **$500**
Imprint: "Eng'd. by Geo. Dunn & Co., Richmond, Va"

				fine	very fine
376.	$500	Printed on white paper. March 23, 1863 bonds converted for Act of February 17, 1864 use.[150]			
		Number issued: 53 (#2352-2404)	Rarity (7+)	$700	$1000
		Dates of issue: unknown			
		Signed by Rose.			

TYPE 188 **$1000**
"Printed by Evans & Cogswell, Columbia S.C."

377.	$1000	Printed on white paper. March 23, 1863 bonds converted for Act of February 17, 1864 use.[151]			
		Number issued: 767 (#14280-15046)	Rarity (6+)	$250	$350
		Dates of issue: unknown			
		Signed by Rose.			

XV. ACT OF JUNE 13, 1864

(amendatory to the Act of May 16, 1861)[152]

Because the July 25, 1861 treasury notes were still being gathered in and because the holders of registered bonds often wanted to exchange them for coupon bonds, the Congress under this act authorized the issue of a series of $100, $500 and $1000 coupon bonds for this purpose. The bonds were apparently engraved by Fred Geese and printed by Evans & Cogswell. The $1000 bonds are readily available, but the properly issued $100 and $500 pieces are quite rare. Remainder bonds are also seldom seen, although there are a number of falsely filled in $500 bonds in the 401-862 number range.

Coupon bonds

CONFEDERATE STATES of AMERICA

No 1189 $1000

LOAN

Authorized by Act of Congress, approved May 16th 1861,
AS AMENDED BY ACT OF CONGRESS, APPROVED JUNE 13, 1864.

On the first day of July, 1874, The Confederate States of America will pay to the bearer of this Bond, at the seat of Government, or at such place of Deposit as may be appointed by the Secretary of the Treasury, the Sum of ONE THOUSAND DOLLARS, with interest thereon from date, at the rate of Eight per Cent per annum, payable Semi-Annually, on the surrender of the annexed Coupons. This Contract is authorized by an Act of Congress, approved June 13, 1864, entitled, "An Act to authorize the Owners of the Registered 8 per Ct. ten year Convertible bonds issued under the provisions of the Act approved May 16, 1861, to exchange the same for Coupon Bonds."

In Witness whereof the Register of the Treasury, in pursuance of regulations prescribed by the Secretary of the Treasury, as authorized by said Act of Congress, hath hereunto set his hand, and affixed the Seal of the Treasury Department, at Richmond, this 1st day of July, 1864.

Entered

Recorded MRS

Ro: Tyler
Register of the Treasury

Evans & Cogswell, Columbia S.C.

C.S. LOAN of MAY 16, 1861. AMENDED JUNE 13, 1864. CONFEDERATE STATES of AMERICA Will pay FORTY DOLLARS to bearer for Six Months Interest, Due July 1, 1874. 8 PR BOND No 1189 for $1000. Ro: Tyler REGR

C.S. LOAN of MAY 16, 1861. AMENDED JUNE 13, 1864. CONFEDERATE STATES of AMERICA Will pay FORTY DOLLARS to bearer for Six Months Interest, Due Jany 1, 1874. 8 PR BOND No 1189 for $1000. Ro: Tyler REGR

C.S. LOAN of MAY 16, 1861. AMENDED JUNE 13, 1864. CONFEDERATE STATES of AMERICA Will pay FORTY DOLLARS to bearer for Six Months Interest, Due July 1, 1873. 8 PR BOND No 1189 for $1000. Ro: Tyler REGR

C.S. LOAN of MAY 16, 1861. AMENDED JUNE 13, 1864. CONFEDERATE STATES of AMERICA Will pay FORTY DOLLARS to bearer for Six Months Interest, Due Jany 1, 1873. 8 PR BOND No 1189 for $1000. Ro: Tyler REGR

TYPE 189 **$100**

Imprint: "Lith. F. Geese"; "Printed by Evans & Cogswell, Columbia S.C."

No.	Denomination	Description	Rarity	fine	very fine
381.	$100	Printed on white paper. Number issued: 75 (#1-75) Dates of issue: unknown Signed by Rose.	Rarity (7+)	$1,000	$1,250

TYPE 190 **$500**

Imprint: "Lith. F. Geese"; "Printed by Evans & Cogswell, Columbia, S.C."

No.	Denomination	Description	Rarity	fine	very fine
382.	$500	Printed on white paper. Number issued: 73 (#1-73)[153] Dates of issue: unknown Signed by Apperson, Jones.	Rarity (7)	$1,000	$1,250

TYPE 191 **$500**

Imprint: "Lith. F. Geese"; "Printed by Evans & Cogswell, Columbia, S.C."

No.	Denomination	Description	Rarity	fine	very fine
383.	$500	Similar, but falsely filled in remainders.[154] Number issued: c. 187 (#701-887) Dates of issue: early 1865 Signed by Rose.	Rarity (7-)	$300	$400

TYPE 192 **$1,000**

Imprint: "Lith. F. Geese"; printed by "Evans & Cogswell, Columbia, S.C."

No.	Denomination	Description	Rarity	fine	very fine
384.	$1,000	Printed on white paper. Number issued: 2,120 (#1-2120) Dates of issue: unknown Signed by Rose, Tyler.	Rarity (4+)	$100	$150

XVI. ACT OF JUNE 14, 1864

(Amendatory to the Act of February 17, 1864)

The Act of February 17, 1864, section twelve, had made provision for 4% coupon bonds without being very specific on that score. To remedy this deficiency, Congress, at Secretary Memminger's behest, made provision for such an issue. A few days after this act was passed, the CSS *Alabama* was sunk off the coast of France near Cherbourg, on June 17, 1864. The bonds were designed by Evans & Cogswell with a vignette of the CSS *Alabama* as a memorial to its loss. Once again, the amounts reported issued do not reflect the amounts actually emitted. This is doubly true of the $1000 denomination. While fifty-seven pieces of the $500 were found in the London hoard, none of the $1000 bonds were discovered there and indeed only one, from a Thian album, has been handled by me since 1957. They are either lurking in some archives or have suffered destruction.

4% coupon bonds

(CSS *Alabama* at center)

TYPE 193 **$500**

Imprint: "Engraved by Evans & Cogswell Columbia South Carolina"

				fine	very fine
385.	$500	Printed on white paper. Number issued: 2,000 (#1-2000) Dates of issue: n/a Signed by Tyler.	Rarity (6-)	$700	$900

TYPE 194 **$1,000**

Imprint similar to the preceding.

386.	$1,000	Printed on white paper. Number issued: 3,000 (#1-3000) Dates of issue: n/a Signed by Tyler.	Rarity (7+)[155]	$7,500	$10,000

XVII. ACT OF NOVEMBER 28, 1864

The final act for which any bonds are known to have been issued was the Act of November 28, 1864. This act called for the mandatory exchange of the 7.30% notes for 6% thirty year bonds. Forms were prepared for use at various depositories to effect this exchange, and some $300,000 of such bonds were reported issued before the end of the war. However, if these bonds were actually issued, none have been seen to date and perhaps some of the section six bonds were used for this purpose. Again, we have no way of knowing.

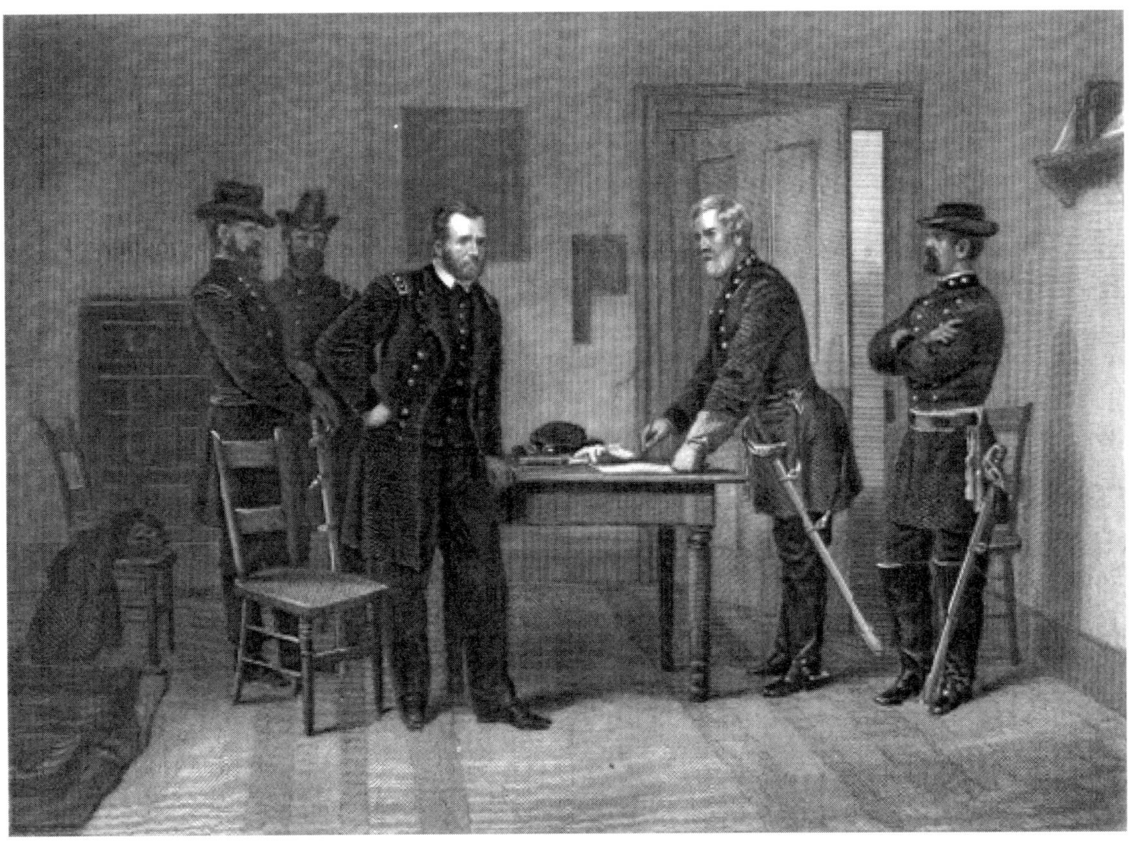

Counterfeit bonds

As I have already noted, availing themselves of the opportunity posed by the British payment of a $20 gold piece for every $1000 face value of Confederate bonds, counterfeiters on the continent, probably in the Netherlands (quite a few have Dutch tax stamps), manufactured additional bonds to meet the demand of the market. Thus it would appear that none of these bonds had anything to do with the Confederacy and were not produced until years later.

Under these circumstances, many collectors do not want such items in their collections, while others continue to desire them. The author's sympathies lie with the first group. However, as a courtesy to the second group, I have listed those bonds that are known to have been copied. All of them are crude, unlike the actually issued bonds, and have poorly forged signatures. For the most part, they are made on a cheap, wood pulp paper that was white and has usually aged to a light or dark tan. Because of its high acidity, the paper is frequently brittle. Frequently, particularly on the Stonewall Jackson bonds, a paper stamp and embossed facsimile seal of the Confederate treasury have been used. If such bonds have been washed, however, the red seal, being made with water soluble ink, has dissolved or become quite faded.

Ball number	Criswell number	Rarity	Value
Ball-C49	(Cr. X-55)	7-	$100
Ball-C50	(Cr. X-82)	6+	$ 80
Ball-C53	(Cr. X-83)	7-	$120
Ball-C62	(Cr. X-85)	7	$120
Ball-C72	(Cr. X-34)	5-	$ 60
Ball-C79	(Cr. X-89)	6+	$ 80
Ball-C105	(Cr. X-95)	7-	$100
Ball-C106	(Cr. X-95A)	7-	$100
Ball-C116	(Cr. X-97)	7-	$100
Ball-C123	(Cr. X-98)	7	$120
Ball-C130	(Cr. X-101)	7-	$100
Ball-C201	(Cr. X-125)	7	$150
Ball-C240A	(Cr. X-122B) "Second series"	3+	$ 50
Ball-C240B	(Cr. X-122C) "Third series"	3+	$ 50
Ball Fantasy	(Cr. XX1)	6+	$250

$1000 Confederate States LOAN of America $1000

Authorized by the Act of Congress C.S.A. of August 19, 1861.

EIGHT PER CENT

JANUARY 1 1868

No.

No.

On the first day of January 1868 The Confederate States of America will pay to the Bearer of this Bond at the Seat of Government or such place of Deposit as may be appointed by the Secretary of the Treasury the sum of One Thousand Dollars, with interest thereon from this date payable at the same places, semi annually, at the rate of Eight per cent per annum, on surrender of the annexed Warrants or Coupons. This debt is authorized by an act of Congress approved August 19 1861 entitled "An Act to Authorize the issue of Treasury Notes and to provide a War tax for their redemption."

In Witness Whereof the Register of the Treasury in pursuance of the said Act of Congress hath hereunto set his hand and affixed the seal of the Treasury at Richmond, this 18 day of June 1862

Entered

Recorded

Register of the Treasury

C.S. Loan of August 19 1861
The Confederate States of America
Will pay to bearer FORTY DOLLARS for six Months Interest due Janry 1 1868 on Bond No for $1000
For the Register of the Treasury

C.S. Loan of August 19 1861
The Confederate States of America
Will pay to bearer FORTY DOLLARS for six Months Interest due July 1 1867 on Bond No for $1000
For the Register of the Treasury

C.S. Loan of August 19 1861
The Confederate States of America
Will pay to bearer FORTY DOLLARS for six Months Interest due Janry 1 1867 on Bond No for $1000
For the Register of the Treasury

C.S. Loan of August 19 1861
The Confederate States of America
Will pay to bearer FORTY DOLLARS for six Months Interest due July 1 1866 on Bond No for $1000
For the Register of the Treasury

C.S. Loan of August 19 1861
The Confederate States of America
Will pay to bearer FORTY DOLLARS for six Months Interest due Janry 1 1866 on Bond No for $1000
For the Register of the Treasury

C.S. Loan of August 19 1861
The Confederate States of America
Will pay to bearer FORTY DOLLARS for six Months Interest due July 1 1865 on Bond No for $1000
For the Register of the Treasury

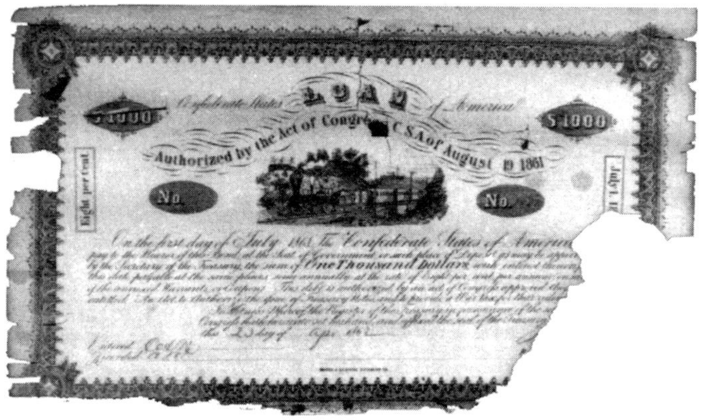
$1000
$1000
Authorized by the Act of Congress C.S.A. of August 19 1861
Eight per Cent
No.
No.

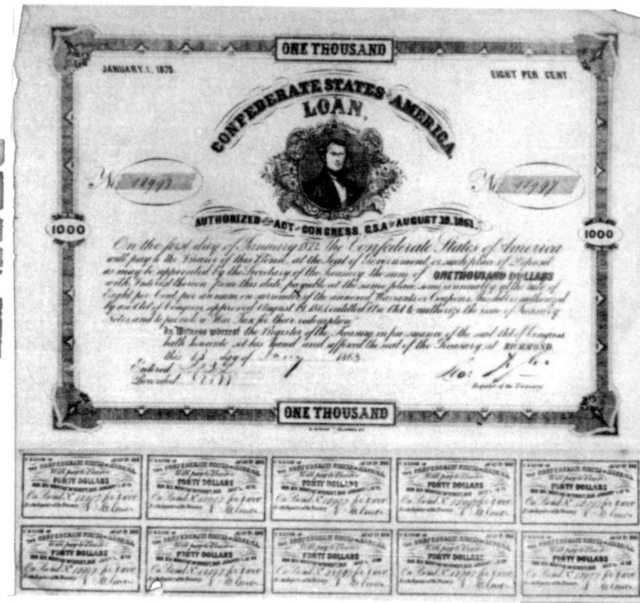
ONE THOUSAND
JANUARY 1, 1879.
EIGHT PER CENT.
CONFEDERATE STATES OF AMERICA
LOAN
1000
1000
AUTHORIZED BY ACT OF CONGRESS, C.S.A. AUGUST 19, 1861.
ONE THOUSAND

ONE THOUSAND
JANUARY 1 1876
EIGHT PER CENT
CONFEDERATE STATES OF AMERICA
LOAN
1000
1000
AUTHORIZED BY ACT OF CONGRESS C.S.A. AUGUST 19, 1861.
ONE THOUSAND

ONE THOUSAND
EIGHT PER CENT.
CONFEDERATE STATES OF AMERICA
LOAN
1000
1000
AUTHORIZED BY ACT OF CONGRESS, C.S.A. AUGUST 19, 1861.
ONE THOUSAND

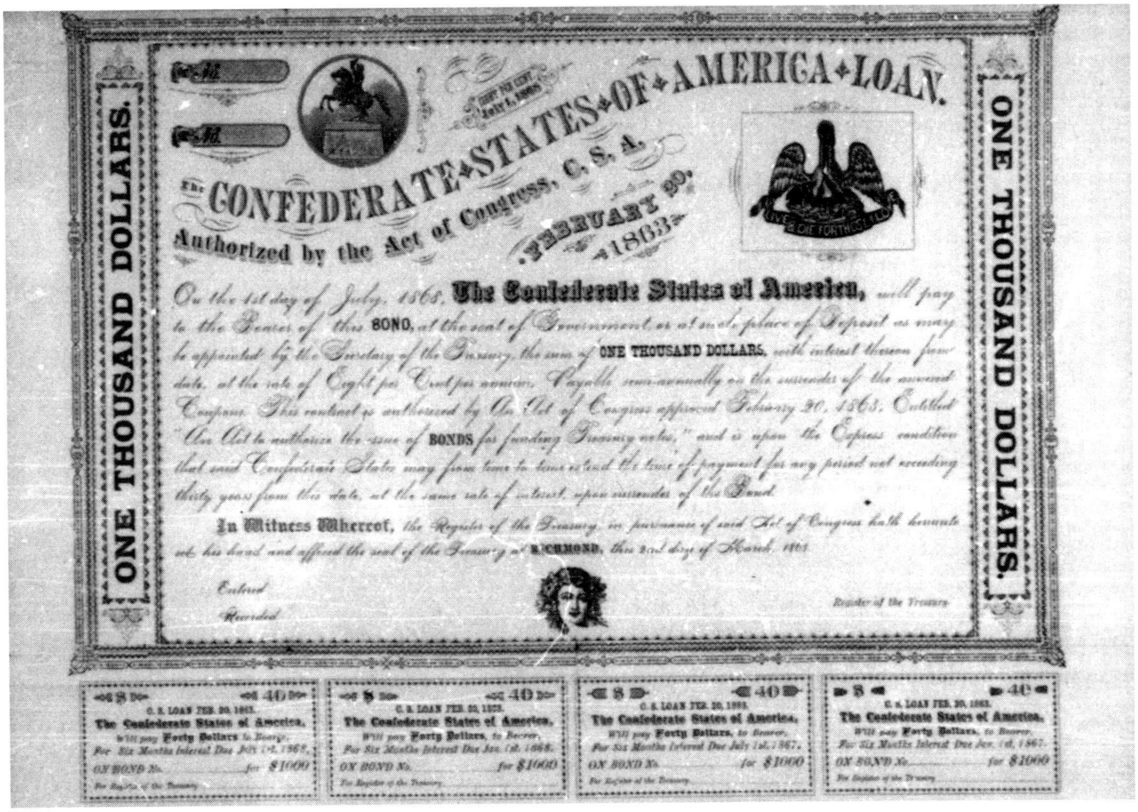

ONE THOUSAND DOLLARS.

THE CONFEDERATE STATES OF AMERICA LOAN.

Authorized by the Act of Congress, C. S. A. February 20, 1863.

On the 1st day of July, 1868, The Confederate States of America, will pay to the Bearer of this BOND, at the seat of Government, or at such place of Deposit as may be appointed by the Secretary of the Treasury, the sum of ONE THOUSAND DOLLARS, with interest thereon from date, at the rate of Eight per Cent per annum, Payable semi-annually on the surrender of the annexed Coupons. This contract is authorized by An Act of Congress approved February 20, 1863, Entitled "An Act to authorize the issue of BONDS for funding Treasury notes," and is upon the Express condition that said Confederate States may from time to time extend the time of payment for any period not exceeding thirty years from this date, at the same rate of interest, upon surrender of the Bond.

In Witness Whereof, the Register of the Treasury, in pursuance of said Act of Congress hath hereunto set his hand and affixed the seal of the Treasury at RICHMOND, this 2nd day of March, 1863.

Entered

Recorded

Register of the Treasury

ONE THOUSAND DOLLARS.

8 — 40	8 — 40	8 — 40	8 — 40
C. S. LOAN FEB. 20, 1863.	C. S. LOAN FEB. 20, 1863.	C. S. LOAN FEB. 20, 1863.	C. S. LOAN FEB. 20, 1863.
The Confederate States of America,	The Confederate States of America,	The Confederate States of America,	The Confederate States of America,
Will pay Forty Dollars, to Bearer,	Will pay Forty Dollars, to Bearer,	Will pay Forty Dollars, to Bearer,	Will pay Forty Dollars, to Bearer,
For Six Months Interest Due July 1st, 1868.	For Six Months Interest Due Jan. 1st, 1868.	For Six Months Interest Due July 1st, 1867.	For Six Months Interest Due Jan. 1st, 1867.
ON BOND No. ______ for $1000	ON BOND No. ______ for $1000	ON BOND No. ______ for $1000	ON BOND No. ______ for $1000
For Register of the Treasury	For Register of the Treasury	For Register of the Treasury	For Register of the Treasury

Other fiscal paper

The forms issued by the Confederate authorities at the treasurer's office, the offices of the assistant treasurers, or at the offices of the pay and funding depositaries throughout the Confederacy, will be included in a second edition of this book or in a separate book as required of this currency series, together with warrants, checks, and other assorted fiscal instruments that fall neither into the bond/call certificate nor currency categories.

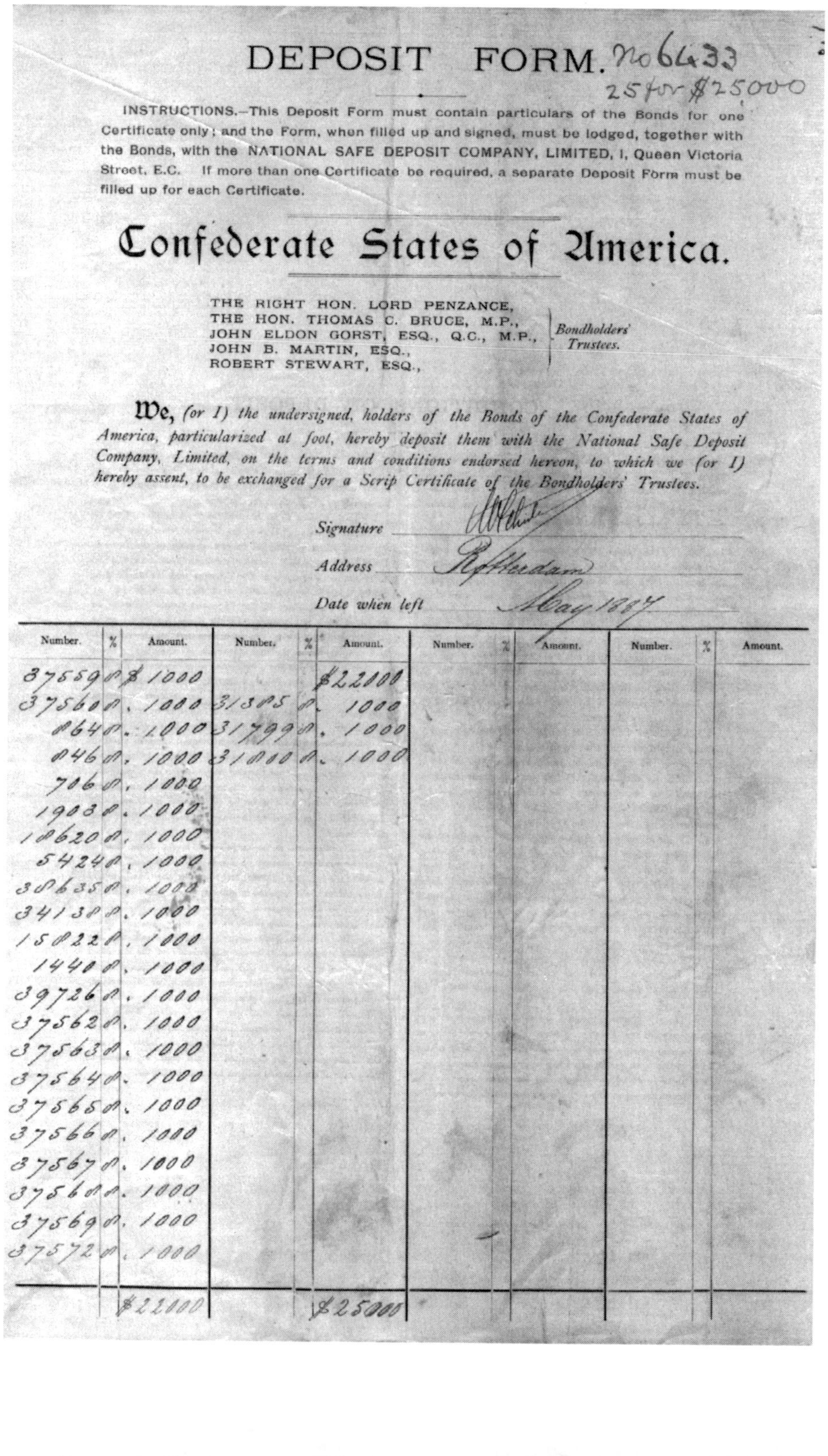

DEPOSIT FORM. No 6433
25 for $25000

INSTRUCTIONS.—This Deposit Form must contain particulars of the Bonds for one Certificate only; and the Form, when filled up and signed, must be lodged, together with the Bonds, with the NATIONAL SAFE DEPOSIT COMPANY, LIMITED, 1, Queen Victoria Street, E.C. If more than one Certificate be required, a separate Deposit Form must be filled up for each Certificate.

Confederate States of America.

THE RIGHT HON. LORD PENZANCE,
THE HON. THOMAS C. BRUCE, M.P.,
JOHN ELDON GORST, ESQ., Q.C., M.P.,
JOHN B. MARTIN, ESQ.,
ROBERT STEWART, ESQ.,
Bondholders' Trustees.

We, *(or I) the undersigned, holders of the Bonds of the Confederate States of America, particularized at foot, hereby deposit them with the National Safe Deposit Company, Limited, on the terms and conditions endorsed hereon, to which we (or I) hereby assent, to be exchanged for a Scrip Certificate of the Bondholders' Trustees.*

Signature [signature]

Address Rotterdam

Date when left May 1887

Number.	%	Amount.	Number.	%	Amount.	Number.	%	Amount.	Number.	%	Amount.
37559	0	$1000			$22000						
37560	0	1000	31385	0	1000						
064	0	1000	31799	0	1000						
046	0	1000	31000	0	1000						
706	0	1000									
1903	0	1000									
10620	0	1000									
5424	0	1000									
30635	0	1000									
34130	0	1000									
15022	0	1000									
1440	0	1000									
39726	0	1000									
37562	0	1000									
37563	0	1000									
37564	0	1000									
37565	0	1000									
37566	0	1000									
37567	0	1000									
37568	0	1000									
37569	0	1000									
37572	0	1000									
		$22000			$25000						

31

CONDITIONS OF DEPOSIT.

1.—The Right Hon. Lord Penzance, the Hon. Thomas C. Bruce, M.P., John Eldon Gorst, Esq., Q.C., M.P., John B. Martin, Esq., and Robert Stewart, Esq., are hereby constituted the Trustees for the Confederate Bondholders, herein called the Trustees, for the following purposes, namely, to deposit the Bonds with the National Safe Deposit Company, Limited, on the terms of these conditions, and to issue Certificates for the Bonds so deposited, with full powers for the Trustees from time to time to agree to any arrangement for settlement of the Bondholders' claims either wholly or partially, to give receipts and discharges, and in all respects to act as the representatives of the Bondholders as the Trustees in their absolute discretion may think fit.

2.—The Trustees have power from time to time to add to their number, to fill up any vacancies in their body and to regulate their meetings and proceedings in every way. All acts herein empowered to be done by the Trustees may be so done by a majority of them.

3.—A body of Bondholders herein called the Subscribers having agreed to find the requisite funds up to £10,000 for expenses, they are hereby empowered to take all such proceedings as they may think fit for the promotion and furtherance of the interests of the Confederate Bondholders, but no settlement shall be made of the Bondholders' claims without the concurrence of the Trustees.

4.—In consideration of the advances to be so made by the Subscribers towards the expenses, and of their services, they are to be entitled to one half the net proceeds realised from or in respect of any of the deposited bonds over and above 5 per cent. on the nominal amount of such bonds, out of which the remuneration of the Trustees is to be provided for; and all bonds deposited are hereby declared to be bound by this condition.

5.—The sterling Bonds to be represented by one style of Certificate, and all the Dollar Bonds (without reference to their different rates of interest or other circumstances) by another style.

6.—The Bonds when deposited not to be withdrawn without the consent of the Trustees before the 1st July, 1888, or such further period as may be determined by a Meeting of the Bondholders to be convened as after mentioned, but when entitled to be so withdrawn under this condition there shall be no claim or lien upon any of the deposited Bonds for expenses, or otherwise. The Bonds represented by this Certificate can only be withdrawn from the National Safe Deposit Company in exchange for this Certificate and the signatures of at least a majority of the Trustees for the time being.

7.—The Trustees to be empowered from time to time to call Meetings of the holders of the deposited Bonds by public advertisement to be inserted in one or more of the London Daily Newspapers, and in such other newspapers in the United Kingdom or elsewhere as the Trustees may in their discretion think fit, and the decisions of such Meetings shall be binding on the holders of the deposited Bonds generally as to all matters not provided for by these conditions or as to any modifications of the conditions not interfering with the proportion of the net proceeds of the Bonds over 5 per cent. which by condition 4 is reserved for the Subscribers. The Trustees shall take the decision of any meeting so called in such way as they in their discretion may think fit, whether by show of hands or by a poll; if the latter, each Bondholder shall on production of his Certificate be entitled to one vote in respect of each £100 of nominal amount of Bonds deposited by him, dollar Bonds being reckoned for this purpose at \$5 to the £. One of the Trustees shall preside at all meetings called under this condition, but if no Trustee be present the holders of the deposited Bonds attending the meeting may elect their own Chairman.

8.—The Trustees to be empowered to fix from time to time the minimum amount of Bonds to be deposited, and to fix the time for such deposit, and to return the Bonds to the Bondholders if the required minimum be not made up within the time so fixed, or such extended time as the Trustees may from time to time think fit to grant.

9.—The National Safe Deposit Company, and not the Trustees, are responsible for the safe custody of the deposited Bonds until withdrawn as aforesaid, and the Trustees shall not be responsible for any misadventure, default, or miscarriage, in the course of the intended negotiations or arrangements.

10.—The Certificate to be given for deposited Bonds shall for all purposes be considered, during the deposit, to be substituted for the Bonds so deposited, and the holder of any Certificate granted for deposited Bonds shall be considered the owner of such Bonds subject to these conditions.

No. 4060

Confederate States of America.

$5000—

SCRIP CERTIFICATE FOR $5000—

This is to Certify that the Bonds particularized in the Deposit Form No. 4060 amounting to Five thousand dollars, have been deposited with the NATIONAL SAFE DEPOSIT COMPANY, LIMITED, London, under and subject to the endorsed Conditions of Deposit. This Certificate passes by delivery, but the Holder for the time being is only entitled to the same rights as the original Depositor named in the said Deposit Note.

Dated this First day of May 1884

Received the above-mentioned Bonds on behalf of the Bondholders' Trustees.

For THE NATIONAL SAFE DEPOSIT COMPANY, LIMITED.

Director.

Manager.

THE RIGHT HON. LORD PENZANCE
THE HON. THOMAS C. BRUCE, M.P.
JOHN ELDON GORST, Esq., Q.C., M.P.
JOHN B. MARTIN, Esq.
ROBERT STEWART, Esq.
} Trustees.

Per Trustee.

The Bonds represented by this Certificate can be inspected on application at the National Safe Deposit Company, Limited, and presentation of this Certificate. No responsibility can be accepted for the genuineness of the deposited Bonds, or otherwise than for their safe custody by the Safe Deposit Company.

During the period when the British bondholders' committee was active, those depositing Confederate bonds with the committee received certificates that would allow them to retrieve their bonds at a future time. These certificates took several forms. We include a picture for those who find such collateral items of interest.

Footnotes

[1] Only three bonds are complete with an odd denomination $1.33_ coupon payable 1 September 1861.
[2] Only three complete bonds are known with a coupon of $2.66_ payable 1 September 1861.
[3] Sold as lot 425 Smythe sale 102, January 24, 1992, for $7,810.
[4] Ordered in New Orleans at ABN, work transferred to New York; partially completed without coupons before the plates were seized by the U.S. government.
[5] This statement was placed on these bonds at the instigation of James D. Denegre, president of the Citizens' Bank. The order for this change came too late for any but the tail run of $500 bonds; Memminger told Denegre not to have the $1,000 bonds thus printed as it was too late to do any good. Denegre to Memminger, June 7, 1861. Clitherall to Denegre, June 12, 1861. Thian, *Correspondence of*, p. 99. First coupon payable September 1, 1861 with the denomination of $13.33_. No complete bonds seen to date.
[6] Sold as lot 426, Smythe sale 102, January 24, 1992, for $4,180.
[7] Bonds #4614-4653 and 7078-7127 were cancelled at or immediately after preparation. Only one complete bond known with a coupon for $26.66 payable September 1, 1861.
[8] In addition, remainder bonds are known from the number range 751-1000 (book 4), several of which turned up in 1983-85.
[9] Only one seen to date.
[10] Only bonds #1-750 were reportedly received; there may be remainders #751-1000 somewhere, though none has been seen to date.
[11] Remainders may exist for bonds #492-1000.
[12] There are a scattered handful of bonds with "Richmond" not written in.
[13] A few bonds have "Montgomery" crossed out but "Richmond" not written in.
[14] The first twelve $5,000 bonds were handwritten and made payable to the Merchants Bank of Cheraw, S.C. (listed as #20).
[15] Owned by the Bank of Charleston, for which an interest certificate (Ball 282, ex Criswell) was issued on January 1, 1865, for $8,000.
[16] Vignettes taken from Bank of Charleston note plates lent to the Confederate treasury in September 1861. First coupon July 1, 1861.
[17] Vignettes taken from Bank of Charleston plates. Coupon on #1-35 not cancelled in error; 36-619 cancelled; 620-799 not cancelled. First coupon July 1, 1861.
[18] Numbered as issued without regard to denomination.
[19] Last original, not transfer certificate, issued June 1, 1864.
[20] #3366 issued to Exchange Bank branch at Richmond.
[21] 600 printed, most cancelled upon redemption or exchange but many still in existence. First coupon for this series July 1, 1862.
[22] 977 printed.
[23] 600 printed. First coupon for this bond July 1, 1862.
[24] 726 printed. First coupon for this bond January 1, 1863.
[25] 985 printed. First coupon for this bond January 1, 1863.
[26] First coupons for this bond series, July 1, 1862.
[27] 616 printed.
[28] 834 printed.
[29] 1,034 printed.
[30] All bonds have coupons starting with January 1, 1863.
[31] Only bond with this portrait. Moore was surgeon general of the Confederacy.
[32] $100 and $500 with coupons starting on July 1, 1862. $1,000 with coupons beginning January 1, 1862.
[33] Coupons for the series begin July 1, 1862.
[34] Border used on the December 24, 1861 call certificates (nos. 143 and 145).
[35] Coupons for this series begin July 1, 1862.
[36] 1,155 printed.
[37] Coupons for these bonds begin on July 1, 1862.
[38] 8,997 were printed from three plates. Coupons for this series began July 1, 1862.
[39] There is no imprint on bond 57, although the style of work is clearly that of Duncan. Coupons for this series began on January 1, 1863.
[40] Wood and Power was a government cotton agent; nothing more is known about the firm.
[41] First coupon dated January 1, 1863.
[42] First coupons dated January 1, 1863.
[43] The coupons of the bonds of this series start July 1, 1862.
[44] The first coupons of this series are dated January 1, 1863.
[45] All bonds with coupons from January 1, 1863.
[46] The first coupons of this series are dated January 1, 1863.
[47] Engraved name of "Osborn" in the plate.
[48] All coupons of this series begin January 1, 1863.
[49] The name "Payne" is engraved in the plate.
[50] The name "Hall" is engraved at the bottom.
[51] The paper ranges from blue-white to light tan.
[52] Coupons on these bonds began January 1, 1863 except for #92 which began July 1, 1863.
[53] "Wright" engraved at the bottom on some bonds. Others are without an imprint.
[54] "Wright" engraved at the bottom on some bonds. Others are without an imprint.
[55] Coupons start January 1, 1863.
[56] The name "Hodge" is engraved at the bottom. General Winder was provost marshal in Richmond until early 1865. On thick and thin paper.
[57] Coupons on these bonds commence January 1, 1863.
[58] Printer initials "PTZ" on some bonds.
[59] Printer initials "PTZ" on some bonds.
[60] The name "Schremp" is engraved at the bottom.
[61] All coupons of this series begin January 1, 1863.
[62] Dabney imprint at bottom.
[63] All coupons of this series commence January 1, 1863.
[64] Coupons commence January 1, 1863.
[65] "Weiss" engraved at the bottom of the plate.
[66] "Lafon" engraved at the bottom of the plate.
[67] Engraved name of "Merrin" at the bottom.
[68] This design is derived from vignettes pulled from a Bank of Charleston, S.C. $5 note plate lent to the Treasury Department in September 1861.
[69] Coupons for this series begin January 1, 1863.
[70] The engraver's name, "Price," appears at the bottom.
[71] Engraved name of "Schremp" at the bottom.
[72] Engraved names of "Hodge" and "Grant" at the bottom.
[73] Coupons for this series begin January 1, 1863.
[74] The plates have the name "Argentier" engraved at the bottom.
[75] The name "Lafon" is engraved at the bottom.
[76] The name "Argentier" is engraved at the bottom.
[77] All coupons of this series commence July 1, 1862.
[78] The precise reason for the rarity of the July due dates on the stock certificates is not known. Evidently, January must have been selected as the due date on the registered bonds.
[79] #3 $50.

[80] #1 $14,300; #2 $350 January 15, 1863.

[81] Most of these were changed to or converted to the loan of December 24, 1861 (6% call certificates).

[82] Only $69,006,870 listed in Thian. Many of these call certificates exist; however, most of the certificates are in the National Archives. Rarity is based on the available market supply. Denominations range from $500 up to $100,000 for the Hoyer & Ludwig piece, and $50,000 for the Paterson ones. Denominations under $1,000 are rare.

[83] Number 1 exists. There are also a few remainders.

[84] By an act passed on February 14, 1863, the appointment of two assistant registers was permitted. This is the first bond on which Rose's signature appears.

[85] Bond #5542 was stolen; bonds #5543-5560 were issued under the Act of April 27, 1863. Excess bonds were printed; the highest seen is #8121, printed by "Weiss." Other bonds bear the imprints of "Ainsworth" and "Mulroy."

[86.] This piece had not been sold since the 1950s until the 1997 Ford sale (RMS No. 165.) lot 1033 when it brought $22,275.

[87] After deducting transfers, only 133 were outstanding on April 1, 1865. Any existing denomination is rarity 8. A total of 1,995 certificates was printed, but no remainders have been seen and these may have been burnt with other obsolete securities in early 1864. A choice specimen of this bond went for $7,700 in 1994. The VF Ford example sold for $12,650 in June 1997.

[88] While 1,000 certificates were prepared, none were issued due to the Erlanger Loan. Four of each certificate (#997-1000) were procured by John J. Ford from the Erlanger firm in London. Two remainders and an issued bond in the 700 range have turned up subsequently. A pair, unissued, was sent to the senate by President Davis in January 1863. The residue, according to Mr. Leo Erlanger, were destroyed upon the merger of his firm with Hill, Samuels, in 1964-5.

[89] Four certificates were procured (#1001-1004) by Mr. John J. Ford, Jr. in London from the Erlanger firm. Only one remainder other than the President Davis piece has turned up.

[90] Last sold as lot 195 of the NASCA Richmond Sale, September 25-6, 1987, where it brought $7,810. Clearly worth more now.

[91] All are signed by Baron Emil Erlanger (loan manager in Paris and Frankfurt); J. Henry Schröder (loan agent in London); Colin J. McRae (CSA European agent); and John Slidell (CSA commissioner to Paris).

[92] Last coupon is hand signed.

[93] Last coupon is hand signed.

[94] Last coupon is hand signed.

[95] Last coupon is hand signed.

[96] Only five are known at present, one in a museum.

[97] About 500 or so were printed. It is known that £222,100 of Erlanger bonds were redeemed with these certificates. As the only one known at present, number 125, is not issued, issued certificates must have been less than that number.

[98] Bonds exist with the engraved names of Carmine and McKenzie.

[99] The number issued does not include the quantities estimated for Ball numbers 172-188 following. Remainders numbered 26997-28636 are also known.

[100] Bonds have been seen with the engraved names of Cook (two varieties), Campbell, Baxter, Mulldoon, McKenzie, McFarlane, and Blackwood, which indicates a minimum of 8 plates for this bond plus one for 191.

[101] Davis portrait, etc., different from other varieties.

[102] Engraver's names at the bottom include Baxter (two varieties), Carine, Strain, Deniven (two) and Swanson. Serial numbers, including remainders, go up to 50,696.

[103] Note that some of these numbers appear on the following Trans-Mississippi varieties.

[104] Engraver's names include Blackwood and Baxter (two varieties). C. Ansell was a London stationer, and this was "house" paper purchased by Major Evans of Evans & Cogswell and sent to the Confederacy.

[105] See the counterfeit section for "second" and "third" series bonds on white paper. These bonds consist of a few properly issued, low numbered bonds and less than a handful of remainders. Evidently, the treasury started using the white paper bonds before the pink paper was delivered to Archer and Daly.

[106] The bonds of this act have ten coupons, two rows of four and a third row of two in the center, starting October 1, 1863.

[107] The nine coupons on the bonds of this series commence with April 1, 1864. For bonds of these types issued under the Act of February 17, 1864, see Ball 375-377.

[108] 8,290 of all three denominations were printed, of which only 958 were used.

[109] Unique; only one completely filled in is known to date. None were in the London hoard. See Ball 372 for serials above 13, issued under the Act of February 17, 1864.

[110] All six pieces have survived. See Ball 373 for serials above 6, issued under the Act of February 17, 1864.

[111] See Ball 374 for serials above 18, issued under the Act of February 17, 1864.

[112] Over 4,000 were printed and remainders exist; most of these certificates are lodged in the National Archives and are not available; the rarity is for the market supply, otherwise the rarity would be 3. The denominations range from $1,000 to $100,000. Higher denominations bring better prices.

[113] Remainders only. Properly issued items were destroyed.

[114] All issued items are known to have been cancelled and destroyed before the evacuation of Richmond. Consequently, the signer or signers are unknown.

[115] Only five are known, including two proofs and three remainders, one falsely filled in. All the issued certificates were certified as destroyed.

[116] Last bond issued of this design; it still exists.

[117] Bond #5542 was lost or mis-prepared and was cancelled.

[118] Some 8,074 bonds were reported as printed by August 14, 1863, with the names of "Mulroy," "Campbell," "Frame," "Carime," "Baxter," and "Sullivan" appearing in the various plates. Some have plate nos. 2, 54, 61. The bonds were sold for a 50% or larger premium. Remainders exist.

[119] Evidently prepared before the final passage of the act that deleted this arrangement. The two sold in 1987 for $577.50 and in 1997 as indicated.

[120] The January 1, 1864 plate was prepared, but never used due to Congress's delay in passing this act until after the interest was due. The plate is now deposited in the Museum of the Confederacy.

[121] Issued certificates into the 500 range were still not distributed on March 31, 1865. Remainders exist.

[122] There are unissued remainders with stubs, at least 200 or so, bearing neither denomination nor series number. These are worth, depending on whether they have the stub or not, $75-$100.

[123] Actually, only 2,675 were reported as properly issued to the various Confederate agents; *bona fide* issued bonds have, however, been seen up to no. 3376. The number given in Thian is for bonds prepared.

[124] Some 4,876 bonds were prepared, according to Thian, by December 20, 1864; bond #1295 was issued March 31, 1865. Fully prepared bonds have been seen up to #5200.

[125] Amounts received from printer; none officially issued. Bonds #7001-9900 have forged "Robert Taylor" (*sic!*) signatures; a stray bond (7900 range) has an "Apperson" signature. These were probably filled in after the war and sold for $10 in gold each to gullible British speculators.
[126] Amounts received from printers; none officially issued.
[127] Amounts received from printers; none officially issued.
[128] Amount received from printers; none officially issued. Fifth and seventh series bonds have not been seen to date and may be extinct. Remnants cut up for use as bill of lading forms by the Greenville and Columbia Railroad turn up from time to time.
[129] Evidently when bond sales could not be effected prior to July 1, 1864, that coupon was dropped from the bond. The bonds with the extra coupon were obviously printed first but were used later, probably to save the trouble of printing new bonds. The use of leftover tint plated bonds was similarly motivated.
[130] 9,577 delivered by printers; only 3,508 reported sold, yet properly issued bonds only up to #10041 have been seen.
[131] 7500 reported prepared by Thian, but the records in the National Archives show only 3,800. #7426 has been seen.
[132] 500 bonds were printed of the $5,000 and $10,000 denominations; all were delivered to Leitch, the Charleston-Columbia assistant treasurer. 200 of the $5,000 were prepared; 100 of the $10,000 were prepared.
[133] Only two pieces, numbers 3 and 4, are known.
[134] Printed two to a sheet, only one issued piece seen.
[135] Printed two to a sheet. Highest officially listed; partially filled in remainders go higher.
[136] See note above.
[137] Highest officially issued; partially filled in remainders go higher. Printed two to a sheet, each certificate is different. The odd numbered certificates end on the fourth line, "FOUR PERCENT." The even numbered certificates end on the fourth line with "of FOUR PER."
[138] Highest officially issued; partially filled in remainders go higher. Printed two to a sheet, each certificate different. The odd numbered certificates end on the fourth line, "FOUR PERCENT." The even numbered certificates end on the fourth line with "of FOUR PER."
[139] Only 292 were officially listed; 444 are reported in Thian, and items numbered up to 492 have been seen. It is possible additional issues occurred without being entered.
[140] Printed four to a sheet.
[141] Some bonds are numbered into the 1000+ level, but none of the lower denominations has been yet seen properly issued. We believe the Thian numbers are for printed bonds or those eligible to be issued, but not those fully prepared. It is thought that issued bonds were paid over to the states, and may exist in some state archives.
[142] Some 11,551 were officially "issued"; the residue were prepared for issue. Certificates were made payable by any pay depositary, assistant treasurer, or treasurer.

It should also be noted that many of the issue figures are incomplete by several days, figures being reported at various dates in March 1865.

There are several varieties of configurations for issued and remainder bonds, which have varying values:

(1) Double sheet, tab cut off, properly issued; *very rare.* 500% premium over single.

(2) Single, properly issued (value as shown for #359).

(3) Full sheet, left tabs, back transfer form. Very rare; 600% of single sheet value.

(4) Single remainder with tab; 40% of issued value.

(5) Double, missing tabs at left or transfer on back; 40% of issued value.

(6) Single, missing tab or transfer form on back; 30% of issued value.

(7) Double, missing tab and transfer form; 30% of single value.

(8) Single, without tab and transfer form; 30% of issued value.
[143] See note above.
[144] Up to 24,650 certificates were prepared, only 12,410 being officially issued.
[145] Some 24,210 were officially issued; the residue were prepared for issue and there are many remainders.
[146] None seen to date. See #'s 269-274.
[147] None seen to date. See #'s 269-274.
[148] Only twenty-two known to date.
[149] Tail end of 266.
[150] Tail end of 262.
[151] Tail end of 267.
[152] This act allowed the holders of stock certificates to exchange them for 8% coupon bonds.
[153] Remainders have appeared falsely filled in to deceive British CSA bond speculators.
[154] Unissued remainders up to number 887 have been seen for this issue.
[155] We have seen only two of these bonds: where all the others are is an interesting question.

Bibliography

Ball, Douglas B. "Confederate Financial Expedients in the Trans-Mississippi Department: The Thayer-Santos Expedition of 1963-4." Carlson, Carl A. and Hodder, Michael, eds., *The American Numismatic Association Centennial Anthology,* Wolfeboro, New Hampshire, Bowers and Merena Galleries, Inc. 1991.

———. *Financial Failure and Confederate Defeat.* Urbana and Chicago, University of Illinois Press 1991.

Criswell, Grover C. *Confederate and Southern States Bonds.* 2nd ed. Citra, Florida, Criswell Publications 1980.

Thian, Raphael P. *Reports of the Secretary of the Treasury of the Confederate States of America 1861-1865.* App III. Washington, D.C., privately published 1878.

———. *Register of the Confederate Debt.* Douglas B. Ball, ed. Boston, Quarterman Publications 1972. Originally published in 1879 as Appendix II to the Thian series.

———. *Correspondence of the Treasury Department of the Confederate States of America 1861-1865.* App. IV. Washington, D.C., privately published 1879.

———. *Correspondence with the Treasury Department of the Confederate States of America 1861-1865.* App. V, parts 1 and 2. Washington, D.C., privately published 1880.

United States Government. Record group 135: Archives of the Confederate Treasury Department 1861-1865. Treasury Department, National Archives, Washington D.C.

Criswell-Ball cross index

Criswell #	Ball #	10M	n/a	48	133	96	110
1	10	10N	n/a	49	31	97	115
1A	11	10O	n/a	50	34	98	118
2	12	10P	n/a	51	37	99	121
2A	13	10Q	n/a	52	40	100	123
3	14	10R	n/a	53	43	101	127
3A	15	10S	19L	54	46	102	135
4	16	10T	n/a	55	49	103	139
4A	17	10U	n/a	56	52	104	138
5	1	11	21	57	55	105	140
5A	2	12	22	58	58	106	137
6	3	12A	23	59	65	107	144
6A	4	13	24	60	68	108	143
7	6	13A	25	61	74	109	145
7A	7	14	27	62	77	110	147, 278
8	9	15	26	63	81	111	148, 279
9A	18A	16	28	64	85	113	150
9B	B	17	45	65	90	114	151
9C	C	18	71	66	93	115	152
9D	D	19	83	67	98	116	156
9E	E	20	87	68	103	117	157
9F	F	21	130	68A	104	118	158
9G	G	22	30	69	108	119	159
9H	H	23	33	70	113	120	212
9I	I	24	36	71	117	121	221
9J	J	25	39	72	120	121A	220
9K	K	26	42	73	123	122	241
9L	L	27	48	74	127	122A	240
9M	M	28	51	75	134	123	165
9N	N	29	54	76	32	123A	166
9O	O	30	57	77	35	124	192
9P	P	31	63	78	38	124A	191
9Q	Q	31A	64	79	41	125	201
9R	R	32	67	80	44	125A	209
9S	S	33	73	81	47	125B	200
9T	T	34	74	82	50	126	241
9U	U	35	76	83	53	127	258
9V	V	36	80	84	56	128	260, 375
10A	19B	37	84	85	62	128A	254
10B	C	38	88	86	66	129	262, 376
10C	D	39	92	87	69	129A	268
10D	E	40	96	88	75	130	264
10E	n/a	41	102	89	79	130A	265
10F	19F	42	107	90	82	130AA	266
10G	G	43	112	91	86	130B	263
10H	H	43A	111	92	91	130C	267, 377
10I	n/a	44	116	93	95	131	269
10J	19I	45	117	94	101	132	271
10K	n/a	46	122	95	105	133	273
10L	19K	47	125	95A	106	134	268

135	275
136	276
137	277
138	280
139	284
140	285
141	286
141A	288
141B	290
141C	292
141D	294
141E	287
141F	289
141G	291
141H	293
141I	295
142	296
142A	303
143	305
143A	307
143B	312
143C	313
143D	314
1431E	315
143F	316
144	317
144A	322
144B	325
144C	327
144D	329
144E	330
144F	331
144G	332
144H	333
144I	334
144J	335
144K	336
145	337
146	339
147	357
148	359
149	360
152	362
153	363
154	366
155	368
156	370
159	355
160	354
161	342
162	343
162A	344
162B	345
162C	346
162D	347
162E	348
162F	349
162G	350
162H	351
162I	352
163	381
164	382
165	383
166	384
167	385
174	20, 29, 130, 136
175	—
X34	C72
X55	C49
X82	C50
X83	C53
X85	C62
X89	C79
X95	C105
X95A	C106
X97	C176
X98	C123
X101	C130
X122B	C241
X122C	C201
X125	C199
X1	Fantasy I

Confederate Bond Legislation

Below are extracts of the relevant portions of Confederate legislation pertaining to bonds.

I. Act of February 28, 1861.

An Act to raise money for the support of the Government and to provide for the defense of the Confederate States of America.

The Congress of the Confederate States of America do Enact, That the President of the Confederate States be, and he is hereby authorized, at any time within twelve months after the passage of this act, to borrow, on the credit of the Confederate States, a sum not exceeding $15,000,000 or so much thereof as in his opinion the exigencies of the public service may require, to be applied to the payment of appropriations made by law for the support of the Government and for the defenses of the Confederate States.

Section 2. The Secretary of the Treasury is hereby authorized, by the consent of the President of the Confederate States, to cause to be prepared certificates of stock or bonds, in such sums as are hereinafter mentioned, for the amount to be borrowed as aforesaid, to be signed by the Register of the Treasury and sealed with the seal of the Treasury; and the said certificates of stock or bonds shall be made payable at the expiration of ten years from the first day of September next; and the interest thereon shall be paid semiannually at the rate of 8 per cent. per annum at the Treasury and such other places as the Secretary of the Treasury may designate. And to the bonds which shall be issued as aforesaid shall be attached coupons for the semiannual interest which shall accrue, which coupons may be signed by officers appointed for the purpose by the Secretary of the Treasury....

Sec. 4. The certificates of stock and bonds shall be issued in such form and such amounts as may be determined by the Secretary of the Treasury, and may be assigned or delivered under such regulations as he may establish; but none of them shall be for a less sum than $50....

II. Act of May 16, 1861

An Act of authorize a loan and the issue of Treasury notes, and to prescribe the punishment for forging the same, and forging certificates of stock and bonds.

The Congress of the Congress of the Confederate States of America, Do Enact, That the Secretary of the Treasury may, with the assent of the President of the Confederate States, issue $50,000,000 in bonds, payable at the expiration of twenty years from their date, and bearing a rate of interest not exceeding 8 per cent. per annum until they become payable, the said interest to be paid semiannually. The said bonds, after public advertisement in three newspapers within the Confederate States for six weeks, to sold for specie, military stores, or for the proceeds of sales of raw produce or manufactured articles, to be paid in the form of specie or with foreign bills of exchange in such manner and under such regulations as may be prescribed by the secretary of the Treasury, with the assent of the President....Nor shall the said bonds be issued in fractional parts of the hundred....

Sec. 2. And be it further enacted, That in lieu of bonds, to an amount not exceeding twenty millions of dollars, the Secretary of the Treasury may issue Treasury notes to the same amount... The holders of the said notes may at any time demand in exchange for them bonds of the Confederate States, payable at the end of ten years, and bearing an interest of eight per cent. per annum, to be paid semiannually. The Secretary of the Treasury is authorized to issue the said bonds, but not in fractional parts of the hundred...

Sec. 3. ...But the Secretary of the Treasury may, upon application of the hold of a bond thus funded, redeem it by giving in exchange treasury notes issued under the provisions of this act, to such extent that the entire amount of notes then issued, together with the amount of the bonds in which they may have been funded, shall not exceed twenty millions of dollars.

Chap. LVIII- act relative to certain Bonds and Treasury Notes under the provisions of the Act approved sixteenth May, eighteen hundred and sixty-one.

The Congress of the Confederate States of America do enact, That the ten year Bonds and two year Treasury Notes...are hereby excepted from the operation the Act [March 23, 1863]...Provided that the said two year treasury Notes now outstanding shall be funded prior to the first day of August, eighteen hundred and sixty-three.

Approved April 30, 1863.

III. Act of August 19, 1861

An Act to authorize the issue of Treasury notes and to provide a war tax for their redemption.

Sec.2. That for the purpose of funding the said notes and of making exchange for the proceeds of the sale of raw produce and manufactured articles, or for the purchase of specie or military stores, the Secretary of the Treasury, with the assent of the President, is authorized to issue bonds, payable not more than twenty years after date, and bearing a rate of interest not exceeding 8 per cent. per annum until they become payable, the interest to be paid semiannually, the said bonds not to exceed, in the whole, $100,000,000 and to be deemed a substitute for $30,000,000 of the bonds authorized to be issued by the act approved May sixteenth, eighteen hundred and sixty-one; and this act is to be deemed a revocation of the authority to issue the said $30,000,000. The said bonds shall not be issued in less sums than $100, nor in fractional parts of a hundred, except when the subscription is less than $100, the said bonds may be issued in sums of $50. They may be sold for specie, military and naval stores, or for the proceeds of raw produce and manufactured articles, in the same manner as is provided by the act aforesaid; and whenever subscriptions of the same have been or shall be made payable at a particular date the Secretary of the Treasury shall have power to extend the time of sales until such date as he shall see fit to indicate.

IV. Act of August 24, 1861

Chap. XL.- An Act to authorize the issue of inscribed stock in the stead of Coupon Bonds.

The Congress of the Confederate States of America do enact, That in all cases where bonds are authorized to be issued under the acts of Congress, ...the Secretary of the Treasury, at the request of the party interested, may cause to be issued, in the stead of bonds, certificates of inscribed stock, payable to the order, transferable at the Treasury for the same amount of principal, at the same rate of interest, and payable at the same dates as are prescribed for the bonds....

V. Act of December 19, 1861

Chapter XIV- An act further supplementary to an act to authorize the issue of treasury notes and to provide a war tax for their redemption.

The Congress of the Confederate States of America do enact, That the Secretary of the Treasury is hereby authorized to pay over to the several banks, which have made advances to the government, in anticipation of the issue of treasury notes, a sufficient amount, not exceeding ten millions of dollars, for the principal, of treasury notes to pay the principal and interest due upon the said advance, according to the engagements made with them.

VI. Act of December 24, 1861

An Act supplementary to an act to authorize the issue of Treasury notes, and to provide a war tax for their redemption.

Sec. 2. The Secretary of the Treasury, with the approval of the President, in addition to the bonds authorized to be issued by the second section of the said act approved August nineteen, one thousand eight hundred and sixty-one, to which this is supplementary, is hereby authorized to issue bonds, not to exceed an any one time an amount of thirty millions of dollars, payable not more than twenty years after date, and to bear an interest not to exceed six per cent. per annum, interest payable semiannually; to be exchange for treasury notes issued under the authority of this act of the act [August 19, 1861] to which this is supplementary, and the said bonds many, at the option of the holders, be reconverted into treasury notes under such rules and regulations as the Secretary of the Treasury may prescribe....

An Act to authorize certain financial arrangements at the Treasury.

Whereas, by the act...[December 24, 1861] Treasury notes to an amount not exceeding thirty million of dollars were authorized to be converted into bonds bearing interest at the rate of six per cent. per annum, which bonds should, at the option of the holders, be reconvertible into Treasury notes; but no appropriation of Treasury notes to be exchanged for said bonds was made.

The Congress of the Confederate States of America Do Enact, That any Treasury notes not otherwise appropriated are hereby appropriated and may be applied by the Secretary of the Treasury to the redemption of the said bonds.

Approved February 2, 1862.

An Act to provide further means for the support of the Government

Sec.2. The Secretary of the Treasury may issue in exchange for any of the Treasury notes which may be issued under this or any other law, bonds or certificates, payable in not more than ten years, at a rate of interest not exceeding 6 per cent. per annum, payable semiannually, to the extent of fifty millions of dollars...the said bonds or certificates to be reconvertible, at the pleasure of the holder, into Treasury notes, and the said exchange and re-exchange to be subject to such regulations to be subject to such regulations as the Secretary of the Treasury may prescribe.

Approved April 18, 1862.

Act to provide for the further issue of Treasury notes.

Sec.2 That the authority given to the Secretary of the Treasury, in the second section of an act..[April 18, 1862] ...to issue in exchange for Treasury notes, bonds, or certificates to be reconvertible in the same at the pleasure of the holder, shall be extended from fifty millions to one hundred millions of dollars but the said authority shall be exercised under all the conditions and limitations prescribed in the said act.

VI. Act of April 18, 1862

An Act to provide further means for the support of the Government.

The Congress of the Confederate States of America Do Enact, That the Secretary of the Treasury be, and he is hereby authorized to issue, in addition to the amounts heretofore authorized to be issued...$165,000,000 certificates of stock and bonds...And provided further, that all bonds issued under this section shall be made redeemable at the pleasure of the Government after the expiration of ten years from their respective dates, but the faith of the Government shall be pledged to redeem the same at the expiration of thirty years from such date...

Sec.2. The Secretary of the Treasury may issue in exchange for any of the Treasury notes which may be issued under this or any other law, bonds or certificates, payable in not more than ten years, at a rate of interest not exceeding 6 per cent. per annum, payable semiannually, to the extent of $50,000,000 which $50,000,000 shall constitute part of the $165,000,000 of stock and bonds above authorized....

VII. Act of October 13, 1862

Chap.LVIII-An Act to reduce the rate of interest on the funded debt of the Confederate States.

The Congress of the Confederate States of America do enact, That all Treasury notes issued after the first day of December next shall be made fundable only in bonds bearing interest at the rate of seven per cent. per annum, but in all other respects similar to the bonds bearing eight per cent interest.

Sec.2. The Secretary of the Treasury shall have authority, by public notice duly advertised, to require the holders of Treasury notes to come in and fund the same in eight per cent. bonds, or stocks within six months of his advertisement. Those Treasury notes which shall not be presented for funding within the said time shall thereafter be issued under the direction of the Secretary of the Treasury bonds bearing interest at the rate of seven per cent. per annum, payable semiannually: Provided, That nothing herein contained shall be construed to revoke the authority heretofore given to issue six per cent., reconvertible bonds.

IX Act of January 29, 1863

An Act to authorize a foreign loan.

The Congress of the Confederate States of America do enact, That the Secretary of the Treasury is authorized to complete and carry into effect a certain contract made at the City of Richmond, on January 8, in the year 1863, with Messrs. Erlanger & Co., of Paris, through Jules Beer, their attorney, for the purpose of raising by loan the sum of seventy-five millions of francs, and to that end he may cause to be issued bonds of the Confederate States, payable twenty years after date, with coupons attached for the payment of interest abroad, at the rate of seven per cent per annum, and also certificates for the delivery of cotton in exchange for the said bonds; the said bonds and certificates to be issued in such form and with such signatures as the said Secretary shall deem proper.

Sec. 2. An agent to superintend and conduct all the details of the said loan shall be appointed by the President, with a compensation of five thousand dollars, payable in Paris, for his services in completing the said loan. The said agent shall have power to sign bonds, coupons and certificates for the delivery of bonds, and to receive and make all payments, and to give and receive all notices, and generally to do all such act and execute all such instruments of writing as may be necessary and proper for carrying the said contract and all things therein required into complete execution. Provided, however, that all bonds issued by the said agent shall be countersigned by the Minister or Commissioner of the Confederate States resident in Paris.

Sec. 3. The said agent shall have power to appoint such clerks and subordinate agents as may be required, not exceeding three, for the performance of the various duties and service[s] in and about the said loan; and one of these clerks may be authorized by him to sign such coupons as may be required for the bonds.

Sec. 4. The Secretary of the Treasury shall have power to regulate the entire management of the said loan and of all business connected therewith, and to prescribe the form of all bonds and certificates, and the modes of issue and transfer, and the appointment and confirmation of all clerks and agents shall be subject to his approval, and they may be dismissed or changed at his discretion; and all officers and agents acting in virtue of this law shall at all times be bound by any regulations or directions which he may see fit to order.

IX. Act of February 14, 1863

Chap. IV.- An Act to authorize the appointment of Assistants to the Register in signing Bonds and Certificates.

The Congress of the Confederate States of America do enact, That the Secretary of the Treasury is hereby authorized to appoint two clerks, if so many be necessary, to assist the Register in signing bonds and certificates of stock, with the salary of principal clerks in the department; and every bond and certificate signed by one of the said clerks for the Register, shall be as valid and effectual, to all intents and purposes, as though the same were actually signed by the Register in his proper handwriting.

X. Act of February 20, 1863

An Act to authorize the issue of bonds for funding Treasury notes.

The Congress of the Confederate States of America Do Enact, That the Secretary of the Treasury be, and he is hereby, authorized to issue coupon bonds and certificates of stocks, with interest, payable semiannually, at the yearly rate of eight per cent. for such amount as may be required in exchange for all Treasury notes which are now fundable in eight per cent. bonds, and also to pay for any subscription to the produce loan which may remain unpaid after exhausting the one hundred million loan.

Sec.2. That the said Secretary is also authorized to issue coupon bonds, and certificates of stock, with interest at the yearly rate of seven per cent., payable semiannually, for such amount as may be required in exchange for all Treasury notes which are now fundable in seven per cent. bonds.

Sec.3 That all bonds issued under this act shall be made redeemable at the pleasure of the Government after the expiration of five years from their respective dates, but the faith of the government shall be pledged to redeem the same at the expiration of thirty years from such dates.

XI. Act of March 23, 1863

An Act to provide for the funding and further issue of Treasury notes.

The Congress of the Confederate States of America do enact, That...All call certificates of every description, outstanding on the first day of July, eighteen hundred and sixty-three, shall after that date be deemed to be bonds bearing an annual interest of six per cent. and payable at a date not exceeding thirty years from the first day of July, eighteen hundred and sixty-three.

Sec.3. After the passage of this act, the authority heretofore given to issue call certificates shall cease, but the notes fundable into six per cent. bonds may be converted at the pleasure of the holder, into call certificates, bearing interest at the rate of five per cent. per annum, from the date of their issue. That every such certificates shall bear upon the face the monthly date of the oldest of the notes which it represents, and be convertible into like notes at any time within six months from the first day of the monthly date, aforesaid. But every certificate not converted within six months from the first day of the monthly date, shall be exchanged for a bond payable at any time not exceeding thirty years from the expiration of the said six months, and bearing interest at the rate of six per cent. per annum. Treasury notes which, by the operation of this act may be converted at the pleasure of the holder, into call certificates, bearing interest at the rate of four per cent. per annum from their date, until reconverted or paid; the said certificates being reconvertible at any time by the holder, into notes fundable in four per cent. bonds...but the certificates may be redeemed by the government after six months from the ratification of a treaty of peace between the Confederate States and the United States.

Sec.4. That all bonds or registered stock authorized to be issued by this act shall be payable not less than thirty years after date; but shall be redeemable five years after date, at the pleasure of the Government and shall in other respects conform to existing laws...

Sec.8. That the Secretary of the Treasury be authorized to sell bonds bearing six per cent. interest per annum, and payable, as heretofore directed, at part for Treasury notes issued since the first of December, eighteen hundred and sixty-two, to such of the Confederate States as may desire the same; or he may sell such bonds, when guaranteed by any of the States of the Confederacy. upon such plan as may be determined by the Secretary of the Treasury, for Treasury notes, on such terms as he may deem advisable, to the highest bidder, and not below par; Provided, however, That the whole amount of such bonds shall not exceed two hundred millions of dollars: And provided further That the Treasury notes thus purchased shall not be reissued, if the effect of such reissue would be to increase the whole amount of Treasury notes, bearing no interest, which are in circulation, to a sum greater than one hundred and seventy-five millions of dollars. And the Secretary is also authorized, at his option, after the first of July, eighteen hundred and sixty-three, to issue and sell, at not less than par, as estimated in Treasury notes, coupon bonds of the Confederate States bearing six per cent. interest per annum, and payable as herein before directed. the said coupons to be paid at the pleasure of the owner, either in the currency in which interest is paid on other bonds or the Confederate States, or else in cotton certificates which pledge the Government to pay the same in cotton of the quality of New Orleans middlings. The said cotton to be paid at the rate of eight pence sterling per pound, and to be delivered at any time within six months after the ratification of a treaty of peace between the Confederate States and the United States, at any or all of the ports of New Orleans, Mobile, Savannah, Charleston or Wilmington, as the Secretary of the Treasury may direct: Provided, however, That the bonds hereby authorized shall not exceed one hundred millions of dollars, and shall be applied only to the absorption of Treasury notes, as prescribed in this act....

XII. Act of April 27, 1863

An Act to authorize the issue of eight per cent. bonds or certificates of stock in certain cases.

The Congress of the Confederate States of America Do Enact, That the secretary of the Treasury be, and he is hereby authorized to issue and deliver bonds or certificates of stock of the Confederate states, bearing eight per cent. interest per annum, to such an amount as may be necessary to discharge all agreements entered into prior to the first day of December, 1862, whereby goods were sold and delivered to the Government, and the vendor, at the time of sale, agreed to receive bonds or stock in payment of the price; and the said bonds or stock may bear date on the day of issue, or on the day the vendor was entitled to receive payment; but if dated on the day of issue, the interest which would have accrued had the bonds or stock been issued on the day the vendor was entitled to received them shall be paid. And the said conditions and restrictions as are provided in the act entitled "An Act to provide further means for the support of the Government, " approved twelfth April eighteen hundred and sixty-two and the Secretary of the Treasury shall also be authorized to issue like bonds to any person who shall actually have paid money into the hands of an agent of the Treasury for the purchase of eight per cent. bonds of the one hundred million loan, prior to the twentieth February, eighteen hundred and sixty-three.

XIII. Act of April 30, 1863

An Act supplementary to an act to provide for the funding and further issue of treasury notes.

The Congress of the Confederate States of America do enact, That in lieu of one hundred millions of dollars in bonds, which, by the eighth section of an act entitled "any act to provide for the funding and further issue of treasury notes," approved March twenty-third, eighteen hundred and sixty-three, the Secretary of the Treasury is authorized to issue, at a rate of interest of six per centum per annum, payable at the pleasure of the owner in the currency in which interest is paid on the other bonds of the Confederate States, or in cotton of the quality of New Orleans middling, valued at eight pence sterling per pound, the said Secretary shall be and is herby authorized to issue two hundred and fifty millions of dollars in bonds, in sums of not less than five hundred dollars each, payable at twenty years from their date, and bearing interest at the rate of six per centum per annum, to be paid at the pleasure of the Government in specie, or in cotton of the quality of New Orleans middling, to be valued at six pence sterling per pound--the said cotton to be delivered, at the pleasure of the Secretary of the Treasury, at either of the ports of New Orleans, Savannah, Charleston, Mobile, Wilmington, Richmond, or Norfolk, under such regulations as the said Secretary may establish. These bonds shall be sold by the Secretary of the Treasury for all outstanding Confederate States treasury notes, at not less than their par value in said treasury notes: Provided, That the Secretary of the Treasury be authorized to apply the proceeds of as many of the said bonds as may be required for the purchase of agricultural products under the act of Congress, approved April twenty-first, eighteen hundred and sixty-two, entitled "an act to authorize the exchange of bonds for articles in kind, and the shipment, sale or hyppothecation of such articles."

XIV. Act of February 11, 1864

An Act to authorize the issue of certificates for interest on the "fifteen million loan."

The Congress of the Confederate States of America Do Enact, That the Secretary of the Treasury be, and he is hereby authorized to cause certificates to be issued, in such form as he shall devise, for the interest which has accrued, or which shall accrue, on the registered stock issued under authority of the act of February the twenty-eighth, eighteen hundred and sixty-one, entitled, "An act to raise money for the support of the Government, and to provide for the defense of the Confederate States of America." The said certificates shall be prepared and signed by the Register of the Treasury, in favor of the persons, respectively, in whose names the said stock shall be standing on the books of the Treasury, or their order, at the designated periods, and shall be sent by him to the Treasurer, assistant treasurers and depositories located the places where said interest is payable. The said certificates shall be signed by the Treasurer, assistant treasurer, or depository, by whom they shall be delivered; and shall be receivable in payment of the export duty on cotton, in the same manner as the coupons of the bonds issued under said act of February twenty-eight, eighteen hundred and sixty-one, now are.

XV. Act of February 17, 1864

Chap. LXIII. An Act of reduce the currency and to authorize a new issue of notes and bonds.

Sec.1. The Congress of the Confederate States of America do enact, That the holders of all Treasury notes above the denomination of five dollars, not bearing interest shall be allowed until the first day of April 1864, east of the Mississippi River, and until the first day of July, 1864, west of the Mississippi River, to fund the same, and until the periods and at the places stated the holders of all such Treasury notes shall be allowed to fund the same in registered bonds payable twenty years after their date bearing interest at the rate of four per cent. per annum, payable on the 1st day of January and July of each year.

Sec.2. The Secretary of the Treasury is hereby authorized to issue the bonds required for the funding provided for in the preceding section; and until the bonds can be prepared, he may issue certificates to answer the purpose. Such bonds and certificates shall be receivable, without interest, in payment of all Government dues payable in the year 1864, except export and import duties....

Sec. 6. That to pay the expenses of the Government not otherwise provided for, the Secretary of the Treasury is hereby authorized to issue six per cent. bonds, to an amount not exceeding five hundred million of dollars, the principal and interest whereof shall be free from taxation; and for the payment of the interest thereon, the entire net receipts of any export duty hereafter laid on the value of all cotton, tobacco, and naval stores, which shall be exported from the Confederate States, and the net proceeds of the import duties now laid, or much thereof as may be necessary to pay annually the interest, are hereby specially pledged; Provided, That the duties now laid upon imports and hereby pledged shall hereafter be paid in specie, or in sterling exchange, or in the coupons of the said bonds.

Sec. 7. That the Secretary of the Treasury is hereby authorized from time to time, as the wants of the Treasury may require it, to sell or hypothecate for Treasury notes said bonds or any part thereof, upon the best terms he can, so as to meet appropriations by Congress and at the same time reduce and restrict the amount of circulation in Treasury notes within reasonable and safe limits.

Sec.8. The bonds authorized by the sixth section of this act may be either registered or coupon bonds, as the parties taking them may elect, and they may be exchanged for each other under such regulations as the Secretary of the Treasury may prescribe. They shall be for one hundred dollars, or some multiple of one hundred dollars, and shall, together with the coupons thereto attached, be in such form and of such authentication as the Secretary of the Treasury may prescribe. The interest shall be payable half yearly, or on the first of January and July in each year-the principal shall be payable not less than thirty years from their date.

Sec. 9. All Call certificates shall be fundable, and shall be taxed in all respects, as is provided for the Treasury notes, into which they are convertible. If not converted before the time fixed for taxing the Treasury notes, such certificates shall, from that time, bear interest upon only sixty-six and two-thirds cents for every dollar promised on their face, and shall be redeemable only in new treasury notes at that rate, but after the passage of this act, no call certificates shall be issued until after the first day of April eighteen hundred and sixty-four....

Sec. 12. That any State holding treasury notes, received before the times herein fixed for taxing said notes, shall be allowed until the first day of January eighteen hundred and sixty-five, to fund the same in six per cent. bonds of the Confederate States, payable twenty years after date, and the interest payable semiannually....

Sec. 14. That the Secretary of the Treasury be and he is hereby, authorized in case the exigencies of the Government should require it, to pay the demand of any public creditor whose debt may be contracted after the passage of this act, willing to received the same in a certificate of indebtedness to be issued by the said Secretary, in such form as he may deem proper, payable semiannually and transferable only by special endorsement under regulations to be prescribed by the Secretary of the Treasury, and said certificate shall be exempt from taxation in principal and interest.

Sec. 18. The Secretary of the treasury is hereby authorized and required upon the application of the holder of any call certificate-which by the first section of the act "to provide for the funding and further issue of treasury notes; approved March twenty-third, eighteen hundred and sixty-three, was required to be hereafter deemed to be a bond-to issue such holder a bond therefore, upon the terms provided by said act.... [6% thirty year bonds].

XV. Act of June 13, 1864

Chap. XI. An Act to authorize the owners of the registered eight per cent. ten year convertible bonds, issued under the provisions of the act approved may sixteenth eighteen hundred and sixty-one, to exchange the same for coupon bonds.

The Congress of the Confederate States of America do enact, That the owners of the registered eight per cent. ten years convertible bonds...are hereby authorized to exchange the same for coupon bonds payable ten years after the first day of July... [1864] and the Secretary of the Treasury...is hereby authorized to prepare and issue the bonds, which bonds, and the coupons attached thereto, may be issued with such authentication as the Secretary of the Treasury may prescribe.

XVI. Act of June 14, 1864

Chap. XLIII. Act to amend an act entitled "an Act to reduce the currency and to authorize a new issue of notes and bonds" approved February seventeenth, eighteen hundred and sixty-four.

The Congress of the Confederate States of America do enact, That instead of six per cent. bonds, authorized to be issued to the states, under the twelfth section of the said act, The Secretary of the Treasury is authorized and required to issue to any State which may desire the same, one half of such amount as the said State is entitled to claim in Treasury notes of the new issue, and the other half in said six per cent. bonds; or at the option of the state in coupon bonds, payable in twenty years, with interest at the rate of four per cent per annum, payable half yearly.

THE
PLURIBUS
UNUM

Great Civil War

Civil War Encased Stamps

by Fred Reed

During the Civil War, governments and merchants alike had to be creative in solving financial difficulties. Both sides experienced severe financial difficulties. Gold and silver coinage was hoarded and disappeared from circulation. Both sides then issued paper money. As amazing as that seems today, that was the first successful use of federal paper money. Fractional currency was created and huge quantities of tokens were issued.

Encased postage stamps were perhaps the most interesting and innovative money of them all. Postage stamps were encapsulated so that they could circulate without deteriorating. The denomination was visible to establish the value and the other side was available for advertising. This was the perfect free enterprise solution, but the introduction of fractional currency ended the need for encased stamps.

Fred Reed has studied Civil War encased stamps in a way that few issues have been studied. He has done the traditional things. He studied collections, auction catalogs, old price lists and the like. He has developed pedigrees and lists. Of course he has also cataloged and evaluated each piece and used computer technology to generate emission models for each issue.

You would expect all of the above in a numismatic catalog. However, he went far beyond that. He researched each issuer in detail and in twenty years he had remarkable results. You will love the text and amazing graphics in this book.

Civil War Encased Stamps by Fred Reed is a monumental new reference. It has been TWENTY YEARS in the making: 558 page, $64 postpaid, satisfaction guaranteed.

Numismatic Books

Comprehensive Catalog of Confederate Paper Money by Grover Criswell.

Confederate paper money has been popular with collectors for more than 100 years! It is interesting as it is popular. For fifty years the leading authority on Confederate paper money has been Grover Criswell. In addition he has been a hobby leader. He served as governor and president of the American Numismatic Association. His books, pamphlets, and even price lists have started many collectors. This version of his Confederate paper money catalog is by far the best that has ever been published. You will like this book.
The *Comprehensive Catalog of Confederate Paper Money* was the Civil War Numismatic Society book of the year and is the standard catalog used by collectors world wide.

- Confederate Treasury notes
- contemporary counterfeits
- standard Criswell numbers
- 6 by 9 inch handbook format
- full color cover
- thousands of varieties
- complete note illustrations
  - — faces and backs
  - — close ups
- complete market values
- Foreword by Fred Schwan
- check lists
- 356 pages/hundreds of photographs
- historic illustrations
- guaranteed satisfaction
- hardbound $35 (plus shipping)
- featuring **Hot Contact List**™

Civil War Numismatic Society book of the year.

BNR Press

our 20th year

132 E. Second Street
Port Clinton, Ohio 43452-1115-04
order via voice or fax
800 793-0683
also (419) 732-NOTE (6683)

Society of Paper Money Collectors

It would be to your advantage to join the Society of Paper Money Collectors, organized in 1961 to further the following objectives:

1. Encourage the collecting and study of paper money.
2. Cultivate fraternal collector relations with opportunities for discussion trading, etc.
3. Furnish information and knowledge through experts, particularly through the Society's *PAPER MONEY* magazine.
4. Promote legislation favorable to collectors, providing it is in accord with the general welfare.
6. Advance the prestige of the hobby.
7. Promote exhibits at numismatic and syngraphic meetings.
8. Encourage realistic and consistent market valuations.

PAPER MONEY, the society bimonthly journal, is sent to all members. In addition to informative articles, it lists new members, the collecting specialty of each, and identifies each as a collector or dealer. Members are encouraged to submit articles for publication.

BOOKS that catalog the obsolete currency of individual states are available to members at reduced prices.

DUES are $20 ($30 outside the United States) per year and are payable in U. S. funds. Members who join the Society prior to October 1 receive the magazines already issued in the year in which they join. Members who join after October 1 will have their dues paid through December of the following year. They will also receive, as a bonus, a copy of the magazine issued in November of the year in which they join.

JUNIOR and LIFE MEMBERS, from 12 to 17 years of age, are required to have a parent or guardian sign their application. The "J" that will precede membership numbers will be removed upon notification to the secretary that the member has reached 18 years of age. Life memberships are $300.

MEETINGS, national and regional, take place throughout the year.

Annual dues in US funds: $24 in the U.S.; $29 for Canada and Mexico; $34 for other countries.

To join the SPMC send dues to SPMC, P. O. Box 117060, Carrollton, TX 75011. For a complimentary copy of *PAPER MONEY,* send $2 for postage and handling.

INTERESTING FACTS REGARDING FORD STOCK CERTIFICATES

Without question, the success of the billionaire, Henry Ford, can justifiably be called one of the greatest, if not *the* greatest, entrepreneurial successes of all time. Accordingly, automotive stock certificates bearing this signature are among the most desirable.

Because of his extreme distrust of Wall Street, Henry Ford only bought stocks in companies in which he was direcetly involved. Therefore, Henry Ford's signature on any

CAPITAL STOCK, $125,000.00

The Ford Motor Company of Canada, Limited

No 91 STOCK CERTIFICATE 19 Shares

This Certifies that Charles Montreuil of Walkerville Ontario is entitled to Nineteen fully paid up shares of One hundred Dollars each, in the Capital Stock of the Ford Motor Company of Canada, Limited

The said shares are transferable on the books of the Company only by him or his Attorney duly constituted, and upon surrender of this Certificate, and as provided for in the By Laws of this Company.

Dated at Walkerville, Ontario, this Sixth day of April 1907

G. M. McGregor SECRETARY. Henry Ford PRESIDENT.

stock certificate is rare. Only two public sales have ever been recorded, both realizing five figures with the last appearance in a R. M. Smythe auction of several years ago. However, by comparison, this offering is much more desirable in that it is an automotive issue--plus being one of the actual Ford companies. Moreover, Henry Ford's signature is on the face of the certificate which is considered to be much more desirable and allows for more effective display.

Ford Canadian operations are now a part of the world-wide Ford company. It was founded (1904) in the year following formation of the Michigan company to avoid import taxes and was dominated by U. S. investors. All twelve original shareholders of the Michigan company were also shareholders in the Canadian company which was located only a few miles across the Detroit River. Both offices of president were give to the largest cash contributor, a Detroit banker named John S. Gray. Henry Ford was only a vice president of both companies and as such did not sign stock certificates. After the death of John S. Gray, Henry Ford was eventually elected president. In the teens Henry Ford gave up the office of president of the Ford Motor Co., to his son, Edsel, who retained the title until his death in 1943 long after the minority stock holders had been bought out. Henry Ford was not a president of the Ford Motor Co. during most of his comparatively long life and only signed a very limited number of stock certificates primarily at a time when he was actually buying out the minority shareholders. The only other known Ford signed automotive certificates are the first, but very small issue of the Michigan company, which are in the Henry Ford Museum archives in Dearborn, Michigan and cannot be obtained under any circumstances.

The signature of Henry Ford is absolutely original and authentic in all respects. It corresponds with the very rare and seldom seen early signature of Henry Ford as contained in the Henry Ford Museum. Interestingly, the famous Ford script logo, which is recognized the world over, was "invented" by one of Ford's most brilliant employees, C. Harold Willis and is well documented. Later in life when he was rich and famous, Henry Ford's signature closely resembled the famous logo.

There are no other known Henry Ford signed Ford company or automobile company stock certificates of any kind in private hands other than this offering. Price $30,000

Colonel Grover Criswell

15001 NE 248th Ave. Road
Salt Springs, FL 32134
(352) 685-2287, 2358
fax (352) 685-1014

Available from the author directly...

Confederate and Southern States Currency, 1992, hardbound 420 page book covers all of the notes issued by the southern states, Indian territories, the Florida Republic and Territory, and the Republic and independent government of Texas. If you need the information mentioned above, this 1992 work has 255 pages of information and you probably cannot afford to be without it. It is out of print, but we have a few copies, autographed at $75.

Confederate and Southern States Bonds, 380 pages, hardbound, published in 1979, lists all CSA bonds plus those issued by the southern states, the Territory of Florida and the Republic of Texas. This book has been long out of print, but again we have a few autographed copies available at $55.

Confederate and Southern States Currency by William W. Bradbeer, New York, 1915. This is a 1956 reprint by Aubrey Beebe. This book is itself a collector's item and is part of the lore of collecting Confederate money. It is seldom available for less than $100, special $75.

Many other rare and hard to find paper money and historical books are available. Send for our complete list of books...FREE

Our latest *Compendium Price List,* 432 page book listing paper money, autographs, slavery material, Army, Navy papers, documents, and etc. is available for $8 postpaid. Prices includes a refund slip good on a $25.00 order or free with any book offered above.

My 50th year in buying and selling
paper money, stocks and bonds, autographs etc.

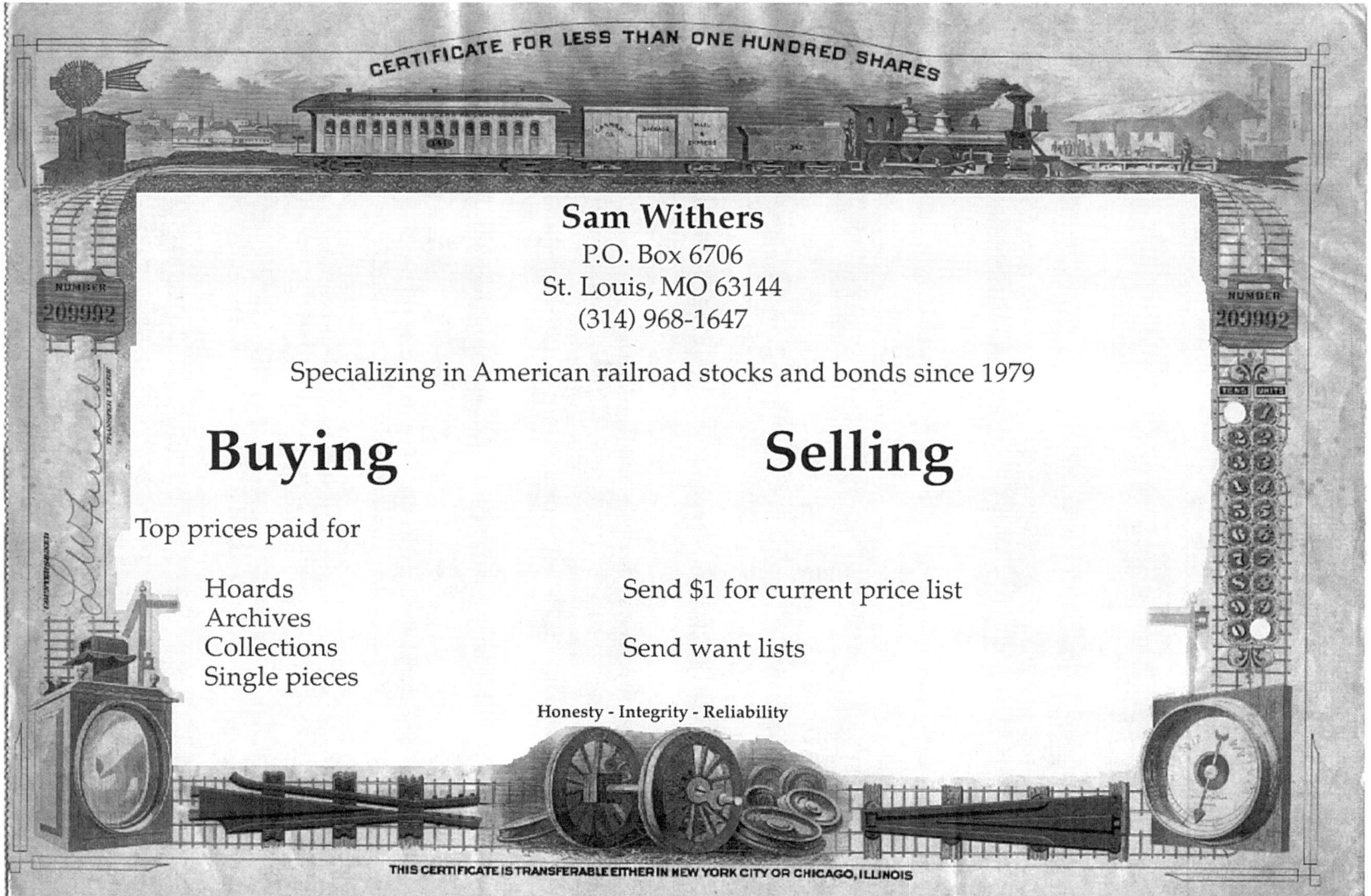
CERTIFICATE FOR LESS THAN ONE HUNDRED SHARES
Sam Withers
P.O. Box 6706
St. Louis, MO 63144
(314) 968-1647
Specializing in American railroad stocks and bonds since 1979
Buying
Selling
Top prices paid for
Hoards
Archives
Collections
Single pieces
Send $1 for current price list
Send want lists
Honesty - Integrity - Reliability
NUMBER
209992
THIS CERTIFICATE IS TRANSFERABLE EITHER IN NEW YORK CITY OR CHICAGO, ILLINOIS

Fun! Fun! Fun!
Annual
FUN SHOW!
every January
Orange County Convention/Civic Center
9800 International Drive ◆ Orlando, Florida
Hotel Reservations
Peabody Hotel
Sheraton World Resort
1-800-327-0363
Quality Inn
1-800-999-8585
Clarion Plaza Hotel
1-800-627-8258
*Mention "FUN 1999" for special convention rates!
Competitive Exhibits
Gene Hynds
4746 S. Atlantic #2
Ponce Inlet, FL 32127
PH: 904-760-0608
Auction by Heritage Numismatic Auctions
Heritage Plaza
100 Highland Park Village, Dallas, TX 75205
1-800-US COINS • (1-800-872-6467)
Consignments now being accepted!
M & M World Travel Service
Travel Arrangements & Car Rental
PH: 800-426-8326
Bourse Information
Cindy Grellman, Chairperson
P.O. Box 951988, Lake Mary, FL 32795-1988
PH: 407-321-8747 • FAX: 407-321-5138
FLORIDA UNITED NUMISMATISTS, INC.
1955

Hot Contact List™

Dealers and resources for collectors [page]

Name	Page	Contact
American Coins & Collectibles	[279]	(800) 865-3562
fax		(318) 868-9876
American Numismatic Association	[282]	(800) 367-9723
Archives International	[286]	(212)426-8494
fax		(212) 426-8800
Dick Balbaton	[255]	(508) 699-2266
BNR Press	[256]	(419) 732-6683
toll free		(800) 793-0683
fax		(419) 732-6683
fax		(800) 793-0683
e-mail		BNRPress@aol.com
Centennial Documents	[259]	(908) 730-6009
fax		(908) 730-9566
e-mail		centdocs@postoffice.ptd.net
Conrad L. Bush	[253]	(904) 243-1638
David Cieniewicz	[259]	(205) 852-7015
Ritchie Clay	[273]	(415) 323-8101
fax		(415) 323 8105
Confederate Treasury	[287]	(615) 721-3303
fax		(615) 721-4155
Cygnet Charters		(800) GO2-FISH
Grover Criswell	[272]	(352) 685-2287
fax		(352) 685-1014
Doric Coins & Currency	[255]	(508) 699-2266
fax		(508) 643-1154
Early American Numismatics	[266]	(619) 459-4159
fax		(619) 459-4373
Lawrence Falater	[262]	(517) 869-2541
		(888) FALATER
fax		(517) 869-2994
FUN (Cindy Grellman)	[283]	(407) 321-8747
fax		(407) 321-5138
Great Lakes Bank Note Company	[275]	(800) 793-0683
Paul, Linda, and Bryan Gibson	[264]	(423) 323-2427
fax		(423) 968-7797
fax		(954) 572-0677
John Kimbrough	[253]	(817) 249-2447
fax		(817) 249-5213
McIntire Rare Collectibles	[258]	(501) 985-1663
Memphis Coin Club	[274]	(901) 754-6118
Hudson McDonald	[253]	(334) 937-6580
Howard Norton (also fax)	[280]	(501) 223-4858
John Parker	[267]	(404) 351-7960
Clarence Rareshide	[261]	(504) 866-4212
John Rowe	[258]	(214) 826-3036
fax		(214) 823-1923
Richie Self	[279]	(318) 868-9077
Robert Schwartz	[286]	(212)426-8494
fax		(212) 426-8800
Fred Schwan		(419) 732-6683
Hugh Shull	[269]	(803) 432-8500
fax		(803) 432-9958
R. M. Smythe [inside front]		(212) 943-1880
toll free		(800) 622-1880
fax		(212) 908-4047
Scott Winslow Associates	[252]	(603) 472-7040
fax		(603) 472-8773
e-mail		SWins82687@aol.com
Sam Withers	[281]	(314) 968-1647
e-mail		SAMWITHERS@aol.com
Crutch Williams	[273]	(281) 334-3297
e-mail		crutch@prodigy.com

Auction companies

Name	Page	Contact
Early American Numismatics	[266]	(619) 459-4159
fax		(619) 459-4373
R. M. Smythe [inside front]		(212) 943-1880
toll free		(800) 622-1880
fax		(212) 908-4047
Scott Winslow Associates	[252]	(603) 472-7040
fax		(603) 472-8773

Publications

Name	Page	Contact
BNR Press	[256]	(419) 732-6683
toll free		(800) 793-0683
fax		(419) 732-6683
fax		(800) 793-0683
e-mail		BNR Press@aol.com
Coin World	[265]	(513) 498-0800
Currency Dealer Newsletter	[284]	(310) 515-7369
Military Trader	[254]	(800) 334-7165

Airline reservations

America West	(800) 235-9292
American	(800) 433-7300
Continental	(800) 525-0280
Delta	(800) 221-1212
Hawaiian	(800) 367-5320
Midwest Express	(800) 452-2022
Northwest	(800) 225-2525
Southwest	(800) 435-9792
TWA	(800) 221-2000
United	(800) 241-6522

Hotel reservations

Best Western	(800) 528-1234
Budgetel	(800) 428-3438
Clarion/Choice Hotels	(800) 221-2222
Clarion Plaza Hotel	(800) 627-8258
Courtyard by Marriott	(800) 321-2211
Days Inn	(800) 325-2525
Doubletree	(800) 528-0444
Drury Inns	(800) 325-8300
Embassy Suites	(800) 362-2779
Excell Inns	(800) 356-8013
Fairmont	(800) 527-4727
Fairfield by Marriott	(800) 228-2800
Hampton Inns	(800) 426-7866
Hilton	(800) 445-8667
Holiday Inn	(800) 465-4329
Hyatt	(800) 233-1234
Inter-Continental	(800) 327-0200
Lowes	(800) 235-6397
Marriott	(800) 228-9290
Marriott & Renissance	(800) 468-3571
Omni	(800) 843-6664
Outrigger Resorts	(800) 733-7777
Peabody	(800) 732-2639
Preferred Hotels	(800) 323-7500
Quality Inn	(800) 999-8585
Radisson	(800) 333-3333
Ramada	(800) 272-6232
Red Lion	(800) 848 9600
Red Roof	(800) 843-7663
Sheraton	(800) 325-3535
Super 8	(800) 800-8000
Sofitel	(800) 763-4835
Westin	(800) 228-3000

Bond quick find list

CIVIL WAR DOCUMENTS AND AUTOGRAPHS

CONFEDERATE BONDS

EXPERIENCE AND LONGEVITY
A COMMITMENT TO THE MARKETPLACE

Since 1985 we have been one of America's largest active buyers and sellers of historical bonds and shares and are recognized as one of the world's leading market makers for good quality American material. We have contributed in large part to the development of many of the finest collections of American material in the world today and understand the needs of both he casual and serious collector.

EXCITING MAIL AND PHONE BID CATALOGS

We conduct some of America's finest mail bid auctions offering a large selection of items in virtually every collecting category imaginable. Our fully illustrated and well researched catalog are an important permanent reference work for serious collectors and dealers alike.

PRIVATE TREATY SALES TO COLLECTORS, DEALERS, AND CORPORATIONS

We maintain a large and diversified inventory of items ranging in price from less than a dollar to in excess of $10,000. Some major categories found in our inventory—autographs, automotive, aviation, banking, early finance, entertainment, insurance, mining, oil, railroad, shipping, telephone and telegraph, utilities

Scott J. Winslow Associates, Inc.

Post Office Box 10240
Bedford, New Hampshire 03110
(800) 255-6233 ~ (603) 472-7040
Fax (603) 472-8773, e-mail SWins82687@aol.com